Head
  hung down, 71, 157, 184, 304
  lop-sided, 158, 178
  shaking, 140, 143, **146-7**, 154, 173 ·
  swelling up, 106, **178**
  tilted, 141, 149, 155, **229**
Hearing with difficulty, **149-50**, 262, 362
Hunching-up back, **229-30**, 249

Legs
  cold, 218
  swollen, 215, 354
  weak (or paralyzed), 218, 226, **229-30**
Lethargic (no pep), 64, 71-2, 75, 81, 111, 184-5, 192, 200, 215, 281
Licking
  at anus, 194
  at coat or skin, 115, 202, **347**
  at penis, 249, 253, **279**
  at vulva, 249, 257, **281**
Limping (lameness), **236,** 243-5, 354
Lips
  bumps on, 113
  chapped or inflamed, 161
  ulcer on, 115, **161-2**
Lumps and bumps, **97,** 115, **354-6**

Mouth
  held open, 155, 161, 174, 181
  irritated, 38, 43, 78
  ulcerated, 68, 152, 170, **173,** 251, 324
Mucus membranes (tongue, gums)
  bluish, 28, 35, 40, 160, 209-10, **214-5**
  bright red, 28, 34, 164
  pale, 46, 64, 75, 160, **220,** 308, 323

Nasal discharge (runny nose), 68, 72, 106, **152-3,** 156-7, 324
Nose-bleed, 42, **155,** 158

Paddling (collapsing and kicking feet wildly), 40, **227,** 308
Paralysis, 41, 45, 77, 218, 222, 226, **229-30**
Pawing
  at ear, 146
  at eye, 120, 126, 128, 130, 133
  at mouth, 77, 173-4
  at nose, 154-5
Penis
  discharge from, 249, **279, 364**
  protruded (extended), 256, 279-80
Phlegm (sputum), 181, **203**
  bubbly red, 214
Pot-bellied look, 55, 112, **185-6,** 215
Pulse, abnormal, 46, 212, 224
Pupils
  constricted, 137
  dilated, 28, 123, 136, **224**

Regurgitating, 180-1
Retching, 180
Rubbing up against, 95, 152, 174, 269

Scooting, 194, 196
Scratching
  at ears, 140, 143, **146,** 147
  at furniture, 344
  at skin, 78, **95-6**
Shivering, 26, 46, 200
Sneezing, 66, 105, 106, 153, **154,** 155-8, 324
Sniffling, 153-4, 157-8
Snoring and snorting, 153-4
Soiling in house, 258, **346-7,** 360
Spasms
  of lips (lip retraction), 65, 77, 308
  of muscles, 40, 104, 227, 308, 313
Spraying, 266, 286-7, **347**
Squinting, **125,** 126-8, 130, 133-4, 136
Staggering, 35, 41-2, 71, 78, 104, 200, 225-6, 308, 325
Stool streaked with blood, 71, 80, 188, 192, 194, 196, 353, 369
Stool, straining at, 188, 191, **194,** 198, 353
Straining to urinate, 249, **253,** 257
Swallowing
  repeatedly, 182, 203, 208
  with difficulty, 65, 161, 172, 175, **181,** 353

Tail, limp, 230, **241**
Teeth, damaged or loose, 164, 169, 245
Thirst, 198-9, 282, 363
Tongue, coated, 173, 252
Tremors of muscles, 40-2, 104, 226
Turning in circles, 149, 225, **229**

Unkempt appearance, 161, 163, 169-70, 173-4, 362
Upset stomach, 184-5
Urinary incontinence (loss of control), 249, 251, 253, **258**
Urinate, straining to, 249, **253,** 257
Urinating frequently, 200, **249,** 251, 253, 257, 281-2, 363
Urinating painfully, 249, 253, 281
Urine, blood in, 42, **249,** 253, 257

Vaginal discharge, 257, **281,** 282, 303, 305, 353
Vomiting, 38, 41-3, 55, 59, 64, 70, 72, 105, 180, **182-5,** 188, 200, 328
  blood, 42, **183**

Weakness, 41-2, 45-6, 56, 64, 80, 198, 200, 224
Weight loss, 51, 72, 75, 81, 169, 185, 198, 200, 215, 220, 251, 348, 364
  in newborns, 316
Wheezing, 59, 104, 153, **202**

CAT OWNER'S
HOME VETERINARY HANDBOOK

"Beware! When least expected a cat will sneak up and steal your heart."
—*Sue Giffin Litwin* and *Sydney Griffin Wiley.*

Cat Owner's HOME VETERINARY Handbook

by
DELBERT G. CARLSON, D.V.M.
and **JAMES M. GIFFIN, M.D.**

FIRST EDITION

HOWELL BOOK HOUSE
New York

HOWELL BOOK HOUSE
Macmillan Publishing Company
866 Third Avenue, New York, NY 10022
Collier Macmillan Canada, Inc.

Library of Congress Cataloging in Publication Data

Carlson, Delbert G.
    Cat owner's home veterinary handbook.

    Includes index.
        1. Cats—Diseases—Handbooks, manuals, etc.
I. Griffin, James M.   II. Title.
SF985.C29   1983   636.8'0896   82-23383
ISBN 0-87605-814-4

Macmillan books are available at special discounts for bulk purchases
for sales promotions, premiums, fund-raising, or educational use.
For details, contact:
                        Special Sales Director
                        Macmillan Publishing Company
                        866 Third Avenue
                        New York, NY 10022

20   19   18   17   16   15   14   13   12   11

Printed in the United States of America

To

Krist Carlson
for your care in handling the animals
at your dad's clinic
and
your special interest in taking the pictures

and to

Katherine Giffin
because
you love cats
and
all animals

This book is lovingly dedicated.

Dr. Delbert G. Carlson.

Dr. James M. Giffin.

The Authors

DELBERT G. CARLSON, D.V.M.

Dr. Del Carlson, co-author of the award-winning book, *Dog Owner's Home Veterinary Handbook* (Howell Book House, Inc.), is a practicing veterinarian with a long-standing experience in the medical and surgical care of cats and dogs. He received his medical degree from the University of Minnesota Veterinary School in 1954 and interned at the Rawley Memorial Hospital in Springfield, Massachusetts.

Stretching back to his early boyhood, Dr. Carlson can't recall when there weren't at least one or two cats sharing his bedroom. He and Mrs. Carlson, both confirmed animal lovers, have at various times bred and shown gaited horses, Afghan Hounds and Borzois—in addition to putting five children through college.

Dr. Carlson is a member of the Missouri Veterinary Medical Association and a past-president of the Greene County Humane Society. He makes his home in Springfield, Missouri.

JAMES M. GIFFIN, M.D.

Dr. Jim Giffin is co-author of the award-winning books, *The Complete Great Pyrenees* and *Dog Owner's Home Veterinary Handbook* (both from Howell Book House, Inc.).

Dr. Giffin received his medical degree from Yale University School of Medicine in 1961 and completed his surgical residency at Barnes Hospital in St. Louis. He served as Chief of Surgery at the 45th Surgical Hospital in Vietnam.

He and Mrs. Giffin founded their Elysee Great Pyrenees Kennel in 1969 and became active in showing and judging the breed. They finished several champions and campaigned a Best in Show winner. Dr. Giffin recently served on the Board of Directors of the Great Pyrenees Club of America, Inc., and remains active in the breed.

Dr. and Mrs. Giffin acquired their first cats during medical school. While pets were not officially allowed in their small upstairs apartment, they managed to keep three cats who went outside onto a closed-in porch through a modified stove-pipe whenever the landlord would put in an appearance.

Dr. and Mrs. Giffin, along with three children and numerous dogs, horses and cats, make their home in Delta, Colorado.

Finding it quick in
CAT OWNER'S HOME VETERINARY HANDBOOK:

A special INDEX OF SIGNS AND SYMPTOMS begins on the inside front cover page for fast referral. Consult this if your cat displays unexplained behavior. It will help you locate the problem.

The detailed CONTENTS beginning on the facing page outlines the organs and the systems, which are the usual sites of disease. If you can locate the problem anatomically, consult this first.

The GENERAL INDEX, which begins on Page 387, provides a comprehensive guide to the book's medical information. (Where a page number is in boldface, it indicates a more detailed coverage of the subject.)

CROSS REFERENCES appear throughout to guide you to supplementary information. Where the cross-reference is indicated in caps and small caps (SKIN) it identifies a chapter title; where the cross-reference is in italics (*Basic Coat Care*), it identifies a subdivision of a chapter.

At start of virtually every chapter, there is a section of general information. These sections not only provide the reader with a helpful introduction to the chapter's subject, but also add up to a fascinating overview of much of the latest medical knowledge regarding cats.

Contents

INDEX OF SIGNS AND SYMPTOMS—*Inside Front Cover*
The Authors, 7
Introduction, 19
Home Emergency and Medical Kit, 22

*Chapter 1—*EMERGENCIES—*P. 23*

Artificial Respiration and Heart Massage, 23
   Artificial Respiration, 23; *Heart Massage,* 25
Burns, 26
Cold Exposure, 26
   Hypothermia (Abnormal Low Temperature), 26; *Frostbite,* 27
Dehydration, 27
Drowning and Suffocation, 27
Electric Shocks and Burns, 28
Handling and Restraint, 28
   Picking Up a Cat, 30; *Restraining for Treatment,* 30; *Transporting an Injured Cat,* 34
Heat Stroke, 34
How to Induce Vomiting, 36
Insect Stings, 36
Painful Abdomen, 36
Poisoning, 37
   General Remarks, 37; *Poisonous Houseplants,* 38; *Outdoor Plants with Toxic Effects,* 38; *Strychnine,* 40; *Sodium Fluroacetate,* 40; *Arsenic,* 41; *Metaldehyde,* 41; *Lead,* 41; *Phosphorus,* 41; *Zinc Phosphide,* 42; *Warfarin,* 42; *Antifreeze,* 42; *Organophosphates and Carbamates,* 42; *Petroleum Products,* 42; *Chlorinated Hydrocarbons,* 43; *Corrosives,* 43; *Garbage Poisoning (Food Poisoning),* 43; *Toad Poisoning,* 43; *People Medicines,* 44
Snake Bites, 45
   Pit Vipers, 45; *Coral Snake,* 45.
Shock, 46
Wounds, 47
   Control of Bleeding, 47 *Treating the Wound,* 48; *Bandaging,* 48.

9

Chapter 2—WORMS (INTESTINAL PARASITES)—*P. 51*

General Information, 51
  Deworming Agents, 52; *Deworming Your Cat*, 52—Kittens, 53; Adults, 53; *How To Control Worms*, 53
Diseases Caused by Certain Worms, 55
  Roundworms, 55; *Hookworms*, 56; *Tapeworms*, 57; *Uncommon Worm Parasites*, 58

Chapter 3—INFECTIOUS DISEASES—*P. 60*

General Information, 60
  Antibodies and Immunity, 60
Vaccinations, 61
  Panleukopenia Vaccine, 62; *Feline Respiratory Disease Vaccines*, 62; *Rabies Vaccine*, 62; *Vaccination Schedule*, 63.
Feline Bacterial Diseases, 64
  Feline Infectious Anemia, 64; *Salmonella*, 64; *Tetanus (Lockjaw)*, 65; *Tuberculosis*, 65
Feline Virus Diseases, 66
  Feline Viral Respiratory Disease Complex, 66; *Feline Panleukopenia*, 69; *Feline Infectious Peritonitis*, 72; *Feline Leukemia Virus Disease Complex* (FeLV), 74; *Rabies*, 76; *Pseudorabies*, 78.
Fungus Diseases, 79
Protozoan Diseases, 80
  Coccidiosis, 80; *Toxoplasmosis*, 80; *Feline Cytauxzoon*, 81

Chapter 4—SKIN—*P. 83*

General Remarks, 83
Basic Coat Care, 85
  Growing a Coat, 85; *Shedding*, 85
How to Avoid Coat and Skin Problems, 86
  Grooming, 86; *Bathing*, 90
  How to Give Your Cat a Bath, 90; *Special Bath Problems*, 93
What To Do if Your Cat Has a Skin Problem, 95
Aids in the Diagnosis of Skin Disease, 95
  Table I—Itchy Skin Disorders, 95; *Table II—Disorders in which Hair is Lost*, 97; *Table III—Painful Skin Disorders with Drainage of Pus (Pyoderma)*, 97; *Table IV—Lumps or Bumps On or Beneath the Skin*, 97
Insect Parasites, 98
  Fleas, 98
  Mites, 99—Demodectic Mange, 100; Head Mange, 100; Cheyletiella Mange (Walking Dandruff), 100; Chiggers, 101; Other Mites, 101
  Ticks, 102; *Lice*, 102
  Flies, 103—Maggots, 103; Grubs 103
  Insecticides, 104—Dipping, 104; Premises Control, 105
Allergies, 105
  General Information, 105; *Food Allergy*, 106; *Flea Allergy Dermatitis*, 106; *Irritant Contact and Allergic Contact Dermatitis*, 107

Fungus Infections of the Skin, 109
   Ringworm, 109; *Sporotrichosis,* 110; *Candidiasis, (Thrush),* 110; *Mycetoma,* 110
Hormone Skin Diseases, 111
   Feline Endocrine Alopecia, 111; *Thyroid Deficiency,* 111; *Cortisone Excess,* 113.
Pyoderma (Bacterial Infection of the Skin), 113
   Impetigo, 113; *Folliculitis,* 113; *Feline Acne,* 113; *Stud Tail,* 114; *Cellulitis and Abscess,* 114.
Lick Granulomas, 115
Lumps and Bumps (Tumors On or Beneath the Skin), 115

Chapter 5—EYES—P. 117

Special Characteristics, 117
Structure of the Eye, 118
What To Do if Your Cat Has An Eye Problem, 120
   How to Examine His Eye, 120; *Signs of Eye Ailment,* 121; *How to Apply Eye Medicine,* 122.
The Eyeball, 123
   Eye out of its Socket, 123; *Bulging Eye,* 123; *Sunken Eye,* 123; *Cross-Eyed Gaze,* 125; *Jerking Eye Movements,* 125.
Eyelids, 125
   Severe Squinting, 125; *Irritated Eyelids,* 125; *Sudden Swelling,* 126; *Foreign Bodies in the Eye,* 126; *Eye Irritation from Lashes,* 126; *Eyelid Rolled Inward,* 128; *Eyelid Rolled Outward,* 128; *Tumors,* 128
The Third Eyelid, 128
   Film over the Eye (Protrusion of the Nictitating Membrane), 128
The Tearing Mechanism, 129
   The Watery Eye, 129—*Inadequate Tear Drainage,* 129; *Tear Stains in Persians,* 129
The Outer Eye, 130
   Pink Eye (Conjunctivitis), 130; *Conjunctivitis in Newborn Kittens,* 132; *Eye Worms,* 132
Cloudy Eye, 132
Cornea, 132
   Corneal Abrasion, 133; *Corneal Ulcers,* 133; *Keratitis,* 133
Inner Eye, 134
   The Blind Cat, 134; *Cataract,* 135; *Hard Eye (Glaucoma),* 136; *Soft Eye (Uveitis),* 137; *Retinal Diseases,* 137

Chapter 6—EARS—P. 139

Special Characteristics, 139
Structure of the Ears, 139
Basic Ear Care, 141
   How to Avoid Ear Problems, 141; *Cleaning the Ears,* 141; *How to Apply Ear Medicines,* 142
Outer Ear Diseases, 143
   The Ear Flap, 143—Bites and Lacerations, 143; Swollen Ear Flap, 143; Ear Allergies, 145; Frostbite, 145; Sunburn, 145; Head mange, 145; Ringworm, 145; Flea Infestation, 145; Tumors, 146

The Ear Canal—Ear Mites, 146; Bacterial Infections, 147; Fungus Infections, 148; Foreign Bodies and Ticks, 148

The Middle Ear, 149
   Infection, 149
Inner Ear, 149
   Infection, 149; *Deafness,* 149

Chapter 7—NOSE—*P. 151*

General Information, 151
Signs of Nasal Irritation, 152
   Runny Nose, 153; *Noisy Breathing,* 153; *Sneezing,* 154; *Reverse Sneezing,* 154
The Nasal Cavity, 155
   Trauma and Nose-bleeds, 155; *Foreign Bodies in the Nose,* 155; *Allergic Rhinitis (Allergies),* 156; *Nasal Infections,* 156; *Sinusitis,* 157; *Nasal Polyps and Tumors,* 158

Chapter 8—MOUTH AND THROAT (Oropharynx)—*P. 159*

General Information, 159
   How to Examine the Mouth, 160; *Signs of Mouth Disease,* 161
Lips, 161
   Inflammation of the Lips, 161; *Rodent Ulcer,* 161; *Lacerations of the Lips, Mouth and Tongue,* 163; *Burns of the Lips, Mouth and Tongue,* 163
Gums, 164
   Sore Gums (Gingivitis), 164; *Growths on the Gums,* 164.
Teeth, 164
   Baby Teeth, 164; *Teething in Kittens,* 166; *Aging a Cat by his Teeth,* 166; *Retained Baby Teeth,* 166; *Abnormal Number of Teeth,* 166; *Incorrect Bite,* 168; *Tooth Decay,* 168;
   Periodontal Disease, 168—Cavities, 169;
   Care of Your Cat's Teeth (Oral Hygiene), 170
Tongue, 170
   Sore Tongue, 170; *Foreign Bodies in the Tongue,* 171; *String Around the Tongue,* 172
Mouth, 173
   Sore Mouth (Stomatitis), 173—Trench Mouth, 173; Ulcerative (Viral) Stomatitis, 173; Thrush, 172
   Foreign Bodies in the Mouth, 174—Porcupine Quills, 175
   Growths in the Mouth, 175
Throat, 175
   Sore Throat, 175; *Tonsillitis,* 175; *Foreign Bodies in the Throat (Choking and Gagging),* 176
Salivary Glands, 176
   Drooling, 176; *Salivary Gland Infections and Cysts,* 178
Swollen Head, 178
   Allergic Reaction, 178; *Head and Neck Abscesses,* 178

Chapter 9—DIGESTIVE SYSTEM—*P. 179*

General Information, 179
Esophagus, 180
Foreign Body in the Esophagus, 181; *Strictures*, 181; *Growths*, 181; *Swallowing Problems in Kittens*, 181
Stomach, 182
Vomiting, 182; *Gastritis (Upset Stomach)*, 184
Bloating (Abdominal Distension), 185
Intestines, 186
Diarrhea, 186—*Enteritis*, 187; *Colitis*, 188; *Malabsorption Syndrome*, 188
Treatment of Diarrhea, 189; *Intestinal Obstruction (Blocked Bowel)*, 189; *Intestinal Foreign Bodies*, 190; *Constipation*, 191; *Chronic Constipation*, 191; *Passing Gas (Flatus)*, 193; *Loss of Bowel Control*, 193
Anus and Rectum, 194
Inflamed Anus and Rectum (Proctitis), 194; *Protrusion of Anal Tissue*, 194
Anal Glands or Sacs, 195
How to Empty the Anal Sacs, 195; *Impaction of Anal Sacs*, 197; *Anal Sac Infection*, 197; *Anal Sac Abscess*, 198; *Polyps and Cancer*, 198
Liver, 198
Causes of Liver Insufficiency, 198
Pancreas, 199
Sugar Diabetes, 199—*Insulin Overdose*, 200

Chapter 10—RESPIRATORY SYSTEM—*P. 201*

General Remarks, 201
Abnormal Breathing, 201
Rapid Breathing, 201; *Slow Breathing*, 202; *Panting*, 202; *Noisy Breathing*, 202; *Croupy Breathing*, 202; *Wheezing*, 202; *Shallow Breathing*, 202; *Meowing*, 203; *Purring*, 203
Cough, 203
Voice Box, 204
Loss of Voice (Laryngitis), 204; *Foreign Objects in the Voice Box*, 206
Breathing Tubes *(Trachea and Bronchi)*, 207
Foreign Bodies in the Windpipe, 207
Bronchitis, 207—*Chronic Bronchitis*, 208
Asthma (Allergic Bronchitis), 209
Lungs, 209
Pneumonia, 209; *Fluid in the Chest Cavity*, 210

Chapter 11—CIRCULATORY SYSTEM—*P. 211*

Heart, 211
Physiology, 211
Heart Failure, 214
Left Heart Failure, 214; *Right Heart Failure*, 215

Feline Cardiovascular Disease, 215
  Congenital Heart Disease, 215; *Feline Cardiomyopathy (Heart Muscle Disease)*,
  216; *Arterial Thromboembolism (Blood Clot in an Artery)*, 218; *Acquired Valvular
  Disease*, 218; *Heartworms*, 218
Anemia, 219

Chapter 12—NERVOUS SYSTEM—*P. 221*

General Remarks, 221
Brain Diseases, 222
  Brain Injuries, 222; *Brain Infections (Encephalitis)*, 225; *Feline Cerebrovascular Dis-
  ease (Stroke)*, 225; *Tumors*, 226; *Other Causes of Central Nervous System Disease*,
  226
Seizure Disorder (Fits), 227
Coma, 228
Vestibular Disorders, 229
Spinal Cord Diseases, 229
  Spinal Cord Injuries, 230; *Infections*, 230; *Malformations*, 230
Nerve Injuries, 232

Chapter 13—MUSCULOSKELETAL SYSTEM—*P. 233*

General Information, 233
Limping (Lameness), 236
Injuries to Bones and Joints, 237
  Sprains, 237; *Tendon Injuries*, 237; *Muscle Strain*, 237; *Dislocated Joint (Luxation)*,
  238; *Broken Bones (Fractures)*, 238; *Bone Infection (Osteomyelitis)*, 243; *Torn Knee
  Ligaments*, 243; *Rubber Band Around the Leg*, 243
Arthritis (Degenerative Joint Disease), 243
Metabolic Bone Disorders, 244
  Parathyroid Bone Diseases, 244—Primary Hyperparathyroidism, 244; Renal Sec-
    ondary Hyperparathyroidism, 244; Nutritional Secondary Hyper-
    parathyroidism, 245; Rickets, 245
Other Nutritional Disorders, 246
  Overdosing with Vitamins, 246; *Pansteatitis (Yellow Fat Disease)*, 246

Chapter 14—URINARY SYSTEM—*P. 247*

General Information, 247
  Urinary Tract Infections, 247
Signs of Urinary Tract Disease, 249
Kidney Diseases, 249
  Infection of the Kidney and Renal Pelvis, 249; *Nephritis and Nephrosis*, 250; *Kidney
  Failure (Uremic Poisoning)*, 250; *Tumors*, 252; *Congenital Defects*, 253
Diseases of the Bladder and Urethra, 253
  Feline Urologic Syndrome (FUS), 253; *Cystitis*, 257; *Bladder Stones*, 257; *Urinary
  Incontinence*, 258

Chapter 15—SEX AND REPRODUCTION—*P. 259*

Breeding, 259
  Pedigreed Cats, 259—Registration, 261
  Genetics and Planned Breeding, 261; *The Queen,* 265; *The Stud,* 266
  The Estrus Cycle (Heat Cycle), 268—Mating Seasons, 268; Signs of Heat, 268
  Hormonal Influences During Estrus, 270—Ovulation, 270
  Fertilization, 271
Mating, 271
  Getting Ready, 271; *Normal Mating Procedure,* 272; *Shy Breeders — Cats that Won't Mate,* 274
Infertility, 275
  Fertility Problems in the Male, 275—Impotence, 276
  Fertility Problems in the Female, 276—Abnormal Heat Cycles, 276; Failure to Ovulate, 277; Fetal Loss During Pregnancy, 277
  Diseases of the Male Genital Tract, 279—Infection of the Prepuce and Penis, 279; Strictured Foreskin, 279; Penis That Can't Retract, 279; Undescended Testicles, 280; Orchitis (Inflammation of the Testicles), 281
  Diseases of the Female Genital Tract, 281—Vaginal Infection, 281; Uterine Infection, 282
Artificial Insemination, 283
False Pregnancy *(Pseudocyesis),* 283
Accidental Pregnancy, 284
Birth Control, 284
  Spaying, 285; *Tubal Ligation,* 285; *Artificial Stimulation of the Vagina,* 285; *Male Castration,* 286; *Vasectomy,* 287

Chapter 16—PREGNANCY AND KITTENING—*P. 289*

Pregnancy, 289
  Gestation, 289; *Determining Pregnancy,* 289; *Morning Sickness,* 291; *Prenatal Checkups,* 291; *Care and Feeding During Pregnancy,* 292; *Kittening Preparations,* 292
Kittening, 294
  Signs of Confinement, 294; *Labor and Delivery,* 294; *Assisting the Normal Delivery,* 296
Prolonged Labor *(Dystocia, Difficult Labor),* 298
  Mechanical Blockage, 298; *Uterine Inertia,* 298; *When to Call the Veterinarian,* 299; *Feline Obstetrics,* 299; *Helping a Kitten Breathe,* 302
Caesarean Section, 302
Post Partum Care of the Queen, 303
  Feeding During Lactation, 303
Post Partum Problems, 304
  Post Partum Hemorrhage, 304; *Acute Metritis,* 304; *Mastitis,* 304; *Inadequate Milk Supply,* 307; *Milk Fever,* 308; *Mothers Who Neglect or Injure Their Kittens,* 308

Chapter 17—PEDIATRICS—*P. 311*

Newborn Kittens, 311
  Physiology, 312; *Why Kittens Die,* 313

Caring for the Newborn, 314
  General Appearance and Vitality, 314
  Body Temperature, 315—Warming a Chilled Kitten, 315
  Importance of Weight Gain, 316—When to Supplement, 316
Raising Kittens by Hand, 316
  The Incubator, 317; *General Care,* 318
  Hand Feeding, 318—Calculating the Amount to Feed, 319; How to Give the Formula, 320; Common Feeding Problems, 321
Kitten Diseases, 323
  Toxic Milk Syndrome, 323; *Newborn Anemia,* 323; *Navel Infection,* 323; *Kitten Septicemia,* 324; *Herpes Virus of Kittens,* 324; *Kitten Mortality Complex,* 325; *Neonatal Feline Panleukopenia,* 325; *Skin Infection of the Newborn,* 325; *Conjunctivitis of the Newborn,* 327
  Congenital or Inherited Defects, 327—Hernia, 328; Cleft Palate, 328; Pyloric Stenosis, 328; Imperforate Anus, 329
Weaning, 329
The New Kitten, 330
  Determining the Sex, 330; *Declawing,* 332

Chapter 18—FEEDING AND NUTRITION—*P. 333*

Types of Cat Food, 333
Feeding Your Cat, 335
  Food Preferences, 336; *How to Feed,* 336; *Tables of Nutritional Requirements for Cats,* 337; *Some Caveats Concerning the Feeding of Cats,* 338; *Switching Diets,* 338; *Common Errors in Feeding,* 338; *Feeding Kittens,* 340

Chapter 19—FELINE BEHAVIOR AND TRAINING—*P. 341*

General Remarks, 341
Training, 342
  General Remarks, 342; *Housebreaking,* 343; *Scratching the Furniture,* 344; *Collars and Leashes,* 344; *Coming When Called,* 345
Behavior Disorders, 346
  Soiling in the House, 346—Failure to Use the Litter Pan, 346; Relapses in a Well-Trained Cat, 346; Spraying, 347
  Energy Release Activities, 347; *Eating Disorders,* 348; *Abnormal Sucking Behavior,* 348; *Aggressive Behavior,* 349; *Sexual Behavior,* 349; *Treatment of Behavior Disorders with Drugs,* 350—Tranquilizers, 350; Progesterones, 350

Chapter 20—TUMORS AND CANCERS—*P. 351*

General Information, 351
  What is Cancer? 352; *Treatment of Tumors and Cancers,* 352; *Cancer in the Cat,* 353
Common Surface Tumors, 354
  Cysts (Wens), 354; *Warts and Papillomas,* 354; *Lipomas,* 354; *Hematomas,* 355; *Tender Knots,* 355; *Skin Cancers,* 356; *Breast Tumors and Swelling,* 357

Chapter 21—GERIATRICS—P. 359

General Remarks, 359
Caring for the Elderly Cat, 360
    Behavioral Changes, 360; *Physical Changes*, 361; *Functional Changes*, 363
Diet and Nutrition, 366
Putting Your Cat to Sleep *(Euthanasia)*, 367

Chapter 22—DRUGS AND MEDICATIONS—P. 368

General Remarks, 368
Anesthetics and Anesthesia, 368
Pain Relievers, 369
Common Household Drugs for Home Veterinary Use, 370
How to Give Medications, 370
    Pills, 370; *Liquids*, 372; *Injections*, 372; *Enemas*, 374; *Suppositories*, 374

Chapter 23—ANTIBIOTICS AND INFECTIONS—P. 375

General Remarks, 375
Antibiotics Your Veterinarian May Prescribe (Chart), 376
Why Antibiotics May Not Be Effective, 378
    Misdiagnosis of Infection, 378; *Inappropriate Selection*, 378; *Inadequate Wound Care*, 378; *Route of Administration*, 378; *Dose and Frequency of Administration*, 378
Complications of Antibiotics, 379
    Allergy, 379; *Toxicity*, 379; *Secondary Infections*, 379; *Emergence of Resistant Strains*, 380; *Use in Pregnancy*, 380
Antibiotics and Cortisone, 380

APPENDIX—P. 381

Normal Physiologic Data, 381
    Normal Temperature—How to Take Your Cat's Temperature, 381; *Pulse*, 382; *Respiration*, 382; *Weight*, 382; *Gestation*, 382
Cat Fancy and Registration Associations, 382
Guide for Buying a Healthy Kitten, 383
    Here Are the Things You Should Look For in a Healthy Kitten, 384; *Grooming, Feeding and Training*, 385

GENERAL INDEX—P. 387

**The American shorthair is an exceptionally strong
and hardy breed. Popular as a dependable mouser, it
has been a permanent resident of American farms for
hundreds of years. Its ancestors may have reached
America aboard the *Mayflower*.**   —*Sydney Wiley.*

**Abyssinians are said to be the direct descendants of the Sacred
Cats of Egypt. Medium in size, lithe and graceful, the body is mid-
way between the extremes of cobby and lengthy type.**
                                                    —*Sydney Wiley.*

Introduction

While it appears that man and dog have been companions for more than 50,000 years, the association of man and cat seems to go back only about 5,000. The exact origin of the domestic cat remains controversial. His fossils are found in Europe, Asia and Africa—but not in America.

The early associations of cat and man are cloaked in legend and myth. The Egyptians held cats in the highest esteem and made them the objects of worship. A famous statue depicts the goddess Pasht, bearing the head of a cat. Other figures cast in gold, bronze and copper, and wall paintings showing cats hunting with their masters, attest to the prominence of cats in Egyptian life.

Phoenician sailors, while trafficking with the Egyptians, probably became enamored with the cat and took him to various ports along the Mediterranean coast. Two thousand years later the Romans, who were well-known for their knowledge of livestock and its uses, having already adapted several breeds of dog for guarding and fighting, no doubt recognized the value of the cat as a means of pest control.

Cats would have been especially useful to the Romans who then were suffering severe depredations at their military granaries due to an uncontrolled proliferation of rats and mice. This theory would account for the sudden surge in popularity of cats, and their appearance throughout Europe in the time of the Roman Empire.

Since the beginning of modern history cats have charmed, baffled, delighted and intrigued. Perhaps no other animal has had such a beguiling influence on the minds of the literary. William Blake saw in the cat a symbol of the metaphysical—allusive, undefinable—yet somehow, by his very existence, affirming the hand of an ultimate creator. Thomas Gray, in quite a different vein, found in the lady cat Selima (who drowned in a tub of goldfish) a parody of human nature. He wrote:

> "Not all that tempts your wand'ring eyes
> And heedless heart is lawful prize;
> Nor all that glitters, gold."

Today there is little doubt that cats are enjoying an explosion in popularity. Twenty-five percent of American households claim at least one cat. There are 35 million cats in the United States, which is only 15 million short of the dog population.

Along with this widespread interest in the cat as a companion and pet, there is a growing awareness on the part of the public that the cat is a very special sort

19

of animal, whose health and medical needs are really quite different from those of other pets. Feline medicine is becoming a specialty all its own. A cat's diet is a matter of such particular importance that pet food companies spend millions trying to find out what should, and should not, be included in their products. You may be surprised to learn that the commonest feline cancer is actually caused by a virus! This is quite a remarkable discovery, especially when you consider that human cancer research has yet to produce so positive a correlation between a cancer effect and its cause.

The average cat now lives 15 years. This was not so a short time back. Most cats died before they were 12. Yet it is not uncommon in veterinary practice to see cats 20 years of age. All this means that the pet owner, and the modern veterinarian, have to know a lot more about the care of aging cats.

Improvements in human medicine are being made at an astonishing rate. The same advances are being adopted almost simultaneously by the small animal practitioner. Today's professionalism in anesthesia and peri-operative management has made high-risk surgery relatively safe. Most of the major feline infectious diseases can be prevented, or attenuated, by vaccinations. For those that cannot, such as the feline leukemia virus, it is only a matter of time before commercial vaccines become available.

In writing this book, we have taken the approach that the cat is indeed a special case in veterinary practice. This book was originally started as a companion to the *Dog Owner's Home Veterinary Handbook*. In organization and presentation it follows the same format which proved so convenient to us before. However, the *Cat Owner's Home Veterinary Handbook* departs from the first book in many important respects. Cats and dogs are not alike. Many veterinary procedures suitable for the dog are not suitable for the cat, or may even be harmful. But where general medical information is the same, we have not made changes.

We have attempted to describe in the cat those signs and symptoms which will help you arrive at a preliminary diagnosis, so you can weigh the severity of the problem. Some health problems are not serious and can be treated at home. Others are not. Knowing when to call your veterinarian can be of great importance. Delays can be costly.

At the same time we have sought to provide guidance for the acute or emergency situations that common sense dictates you should handle on your own. Life-saving procedures such as *Artificial Respiration, Heart Massage, Obstetrical Emergencies, Poisonings,* and the like are illustrated and explained in a step-by-step fashion.

A Veterinary Handbook is not intended to be a substitute for professional care. Book advice can never be as helpful or as safe as medical assistance. No text can replace the interview and physical examination, during which the veterinarian elicits the sort of information which leads to a speedy and accurate diagnosis. But the knowledge provided in this book will enable you to work in better understanding and more effective cooperation with your veterinarian.

You'll be more alert to the symptoms of diseases and better able to describe them to him.

In this book you will find the basics of health care and disease prevention for the young and old. A well-cared-for cat suffers fewer illnesses and infirmities as he grows older.

Chapters on *Sex and Reproduction, Pregnancy and Kittening, Feline Behavior and Training, Pediatrics,* and care of the elderly, provide comprehensive coverage on matters of importance to all cat owners and breeders.

The combined efforts of many people make this book possible. We are indebted to Krist Carlson and Dr. James Clawson for their splendid photographs showing techniques in handling and medicating cats; and to Nancy Wallis for her aid in the grooming pictures.

Sydney Giffin Wiley created many fine drawings, as did Rose Floyd.

Shirley Hollis and Margaret Rudnick deserve our sincere thanks for their devoted service in the typing of the manuscript.

Recognition would not be complete without mentioning the many researchers, clinicians, and educators whose work served as a source for our information. Among them are *Current Veterinary Therapy* (edited by Robert W. Kirk, D.V.M.); *Small Animal Dermatology* (George W. Muller, D.V.M. and Robert W. Kirk, D.V.M.); and the numerous contributors to *The Veterinary Clinics of North America* (W. B. Saunders Company).

To Elsworth S. Howell and Ab Sidewater, who gave us the opportunity to produce this work, and who did such a splendid job on our earlier publication, we are indeed grateful.

—Delbert G. Carlson
—James M. Giffin

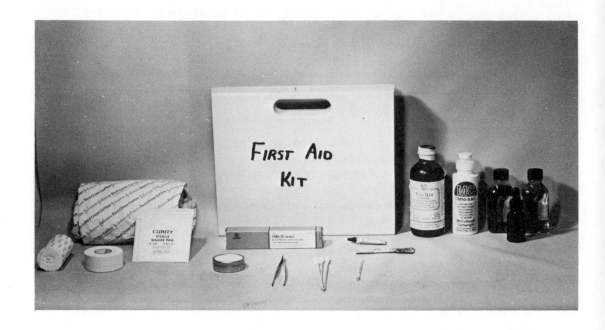

HOME EMERGENCY and MEDICAL KIT

Adhesive tape - 1 inch roll
Container for kit
Cotton-tipped applicators
Eyedropper (plastic)
Furacin ointment
Gauze pads - 3 x 3 inch
Gauze roll - 3 inch
Hairball remedy (Commercial,
   Petroleum jelly—not carbolated)
Hemostat (curved or straight)

Plaster splint
Rubbing alcohol
Scalpel and Scissors
Surgical soap (e.g. pHisoHex,
   Weldol)
"Tamed" iodine (or other
   antiseptic)
Thermometer
Tweezers (thumb forceps)

Note: Common household drugs for home veterinary use are listed in the chapter Drugs and Medications.

1

Emergencies

ARTIFICIAL RESPIRATION and HEART MASSAGE

Artificial respiration is an emergency procedure used to assist breathing in an unconscious cat. Heart massage is used when no heartbeat can be heard or felt. When combined with artificial respiration, it is called *cardiopulmonary resuscitation.* As cessation of breathing is soon followed by heart stoppage and vice versa, cardiopulmonary resuscitation frequently is required to sustain life. Heart massage by itself provides for both movement of air and pumping of blood. For best results, combine heart massage with forced mouth to nose breathing. This requires two people, one to administer heart massage and one to give mouth to nose breathing.

The following emergencies may require artificial respiration and/or heart massage:

Shock	Head Injury
Poisoning	Electric Shock
Prolonged Seizure	Obstructed Airways (Choking)
Coma	Sudden Death

Artificial Respiration

Two methods are used. The *chest compression* technique consists of applying force to the chest wall, which pushes air out and allows the elastic recoil of the chest to draw air back in. It is the easiest to perform.

Mouth to nose forced respiration is used when the compression technique is ineffective, or when the chest is punctured (*pneumothorax*).

Steps in Chest Compression:

1. Feel for pulse or heart beat.
2. Open mouth and clear away secretions. Check for a foreign body. If found, remove if possible. If impossible to reach, execute the *Heimlich Maneuver* (see RESPIRATORY SYSTEM: *Foreign Object in the Voice Box*).
3. Lay the cat on a flat surface with his *right* side down.

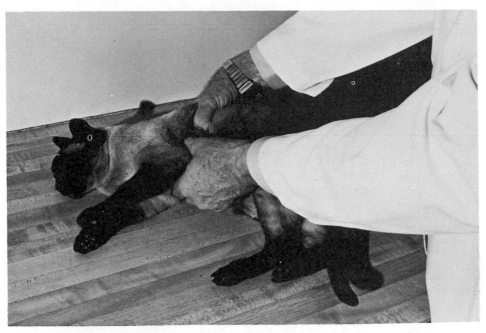

The *chest compression* technique for giving artificial respiration.
—J. Clawson.

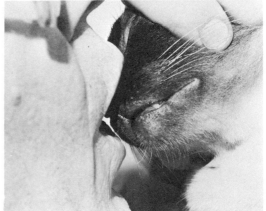

Mouth to nose resuscitation. Leaving the mouth uncovered avoids the problem of overinflation.
—J. Clawson.

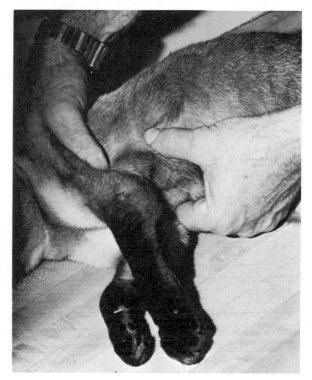

Heart Massage. Note the placement of the fingers and thumb on either side of the sternum behind the elbow. Heart massage alone provides for movement of air as well as pumping of blood.
—*J. Clawson.*

4. Squeeze the chest sharply from side to side. Release quickly. Repeat every four seconds. If properly performed, you should be able to hear air moving in and out. If you can't, proceed with mouth to nose resuscitation.
5. Continue until the cat breathes on his own, or as long as the heart beats.

Steps in Mouth to Nose Resuscitation:

1. Perform steps 1 and 2 in *Chest Compression*.
2. Pull the tongue forward and close the mouth. Seal the lips with your hand.
3. Place your mouth over the cat's nose and blow in steadily for three seconds. The chest will expand. Release to let the air come back out.
4. Continue until the cat breathes on his own, or as long as the heart beats.

Heart Massage

1. Perform steps 1 and 2 in *Chest Compression*.
2. Lay the cat on his *right* side. Place your thumbs on one side of his sternum and your fingers on the other, just behind the elbows.
3. Compress the chest firmly six times. Wait five seconds to let the chest expand; then repeat.
4. Continue until the heart beats on its own, or until no heart beat is felt for five minutes.

BURNS

Burns are caused by heat, chemicals, electric shocks, and radiation. Sunburn is an example of a radiation burn. It occurs on the ear flaps of cats with white coats (see EARS: *Sunburn*); and on the skin of white-coated cats who are sheared in summer.

A cat may be scalded by having hot liquid spilled on him or by being involved in some other household accident. A common type of burn occurs on the foot pads after walking on a hot surface such as a tin roof, stove top, or freshly tarred road.

The depth of injury depends upon the length and intensity of exposure. With a superficial burn you will see redness of the skin, occasionally blistering, perhaps slight swelling; and the burn is tender. With deep burns the skin appears white, the hair comes out easily when pulled, and pain is severe. If more than 15% of the body surface is involved by a deep burn, the outlook is poor. Fluid losses are excessive. Shock can occur.

Treatment: Apply cold water soaks or ice packs to small burns for 20 minutes to relieve pain. Clip away hair and wash gently with a surgical soap. Blot dry. Apply a topical antibiotic ointment (Furacin). Protect the area from rubbing by wrapping it with a loose-fitting gauze dressing.

Treat chemical burns by flushing them with copious amounts of water. Acid on the skin is neutralized by rinsing with baking soda (four tablespoons to a pint of water). Alkali is neutralized by rinsing with a weak vinegar solution (two tablespoons to a pint of water). To be effective, this must be done within five minutes. Blot dry and apply antibiotic ointment. Bandage loosely.

COLD EXPOSURE

Hypothermia (Abnormal Low Temperature)

Prolonged exposure to cold results in a drop in body temperature. It is most likely to occur when a cat is wet. Hypothermia also occurs in shock, after a long anesthetic, and in newborn kittens. Prolonged chilling burns up the available energy and predisposes to low blood sugar.

The signs of hypothermia are: violent shivering followed by listlessness and lethargy; a rectal temperature below 97 degrees F (which is diagnostic); and finally, collapse and coma.

Treatment: Wrap your cat in a blanket or coat and carry him into the house. If he is wet (having fallen into icy water), give him a warm bath. Rub him vigorously with towels to dry his skin.

Warm a chilled cat by applying warm water packs to the axilla (armpits), chest and abdomen. The temperature of the pack should be about that of a baby bottle (warm to the wrist). Continue to change the packs until the rectal temperature reaches 100 degrees F. Warming with a hair dryer or air comb works well.

As the cat begins to move about, give him some honey or glucose (four teaspoons of sugar added to a pint of water).

How to warm a chilled kitten is discussed in PEDIATRICS: *Warming a Chilled Kitten*.

Frostbite

Frostbite often involves the toes, ears, scrotum and tail. These areas are the most exposed, and only lightly protected by fur. At first the skin is pale and white. With return of circulation, it becomes red and swollen. Later it may peel. Eventually, it looks much like a burn, with a line of demarcation between live and dead tissue. The dead skin separates in one to three weeks.

Frostbite of the ear flaps is discussed in the chapter EARS.

Treatment: Apply warm water soaks to the frostbitten parts. Prevent infection by applying an antibiotic ointment. Wrap loosely (see *Bandaging*).

DEHYDRATION

Dehydration is excess loss of body fluids. Usually it involves loss of both water and *electrolytes* (which are minerals such as sodium, chloride, potassium). During illness, dehydration may be due to an inadequate fluid intake. Fever increases the loss of water. This becomes significant if the cat does not drink enough to offset it. Other common causes of dehydration are prolonged vomiting and diarrhea.

One sign of dehydration is loss of skin elasticity. When the skin along the back is picked up into a fold, it should spring back into place. In dehydration, the skin stays up in a ridge. Another sign is dryness of the mouth. Late signs are sunken eyeballs and circulatory collapse (shock).

Treatment: If your cat is noticeably dehydrated, he should receive prompt veterinary attention. Treatment is directed at replacing fluids and preventing further losses.

In mild cases without vomiting, fluids can be given by mouth. If the cat won't drink, he can be given an electrolyte solution by bottle or syringe into his cheek pouch (see DRUGS AND MEDICATIONS). Balanced electrolyte solutions for treating dehydration in children are available at drug stores. Ringer's lactate with 5% Dextrose in water, and a solution called Pedialyte, are suitable for cats. They are given at the rate of two to four cc per pound body weight per hour depending on the severity of the dehydration (or as directed by your veterinarian).

The treatment of dehydration in infant kittens is discussed in PEDIATRICS: *Common Feeding Problems*.

DROWNING and SUFFOCATION

Conditions which prevent oxygen from getting into the lungs and blood cause *asphyxiation*. They are: carbon monoxide poisoning; inhalation of toxic fumes (smoke, gasoline, propane, refrigerants, solvents); drowning; and smothering (which can happen when a cat is left too long in an airtight space). Other causes are foreign bodies in the airways and injuries to the chest which interfere with breathing.

A cat can get his collar snagged on a fence and strangle while struggling to get free. Be sure to provide your cat with an elastic collar which can stretch and slip over his head in an emergency.

Cats are natural swimmers and can negotiate short distances well. However, they can't climb out of water over a ledge. They might drown in a swimming pool if a ramp exit is not provided.

The symptoms of oxygen lack are: straining to breathe; gasping for breath (often with the head extended); extreme anxiety; and weakness progressing to loss of consciousness as the cat begins to succumb. The pupils begin to dilate. The tongue and mucous membranes turn blue, which is a reflection of insufficient oxygen in the blood. One exception to the blue color is carbon monoxide poisoning, in which the membranes are a bright red.

Treatment: The most important consideration is to provide your cat with fresh air to breathe. (Better yet, give him oxygen, if available.) If respirations are shallow or absent, immediately give mouth to nose respiration.

If the cat has an open wound into his chest (which you can diagnose if you hear air sucking in and out as he breathes) seal off the chest by pinching the skin together over the wound.

When the situation is one of drowning, turn the cat upside down, suspend him by his legs, and let the water run out of his windpipe. Then position the cat with his head lower than his chest (on a slope, or with a roll beneath his chest) and begin artificial respiration. Mouth to nose forced respiration may be required. With heart stoppage, heart massage should be attempted. Continue efforts to resuscitate until the cat breathes on his own or until no heartbeat is felt for five minutes (see *Artificial Respiration and Heart Massage* in this chapter).

Once the immediate crisis is over, veterinary aid should be sought. Pneumonia from inhalation is a frequent complication.

ELECTRIC SHOCKS and BURNS

Electric shocks occur in kittens who chew on electric cords. Occasionally a cat comes into contact with a downed wire or is struck by lightning.

Cats who receive an electric shock may be burned, or the electric shock may cause irregular heartbeat with signs of circulatory collapse. Electric current also damages the capillaries of the lungs and leads to the accumulation of fluid in the air sacs (*pulmonary edema*). The signs are those of difficulty in breathing.

Treatment: If your cat is unconscious and not breathing, administer artificial respiration. Pulmonary edema has to be treated by a veterinarian.

Burns of the mouth from electric cords are discussed in the chapter MOUTH AND THROAT.

HANDLING and RESTRAINT

There are several effective methods to handle and restrain a cat. Your choice will depend upon whether the individual is tranquil and cooperative or frightened and aggressive.

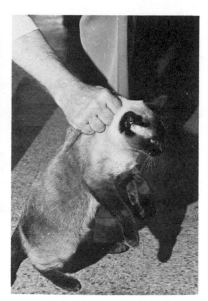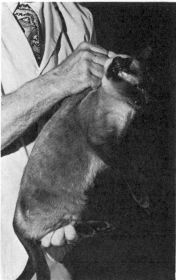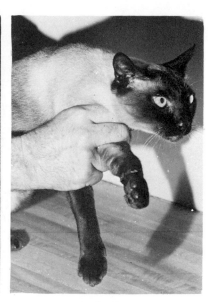

Picking up a cat. Reach down and grasp the cat by the scruff of the neck. Secure the back feet with your other hand. Note the position of the fingers, which securely immobilize the front legs. —*J. Clawson.*

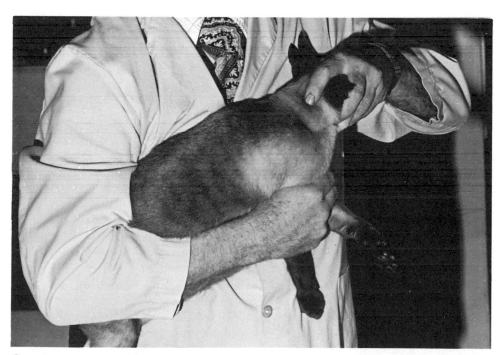

Carrying a cat. Hold him firmly against your body with his rear feet pressed out behind. Cover his eyes and ears with your other hand. —*J. Clawson.*

Picking Up a Cat

As a general rule, it is advisable to reach down and pick a cat up from above. A face to face confrontation might provoke a cat into becoming uncooperative or aggressive.

Cooperative Cat: Place one hand around his abdomen beneath his chest and take hold of his front legs so they cross over each other, keeping your index finger between them for a secure grip. Pick him up and snuggle him close to your body. Cradle his chin with your other hand.

Apprehensive Cat: Reach down and lift the cat up by the scruff of his neck. Most cats go limp—as they did when their mothers carried them as kittens.

Frightened Cat: Cover the cat with a towel. After a minute or two, as he calms, slide the rest of the towel underneath him and lift him up as a bundle.

Aggressive Cat: Make a loop with a leash or piece of rope and slip it over his head and *one* front leg. Then lift the cat up by the leash and set him down on a table, or lower him into a cat carrier or box. This method should be used only as a last resort. It will certainly agitate the cat further.

Restraining for Treatment

Routine procedures such as grooming, bathing, or even medicating when the individual is cooperative, are best carried out with a minimum of physical restraint. Approach the cat with confidence and handle him gently. Most cats can be coaxed into accepting the procedure and do not need to be restrained.

Cooperative Cat: Lift him up onto a smooth surface such as a table top where he is less secure—but still not frightened. Soothe him and speak to him in a calm voice until he relaxes. Place one hand around the front of his chest to keep him from moving forward. Use your other hand to administer the treatment.

Uncooperative Cat: Depending upon his degree of agitation, several methods are available.

If the cat is sufficiently cooperative to permit handling, grasp him by the scruff of his neck and press him down firmly against the top of the table so that he *stretches out*. This is to prevent him from scratching you with his rear claws.

When help is available, have your assistant stand behind the cat and place both his hands around the cat's neck or front legs while pressing his arms against the cat's sides. Wrapping a towel or blanket around the cat has a calming effect and is useful for short procedures such as giving medications. An assistant is required to steady the cat and hold the wraps in place.

A coat sleeve makes an excellent restraint. The cat will often scoot up into it willingly. Hold the end of the sleeve securely around the cat's neck. Now you can treat his head or tail.

For more extended procedures in which the cat cannot be managed by the above methods, lift the cat straight up from behind by the scruff of his neck with one hand and hold his rear paws together with the other. Press him down firmly on the table top so he is lying on his side with his body extended. Now have an

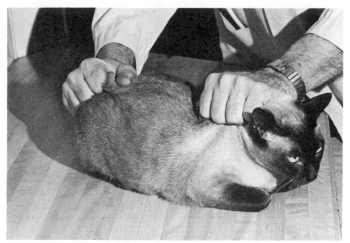

Restraining for treatment. **Hold firmly for any treatment which might prove unpleasant.** —*J. Clawson.*

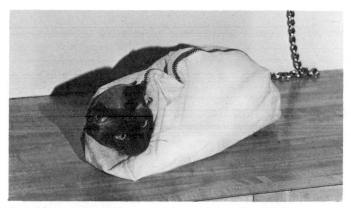

A cat bag restraint is useful for treating the head. —*J. Clawson.*

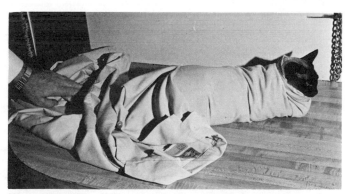

Wrapping the cat has a calming effect. A coat sleeve is an excellent restraint which a cat will go into willingly. —*J. Clawson.*

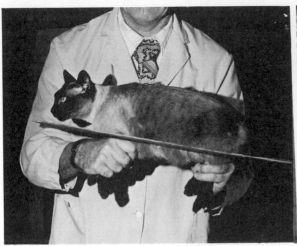 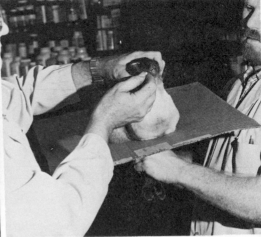

A simple restraint can be made from a piece of cardboard. It is useful for a short procedure, such as giving a pill.
—*J. Clawson.*

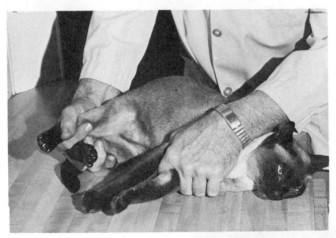

Another method of restraining for a short procedure. An assistant is required.
—*J. Clawson.*

An unruly cat who requires more extended treatment can be immobilized by taping his legs.
—*J. Clawson.*

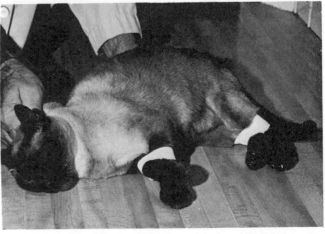

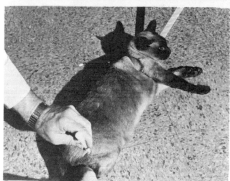

A leash and loop restraint. The cat is immobilized by drawing the leash taut. To keep the cat from being choked, the loop should include one leg. —*J. Clawson.*

Transporting an injured or aggressive cat. Lift up the cat as described in the text, and lower him into a sack or pillow case. —*J. Clawson.*

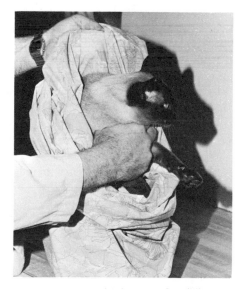

assistant wrap his front legs together with adhesive tape, taking two or three turns below the elbows. Secure the rear legs by wrapping with tape above the hocks. Calm him by covering his head with a towel or cloth.

When properly restrained, cats usually settle down and accept the treatment. When released, they soon forget the unpleasant experience.

Transporting an Injured Cat

When a cat is severely injured or in pain, he cannot be held responsible for his actions. No matter how docile his basic nature, you should recognize that under such circumstances he may scratch or bite.

DO NOT continue to struggle unsuccessfully with a weak or injured cat. This could tire him out quickly and produce further shock and collapse.

If able to handle, pick the cat up as described for *Cooperative Cat* and then settle him over your hip so that his rear claws project out behind where they can do no harm. Press the inside of your elbow and forearm against the cat's side and hold him firmly against your body. Cover his eyes and ears with your other hand.

If the cat is frightened or in pain, you should take precautions to avoid injury. Lift him up at once from behind by the nape of his neck and lower him into a cat carrier or a cloth bag such as a pillow case. The material must not be airtight or the cat will smother. Once inside where he can't see out, the cat will feel secure and begin to relax. Transport him to the veterinary hospital.

If unable to handle, throw a towel over the cat to calm him; then set a box on top. Raise the edge of the box and slide the top underneath. The cat is now enclosed and can be transported.

HEAT STROKE (Overheating)

Heat stroke is an emergency which requires immediate recognition and prompt treatment. Cats do not tolerate high temperatures as well as humans. They depend upon rapid breathing to exchange warm air for cool air. Heat-stressed cats drool a great deal and lick themselves to spread the saliva on their coats. The evaporation of saliva is an important additional cooling mechanism. But when air temperature is close to body temperature, cooling by evaporation is not an efficient process. Cats with airway disease also have difficulty with excess heat.

Common situations which predispose to overheating or heat stroke are:
1. Being left in a car in hot weather.
2. Being confined on concrete runs without shade in hot weather.
3. Being of a short-nosed breed, especially a Persian.
4. Suffering from airway disease; being overweight; or any condition which impairs breathing.

Heat stroke begins with rapid frantic noisy breathing. The tongue and mucous membranes are bright red; saliva is thick and tenacious; and the cat often vomits. His rectal temperature rises, sometimes to over 106 degrees F. The cause

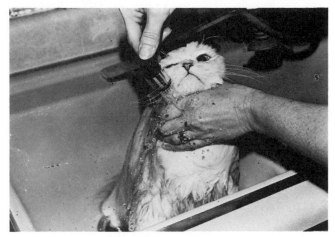

Heat stroke is an emergency. Cool the cat with a spray, or immerse him in a tub of cold water.

of the problem usually is evident by the typical appearance of the cat; it can be confirmed by taking his temperature.

If the condition is allowed to go unchecked, the cat becomes unsteady and staggers; he has diarrhea which often is bloody; and he becomes progressively weaker. His lips and mucous membranes become a pale blue or gray. Coma and death ensue.

Treatment: Emergency measures must begin at once. Mild cases respond to moving the cat to cooler surroundings such as an air-conditioned building or car. If his temperature is over 104 degrees F, or if he becomes unsteady on his feet, he should be cooled by immersing him in a tub of cold water; or wrap him in cold wet towels. As an alternative, hose him down with a garden hose. Ice packs can be applied to his head. For temperature over 106 degrees F, or if he is near to collapse, give him a cold water enema. A more rapid temperature drop is imperative.

Heat stroke can be associated with swelling of the throat. This aggravates the problem. A cortisone injection by your veterinarian may be required to treat this.

Prevention:

1. Do not expose cats with airway disease or impaired breathing to prolonged heat.
2. Don't leave a cat in a car with the windows closed, even though the car may be parked at first in the shade.
3. If traveling in a car, crate the cat in a well ventilated cat carrier, or better yet an open wire cage, so the windows can be left open.
4. Provide shade and cool water to cats living outdoors in runs.

HOW TO INDUCE VOMITING

DO NOT induce vomiting if your cat:

1. Swallows an acid, alkali, solvent, or heavy duty cleaner;
2. Is severely depressed or comatose;
3. Swallows a petroleum product;
4. Swallows tranquilizers (which prevent vomiting);
5. Swallows a sharp object (which could lodge in his esophagus or perforate his stomach);
6. Or if more than two hours have passed since the poison was swallowed.

Induce vomiting by giving:

1. Hydrogen peroxide 3% (most effective): One teaspoon every ten minutes; repeat three times.
2. One-fourth teaspoonful of salt, placed at the back of the tongue.
3. Syrup of Ipecac (one teaspoonful per ten pounds body weight).

INSECT STINGS

The stings of *bees, wasps, yellow jackets and ants* all cause painful swelling at the site of the sting. If an animal is stung many times, he could go into shock as the result of absorbed toxins. Rarely, hypersensitivity reactions develop in cats who have been stung before (see SKIN: *Allergies*).

The stings of *Black widow* and *Missouri brown* spiders, and *tarantulas,* also are toxic to animals. The signs are sharp pain at the sting site. Later the cat can develop chills, fever, labored breathing. Shock can occur.

The stings of *centipedes* and *scorpions* cause local reaction and at times severe illness. These bites heal slowly.

Other common insect parasites are discussed in the SKIN chapter.

Treatment of insect bites:

1. Identify the insect.
2. Remove a stinger, when accessible, with tweezers. (Only bees leave their stingers behind.)
3. Make a paste of baking soda and apply it directly to the sting.
4. Ice packs relieve swelling and pain.
5. Calamine lotion relieves itching.

If there are signs of generalized toxicity, take your cat to the veterinarian.

PAINFUL ABDOMEN (Acute Abdomen)

An acute abdomen is an emergency that can lead to the death of the cat unless treatment is started as soon as possible.

The condition is characterized by the *sudden onset* of abdominal pain along with vomiting; retching; extreme restlessness and inability to find a comfortable

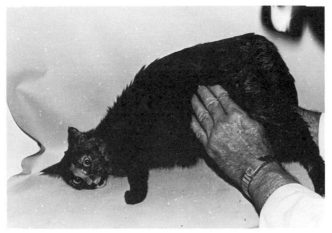

A *painful abdomen* indicates the need for immediate veterinary attention.

position; purring; meowing and crying; grunting; and labored breathing. The abdomen is extremely painful when pressed on. A characteristic position is sometimes seen in which the cat rests his chest against the floor with his rump up in the air (prayer position). As the condition worsens, his pulse becomes weak and thready, his mucous membranes appear pale, and he goes into shock.

One of the following may be the cause:

Urinary stones
Trauma to the abdomen with internal injury
Rupture of the bladder
Perforation of the stomach and intestines
Poisoning
Rupture of a pregnant uterus
Acute peritonitis
Acute pancreatitis
Intestinal obstruction.

A cat with an acute abdomen is critically ill. He should have immediate veterinary attention.

POISONING

General Remarks

A poison is any substance harmful to the body. Animal baits are palatable poisons that encourage ingestion. This makes them an obvious choice for intentional poisoning.

Cats by nature are curious and have a tendency to hunt small game, or explore out of the way places such as wood piles, weed thickets, and storage ports. This puts them into contact with insects, dead animals and toxic plants. It also means that in many cases of suspected poisoning the actual agent will be un-

known. The great variety of potentially poisonous plants and shrubs makes identification difficult or impossible, unless the owner has direct knowledge that his
cat has eaten a certain plant or product. Most cases suspected of being malicious
poisoning actually are not.

In some types of vegetation only certain parts of the plant are toxic. In
others, all parts are poisonous. Ingestion causes a wide range of symptoms. They
include: mouth irritation; drooling; vomiting; diarrhea; hallucinations; seizures;
coma; and death. Other plant substances cause skin rash. Some toxic plants have
specific pharmological actions which are used in medicines.

Tables of toxic plants, shrubs, and trees are included for reference. This list
is a collection of common toxic plants. It is not a list of all poisonous plants.

POISONOUS HOUSEPLANTS

Toxic Houseplants

A. That give rash after contact with the skin or mouth:

Chrysanthemum	Weeping fig	Pot mum
Creeping fig	Poinsettia	Spider mum

B. Irritating (toxic oxalates); especially the mouth gets swollen; tongue
pain; sore lips:

Arrowhead vine	Heart leaf	Pathos
Boston Ivy	(Philodendrum)	Red Princess
Colodium	Marble Queen	Saddle leaf
Drunk cane	Majesty	(Philodendrum)
Emerald Duke	Neththyis	Split leaf
	Parlor Ivy	(Philodendrum)

C. *Toxic plants*—may contain wide variety of poisons. Most cause vomiting, abdominal pain, cramps. Some cause tremors, heart and
respiratory and/or kidney problems, which are difficult for an owner to
interpret:

Amaryllis	Elephant ears	Pot mum
Asparagus fern	Glocal Ivy	Ripple Ivy
Azalea	Heart Ivy	Spider mum
Bird of paradise	Ivy	Sprangeri Fern
Creeping Charlie	Jerusalem Cherry	Umbrella plant
Crown of thorns	Needlepoint Ivy	

OUTDOOR PLANTS WITH TOXIC EFFECTS

A. *Outdoor plants* that produce vomiting and diarrhea in some cases:

Delphinium	Skunk Cabbage	Larkspur
Daffodil	Poke weed	Indian Tobacco
Castor bean	Bittersweet woody	Wisteria
Indian turnip	Ground cherry	Soap berry
	Fox glove	

B. *Trees and shrubs* which are poisonous and may produce vomiting, abdominal pain, and in some cases diarrhea:

Horse chestnut	Western Yew	Apricot, almond
Buckey	English Holly	Peach, cherry
Rain tree	Privet	Wild cherry
Monkey pod	Mock orange	Japanese plum
American Yew	Bird of Paradise	Balsam Pear
English Yew	bush	Black locust

C. *Outdoor plants* with varied toxic effect:

Rhubarb	Buttercup	Moonseed
Spinach	Nightshade	May apple
Sunburned potatoes	Poison Hemlock	Dutchman's breeches
Loco weed	Pig weed	Angel's trumpet
Lupine	Water Hemlock	Jasmine
Dologeton	Mushrooms	Matrimony vine

D. *Hallucinogens:*

Marijuana	Nutmeg	Peyote
Morning glory	Periwinkle	Loco weed

E. *Convulsions:*

China berry	Moonweed	Water Hemlock
Coriaria	Nux vomica	

If you think that your cat may have been poisoned, the first thing to do is try to identify the poison. Most products containing chemicals are labeled for identification. Read the label. If this does not give you a clue to its possible toxicity, call the emergency room of your local hospital and ask for information from the *Poison Control Center.* (In addition, the *University of Illinois* provides a unique service called *Toxicology Hotline for Animals.* Day or night, a caller can obtain information and advice about known or suspected cases of poisoning or chemical contamination by calling the hotline number: 217-333-3611. The hotline is manned 24 hours a day, seven days a week.)

The first step in treatment is to eliminate the poison from your cat's stomach by making him vomit (see *How to Induce Vomiting* earlier in this chapter). The second step is to delay absorption of the poison from his intestinal tract by coating it with a substance which binds it. This should be followed by a laxative to speed its elimination.

How to Delay or Prevent Absorption:

1. Mix activated charcoal with water (5 grams to 20 cc). Give one teaspoonful per two pounds body weight.
2. Thirty minutes later, give sodium sulphate (glauber's salt), one teaspoonful per ten pounds body weight, or Milk of Magnesia, one teaspoonful per five pounds body weight.

Note: If these agents are not available, coat the bowel with milk, egg whites, vegetable oil; and give a warm water enema.

If your cat has a poisonous substance on his skin or coat, wash it well with soap and water or give him a complete bath in *lukewarm* (not cold) water, as described in the SKIN chapter. Even if the substance is not irritating to the skin, it should be removed. Otherwise he may lick it off and swallow it. Soak gasoline and oil stains with mineral or vegetable oil. Work in well. Then wash with a mild detergent, such as Ivory soap.

If your cat begins to show signs of nervous system involvement, he is in deep trouble. At this point, your main objective is to *get your cat to a veterinarian as quickly as possible.* Try to bring with you a sample of vomitus, or better yet the poison in its original container. Do not delay to administer first aid—unless it is life saving. If the cat is convulsing, unconscious, or not breathing, see *Artificial Respiration and Heart Massage.* See also *Fits* and *Loss of Consciousness* in the NERVOUS SYSTEM chapter.

The poisons discussed below are included because they are among the most frequently seen by veterinarians.

Strychnine

Strychnine is used as a rat, mouse, and mole poison. It is available commercially as coated pellets dyed purple, red, or green. Signs of poisoning are so typical that the diagnosis can be made almost at once. Onset is sudden (less than two hours). The first signs are agitation, excitability, and apprehension. They are followed rather quickly by intensely painful tetanic seizures which last about 60 seconds, during which the cat throws back his head, can't breathe, and turns blue. The slightest stimulation, such as tapping the cat or clapping the hands, starts a seizure. This characteristic response is used to make the diagnosis. Other signs associated with nervous system involvement are: tremors; champing; drooling; uncoordinate muscle spasms; collapse; and paddling of the legs.

Seizures due to strychnine and other central nervous system toxins sometimes are misdiagnosed as epilepsy. This would be a mistake, as immediate veterinary attention is necessary. Epileptic seizures are usually self-limited; the signs always appear in a certain order, and each attack is the same. They are over before the cat can get to a veterinarian. Usually they are not considered emergencies (see NERVOUS SYSTEM: *Epilepsy).*

Treatment: If your cat is showing signs of poisoning and hasn't vomited, induce vomiting as discussed above.

With signs of central nervous system involvement, don't take time to induce vomiting. It is important to avoid loud noises or unnecessary handling which might trigger a seizure. Cover your cat with a coat or blanket and drive him to the nearest veterinary clinic.

Sodium Fluroacetate (1080)

This chemical, used as a rat poison, is mixed with cereal, bran, and other rat feeds. It is so potent that cats and dogs can be poisoned just by eating a dead rodent. The onset is sudden and begins with vomiting—followed by agitation, straining to urinate or defecate, a staggering gait, atypical fits or true convulsions, and then collapse. Seizures are not triggered by external stimuli as are those of strychnine poisoning.

Treatment: Immediately after the cat ingests the poison, induce vomiting. Care and handling is the same as for strychnine.

Arsenic

Arsenic is combined with metaldehyde in slug and snail baits, and may appear in ant poisons, weed killers, and insecticides. Arsenic is also a common impurity found in many chemicals. Death can occur quickly before there is time to observe the symptoms. In more protracted cases the signs are thirst, drooling, vomiting, staggering, intense abdominal pain, cramps, diarrhea, paralysis and death. The breath of the cat has a strong odor of garlic.

Treatment: Induce vomiting. A specific antidote is available. See your veterinarian.

Metaldehyde

This poison (often combined with arsenic) is used commonly in rat, snail, and slug baits. The signs of toxicity are excitation, drooling and slobbering, uncoordinated gait, muscle tremors, and weakness which leads to inability to stand in a few hours. The tremors are not triggered by external stimuli.

Treatment: Immediately after the cat ingests the poison, induce vomiting. The care and handling are the same as for strychnine.

Lead

Lead is found in insecticides and serves as a base for many commercial paints. Intoxication mainly occurs in kittens and young cats who chew on substances coated with a lead paint. Other sources of lead are: linoleum; batteries; plumbing materials. Lead poisoning can occur in older cats following the ingestion of an insecticide containing lead. A chronic form does occur.

Acute poisoning begins with abdominal colic and vomiting. A variety of central nervous system signs are possible. They include fits, uncoordinated gait, excitation, attacks of hysteria, weakness, stupor, and blindness.

Treatment: Immediately after ingestion, induce vomiting. If some time has elapsed, coat the bowel as described above. Specific antidotes are available through your veterinarian.

Phosphorus

This chemical is present in rat and roach poisons, fireworks, matches and matchboxes. A poisoned cat may have a garlic odor to his breath. The first signs of intoxication are vomiting and diarrhea. They may be followed by a free interval—then by recurrent vomiting; cramps; pain in the abdomen; convulsions and coma.

There is no specific antidote. Treat as you would for strychnine.

Zinc Phosphide

This substance also is found in rat poisons. Intoxication causes central nervous system depression; labored breathing; vomiting (often of blood); weakness; convulsions; and death. There is no specific antidote. Treat as you would for strychnine.

Warfarin (Decon; Pindone)

Warfarin is incorporated into grain feeds for use as rat and mouse poisons. It causes death by interfering with the blood clotting mechanism. This leads to spontaneous bleeding. There are no observable signs of warfarin poisoning until the cat begins to pass blood in his stool or urine, bleeds from his nose, or develops hemorrhages beneath his gums and skin. He may be found dead without apparent cause. A single dose of warfarin is not as serious as repeated doses.

Treatment: Induce vomiting. Vitamin K is a specific antidote. It is given intramuscularly (or in cases where there are no symptoms it can be given by mouth as a preventative).

Antifreeze *(Ethylene glycol)*

Poisoning with antifreeze is one of the most common poisoning conditions found in cats. This is because *ethylene glycol* has a sweet taste that appeals to cats and dogs. One teaspoon of antifreeze can kill an average size cat! Signs of toxicity, which appear suddenly, are vomiting, uncoordinated gait (seems "drunk"), weakness, mental depression and coma. Death occurs in 12 to 36 hours. Convulsions are unusual. Cats who recover from the acute poisoning may have damage to their kidneys and go on to kidney failure.

Treatment: Induce vomiting. Coat the bowel to prevent further absorption. Intensive care in an animal hospital may prevent kidney complications.

Organophosphates and Carbamates

These substances are used on cats to kill fleas and other parasites. The common ones are *Dichlorvos, Ectoral, Malathion,* and *Sevin,* but there are others. They are also used in garden sprays and in some dewormers. Improper application of insecticides to the cat can lead to absorption of a toxic dose through the skin. These drugs affect the nervous system primarily. Insecticides are discussed in the SKIN chapter.

Petroleum Products (Gasoline, Kerosene, Turpentine)

These volatile liquids can cause pneumonia if aspirated or inhaled. The signs of toxicity are vomiting, difficulty in breathing, tremors, convulsions and coma. Death is by respiratory failure.

Treatment: Do not induce vomiting. Administer one ounce of mineral oil, olive oil, or vegetable oil by mouth; then follow it in 30 minutes with glauber's salt (one teaspoon per 10 pounds body weight), or Milk of Magnesia (one teaspoon per five pounds body weight). Be prepared to administer artificial respiration.

Chlorinated Hydrocarbons

These compounds, like the organophosphates, are incorporated into some insecticide preparations (not for use on cats). The common products in veterinary use are *Chloradane, Toxaphene, Lindane,* and *Methoxychlor.* Accidental application to cats produces muscle twitching, excitation and convulsions. Bathe the animal immediately to remove the substance from his coat. Veterinary attention is imperative.

Corrosives (Acid and Alkali)

Corrosives and caustics are found in household cleaners, drain decloggers, and commercial solvents. They cause burns of the mouth, esophagus and stomach. Severe cases are associated with acute perforation (or late stricture) of the esophagus and stomach.

Treatment: If an acid is ingested, rinse out your cat's mouth. Then administer an antacid (Milk of Magnesia or Pepto-Bismol) at the rate of one to two teaspoons per five pounds body weight.

In the case of an alkali, use vinegar or lemon juice. Vinegar is mixed one part to four parts of water.

In either situation, do not induce vomiting. This could result in rupture of the stomach or burns of the esophagus.

Garbage Poisoning (Food Poisoning)

Cats are more particular about what they eat than dogs. Nevertheless, they too are scavengers and come into contact with carrion, decomposing foods, animal manure and other noxious substances (some of which are listed in DIGESTIVE SYSTEM: *Common Causes of Diarrhea*). Cats are more sensitive to food poisoning than dogs and show effects at lower levels. Signs of poisoning begin with vomiting and pain in the abdomen. Two to six hours later, in severe cases, they are followed by a diarrhea which is often bloody. Shock may occur—particularly if the problem is complicated by bacterial infection. Mild cases recover in a day or two.

Treatment: Induce vomiting. Afterwards, coat the intestines to delay or prevent absorption as described above. Antibiotics may be required.

Toad Poisoning

All toads have a bad taste. Cats who mouth them slobber, spit and drool. In southern states a tropical toad (*Bufo marinus*) secretes a potent toxin which appears to affect the heart and circulation, bringing on death in as short a time as 15 minutes. There are 12 species of "Bufo" toads distributed world-wide.

Symptoms in cats depend upon the toxicity of the toad and the amount of poison absorbed. They vary from merely slobbering to convulsions, blindness and death.

Treatment: Flush out your cat's mouth with a garden hose and attempt to induce vomiting. Be prepared to administer artificial respiration.

People Medicines

Veterinarians frequently are called because a cat has swallowed pills intended for his owner, or has eaten too many of his own pills. (Some cat pills are flavored to encourage cats to eat them.) Drugs most often involved are antihistamines, pain relievers, sleeping pills, diet pills, heart preparations, and vitamins.

Cats appear to be unusually sensitive to drugs and medications. The reasons for this are discussed in the chapter DRUGS AND MEDICATIONS. Common household items considered safe for humans may be toxic to cats. All cases of drug ingestion should be taken seriously.

Treatment: Induce vomiting and coat the bowel as described above to prevent further absorption. Discuss the potential side effects of the drug with your veterinarian.

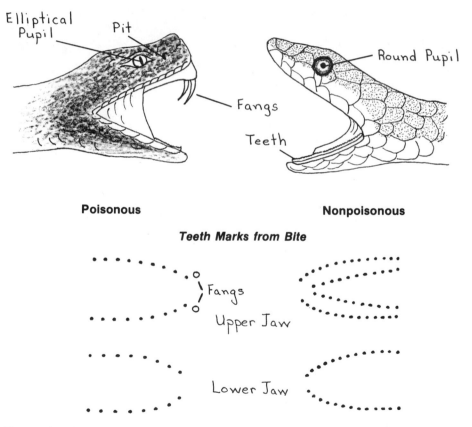

Poisonous   **Nonpoisonous**

Teeth Marks from Bite

Except for the coral snake, all poisonous species in North America are pit vipers. Note the elliptical pupil, pit below the eye, large fangs, and characteristic bite.
—Rose Floyd.

SNAKE BITES

If your cat is bitten by a snake, there may be no cause for concern as the majority of snakes are not poisonous. The bites of harmless snakes show teeth marks in the shape of a horseshoe—but there are no fang marks.

In the United States there are four poisonous varieties: Cotton mouth moccasins, Rattlesnakes, Copperheads, and Coral snakes. The diagnosis of poison snake bite is made by the appearance of the bite; the behavior of the animal; and by identification of the species of snake. (Kill it first, if possible.)

Pit Vipers (Rattlesnakes - Moccasins - Copperheads)

Identify these species by their large arrow-shaped heads, pits below and between the eyes, elliptical pupils, rough scales, and the presence of fangs in the upper jaws.

The bite: There are two puncture wounds in the skin (fang marks). Signs of local reaction appear quickly and include swelling; excruciating pain; redness; and hemorrhages in the skin.

Behavior of the animal: Signs and symptoms depend on the size and species of the snake, location of the bite, and amount of toxin absorbed into the system. The first signs are extreme restlessness, panting, drooling, and weakness. These are followed by diarrhea, collapse, sometimes seizures; shock; and death in severe cases.

Coral Snake

Identify this snake by its rather small size, small head with black nose, and vivid-colored bands of red, yellow, white and black—the red and yellow bands always next to each other. Fangs are present in the upper jaw.

The bite: There is less severe local reaction but the pain is excruciating. Look for the fang marks.

Behavior of the animal: Coral snake venom primarily is neurotoxic (destructive to nerve tissue). Signs include vomiting, diarrhea, urinary incontinence, paralysis, convulsions and coma.

Treatment of All Bites:

First identify the snake and look at the bite. If it appears that your cat has been bitten by a poisonous snake, proceed as follows:

1. Restrain the cat. Snake bites are extremely painful.
2. Apply a flat tourniquet above the bite. It should not be as tight as an arterial tourniquet (see *Wounds*), but should be tight enough to keep venous blood from returning to the heart.
3. Use a knife or razor blade and make parallel cuts one-fourth inch deep through the fang marks. On a leg, make them up and down. Blood should ooze from the wound. If not, loosen the tourniquet.
4. Apply mouth suction to the wound unless you have a cut or open sore in your mouth. Spit out the blood. If poison is swallowed, the stomach will inactivate it. Continue for 30 minutes.

5. Loosen the tourniquet for 30 seconds every half hour.
6. KEEP THE CAT QUIET. Excitement, exercise, struggling—all these increase the rate of absorption. Carry him to your veterinarian.

Specific antivenoms are available through veterinarians. Snake bites become infected. Antibiotics and dressings are indicated.

SHOCK

Shock is lack of adequate blood flow to meet the body's needs. Adequate blood flow requires effective heart pumping, open intact vessels, and sufficient blood volume to maintain flow and pressure. Any condition adversely affecting the heart, vessels, or blood volume, can induce shock.

At first the body attempts to compensate for the inadequate circulation by speeding up the heart, constricting the skin vessels, and maintaining fluid in the circulation by reducing output of urine. This becomes increasingly difficult to do when the vital organs aren't getting enough oxygen to carry on these activities. After a time, shock becomes self-perpetuating. Untreated, shock causes death.

Common causes of shock are: dehydration (prolonged vomiting and diarrhea); heat stroke; severe infections; poisoning; and hemorrhage. Falling from a height, and being hit by a car, are the most common causes of traumatic shock in the cat.

The signs of shock are: a drop in body temperature; shivering; listlessness and mental depression; weakness; cold feet and legs; pale skin and mucous membranes; and a weak faint pulse.

Treatment: First evaluate the cat. Is he breathing? Does he have a heartbeat? What are the extent of his injuries? Is he in shock? If so, proceed as follows:
1. If not breathing, proceed with *artificial respiration.*
2. If no heart beat or pulse, administer *heart massage.*
3. If unconscious, check to be sure his airway is open. Clear secretions from his mouth with your fingers. Pull out his tongue to keep his airway clear of secretions. Keep his head lower than his body.
4. Control bleeding (as described below under *Wounds*).
5. To prevent further aggravation of shock:
   a. Calm him, and speak soothingly.
   b. Let him assume the most comfortable position. He will naturally adopt the one of least pain. Don't force him to lie down—it may make his breathing more difficult.
   c. When possible, splint or support broken bones before moving the cat (see MUSCULOSKELETAL SYSTEM: *Broken Bones).*
   d. Wrap the cat in a blanket to provide warmth and protect injured extremities. How to handle and restrain an injured cat for transport to the veterinary hospital is discussed above (see *Handling and Restraint).* Do not attempt to muzzle a cat. This may impair his breathing.

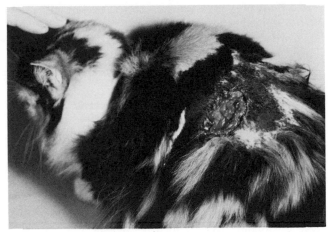

An infected cat-fight wound. It should be treated as described in the text.

WOUNDS

In the care of wounds, the two most important considerations are (*a*) first stop the bleeding, and (*b*) then prevent infection. Be prepared to restrain before you treat the wound (see *Handling and Restraint*).

Control of Bleeding

Bleeding may be *arterial* (the spurting of bright red blood), or *venous* (oozing of dark red blood) or sometimes both. Do not wipe a wound which has stopped bleeding. This will dislodge the clot. Don't pour peroxide on a fresh wound. Bleeding then will be difficult to control.

The two methods used to control bleeding are the pressure dressing and the tourniquet:

The Pressure Dressing: Take several pieces of clean or sterile gauze, place them over the wound, and bandage snugly. Watch for swelling of the limb below the pressure pack. This indicates impaired circulation. The bandage must be loosened or removed.

If material is not available for bandaging, place a pad on the wound and press it firmly. Hold it in place until help arrives.

A method to temporarily control arterial bleeding is to apply pressure over the artery in the groin or axilla. (See CIRCULATORY SYSTEM: *Pulse*). Often this will stop bleeding long enough to permit an assistant to apply a pressure dressing.

The Tourniquet: A tourniquet may be needed to control a sputting artery. It can be applied to the leg or tail above the wound (between the wound and heart). Take a piece of cloth or gauze roll and loop it around the limb. Then tighten it by hand, or with a stick inserted between the loop, and twist it around until bleeding is controlled. If you see the end of the artery, you might attempt to pick it up with tweezers and tie it off with a piece of cotton thread. When possible, this should be left to a trained practitioner.

A tourniquet should be loosened every 30 minutes, for two to three minutes, to let blood flow into the limb.

Treating the Wound

All wounds are contaminated with dirt and bacteria. Proper care and handling will prevent some infections. Before handling a wound, make sure your hands and instruments are clean. Starting at the edges of a fresh wound, clip the hair back to enlarge the area. Cleanse the edges with a damp gauze or pad. Irrigate the wound with clean tap water. Apply antibiotic ointment. Bandage as described below.

Older wounds with a covering of pus and scab are cleaned with 3% hydrogen peroxide solution or surgical soap. Blot dry. Apply antibiotic ointment and either leave open or bandage as described below.

Dressings over infected wounds should be changed frequently to aid in the drainage of pus and allow you to apply fresh ointment.

Fresh lacerations over ½ inch long should be sutured to prevent infection, minimize scarring, and speed healing.

Wounds older than 12 hours are quite likely to be infected. Suturing is questionable.

Bites are heavily contaminated wounds. Often they are puncture wounds. They are quite likely to get infected. They should not be sutured. Antibiotics are indicated. Most wounds incurred in a cat fight are of the puncture variety.

With all animal bites, the possibility of rabies should be kept in mind (see IN-FECTIOUS DISEASES: *Rabies*).

Bandaging

Bandages are more difficult to apply to cats than to dogs; and once applied more difficult to keep in place. Cats who do not tolerate bandages and continually remove them may be helped by tranquilization. Wounds about the head, and wounds draining pus, are best left open to facilitate drainage and ease of treatment.

When a cat claws and macerates a wound, or continually scratches at a skin condition, treatment can be facilitated by bandaging his back feet or clipping his nails.

Bandaging is made much easier when a cat is gently but firmly restrained as discussed earlier in this chapter. The bandaging equipment you will need is listed in the *Home Emergency and Medical Kit* at the beginning of the chapter.

Foot and Leg Bandages: To bandage a foot, place several sterile gauze pads over the wound. Insert cotton balls between the toes and hold in place with adhesive tape looped around the bottom of the foot and back across the top until the foot is snugly wrapped.

For leg wounds, begin by wrapping the foot as described. Then cover the wound with several sterile gauze pads and hold in place with strips of adhesive

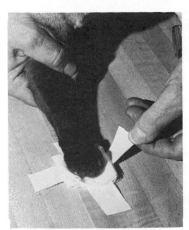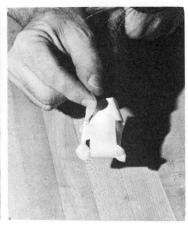

A method of applying a foot bandage. Tape loosely to allow for good circulation.
—*J. Clawson.*

tape. Wrap the tape around the leg but don't overlap it, so that the tape sticks to the hair. This keeps the dressing from sliding up and down, as often happens when a roll gauze bandage is used. Flex the knee and foot several times to be sure the bandage is not too tight and there is good circulation and movement at the joints.

When a dressing is to be left in place for some time, check on it every few hours to be sure the foot is not swelling. If there is any question about the sensation or circulation to the foot, loosen the dressing. Cats will frequently attempt to lick at, bite at, or remove dressings which are too tight and uncomfortable.

Many-Tailed Bandage: This bandage is used to protect the skin of the abdomen, flanks or back from scratching and biting, and to hold dressings in place. It is made by taking a rectangular piece of linen and cutting the sides to make tails. Tie the tails together over the back to hold it in place.

A many-tailed bandage may be used to keep kittens from nursing infected breasts.

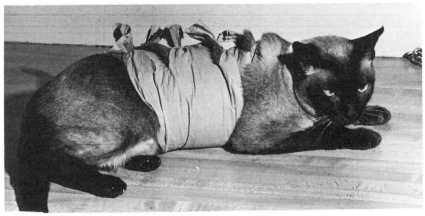

Many-tailed bandage.—*J. Clawson.*

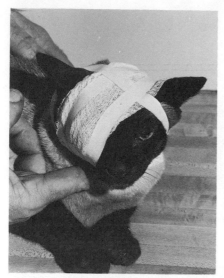

Eye bandage. **Wrap a gauze roll around the eye. A pad may be placed beneath. Secure with tape to the hair. The ears should be free.**
—*J. Clawson.*

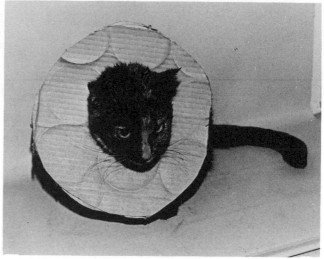

Elizabethan collar.

Eye Bandage. At times your veterinarian may prescribe an eye bandage in the treatment of an eye ailment. Place a sterile gauze square over the affected eye and hold it in place by taping around the head with one inch adhesive. Be careful not to get the tape too tight. Apply the dressing so that the ears are free.

You may be required to change the dressing from time to time to apply medication to the eye.

Ear Bandage. These dressings are difficult to apply. Most ear injuries can be left open. To protect the ears from scratching, an Elizabethan collar can be applied.

Elizabethan Collar. The Elizabethan collar, named for the high neck ruff popular in the reign of Queen Elizabeth, is a useful device to keep a cat from scratching at his ears and biting at a wound or skin problem. They can be purchased from some veterinarians or pet stores, or can be made from a piece of heavy flexible cardboard. Cut out a circle 12 inches in diameter. In the center, cut out a hole four to five inches in diameter. Cut out a wedge (like a piece of pie) one-quarter of the circumference of the circle. Fit the collar around the cat's neck and secure the sides with adhesive tape. Make sure the collar is not too tight around the neck. Fasten the device to the cat's leather collar by strings passed through holes punched in the sides of the cardboard. Many cats cannot or will not drink while wearing an Elizabethan collar. In that case, temporarily remove the collar.

2

Worms (Intestinal Parasites)

GENERAL INFORMATION

Most owners assume that if a cat is found to have parasites in his stool, then he must be suffering from a disease state.

This is not necessarily the case. Most cats are infested at one time or another with intestinal parasites. Some are born with them and others acquire them later in life. When they recover, they develop a certain amount of immunity. This helps to keep the worms in check.

If worms are causing a disease, there should be some change in the appearance of the stool. In turn, this is reflected by a decline in the general health of the cat. You should note decreased appetite, loss of weight, sometimes protrusion of the third eyelid, diarrhea, anemia, and the passage of mucus or blood.

It is probable that cats, like dogs, develop a resistance to certain intestinal parasites that have larvae which migrate in their tissues (e.g., roundworms, hookworms)—although this has not been proven in the cat. Tapeworms have no migratory phase and thus cause little build-up of immunity.

Roundworms, tapeworms and hookworms are the most common internal worm parasites in cats.

Resistance to roundworms appears age related. Kittens and young cats show less resistance and in consequence may experience a heavy infestation. This can lead to marked debility or even death. Cats over six months of age are less likely to show significant clinical signs.

Immunosuppressive drugs such as cortisone have been shown to activate large numbers of hookworm larvae lying dormant in an animal's tissues. Stressful events such as trauma, surgery, severe disease, and emotional upsets (i.e., shipping), also can activate dormant larvae. This leads to the appearance of eggs in the stool.

During lactation, round and hookworm larvae are activated and appear in the queen's milk. Therefore a heavy parasite problem might develop in the litter even when the mother was effectively dewormed. This can happen because none of the deworming agents are effective against larvae encysted in the tissue.

51

Deworming Your Cat

Although some deworming preparations are effective against more than one species of worms, there is no preparation that is effective against them all. Accordingly, for a medication to be safe and effective, a precise diagnosis is required. It is also important that the medication be given precisely as directed. Natural side-effects, such as diarrhea and vomiting, must be distinguished from toxic reactions. For these reasons, it is advisable to deworm only under veterinary supervision.

Deworming agents effective against various species of worms are given in the accompanying table.

DEWORMING AGENTS

DRUG	TYPE OF WORM INVOLVED				COMMENTS
	Hook	*Ascarid*	*Tape*		
Piperazine	—	***	—		Inexpensive. Safe. Do not over-dose.
Caricide (*Diethylcarbamazine*)	—	***	—		Piperazine derivative; less effective.
Task (*Dichlorvas*)	****	****	—		May potentiate effects of insecticides in coat preparations and flea collars.
Vermiplex (*Methylbenzene* and *Dichloraphene*)	***	****	***		Don't use if animal has diarrhea.
Yomesan (*Niclosamide*)	—	—	*** *	(Taenia) (D. caninum)	Vomiting often occurs.
Scolaban (*Bunamidine*)	—	—	**** **	(Taenia) (D. caninum)	
N - butyl chloride	**	***	—		Cathartic recommended. Not too effective.
DNP (*Disophenol*)	****	—	—		Given by injection. Do not use in debilitated animal.
Nemex (*Pyrantel pamoate*)	****	****	—		Safe but not cleared by USDA for use on cats at this time.
Telmintic (*Mebendazole*)	****	****	*** —	(Taenia) (D. caninum)	Safe but not cleared by USDA for use on cats at this time.
Droncit (*Praziquantel*)	—	—	****		

**** Excellent   *** Good   **Fair   *Poor   — No effect

Kittens — Many kittens are infested with roundworms. Other worms may be present, too. It is advisable to have your veterinarian check your kitten's stool before treating him for roundworms. Otherwise, other worms may go undetected.

Worm infestations are particularly harmful in kittens subjected to overfeeding, chilling, close confinement and a sudden change in diet. Stressful conditions such as these should be corrected before administering a deworming agent. Do not deworm a kitten with diarrhea or other signs of illness unless your veterinarian has determined that his illness is caused by an intestinal parasite.

Kittens with roundworms should be dewormed at two to three weeks of age and again at five to six weeks. If eggs or worms are still found in the stool, subsequent courses should be given.

Adults — Most veterinarians recommend that adult cats be dewormed only when there is specific evidence of an infestation. A stool examination is the most effective way of making an exact diagnosis and choosing the best agent.

It is not advisable to deworm a cat suffering from some unexplained illness which is assumed to be caused by "worms". All dewormers are poison—meant to poison the worm but not the cat. Cats who are debilitated by another disease may be too weak to resist the toxic effects of the deworming agent.

Cats of all ages, particularly those that hunt and roam freely, can be subject to periodic heavy worm infestations. These cats should be checked once or twice a year. If parasites are identified, they should be treated.

The Breeding Queen — Before breeding your female have her stool checked. If parasites are found, she should receive a thorough deworming. This will not protect her kittens from all worm infestation. However, it will help to put her in the best condition for a healthy pregnancy.

How to Control Worms

The life cycles of most worms are such that the possibility of reinfestation is great. To keep worms under control, you must destroy eggs or larvae *before* they reinfest the cat. This means good sanitation and maintaining clean dry quarters for your cat.

Cats should not be crowded together on shaded earth runways which provide ideal conditions for seeding eggs and larvae. A water-tight surface, such as cement, is the easiest to keep clean. Hose it down daily and allow it to dry in the sun. Gravel is a good substitute. Usually it provides effective drainage and it is easy to remove stools from gravel. Concrete and gravel surfaces can be disinfected with lime, salt or borax (one ounce to 10 square feet). Remove stools from the pens daily. Lawns should be cut short and watered only when necessary. Stools in the yard should be removed at least twice a week.

The litter box should be kept clean and dry and should be washed thoroughly every four days with detergents and boiling water.

Fleas, lice, cockroaches, beetles, waterbugs, and rodents are intermediate hosts of tapeworms and/or roundworms. It is necessary to get rid of these pests in order to control reinfestation (see *Premises Control*).

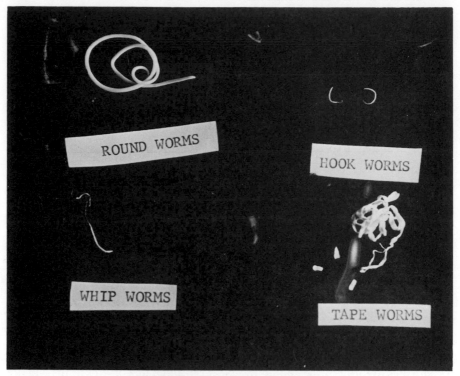

Common adult feline worms.

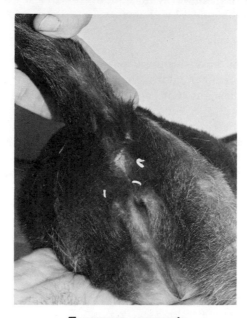

Tapeworm segments.

Many internal parasites spend the young stages of their life cycle in another animal and can only infect the cat and develop into adults when the cat preys on and eats this other animal. Accordingly, cats should not be allowed to roam and hunt. Be sure to cook thoroughly all fresh meat before feeding it to your cat.

Catteries that have continuous problems with worms often have other problems, too. They include skin, bowel and respiratory difficulties. Steps should be taken to improve the management of the cattery, especially sanitation measures.

DISEASES CAUSED BY CERTAIN WORMS

Roundworms

Ascarids are the most common worm parasite in kittens. There are three species which infest the cat. Adult roundworms live in the stomach and intestine and attain lengths up to five inches. The eggs are protected by a hard shell. They are extremely hardy and can live for months or years in the soil. They become infective in three to four weeks.

Cats acquire the disease through contact with soil containing the eggs or by eating an abnormal host, such as a beetle or rodent, who has acquired encysted larvae in its tissues. The larvae are released in the cat's digestive tract.

Larvae of the common feline roundworm *Toxocara cati* are capable of migrating in tissues. Eggs, entering via the oral route, hatch in the intestines. Larvae are carried to the lungs by the bloodstream. Here, they become mobile, crawl up the windpipe and are swallowed. This may cause bouts of coughing and gagging. They return to the intestine and develop into adults.

In the older cat, only a few larvae return to the intestine. The others encyst in tissues and remain dormant. During lactation, these dormant larvae are released, re-enter the circulation, and get to kittens via the breast milk.

Deworming the queen before or during pregnancy does not prevent roundworm infestation of kittens. Medications do not work on encysted larvae.

Roundworms usually do not produce a heavy infestation in adult cats, but may do so among those who do a lot of hunting. In kittens, a heavy infestation can result in severe illness or even death. Such kittens appear thin and have a pot-bellied look; sometimes cough or vomit; experience diarrhea; and may come down with pneumonia as the worms migrate from the blood vessels to the air sacs of the lungs. Worms may be found in the vomitus or passed in the stool. Typically, they look like white earthworms or strands of spaghetti which are alive and moving.

Roundworms can cause a disease in humans called *visceral larva migrans*. Most of them are caused by the dog roundworm, *Toxocara canis,* but the cat roundworm also can produce this disease. Only few cases are reported each year, usually from areas with a mild climate. There is often a history of dirt-eating (of soil contaminated by the eggs). Children are most likely to be affected. Because man is not the normal host, the immature worms do not become adults. Instead, they migrate in the tissues and wander aimlessly, causing fever, anemia, liver enlargement, pneumonia and other ill effects. The disease runs its course in about a year. It is best prevented by controlling infestation in dogs and cats through periodic deworming and good sanitation (see *Premises Control*).

Treatment: A Piperazine compound (*Antepar*) is the safest dewormer for roundworms and for this reason is the agent of choice for kittens. Kittens should be dewormed by three weeks of age to prevent contamination of their quarters by roundworm eggs. A second course should be given two to three weeks later to kill any adult worms which were in the larval stage at the first deworming. Subsequent courses are indicated if eggs or worms are found in the stool.

Piperazine dewormers can be obtained from your veterinarian or a pet shop. You do not have to fast your cat before using this agent. Be sure to follow the directions of the manufacturer in regard to dosage.

Dichlorvos (*Task*) is effective against roundworms, hookworms and whipworms. It is somewhat harsher than Piperazine. Cats who have just been medicated with insecticides, or who wear flea collars, should not be treated within a week. Use under veterinary guidance.

Telmintic (*Mebendazole*) is effective against roundworms, hookworms, tapeworms and whipworms. Although it has not been approved for cats at this time, it may be in the near future. One disadvantage is that it must be given for three to five consecutive days. It should be used under veterinary guidance.

Hookworms (Ancylostoma)

There are four species of hookworm which afflict the cat. Hookworms are not as common in cats as they are in dogs. They are most prevalent in areas of high temperature and humidity (for example, in the southern United States), where conditions are favorable for rapid development and spread of larvae.

Hookworms are small thin worms about one-fourth to one-half inch long. They fasten to the wall of the small intestine and draw blood from the host.

The cat acquires the disease by ingesting infected larvae in soil or feces, or by direct penetration of the skin (usually the pads of the feet). The immature worms migrate to the intestine where they become adults. In about two weeks, the cat begins to pass eggs in the feces. The eggs incubate in the soil. Depending upon conditions, larvae can become infective within two to five days.

Newborn kittens can acquire the disease from the milk of an infected queen.

The typical signs of *acute* hookworm infestation are anemia and diarrhea. With a heavy infestation stools might be bloody, wine-dark or tarry-black, but this is uncommon. A hookworm infestation can be fatal in very young kittens.

Chronic infection usually is not a problem in the adult cat. When it occurs, the signs are diarrhea, anemia, weight loss and progressive weakness. The diagnosis is made by finding the eggs in the feces.

Many cats who recover from the disease become carriers via cysts in the tissue. During periods of stress or some other illness, a new outbreak can occur as the larvae are released.

A disease in humans called *cutaneous larvae migrans* (creeping eruption) is caused by the hookworm (*A. brasiliense*). It is due to penetration of the skin by larvae present in the soil. It causes lumps, streaks beneath the skin, and itching. The condition is self-limited.

Treatment: A number of agents are effective against hookworms. Disophenol (DNP) is a preparation which must be given by subcutaneous injection. Dichlorvos (Task) and Methylbenzene (Vermiplex) are effective against both hookworms and roundworms. Nemex and Telmintic also are effective against hookworms and roundworms, but not cleared for use on cats at this time. Consult your veterinarian before using any of these agents.

To prevent reinfestation, see *How to Control Worms.*

Kittens with acute signs and symptoms require intensive veterinary management.

Tapeworms (Cestodes)

Tapeworms are the most common internal parasite in the adult cat. They live in the small intestine. The scolex (head) of the parasite fastens itself to the wall of the gut by hooks and suckers. The body is composed of segments containing the egg packets. Tapeworms vary in length from less than an inch to several feet. To eliminate tapeworm infection, the head must be destroyed. Otherwise, the worm will regenerate.

The body segments containing the eggs are passed in the feces. Fresh moist segments are capable of moving. They are about a quarter of an inch long. Occasionally you might see them adhering to the fur about your cat's anus, or in his stool. When dry, they resemble kernels of rice.

There are two common tapeworm species in the cat. Both are transmitted via an intermediate host. The worm *Diphylidium caninum* is acquired from fleas or lice which harbor immature tapeworms in their intestines. These insects acquire the parasite by eating tapeworm eggs. The cat must bite or swallow the insect.

The tapeworm *Taenia taeniaformis* is acquired by eating uncooked meat, raw fresh water fish, or discarded animal parts.

Dibothriocephalus latus and *Spirometra mansanoides* are two uncommon tapeworms cats might acquire from eating uncooked fresh water fish or a water snake.

A child could acquire a tapeworm if he accidentally swallowed an infective flea. Except for this unusual circumstance, cat tapeworms do not present a hazard to human health.

Treatment: Droncit is one of the most effective preparations against both common species of cat tapeworm. Other suitable remedies are Yomesan and Scolaban. Use under veterinary guidance. Deworming must be combined with control of fleas and lice in the case of *D. caninum* (see *How to Control Worms),* and by preventing roaming and hunting in the case of other tapeworms.

Uncommon Worm Parasites

Pinworms are a common cause of concern to families having cats and children. Cats do not present a source of human pinworm infection as they do not acquire or spread this disease.

Eye worms occur among cats living on the West Coast of the United States. They are discussed in the chapter EYES.

Trichinosis is a disease acquired through ingestion of uncooked pork containing the encysted larvae of *Trichina spiralis.* It is estimated that 15% of people living in the United States have at some time acquired trichinosis— although only a few clinical cases are reported each year. The incidence is probably somewhat higher in cats and dogs. Prevent this disease in your cat by keeping him from roaming, particularly if you live in a rural area. Cook all fresh meat (both your own and your cat's).

Whipworms are slender parasites two to three inches long which live in the cecum (first part of the large intestine). Since they are thicker at one end, they give the appearance of a whip. Whipworm infestation is uncommon.
Eggs in the soil become infective in two to four weeks. When ingested, they develop into larvae. The signs of infestation are intermittent diarrhea and the passage of mucus or blood. These are non-specific. Accordingly, the diagnosis is made by finding the eggs in the feces. Whipworm eggs can easily be confused with those of the lungworm.
A number of dewormers are effective against this parasite.

Flukes are flatworms ranging in size from a few millimeters up to an inch or more in length. There are several species which parasitize different parts of the cat's body including the lung, liver and small intestine. Flukes are acquired by eating infected raw fish and small prey such as snails, frogs, crayfish.
Signs of fluke infestation are variable. Professional diagnosis is required. Drug treatment is difficult and not always successful. Infection should be prevented by cooking fish and restricting hunting.

Heartworms are common in dogs but rare in cats. They are discussed in the chapter CIRCULATORY SYSTEM.

Lungworms are slender hair-like parasites about one centimeter in length. There are several species of lungworm, but only two commonly affect cats. *Aeleurostrongylus abstrussus* has a complicated life-cycle. Larvae are passed in the feces. They are taken up by snails and slugs which, in turn, are eaten by birds, rodents, frogs. When these transport hosts are eaten by the cat, eggs hatch in the intestine. Adult worms migrate to the lungs and lay eggs. Larvae migrate up the windpipe, are swallowed, and pass in the feces. The second common lungworm, *Capillaria aerophila,* is acquired by the direct ingestion of infective eggs or a transport host.

Most cats do not show signs of clinical infection. Others may exhibit a chronic cough. Occasionally a cat will experience fever, weight loss, wheezing, nasal discharge. The symptoms might suggest some other respiratory illness. A chest x-ray may show scarring, due to the effects of the worms.

Microscopic diagnosis is made by finding coiled or comma-shaped larvae in feces or sputum (*A. abstrussus*). The ova of *C. aerophilia* are easily confused with the eggs of whipworms. Many cases thought to be whipworm infestation probably are due to lungworms.

Lungworms are difficult to eliminate. Veterinary management is required.

Stomach worms are most likely to affect cats living in the southwestern United States. There are three species of stomach worm that affect cats. The infection is acquired by eating beetles (cockroaches, crickets) that have ingested eggs from the soil.

Recurrent vomiting is the most common symptom. Veterinary diagnosis is necessary to distinguish stomach worms from other causes of vomiting. Piperazine derivatives are effective in treatment. Prevent this disease by keeping your cat from roaming and hunting.

Bladder worms are common in Australia but rare in the United States. The life-cycle is unknown. Worms live in the urinary bladder and pass eggs in the urine. The eggs resemble those of the whipworm. The infection causes few if any problems.

3

Infectious Diseases

GENERAL INFORMATION

Infectious diseases are caused by bacteria, viruses, protozoa and fungi which invade the body of susceptible host and cause an illness.

Infectious diseases are often transmitted from one cat to another by contact with infected feces and other bodily secretions, or inhalation of germ-laden droplets in the air. A few are transmitted via the genital tract when cats mate. Others are acquired by contact with spores in the soil which get into the body through the respiratory tract or a break in the skin.

Bacteria are single-celled germs, while the virus, the tiniest germ known and even more basic than a cell, is simply a packet of molecules. Although germs exist virtually everywhere, only a few cause infection. Fewer still are contagious—i.e., capable of being transmitted from one animal to another. Many infectious agents are able to survive for long periods outside of the host animal. This information is especially useful in controlling the spread of infectious diseases.

Antibodies and Immunity

An animal who is *immune* to a specific germ has chemical substances in his system called antibodies which attack and destroy that germ before it can cause an illness.

Natural immunity exists which is species-related. A cat does not catch a disease which is specific for a horse, and vice versa. Some infectious diseases are not specific. They are capable of causing illness in several species of animals.

If an animal is susceptible to an infectious disease and is exposed, he will become ill and begin to make antibodies against that particular germ. When he recovers, these antibodies afford protection against reinfection. They continue to do so for a variable length of time. He has acquired **active immunity**.

Active immunity can be induced artificially by vaccination. Through vaccination the animal is exposed to heat-killed germs, live and attenuated germs rendered incapable of producing disease, or toxins and germ products. They stimulate the production of antibodies which are specific for the vaccine.

Since active immunity tends to wane with the passage of time, booster shots should be given at regular intervals to maintain a high level of antibody in the system.

Antibodies are produced by the *reticuloendothelial system*. It is made up of white blood cells, lymph nodes, and special cells in the bone marrow, spleen, liver and lungs. The special cells act along with antibodies and other substances in the blood to attack and destroy germs.

Antibodies are highly specific. They destroy only the type of germ that stimulated their production. Some drugs depress or prevent antibody production. They are called immunosuppressive drugs. Cortisone is such a drug.

Run-down, malnourished, debilitated cats may not be capable of responding to a challenge by developing antibodies or building immunity to germs. Such cats can be vaccinated but should be revaccinated when in a better state of health.

Kittens under two weeks of age may not be able to develop antibodies because of physical immunity.

There is another type of immunity called **passive immunity**. It is acquired from one animal to another. A classic example is the immunity kittens acquire from the colostrum, or first milk of the queen. Kittens are best able to absorb these special proteins through their intestines during the first 24 to 36 hours after birth. The length of protection is dependent upon the antibody level in the blood of the queen when the kittens were born. Queens vaccinated within a few months have the highest levels. The maximum length of protection is 16 weeks. If the queen was never vaccinated against the disease, her kittens would receive no protection against it.

Passive antibodies can "tie-up" vaccines given to stimulate active immunity, rendering them ineffective. This is one reason why vaccinations do not always "take" in very young kittens.

Another method of providing passive antibodies is to inject a cat with a serum from another cat who has a high level of type-specific antibody. Antitoxins and antivenoms are examples of such *immune serums*.

VACCINATIONS

Vaccines are highly effective in preventing certain infectious diseases in cats, but failures do occur. They can be due to improper handling and storage, incorrect administration, or the inability of the cat to respond. Trying to stretch out the vaccine by dividing a single dose between two cats is another reason for failure to take.

If the cat is already infected, vaccinating him will not alter the course of the disease.

Because each kitten is an individual case, proper handling and administration of the vaccine is important. Vaccinations should be given only by those familiar with the technique. When you go to your veterinarian for a booster shot, your cat will get a physical check-up. The veterinarian may detect some important change that you have overlooked.

Young kittens are highly susceptible to certain infectious diseases and should be vaccinated against them as soon as they are old enough to build an immunity. These diseases are Panleukopenia, the Feline Viral Respiratory Disease Complex, and Rabies. Feline Leukemia virus vaccine is not yet available commercially; it may be so in the near future. Discuss this with your veterinarian.

To be effective, vaccinations must be kept current (see *Suggested Vaccination Schedule*).

Panleukopenia *(Feline Infectious Enteritis)* Vaccine

The first panleukopenia shot should be given shortly after weaning and before a kitten is placed in a new home where he will be exposed to other cats. If a kitten is at a particular risk in an area where the disease has occurred, he can be vaccinated at six weeks of age, but may need to be re-vaccinated at two to three week intervals until he reaches 16 weeks of age. Discuss this with your veterinarian.

Two types of vaccines are available. One contains dead virus; the other a live but attenuated strain.

Panelukopenia vaccine is often combined with two feline viral respiratory disease vaccines and given as a single injection.

A booster given at one to two years of age may be sufficient in cats who mix with others, as exposure to the disease will boost their immunity naturally. However, a yearly booster is a sensible precaution.

Feline Respiratory Disease Vaccines

Your veterinarian may recommend an injectable vaccine containing weakened strains of the rhinotracheitis virus (FVR) and calicivirus (FCV). Usually they are combined with panleukopenia vaccine and given as a single injection twice, with the last vaccination after 14 weeks of age. Vaccines also may be given as drops into the eyes and nose. Occasionally this is followed by bouts of sneezing or an eye discharge two to three days later.

Although respiratory disease vaccines are highly effective, they may not prevent all cases of illness. The cat may be exposed to individual strains of virus that aren't countered by the vaccine; or the infection could be so severe that it overcomes the cat's protection against it. However, when this happens, the disease usually is of a milder nature.

Annual booster vaccinations are advisable.

Feline pneumonitis vaccine (FPN) may be advisable in areas where Feline Pneumonitis is prevalent; or where many cats are living together.

Rabies Vaccine

There are two general types of rabies vaccines. One is a modified live virus preparation and the other is a killed virus. *All vaccinations must be given in the muscle.*

Cats can be immunized effectively with both types of vaccine, but live virus vaccines tend to provide higher immunity. There is one type of live virus vaccine—the so-called LEP Flury strain—that should not be administered to cats since it has been known to cause actual rabies.

Most veterinarians advise that all rural cats be immunized against rabies. If it is certain that the cat will never be permitted to roam and hunt (for example, if he lives in an urban apartment), the consideration might be given to omitting this vaccination. Discuss this with your veterinarian.

Rabies vaccines cannot be given successfully before twelve weeks of age. If a kitten is vaccinated before three months of age, he should be re-vaccinated at six months.

Repeat the rabies vaccination annually. This applies to both the live virus vaccine and the killed variety.

A cat being shipped across *some* state lines must have a current rabies vaccination.

Vaccination Schedule

This suggested vaccination schedule should provide protection at minimum cost. It should be modified under the following circumstances:

1. Brood females who have not been immunized within a year should be given a rhinotracheitis (FVR), calicivirus (FCV), and panleukopenia (FPL) booster shot *before* being bred.

2. Live virus vaccines should not be given to pregnant queens because of possible harmful effects on the fetus. A queen who was not vaccinated before being bred can still be immunized—provided *killed* virus preparations are utilized. Discuss this with your veterinarian.

3. Feline pneumonitis vaccine (FPN) may be indicated in certain areas. Discuss this with your veterinarian. The vaccination schedule for FPN is included below.

4. Additional booster shots are a sensible precaution before boarding a cat or taking him to his first show of the year. Panleukopenia, and FVR plus FCV, should be given four weeks in advance of potential exposure.

SUGGESTED VACCINATION SCHEDULE*

Age of Cat	Vaccine Recommended
9 to 10 Weeks	Panleukopenia (FPL) Rhinotracheitis (FVR) Calicivirus (FCV) Feline Pneumonitis (FPN)
14 to 16 Weeks	FPL, FVR, FCV, FPN Rabies
At 12 Months and Annually	Repeat all the vaccinations given at 14 weeks.

*Note: The age of the cat, type of vaccine, and route of administration influence the effectiveness of the vaccine and the number of vaccinations required. Be sure to follow your veterinarian's recommendations.

FELINE BACTERIAL DISEASES

Feline Infectious Anemia

This disease is most common in male cats one to three years of age. It is caused by a microorganism called *Hemobartonella felis*. It attaches itself to the surface of red blood cells and destroys these cells, producing a hemolytic anemia.

The exact method of transmission of this disease is not known. It has been suggested that it may be transferred from one cat to another by the bite of a blood-sucking insect such as a flea; or by the bite of an infected cat. Unborn kittens may be infected by placental transmission if the mother harbors the microorganism. Such kittens may be stillborn; or they may die within a few hours. Experimentally, the disease can be transmitted from one cat to another by a blood transfusion.

Many cats in the general population carry the infection in a latent form. The disease becomes manifest when the individual's immune response is weakened by some other illness. Hemobartonella infections often accompany leukemia.

A cat with infectious anemia occasionally exhibits fever (103 to 106 degrees F), suffers rapid loss of appetite and condition, appears weak and lethargic, and may show signs of anemia (pale gums and mucous membranes). Jaundice can occur. It is due to rapid destruction of red blood cells. Often the anemia is recurrent, with improvement between attacks.

Any cat with anemia can be suspected of having feline infectious anemia. Your veterinarian can make the diagnosis by finding Hemobartonella organisms on a smear of blood taken from the cat. At times the organisms disappear from the circulation and may not be seen. Accordingly, more than one blood smear might be required to make the diagnosis.

Treatment: Tetracycline is effective in about half the cases. Chloromycetin has been recommended. Many cats get better on their own, and treated cases frequently relapse. Cats who recover become carriers.

The cat's general condition should be improved by appropriate nutritional support. Blood transfusions are indicated if the anemia is severe. Associated illnesses should be treated. Steroids are sometimes prescribed when the infection cannot be told apart from other forms of hemolytic anemia that respond to steroids.

Salmonella

This disease is caused by a type of salmonella bacteria which produces gastrointestinal infection in susceptible animals. It tends to afflict kittens housed in crowded, unsanitary surrounding, and cats whose natural resistance has been weakened by a virus infection, malnutrition, or some other stress.

Signs of infection are high fever, vomiting and diarrhea (90 percent of cases), dehydration and weakness. Death will occur in about half the cases. Abortions have been reported.

Cats (and dogs) often are asymptomatic carriers. The bacteria they shed in their feces can, under appropriate conditions, produce active infection in domestic animals and man.

Diagnosis is made by identifying salmonella bacteria in stool cultures (carrier state); or in the blood, feces, and infected tissues of cats suffering acute infection.

Treatment: A number of antibiotics are effective against Salmonella bacteria. Most strains are sensitive to Chloromycetin.

The disease can be prevented by housing cats under sanitary conditions where they can be well cared-for and fed.

Tetanus (Lockjaw)

This disease is caused by a bacteria called *Clostridium tetani.* It is rare in cats, owing to the fact that cats possess a high natural immunity. However, it occurs in all warm-blooded animals.

Bacteria enter the skin via an open wound such as a bite or puncture. The rusty nail is the classical example. But any cut or injury to the full-thickness of the skin can act as a point of entry.

The tetanus bacteria is found in soil contaminated by horse and cow manure. It is present in the intestinal tract of most animals where it does not cause a disease.

Symptoms appear as early as a few days after the injury but can be delayed for as long as several weeks. Tetanus bacteria grow best in tissues where the oxygen level is low (anaerobic conditions). The ideal environment is a deep wound which has healed over, or one in which there is devitalized tissue heavily contaminated with filth. The bacteria make a toxin which affects the nervous system.

Signs of disease are due to the neurotoxin. They include spastic contractions and rigid extension of the legs; difficulty opening the mouth and swallowing; retraction of the lips and eyeballs. The tail sometimes stands straight out. Muscle spasms are triggered by almost anything that stimulates the cat.

Treatment: Tetanus cannot be treated at home. Fatalities may at times be avoided by prompt early veterinary care. Tetanus antitoxins, antibiotics, sedatives, intravenous fluids, and care of the wound alter the course for the better. The disease can be prevented by prompt attention to skin wounds (see *Wounds*).

Tuberculosis

This disease is caused by the *tubercle bacillus.* There are three strains of bacilli that produce disease in man—but only the *bovine* type also infects the cat. The cat, unlike the dog, is resistant to infection by the *human* tubercle bacillis; but cats are considerably more sensitive than dogs to the bovine type.

Tuberculosis in cats usually is acquired by ingesting infected cow's milk or by eating contaminated uncooked beef. Even though there has been a steady decline in tuberculosis with the elimination of this disease from dairy herds, it has not been completely wiped out.

Bovine tuberculosis is primarily a gastrointestinal problem. A common finding is low grade fever with chronic wasting and loss of condition in spite of good care and feeding. Abscesses form in the intestinal lymph nodes and liver.

However, lung infection does occur. Occasionally an open wound becomes infected, leading to skin involvement with draining sinuses, and a discharge containing bacteria.

Respiratory tuberculosis causes a persistent cough, labored breathing, shortness of breath, and the production of bloody sputum.

Treatment: The finding of tubercle bacilli in the feces, sputum, or in drainage from a wound, makes the diagnosis. A chest x-ray may be suggestive. Treatment, which involves antituberculus drugs, is difficult and prolonged. The hazard to human health makes euthanasia the wisest choice.

FELINE VIRUS DISEASES

Feline Viral Respiratory Disease Complex

Feline viral respiratory diseases are highly contagious, often se-ious illnesses of cats that spread rapidly through a cattery and are transmitted from one cat to another. They are one of the most common infectious disease problems a cat owner is likely to encounter.

Recently it has been recognized that two major viral groups are responsible for the majority of clinical upper respiratory infections in cats (80-90 percent). The first is the *herpes* virus group which produces *Feline Viral Rhinotracheitis* (FVR). The second is the *Calici* virus group which produces *Feline Calici Viral Disease* (FCV).

At one time the *Chlamydia* was considered to be a major cause of feline respiratory disease. However, current research has shown that this bacteria-like organism is primarily a conjunctival disease producer. Its importance as a cause of respiratory infection is relatively minor.

Other viral agents (especially those of the *Reovirus* group) have been found to cause feline viral respiratory illness. They account for a minority of cases.

There are two distinct stages in the feline viral respiratory disease complex. They are the **acute** stage followed by the **chronic carrier** state.

Acute Respiratory Infection

There is considerable variation in the severity of illness among affected cats. Some have only mild symptoms while in others the disease is rapidly progressive and sometimes fatal.

Regardless of which viral group is responsible for the infection, the signs are so similar that they cannot be told apart except by virological or serological tests. These special tests are not always available to practitioners in time to be of use in planning treatment.

The disease is transmitted from cat to cat by direct contact with infected sputum, nasal secretions or eye discharges; and by contaminated litter pans and water bowls; by human hands; and rarely by air-borne droplets. The virus may be stable outside the host for as little as 24 hours or as long as ten days.

Clinical signs usually appear two to 17 days after exposure and reach their maximum ten days later. The first signs are fever and bouts of sneezing. This may

Acute upper respiratory infection, typified by ocular and nasal discharge.

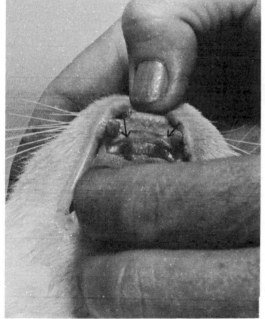

Ulcers on the roof of the mouth, produced by *acute viral respiratory infection.*

Feline upper respiratory infection is a common cause of conjunctivitis in kittens. Typically, these eyelids are pasted shut.

at first suggest a "cold" or the "flu". (However, cats don't catch "people" colds.)

Next you may see nasal and/or eye discharge. At first it is clear. Later it becomes mucoid (containing mucus) or purulent (containing pus). This signifies secondary bacterial infection. Open-mouth breathing develops in cats with obstructed nasal passages.

At times you may see ulceration of the mucous membranes of the mouth (*Stomatitis*). It is particularly disabling, as the cat loses his taste for food. He might refuse to eat and drink. Drooling is common.

With particularly severe viral involvement of the surface of the eye, the cat could develop keratitis or corneal ulceration. These conditions are discussed in the EYES chapter. They can produce partial or complete blindness.

Airway obstruction and/or bacterial pneumonia, dehydration, starvation and weight loss are all complicating factors which can lead to death.

Feline respiratory diseases are particularly serious in young kittens and old cats, and in those who are in poor general condition. In these individuals the mortality is high.

A diagnosis can be suspected from the clinical signs. It can be confirmed by isolating the virus from the throat; or by special serological blood tests. These tests are most important when the disease involves a cattery or a multiple-cat household.

Treatment: Cats suspected of having the disease should be isolated so as not to infect others.

Rest and proper humidification of the atmosphere are important items in treatment. Confine your cat in a warm room and use a home vaporizer. A cold steam vaporizer offers some advantage over a heat vaporizer because it is less likely to cause additional breathing problems due to the heat.

As dehydration and loss of caloric intake seriously weaken a cat, it is important to encourage oral intake. Feed highly palatable food, or strained baby food, diluted with water. Supplemental fluids can be given by cheek pouch (see *How To Give Medications* in the chapter DRUGS AND MEDICATIONS).

Remove purulent secretions from the eyes, nose and mouth with moist cotton balls.

Nasal congestion can be relieved by using Afrin Pediatric Nasal Spray. Avoid prolonged use of decongestants as they may dry out the mucous membranes.

Antibiotics are important in the management of viral respiratory illnesses. They are used to prevent secondary bacterial invaders rather than to treat the respiratory virus which is not sensitive to antibiotics. Chloromycetin or Ampicillin is a good choice.

In serious cases the prognosis is guarded. Once the cat begins to eat and drink on his own, the worst of the danger is past.

Chronic Carrier State

Many cats who recover from the acute illness become chronic carriers.

The herpes virus (FVR) lives and multiples in the lining cells of the throat. During periods of stress (such as illness, anesthesia, surgery, lactation, administration of steroids) the cat's immunity breaks down and virus is shed in the mouth secretions. At such times the cat may exhibit signs of a mild upper respiratory illness.

Calici virus may be shed continuously. Cats infected with FCV therefore present an especially serious hazard to others living on the premises. Periodic outbreaks of respiratory infection are likely to occur.

Prevention: Elimination of virus-positive cats from a breeding colony or household of cats may be difficult. Several months of testing and segregation, at considerable cost and inconvenience to the owner, may be required. New cats entering the colony present a further source of potential contamination and infection. Isolation and serological testing often is not practical. When a cat is admitted as a boarder he should, insofar as possible, be housed in separate quarters and be handled and fed separately from the other cats.

Well-ventilated surroundings, and ample living space for each cat to avoid crowding, are important to good cattery management.

By far the most effective step that can be taken to control feline viral respiratory infection is to vaccinate all cats. This may not eliminate all cases of respiratory disease, but it will certainly reduce their incidence and severity.

Vaccination against FVR and FCV can be given by injection; or by the oculonasal route (i.e., by nose or eye drops). The oculonasal route produces immunity in a shorter period of time (48 hours as opposed to one week); it also appears to increase local immunity in the eyes and nose. The intramuscular injection confers immunity to both strains of respiratory virus. Usually it is combined with panleukopenia vaccine.

Kittens should be vaccinated at nine to ten weeks of age and again at 14 to 16 weeks. Repeat all vaccinations annually. Brood queens should be re-vaccinated prior to breeding.

Feline pneumonitis vaccine is recommended by some authorities. It is now available for intramuscular use. It may be advisable to use it when many cats are living together. Give it according to the schedule mentioned above (see *Suggested Vaccination Schedule*).

Feline Panleukopenia (FPL)

Feline Panleukopenia, also called *feline infectious enteritis,* is one of the most serious and widespread viral diseases of the cat. It is a leading cause of infectious disease deaths in kittens. It has been incorrectly called feline "distemper". However, FPL bears no relation to the virus that causes distemper in dogs.

Panleukopenia virus is present wherever there are susceptible animals. Wild felines and raccoons also can be infected. The virus is highly contagious. It is spread by direct contact with an infected cat or his secretions; and by the airborne route. Other routes of spread are by exposure to contaminated utensils such as food pans and litter boxes; and via the clothes or hands of personnel who have treated an infected cat. The bite of an infected flea or other external parasite also can transmit the disease.

The FPL virus is extremely hardy. It can live in carpets, cracks and furnishings for at least a year. It is resistant to ordinary household disinfectants.

Feline pneumonitis begins with swelling of the eyelids and a water or mucus discharge from the eyes. Nasal congestion is not as common as it is with upper respiratory disease.

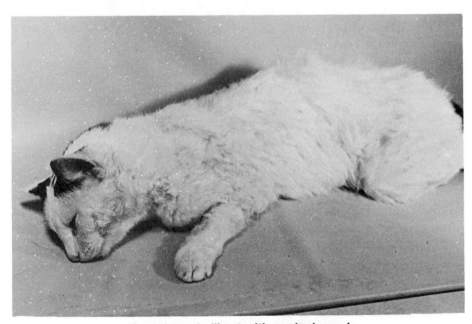

An extremely ill cat with *panleukopenia*.

Signs of acute illness appear two to ten days after exposure. Early signs are loss of appetite, depression, and fever (up to 105 degrees F). The cat usually vomits repeatedly and brings up frothy yellow-stained bile. Often he seems to want water but is unable to drink it—or if he does, vomits it immediately. Characteristically, the cat may be seen crouching in pain over his water bowl with his head hanging a few inches above the surface. Owing to pain in the abdomen, he cries plaintively.

Diarrhea may appear early in the course of the disease but frequently comes on later. The stools are yellow and/or blood-streaked.

In young kittens (and some older cats) the onset can be so sudden that death occurs even before the owner realizes his cat is ill. The cat may have been believed to have been poisoned.

The FPL virus has a special affinity for attacking rapidly dividing cells—such as those that line the surfaces of the gastrointestinal tract. Destruction of circulating white cells (leukopenia) gives the disease its name. Retinal involvement may occur. Cats who recover can suffer partial or complete loss of sight.

Panleukopenia can be transmitted in utero to unborn kittens; and to kittens shortly after birth. In such cases the mortality is high (90%). Kittens recovering from neonatal infection may have cerebellar brain damage and exhibit a wobbly, jerky, uncoordinated gait which is first noted when they begin to walk.

Secondary bacterial infections and complications are common. This is due in part to a reduction in circulating white blood cells (which normally fight bacteria); and to the general weakness of the cat. They are sometimes the cause of death.

Cats who survive may become carriers. In a population of cats, this leads to repeated exposure. It helps to boost immunity among cats who have already acquired protective antibodies.

Treatment: Detection of panleukopenia *early* in the course of the illness is of prime importance. Intensive treatment must be started at once to save the life of the cat. It is better to consult your veterinarian on a "false alarm" than to wait until the disease is full-blown, at which time a cat might be desperately ill. A white blood cell count serves to confirm the diagnosis.

Supportive measures include fluid replacement, antibiotics, maintenance of nutrition, and occasionally blood transfusions. Immune serums are available. They contain a high level of antibody against the virus. They may be effective—especially when given early in the course of the illness.

Prevention: Most cats are exposed to panleukopenia sometime during their life. Vaccination is the most effective method of preventing serious infection.

Kittens should be vaccinated at nine to ten weeks of age and again at 14 to 16 weeks. Annual booster vaccinations are required. When a young kitten is at a particular risk, he can be vaccinated at six weeks of age. Subsequent vaccinations every two weeks until 14 weeks are still necessary as the first vaccinations might have been "blocked" by maternal antibodies in the kitten. This could interfere with the development of active immunity.

After vaccinating your kitten, you should still keep him away from other cats (who might carry the virus) until he is four months old. Wait at least three to six months before introducing a new cat into a household in which infection has occurred.

A brood queen should be vaccinated before she is bred. (This can be done later if a killed vaccine is used.) This affords better protection for her kittens during their first few weeks of life.

Control measures also are necessary. They involve sanitation and good housecleaning practices. Contaminated utensils and equipment should be disinfected by soaking them in Formalin. Fleas and other external parasites should be eliminated from the cat and his environment.

Feline Infectious Peritonitis (FIP)

This common disease of wild and domestic cats is caused by a member of the Corona virus group. The virus is quickly and easily spread among cats. The incubation period is two to six weeks. However, the majority (75 percent) of those exposed experience no apparent infection. Among those who do, a mild respiratory infection, with perhaps a runny nose or eye discharge, is the most common sign of illness. Less than 5% develop the secondary disease we know as FIP.

Why some cats develop FIP while others don't is not entirely understood. We do know that the disease tends to affect cats younger than three years of age and over ten. There is a higher rate of clinical infection in catteries. Here living conditions are apt to be crowded and there is greater opportunity for continuous and prolonged exposure. Cats who are poorly nourished, debilitated, run-down, or suffering from other illnesses (especially the feline leukemia virus), are more susceptible. These factors may lower the cat's natural resistance to FIP. Then, too, the virulence of the particular strain, the size of the inoculum, and the genetic predisposition of the cat, also may play a role. Most cats who recover from the mild primary infection become carriers. They are capable of transmitting the disease to other cats who are not immune.

Feline infectious peritonitis, despite its name, is not strictly a disease of the abdominal cavity. The virus acts on capillary blood vessels throughout the body—particularly those of the abdomen, chest cavity, eyes, brain, internal organs and lymph nodes. Loss of fluid into tissues and spaces results from damage to these minute blood vessels. FIP tends to run a prolonged course. It may go on for weeks before the signs are noticed.

FIP occurs in two forms—both of which are invariably fatal:

Wet Form. Early signs are non-specific and mimic other feline disorders. They include loss of appetite, weight loss, listlessness and depression. The cat appears chronically ill. As fluid begins to accumulate in his body spaces you may notice labored breathing (from fluid in the chest); or abdominal enlargement (from fluid in the abdomen). Sudden death may occur from fluid in the heart sac. Other signs which accompany the wet form are fever (up to 106 degrees F), dehydration, anemia, vomiting and diarrhea. Jaundice and dark urine are caused by liver failure.

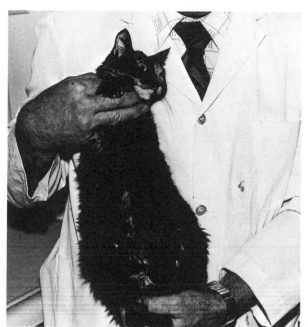
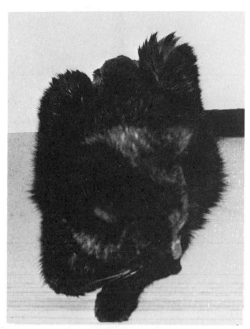

Abdominal enlargement in a cat with the wet form of *feline infectious peritonitis.* Note the extreme depression, muscular wasting, and prominence of the backbone.

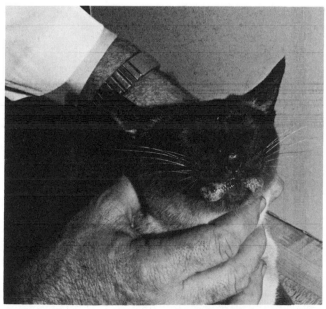

Pseudorabies is typified by excessive drooling and slobbering.

Dry or Disseminated Form. Early signs are like those of the wet form except fluid is not produced. The disseminated form is even more difficult to diagnose. It affects a variety of organs including the eyes (25% of cases), brain, liver, kidney, pancreas. At surgical exploration, which may be necessary to make the diagnosis, sticky mucus or strands of fibrin may be found on the surface of the liver, spleen or intestines. Fifty percent of cats with the dry form also are infected with the feline leukemia virus. This undoubtedly lowers their resistance to FIP.

While FIP can be suspected by the clinical signs, special diagnostic studies usually are necessary to confirm the diagnosis. Antibodies to the virus can be measured by an indirect fluorescent blood test. A single positive test does not mean the cat has FIP, will become ill from FIP, will die from FIP, or will necessarily become a carrier. If a second blood test is higher than the first, then probably the cat has active infection—while a drop in titer suggests the cat is an immune carrier. A *low* titer (under 1:400) suggests that the cat has had the disease and recovered; or is an immune carrier.

Treatment: Unfortunately, once a cat develops the secondary disease (wet or dry form), he will die within a few weeks. He can be made more comfortable by medications; and at times his life can be prolonged by chemotherapy and/or cortisone.

Prevention: There is no vaccine for FIP. But as physical and environmental stresses do play a role in lowering a cat's immunity, and thus increasing his susceptibility to the virus, it is important to maintain good nutrition, control parasites, treat illnesses promptly and groom regularly.

FIP presents its greatest hazard to multiple cat families, boarding establishments, and catteries. Fortunately, the virus is easily killed by household disinfectants. Ammonia or bleach (1:32) is a good disinfectant. Disinfect cat-quarters at regular intervals. Provide a spacious enclosure for each cat; and allow ample opportunity for exercise.

Routine FIP testing for all cats in a multiple cat family or cattery is advisable. Isolate all new arrivals for two weeks, until tests are complete. FIP positive and negative cats should be housed in separate facilities.

Recently the FIP virus has been implicated as a cause of an entire syndrome of reproductive failures called the *Kitten Mortality Complex.* It is discussed in the PEDIATRICS chapter.

Feline Leukemia Virus Disease Complex (FeLV)

This virus, which may produce an active or chronic illness in cats, is also the most important cause of feline cancer. In addition, it contributes to the severity of several other cat diseases.

It is believed that the virus is transmitted from one cat to another by infected saliva, blood, feces or urine. Thus sharing water bowls, feed dishes, exchange grooming, or even bites could lead to spread of the disease. Kittens may acquire the virus from their mothers in utero, or via infected milk.

The incidence of infection is quite variable. In rural areas the incidence is quite low—perhaps only five percent. In heavily populated urban areas 25 to 60 percent of free-roaming cats are infected. And where conditions are even more crowded, such as in a cattery, nearly 100 percent become infected. Repeated or continuous exposure appears to be necessary for transmission of the disease. The virus does not appear in the blood until a cat has been exposed to it for at least four weeks. After 20 weeks of exposure, 80 percent of cats are infected; while in others it may take up to a year. Environmental stresses, such as illness, overcrowding and poor sanitation, undoubtedly play a role in weakening a cat's resistance to the virus, making infection more likely.

Once exposed, a cat may or may not become ill. Even though a cat does not become ill, he can still become a carrier. Depending upon the number of cats in the exposed population, the carrier rate varies from less than one percent to as high as 30 percent. Seventy to 90 percent of cats who become ill will recover. However, the more severe the illness, the greater the likelihood the cat will become a chronic carrier and/or eventually die.

More than half the cats who become chronic carriers will die within three years. In many cases death is caused by some other disease. The FeLV virus produces suppression of a cat's immunity, allowing other diseases to develop. Diseases which are potentiated by the FeLV virus include Feline Infectious Peritonitis, Feline Infectious Anemia, Feline Viral Respiratory Disease Complex, chronic cystitis, periodontal disease, and various bacterial infections. Only a small percentage of cats develop a virus related cancer.

Signs of Illness. The initial illness usually lasts two to 16 weeks. Signs of illness are non-specific. They include fever, apathy, loss of appetite, and weight loss. Other signs are constipation and/or diarrhea, and vomiting. Some cats develop enlarged lymph nodes, or pale mucus membranes (from anemia).

Maternal infection might be responsible for some cases of reproductive failure including repeated abortions, stillbirths, fetal reabsorptions, and the "fading kitten" syndrome—a disorder in which neonatal kittens grow weak and die rapidly.

A small number of cats develop a cancer months to years after exposure. *Lymphosarcoma* is the most common variety. One or more painless masses may be felt in the abdomen. There may be enlargement of lymph nodes in the groin, axilla, neck or chest. The cancer may spread to the eye, brain, skin, kidney or other tissues producing a variety of symptoms.

Leukemia is another malignant manifestation. It can be defined as rapid and uncontrolled growth of white blood cells. It may be accompanied by anemia and other changes in the blood-cell picture. It is much less common than lymphosarcoma.

The FeLV complex often presents the clinician with a difficult diagnostic problem. There are a number of blood tests available which can be used to tell whether the cat has virus in his blood, whether he is likely to be infective, and whether he is likely to get a virus related tumor. A single test is not always reliable because the cat could be incubating the disease, or the virus could be latent in his tissues. Accordingly, several tests may be required. Other diagnostic studies often are necessary to confirm the diagnosis. They include a bone marrow examination; or possibly a biopsy of a lymph node or an unusual mass.

Treatment: Cancers produced by the FeLV virus are not curable. Early diagnosis may allow successful palliation (relief but not cure) in some individuals. Palliative measures include the administration of steroids, antibiotics, vitamin-mineral supplements, transfusions, and anti-cancer drugs. Cats that respond to the medications may be made more comfortable and their lives may be prolonged. Unfortunately, there is no way to tell which cats are likely to respond. Such cats will continue to shed virus and thus present a hazard to the health of others with whom they come in contact. Many veterinarians advise putting a cat to sleep as soon as the diagnosis of cancer is confirmed.

Prevention: An effective vaccine has been developed. It is undergoing tests but is not commercially available at this time.

The following steps may prevent spread of infection in a cattery or isolated cat colony:

1. First, virus-test all cats on the premises. The most sensitive blood test for the detection of virus is the ELISA. Two negative tests, three months apart, indicate the cat is free of virus. (*Note:* It is necessary to retest all negative cats after three months to see if any were incubating the virus during the first test. If all stay negative, you can consider them free of FeLV.)
2. Isolate all cats who were virus positive. If symptoms do not appear within three months, repeat the blood test. If it converts to negative, the cat is no longer a danger to other cats.
3. Toms and queens should be certified free of virus before being used for breeding.
4. Discard all toys, feeding bowls and litter pans of infected cats. Clean and disinfect the house and cat-quarters with an ordinary household detergent or bleach solution. The FeLV virus is not very hardy and easily killed. Be sure to disinfect spots the cat might have soiled with urine, saliva or feces.
5. Wait 30 days before bringing a new cat onto the premises.

While there is no evidence that FeLV is capable of causing disease in humans, as a sensible precaution young children and women of child-bearing age should not handle virus-positive cats.

Rabies

Rabies is a fatal disease that occurs in nearly all warm blooded animals although rarely among rodents. The main source of infection for humans is a bite from an infected dog or cat. However, skunks, bats, foxes, raccoons, cattle, horses and other wild and domestic animals can serve as a reservoir for the disease, thereby accounting for sporadic cases. Any wild animal that allows you to approach it without running away from you is acting abnormally. Rabies should be suspected. Do not pet, handle, or give first aid to such an animal.

The virus, which is present in infected saliva, usually enters at the site of a bite. Saliva on an open wound or mucous membrane also constitutes exposure to rabies. Animals suspected of having rabies should be handled with great care— or preferably not at all!

The incubation period is 14 to 60 days. The virus travels to the brain along nerve networks. The further the bite is from the brain, the longer the incubation period. Virus then travels back along nerves to the mouth where it enters the saliva.

The signs and symptoms of rabies are due to encephalitis (inflammation of the brain). The first signs are quite subtle and consist of personality changes. Affectionate and sociable cats often become increasingly irritable or aggressive. Shy and less outgoing cats may become overly affectionate. Soon the animal becomes withdrawn and stares off into space. He avoids light which hurts his eyes (photophobia). Finally he resists handling. Fever, vomiting and diarrhea are common.

Cats are inclined to hide when they are ill and thus may die and never be discovered.

There are two characteristic forms of encephalitis. One is the so-called "furious" form and the other is the "paralytic" form. A rabid cat may show signs of one or a combination of both forms, but the furious form is the most common.

The *furious form* is the "mad dog" type of rabies. It lasts one to four days. Here the cat becomes frenzied and vicious, attacking anything that moves. The muscles of the face are in spasm, drawing the lips back to expose the teeth. When running free he shows no fear and snaps and bites at any animal in his path.

In the *paralytic form*, which is common in the dog but uncommon in the cat, the swallowing muscles become paralyzed, which may cause drooling, coughing spells and pawing at the mouth. As encephalitis progresses, the cat loses control of his rear legs, collapses and is unable to get up. Death occurs in one to two days. Because of the rapid course in the cat, paralysis may be the only sign noted.

Public Health Considerations: Nationwide there has been a tremendous increase in animal bites. One percent of hospital emergency room visits are for animal bites (80 to 90% for dogs). Each of them needs to be evaluated with rabies in mind.

Any bite of a *wild* animal, whether provoked or not, should be regarded as having the potential for rabies. Rodent bites also should be evaluated; but as rodents rarely have rabies, their bites need not cause as much concern.

The World Health Organization has established certain guidelines for practitioners to follow in the appropriate management of people who are exposed to a potentially rabid animal. The treatment schedule depends upon the nature of the exposure (lick, bite), severity of the injury, and the condition of the animal at the time of exposure and during a subsequent observation period of ten days.

If there is the slightest possibility that a dog or cat is rabid, and if there has been any sort of human contact, *impound the animal immediately and consult your physician and veterinarian.* This holds true even if the animal is known to be vaccinated for rabies. Depending upon the nature of the exposure, a victim of a biting animal may have to undergo a series of injections—either antirabies serum, rabies vaccine, or both. Often these injections are started at once but can be stopped if the animal remains healthy.

As an alternative, in the case of a feral cat or one whose owner is unknown, the cat can be killed immediately. Should the cat escape, there is no way to prove it was not rabid. In most cases a full course of treatment will have to be given.

When an animal is killed or dies during confinement, its brain is removed and sent to a laboratory equipped to diagnose rabies from special antibody studies.

Treatment: The emergency treatment for any animal bite involves a thorough washing of the wound with soap or detergent. Flush it repeatedly, using copious amounts of water, and apply tincture of iodine. If the victim is a person, contact a physician at once.

There is no effective treatment for rabies in cats. To protect the health of your pet be sure he is vaccinated at three to six months of age and repeat annually. It is important that cats be vaccinated only by a qualified professional. To be effective, the vaccine must be given in the proper location; it must be kept refrigerated; it must not be out of date; it must be intended specifcially for use in cats (other vaccines may actually produce the disease); and it can be hazardous to people who handle it improperly. Furthermore, a veterinarian can provide legal proof of vaccination should the need arise.

Rural cats are at the highest risk for rabies because of the potential for wildlife exposure.

Pseudorabies

While this disease bears no actual relationship to rabies, it can at times be confused with the *furious form* of that disease. It is caused by a herpes virus which infects dogs and cats. The disease is not common in the United States.

The exact mode of transmission is unknown. Pigs, cows, rats, and some other domestic animals appear to serve as a reservoir for the virus. The disease can be produced by eating infected raw pork. It is believed that cats become infected by feeding on, or coming into contact with, infected livestock.

Pseudorabies is an acute, highly fatal disease which involves the nervous system and comes on three to four days after exposure. The first signs are restlessness followed almost at once by intense pain. The cat meows and crouches down in agony. He may drool excessively and act as though he had something caught in his throat. He develops intense itching on his head, shoulders, or within his mouth—sites where the virus apparently enters his system. The cat scratches frantically and turns the area raw. In a short time he staggers about, collapses and falls into a coma. Death occurs within 24 hours.

These symptoms may at first suggest the possibility of rabies, but the shorter course (matter of hours), lack of vicious attacks, and the intolerable itching distinguish the two conditions. Pseudorabies does not present a hazard to human health.

There is no vaccine available for the protection of dogs and cats in the United States. The only means of control is to prevent pets from roaming and coming into contact with infected livestock and eating raw meat.

FUNGUS DISEASES

Fungus diseases may be divided into two groups. In the first, the fungus affects just the skin or mucous membranes. Examples are ringworm and yeast stomatitis. In the second the disease can be widespread, in which case it is called *systemic*.

Systemic fungal diseases are not common in the cat. They tend to occur in chronically ill or poorly nourished individuals. Prolonged treatment with steroids and/or antibiotics can change an animal's pattern of resistance and allow a fungus infection to get established. Some cases may be associated with the feline leukemia virus. Occasionally, a cat in good health can come down with one of the systemic fungal diseases.

Cryptococcosis, Norcardiosis and Blastomycosis are diseases caused by fungi that live in soil and organic material. Spores, which resist heat and can live for long periods without water, gain entrance through the respiratory system or through the skin at the site of a puncture. Respiratory signs resemble those of tuberculosis. They are: chronic cough, recurrent bouts of pneumonia, difficulty in breathing, weight loss, muscle wasting and lethargy. Up and down fever may be present.

Fungal diseases are difficult to recognize and treat. X-rays, biopsies, and fungus cultures are used to make the diagnosis. A fungus infection should be suspected when an unexplained illness fails to respond to a full course of antibiotics.

Systemic fungus infections do not respond to conventional antibiotics and require intensive veterinary management. Some fungi that cause disease in cats also can cause illness in man.

The following systemic fungal diseases can occur in the cat:

Cryptococcus. This disease, caused by the yeast-like fungus *Cryptococcus neoformans,* is the most common systemic fungal infection of cats. It tends to occur in mature cats.

Masses of inflamed draining tissue (granulomas) can occur in the nasal passages and sinuses. They may penetrate into the brain, producing a fatal meningitis. Lung and bone involvement can occur. Skin infection is characterized by open draining sores.

Cryptococcal meningitis is a serious, often fatal disease in humans, caused by the same fungus.

Norcardiosis. This respiratory or skin infection occurs most commonly in young cats. The fungus also affects the lymph nodes, brain, kidney and other organs. Large tumorous masses which discharge a material that looks like sulfa granules can appear on the legs or body.

Blastomycosis. This disease is found in the central United States. The skin form is characterized by nodules and abscesses which ulcerate and drain. The systemic form is similar to Norcardiosis. This disease is difficult to treat.

PROTOZOAN DISEASES

Protozoans are one-celled animals. They are not visible to the naked eye but may be seen under the microscope. A fresh stool specimen is required to find the parasites.

The life cycle of protozoans is complicated. Basically, infection results from the ingestion of the cyst form (*oocyst*). Cysts invade the lining of the bowel where they mature into adult forms and are shed in the feces. Under favorable conditions they develop into the infective form.

Coccidiosis

This protozoan disease usually produces infection in young kittens, although adult cats may be affected also.

Coccidiosis is transmitted from cat to cat, usually through feces containing oocysts. Other animals and birds also can act as intermediate or transport hosts, although feline coccidia do not complete their sexual cycle until the transport host is eaten by the cat. Kittens can acquire the disease from their mother, if she is a carrier; and can re-infect themselves from their own feces.

Coccidiosis in kittens usually is a mild disease. However, when sanitation is poor, a large number of oocysts can be ingested, producing a significant illness. Cats who recover develop a degree of immunity.

Five to seven days after the ingestion of oocysts, infective cysts appear in the feces. The entire life cycle is complete in a week. Diarrhea is the main sign of infection. Usually it is mild but in severe cases the feces become mucus-like and bloody. Such cases are complicated by weakness, dehydration and anemia.

Coccidia can be found in the stools of kittens without causing problems until some stress factor such as an outbreak of roundworms or shipping reduces their resistance. Cats that recover can become carriers. Carriers and cats with active infection can be identified by finding adult oocysts in a microscopic slide of fresh stool.

Treatment: Stop the diarrhea with Kaopectate. A severely dehydrated or anemic cat may need to be hospitalized for fluid replacement and blood.

Supportive treatment is important since in most cases the acute phase of the illness lasts a few days, perhaps ten days, and is followed by recovery.

Sulfonamides have been used to treat coccidiosis. Response is slow once the signs of disease are apparent.

Known carriers should be isolated and treated. At the same time their quarters and runs should be washed down daily with lysol and *boiling water* to destroy oocysts. Otherwise they will re-infect themselves.

Toxoplasmosis

This disease is caused by the protozoan Toxoplasma gondii. Although the exact mode of transmission is not known, cats are likely to acquire the infection from consuming infected birds or rodents, or by ingesting oocysts in contaminated soil.

Evidence strongly suggests that people (and cats) also can get the disease from eating raw or undercooked pork, beef, mutton or veal that contains toxoplasma organisms. The feces of infected cats undoubtedly present another source of infection. Cats and humans can transmit toxoplasma in utero to their unborn offspring.

Toxoplasmosis usually is asymptomatic. When symptomatic it affects the brain, lymphatic system and lungs. Signs include fever, lethargy, loss of appetite, weight loss, diarrhea, coughing, difficulty breathing. Lymph nodes may enlarge. Kittens may exhibit encephalitis, liver insufficiency or pneumonia. Prenatal infection may be responsible for abortion or still-births.

Serologic blood tests will show whether a cat has ever been exposed. A positive test in a healthy cat signifies that he has acquired active immunity and is unlikely to be a source of human contamination.

The most serious danger to human health is congenital toxoplasmosis. About half the human adult population shows serological evidence of having been exposed in the past. A woman with protective antibodies probably will be immune to infection. However, the disease is a particular hazard when a pregnant woman without prior immunity is exposed to it. Birth defects, largely involving the central nervous system, do occur.

Treatment: This disease is difficult to recognize in the cat. Effective medications are available but should be used under veterinary supervision.

Prevention: The disease can be prevented by keeping a cat from roaming and hunting. Thoroughly cook all fresh meat (both yours and your cat's), maintaining a temperature of at least 140 degrees F throughout.

Wear disposable plastic gloves when handling your cat's litter. Remove stools from the litter box daily. Dispose of the litter carefully so that others will not come into contact with it. Clean and disinfect litter trays every two or three days using boiling water or 10% ammonia solution—or better yet, use disposable liners. Cover children's sandboxes when not in use to keep them from being a potential source of infection.

Feline Cytauxzoon

This is a fatal parasitic disease of cats. It was first described in 1976 in southwest Missouri. Cases have now been reported throughout the southern United States.

The cytauxzoon organism attacks red blood cells and those of the reticuloendothelial system. Symptoms include high fever, anemia, jaundice and dehydration. Death occurs in less than one week.

The diagnosis is made by staining a blood smear and examining it under a microscope, looking for the characteristic organisms.

The mode of transmission is not known. At present there is no effective treatment.

Groom a short-haired cat once or twice a week to remove loose hair and keep his skin and coat free of parasites. —*Sydney Wiley.*

Long-haired cats need to be brushed every day to keep their coats from matting and tangling, and to lessen the possibility of hairballs. —*Sydney Wiley.*

4

Skin

GENERAL REMARKS

Skin disease is a common problem in cats and the condition of the skin can often tell you a great deal about your cat's general health and condition.

Unlike the skin of people, your cat's skin is thinner and more sensitive to injury. It is easily damaged by careless or rough handling with the wrong kind of grooming equipment. Because it is loosely applied to the underlying muscle, most bites and lacerations are rather superficial.

There are many functions served by the skin. Without an intact skin, water from the cat's tissue would quickly evaporate, draining him of body heat and water and leading to his death from cold and dehydration. Skin is a barrier which keeps out bacteria and other foreign agents. It is involved in the synthesis of essential vitamins. It provides sensation to the surface of the body. It gives form to the body and insulates the cat against extremes of heat and cold.

The outer layer is the *epidermis*. It is a scaly layer which varies in thickness in different parts of the cat's body. It is thick and tough over the nose and foot pads and thin and most susceptible to injury in the creases of the groin and beneath the arms.

The *dermis* is the next layer inward. Its main function is to supply nourishment to the epidermis. It also gives rise to the *skin appendages* which are the hair follicles, sebaceous glands, sweat glands and toenails. They are modifications of the epidermis to serve special functions.

The skin follicles produce three different types of hair. The first, called primary hair, is exemplified by long *guard hair,* which makes up the top coat. Each guard hair grows from its own individual root. Tiny muscles connected to the roots of guard hairs enable the cat to fluff out his coat in cold weather, thus trapping warm air and providing better insulation.

Secondary hair or *underfur* is much more abundant. Its function is to provide added warmth and protection. Secondary hair grows in groups from a single opening in the dermis. This type can be further subdivided into awn hair and wool hair.

Whiskers, eyelashes, and *carpal hair* (which is found on the backs of the front legs), are a third type of hair which is especially modified to serve the sense of touch. The whiskers are long stiff hairs which can be fanned-out to make contact with the surroundings. Along with other tactile hair, they supplement the cat's keen sense of smell and hearing. They aid in the detection of air currents and are of importance in sensing and investigating objects close to the cat.

The function of sebaceous glands is to secrete an oily substance called *sebum* which coats the hair and waterproofs the coat, giving it a healthy shine. Skin oil is influenced by hormone levels in the blood. Large amounts of estrogen (the female hormone) reduce oil production, while small amounts of androgen (the male hormone) increase it.

Specialized *apocrine* sweat glands, found all over the body but particularly at the base of the tail and on the sides of the face, produce a milky fluid whose scent may be involved in sexual attraction.

In man, the skin is well supplied with *eccrine* sweat glands which help to regulate loss of heat from the body through evaporation. In the cat, eccrine sweat glands are found only on the foot pads. They secrete when the cat is overheated, frightened or excited, leaving damp footprints.

Moisture at the tip of the nose is not caused by sweat but by fluid secreted from the mucous membrane of the nostrils. A cat cools himself by panting and licking his fur. Cooling is due to the evaporation of water.

Nails and foot pads are other specialized structures of the epidermis. The front paws are equipped with five toe pads and five claws, plus two metacarpal pads which normally don't make contact with the ground. The back feet have four toe pads and four claws, plus a large metatarsal pad. The claws can be retracted beneath the skin folds.

The skin of the foot pads is rough for traction and extraordinarily thick—75 times thicker than on other parts of his body. Yet it is remarkably sensitive to touch. A cat will extend one paw and gently feel an unfamiliar object to test its size, texture, and its distance from his body. Such tactile sensitivity is due to the presence of numerous touch-organs located in the deeper layers of his pads.

A cat's toenails are composed of keratin, a solid protein-like substance encased in a hard sheath (*cuticle*). Beneath it is the *quick,* or pink part of the claw, containing blood vessels, nerves, and the germinal cells which are responsible for growth. Nails grow continuously. When not worn down by activity or self-grooming, they should be trimmed.

BASIC COAT CARE

Growing a Coat

The growth of a cat's coat is controlled by a number of factors. Some cats, by selective breeding, carry a more abundant or more stylish coat.

Cat hair, unlike human scalp hair, does not grow continuously. It grows in cycles. Each follicle has a period of rapid growth followed by a slower one; and then a resting phase. Cat hair grows at a rate of about one-third of an inch a month. During the resting phase, mature hair remains in the follicles but becomes detached at the base. As the cycle begins anew, young hair pushes out the old, causing it to shed.

Too much female hormone in the system can slow the growth of hair. Too little thyroid hormone often impairs the growth, texture and luster of a cat's coat. Ill health, a run-down condition, hormone imbalance, vitamin deficiency, or parasites on the cat or within his system may cause the coat to be too thin and brittle. If you suspect that your cat's coat is below par, you should take him to your veterinarian for a general checkup.

Environmental factors have a definite influence on the thickness and abundance of a cat's coat. Cats living outdoors continuously in cold weather grow a heavy coat for insulation and protection. Some additional fat in the diet is indicated in winter to build up the subcutaneous layer of fat and provide more insulation for cats living outdoors. Bacon grease may be added. This improves the palatability of the food and also encourages the appetite. As an alternative feed natural corn oil. It is well tolerated by the digestive tract of cats and adds calories. Give one teaspoon a day.

Nutritional supplements, reported to build coat and improve skin health and hair sheen, are of questionable value in the healthy well-nourished cat.

Shedding

Many people believe that it is the seasonal change in temperature which governs when a cat sheds his coat. However, shedding is influenced more by changes in surrounding light. The more the exposure to light, the greater the shedding.

For cats who spend all of their time outdoors, the lengthening of the hours of sunlight in late winter and early spring activates a shedding process which lasts for many weeks. In fall, as the days grow shorter, the coat begins to thicken for winter. Indoor cats who are exposed to a constant light may shed all year around.

Cats who go outdoors part of the day normally shed at the beginning of summer.

Most cats have a double coat composed of long, coarse outer guard hair and soft, fine woolly underfur. The Rex breed is an exception. Rex cats have a single coat made up of fine curly hair. These cats shed very little.

When a cat with a double coat begins to shed, his appearance may be quite alarming and at first suggests a skin disease. This is because the undercoat is shed in a mosaic or patchy fashion, giving rise to a moth-eaten look. This is perfectly normal. Cats do not shed their coats evenly or in waves.

When shedding begins, prevent skin irritation by removing as much of the dead hair as possible by daily brushings.

HOW TO AVOID COAT AND SKIN PROBLEMS

Grooming

A cat's tongue has a spiny surface which acts much like a comb. As the cat washes himself, he wets his fur with saliva and then licks it dry, catching dirt and pulling out loose hair. Mothers teach their kittens how to do this while still in the nest. When two cats live together, grooming often becomes a mutual activity.

Even though your cat keeps himself relatively clean, you should still brush him at regular intervals. The more hair you remove, the less he can lick off and swallow; or shed about the house. This helps to reduce the problem of hairballs. Frequent grooming also keeps the coat sleek and glowing, free of parasites and other skin problems.

Kittens should be groomed daily, beginning shortly after they are weaned. This is good training. An adult cat who has not grown accustomed to being groomed can present a difficult problem when tangles and mats have to be removed. Keep the sessions relatively brief. If the kitten learns to dislike the basic routine, then a simple procedure is made most difficult.

How often to groom an older cat depends upon the thickness and length of his coat and the condition of his hair and skin. Short-haired cats usually need less grooming. Once a week may be sufficient. Long-haired cats with thick coats—such as Persians, Himalayans and Angoras—should be combed every day to keep their coats from matting and tangling.

Grooming tools you will find especially useful are listed below. The choice depends upon the breed or variety of cat and the nature of his coat.

Grooming Table: It should be solid with a non-slippery surface. The correct height of the table is that at which you can work on your cat comfortably without having to bend. Some people prefer to hold their cats on their laps.

Comb: Purchase a comb with smooth round teeth designed especially to avoid trauma to the skin. You should have a narrow-toothed comb to remove dirt and fleas. A wide-toothed comb is best for grooming long hair. You can buy a combination comb that has narrow teeth on one side and wide teeth on the other.

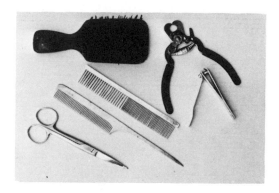

Grooming and bathing equipment.

Brush: Brushes with natural bristles produce less static electricity and broken hair than those of the nylon type. A rubber brush is handy for short-haired cats. For Rex cats, an ultra short-bristled brush is most desirable; this breed is prone to excess loss of hair if brushed too vigorously.

Hound Glove: This is used on short-haired cats to remove dead hair and polish the coat. A piece of chamois leather or nylon stocking also works well.

Scissors: They are used to cut out mats. Purchase a pair that has a blunt tip, or rounded bead, on the end of the lower jaw.

Nail Clippers: Pet stores sell several types. We prefer those that have two cutting edges.

Brush a short-haired cat with the lay of the coat.

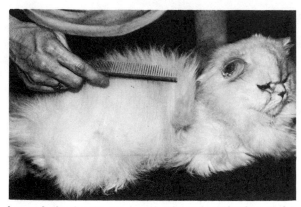

Long-haired cats are combed *against* the lay of the hair.

When brushing a *short-haired* cat, begin at the head and work toward the tail, drawing a narrow-toothed comb carefully through the fur. Then brush in the same direction with a bristle or rubber brush. Finally, using a hound glove or chamois cloth, polish the coat to give it a sheen.

With a *long-haired cat,* use a wide-toothed comb and work against the lay of the hair to fluff out the coat. Work upward over the legs and sides of the chest, the back, flanks and tail. Then use a brush in the same fashion. The fur around the head is brushed up to form a frame for the face.

Should your cat's coat appear greasy, you can sprinkle him with corn starch or baby powder. Work the powder into the coat and allow it to remain for 20 minutes to absorb the oils. A discoloration at the base of the tail, which may be accompanied by loss of hair, is caused by overactivity of the large oil producing glands at the base of the tail. It is most common in the tom but may occur in other cats. It is discussed elsewhere in this chapter (see *Stud Tail*).

When brushing your cat, use special care to see that any soft wooly hair behind the ears and under the legs is completely brushed out. These are two areas where lumps of fur do form if neglected. If such lumps are present, they should be removed. Commercial tangle remover liquids and sprays are available which may soften the lumps and facilitate their removal with a wide-toothed comb. In many cases, however, they will need to be cut out. Use sharp scissors and *carefully* cut away from the skin into the fur ball in narrow strips; then tease it out with your fingers. Slide a comb under the mat and cut on top to avoid cutting the skin. Cats with badly matted coats may need to have this done by a veterinarian.

The cat's ears should be inspected weekly. To remove dirt and debris, see EARS: *Basic Ear Care.*

Routine inspection of the teeth will tell you if there is any buildup of tartar or calculus. To learn how to remove calculus, see *Care of Your Cat's Teeth.*

Inspection of the anal sacs may disclose a build-up of secretions. To care for the anal sacs, see *Anal Glands or Sacs.*

A show cat may require special care and grooming. Most breed books provide more information on this subject. If you plan to show your kitten, it is a good idea to ask your breeder to give you a demonstration.

Trimming the Claws: Indoor cats should be trained to use a scratching post to keep their front claws worn down (see *Scratching the Furniture* in FELINE BEHAVIOR AND TRAINING). When training has not been successful you might need to trim them - particularly if the cat is scratching up your upholstery or

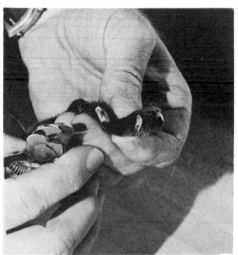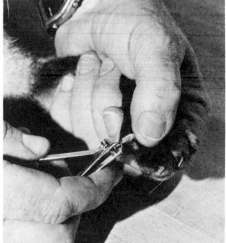

Clipping the nails. **Squeeze the toe between thumb and finger to extend the nail. Cut the clear part of the nail ahead of the quick, just in front of the point where it curves downward.**   —*J. Clawson.*

inflicting painful injuries. In such cases the claws should be trimmed as necessary; not necessarily at regular intervals.

Outdoor cats do not need to have their claws trimmed. Activity keeps them worn down. In addition, they may be needed as defensive weapons.

As a rule, you will need to clip only the front nails. Most cats chew their back claws as a natural part of grooming. They split the old sheaths and pull them off. This keeps them relatively short. Get your pet used to having his nails trimmed while he is still a kitten. Older cats who have not grown accustomed to the procedure might be difficult to manage. Veterinary assistance may be required.

Nail clippers with two cutting edges are the most satisfactory. Lift up your cat's front paw and squeeze one toe between your thumb and finger to extend the nail. Next identify the pink part of the nail which contains the nerves and blood vessels. But sure to cut the clear part of the nail well ahead of the pink part (*quick*). If you can't see the quick, cut the nail just in front of the point where it starts to curve downward. Should you accidentally cut into the quick, the cat will feel pain and his nail will begin to bleed. Hold pressure over it with a cotton ball. The blood will clot in a few minutes. If it persists, a styptic (such as used for shaving) can be used.

Declawing is an operation that might be considered for indoor cats in whom scratching has not been successfully managed by other methods. It is discussed in the chapter PEDIATRICS.

Bathing

While many cats groom their coats and keep themselves relatively clean, there are times when any cat might get dirty and will need to have a bath.

Exhibition cats are bathed periodically in preparation for cat shows. If you plan to show your kitten, it is a good idea to get him used to this routine.

Kittens can be safely bathed after they are three months old.

It is difficult to lay down specific guidelines on bathing since this depends upon the coat type and fastidiousness of the individual cat. Over-bathing can remove natural oils which are essential to the health of the coat. Many owners prefer to bathe only for a specific purpose. Others bathe as often as once a month. Periodic grooming will keep the coat sleek and glowing. This helps to eliminate the need for frequent bathing.

However, when the coat is badly stained or has a strong odor, when it appears oily in spite of a thorough brushing, the only solution is a complete bath. Cats with skin problems may need to be bathed with medicated shampoos.

How to Give Your Cat a Bath

This can be quite a challenge—particularly if you cat has not gotten used to being bathed as a kitten. Cats basically dislike water. You can expect to meet some resistance. If possible have someone hold and soothe the cat while you wash

BATHING THE CAT

—photos by Krist Carlson.

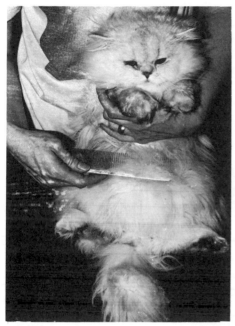

Before bathing, comb out thoroughly.

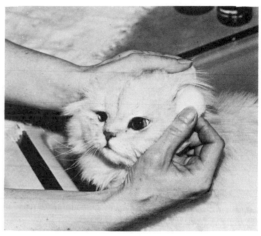

Plug the ears with cotton to keep out water.

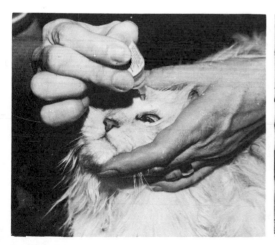

Instill ointment into the eyes to prevent soap burn.

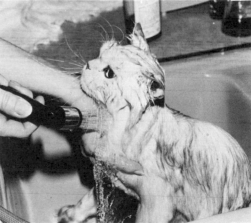

Keep the spray out of the cat's face.

Rinse well to remove all lather.

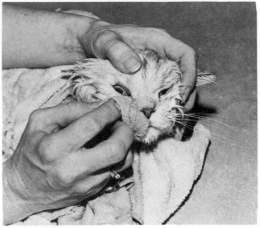

Wrap in towel and pat dry. Wash the face with a damp cloth.

Blow dry with a hair dryer.

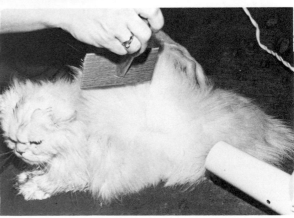

As a final step, fluff out the coat with a brush.

him. Occasionally a cat who is unmanageable will have to be tranquilized. Alternately, you can have him bathed by your veterinarian or a professional groomer.

Begin by brushing out the coat to remove knots or mats. Matted hair tends to "set" when wet. This makes it more difficult to brush out. Plug the ears with cotton to keep out water. Instill ointment into the eyes to prevent soap burn. A drop of mineral oil in each eye works well (see *How to Apply Eye Medicine*).

The next question is what shampoo to use. Dog shampoos are too alkaline and should not be used on cats. It is safe to use a gentle baby shampoo, or a good commercial cat shampoo.

Place a rubber mat or a piece of screen on the bottom of a tub or basin so the cat can have a non-slippery surface to grip with his claws. Fill the tub with soapy warm water to a depth of four inches. Hold the cat gently but firmly by the back of his neck and lower him into the basin with his back toward you (so you won't get clawed). Rub lather into his fur, keeping it out of his eyes and ears. Rinse well with warm tap water, or use a spray, and remove all traces of lather. Soap left behind dulls the coat and irritates the skin. If the coat is especially dirty, you may need to give him a second sudsing.

Special creme rinses are sometimes recommended to bring out the coat for show purposes. If you plan to use one, use it now—and then rinse it out completely. Do not use vinegar, lemon or bleach rinses. They are either too acidic or too basic and will damage the coat and skin. Alpha-Keri bath oil (one teaspoon per quart of water) may be added to the final rinse to give luster to the coat.

Now dry the coat gently with towels. If your cat does not object to it, you can dry him with an air comb. A cat's coat will take an hour or two to dry. He should be kept indoors until completely dry to avoid chilling.

Cats with an oily coat are especially prone to collect dirt. In such cases, a method of dry cleaning the coat between baths is desirable. A number of products have been used successfully as dry shampoos. Calcium carbonate, talcum or baby powder, Fuller's earth, and cornstarch are all effective. They can be used frequently without danger of removing essential oils or damaging the coat or skin. Work the powder into the coat and leave it for 20 minutes to absorb oils. If you plan to show your cat, you must remove all traces of powder before you enter the ring for judging.

Special Bath Problems:

Skunk Oil. Skunk oil can be removed from your cat's coat by soaking it in tomato juice and then giving him a bath as described above. An alternative is to make up a dilute solution of ammonia in water. Use it as a rinse and follow it with a complete bath.

Tar and Paint. Trim away excess coat containing tar, oil or paint, when feasible. Soak the tarry parts of the coat in vegetable oil overnight. Then give him a complete bath. If the substance is on his feet, apply nail polish remover and follow it with a good rinsing. Do not use petroleum solvents such as gasoline, kerosene, or turpentine; they are extremely harmful to the skin.

Scratching is a sign of fleas or other *itchy skin disorder.*
—*Sydney Wiley.*

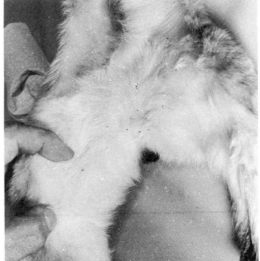

Fleas are easier to see in the groin area.

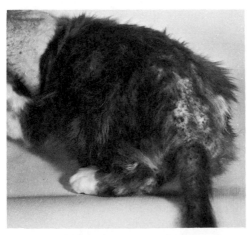

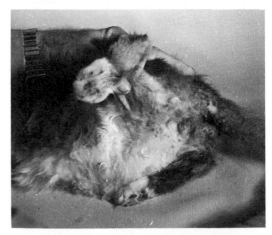

Flea allergy dermatitis. Typical appearance with small crusts and bumps. Hair loss is due to licking and scratching.

WHAT TO DO IF YOUR CAT HAS A SKIN PROBLEM

If your cat begins to scratch at himself continuously, or if he licks, bites at his skin and rubs up against things to relieve his discomfort, then you are faced with an *itchy skin disorder* and should attempt to determine the cause. See *Table I*.

There is another group of skin conditions which have to do with the appearance of the coat and hair. These diseases do not cause your cat much discomfort—at least not at first. *Hair loss* is the main sign. It may appear as impaired growth of new hair or you may notice a patchy loss of hair from specific areas of the body. At times, you may notice that the coat does not look or feel right. It may be greasy; or coarse and brittle. To determine the possible cause, see *Table II*.

When your cat has a painful skin condition and you can see pus and other signs of infection on or beneath the skin, then he is suffering from *pyoderma*. Some cases are caused by self-maceration. They are late consequences of scratching and biting. Other pyodermas are specific skin diseases that occur by themselves. See *Table III*.

During the course of grooming, playing with or handling your cat, you may discover a *lump or bump* on or beneath the skin. To learn what it might be, see *Table IV*.

If you suspect that your cat is suffering from a skin ailment, conduct a thorough examination of his skin and coat. On short-haired cats, run a fine-toothed comb against the lay of the hair to expose the skin. On long-haired cats use a bristle brush. Check the appearance of the skin and examine the scraping found on the comb and brush. In many cases a typical finding makes the diagnosis obvious.

AIDS IN THE DIAGNOSIS OF SKIN DISEASE

Table I—ITCHY SKIN DISORDERS
(Crusty Areas Produced by Scratching)

Fleas: Itching and scratching along back, around tail and hindquarters. Fleas and/or black and white gritty specks in hair (flea feces and eggs).

Head Mange Mites *(Scabies):* Intense itching about head and face with hair rubbed off. Rarely affects other parts of the body. May be complicated by *pyoderma*.

Walking Dandruff *(Cheyletiella Mange):* Tremendous amounts of dry scaly dandruff over back, neck and sides. Mild itching.

Chiggers: Itching and severe skin irritation between toes, about ears and mouth. Look for barely visible red, yellow, or orange chiggers (larvae).

Ear Mites *(Ododectes):* Head shaking and scratching at ears. Excessive brown waxy or purulent material in ear canals.

Ticks: Large insects attached to skin. May swell up to pea-size. Often found about ears, along back and between toes.

Lice: Two millimeter long insects, or white grains of sandy material (nits) found attached to hair. Found beneath matted hair in poorly kept cats. May have bare spots where hair rubbed off.

Maggots *(Myiasis):* Soft-bodied legless fly larvae found in badly soiled damp, matted fur. May be complicated by *pyoderma*.

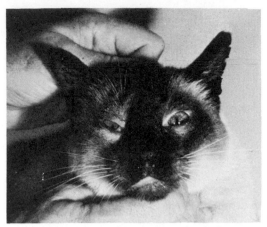

The moth-eaten look of hair loss around the eyes is characteristic of *localized demodectic mange.*

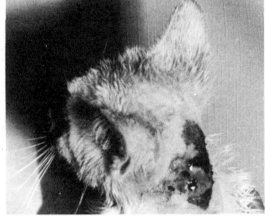

A neck abscess produced by automutilation. *Feline scabies* was the cause of the intense itching and scratching.

Engorged female tick.

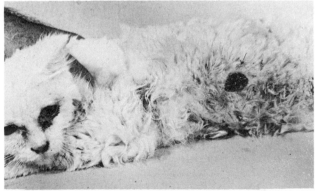

Maggots are the larvae of blow flies. They hatch on dirty and infected skin.

Food Allergy: Severe itching, hives and skin irritation. May be accompanied by sneezing, swelling of eyelids, runny nose, pawing, diarrhea or vomiting. Often complicated by *pyoderma* and hair loss, due to scratching and biting.

Flea Allergy Dermatitis: Follows flea infestation. Pimple-like rash along the back and around neck. Scratching continues after fleas have been killed. May be complicated by *lick ulcers* and/or *pyoderma*.

Irritant Contact Dermatitis: Itching and skin irritation at site of contact with chemical, detergent, paint, etc. May have scaliness and hair loss.

Allergic Contact Dermatitis: Requires repeated or continuous contact with allergen (i.e., flea collar). Appearance similar to *contact dermatitis* but rash may spread beyond area of contact.

Table II—DISORDERS IN WHICH HAIR IS LOST

Lick Granulomas *(Ulcers)*: Red shiny patches of hairless skin on the middle of the upper lip *(Rodent Ulcer)*; or on the back of the legs, abdomen and feet *(Linear Granuloma)*. Progresses through constant licking.

Ringworm: Scaly, crusty or red circular patches with central hair loss. Sometimes just broken hairs around the face and ears. Highly contagious.

Demodectic Mange: Thinning and loss of hair around the eyes and eyelids giving *moth-eaten* appearance. Rare in cats.

Feline Endocrine Alopecia: Thinning of coat or balding on insides of back legs and lower abdomen. Distribution is symmetrical (mirror image). Occurs most often in neutered males.

Hypothyroidism: Dry skin and thinning of hair coat. Hair may become dull or brittle. Uncommon.

Cortisone Excess: Loss of hair in symmetrical pattern over trunk. Can be due to prolonged medication with steroids.

Stud Tail: Greasy, waxy-brown material at base of tail; usually in intact toms. Hair may fall out.

Table III—PAINFUL SKIN DISORDERS WITH DRAINAGE OF PUS (PYODERMA)

Feline Acne: Pimple-like bumps on the underside of the chin and edges of lips.

Impetigo: Pus-filled blisters on abdomen and hairless areas of newborn kittens.

Cellulitis or Abscess *(Pyoderma)*: Painful hot inflamed skin; or pockets of pus beneath the skin. Often caused by self-maceration. Look for underlying cause (i.e., itchy skin disorder, foreign body, puncture wound).

Candidiasis *(Thrush)*: Moist white plaques which bleed easily when rubbed. Most common on mucous membranes.

Table IV—LUMPS OR BUMPS ON OR BENEATH THE SKIN

Papillomas and Warts: Grow out from the skin and look like warts or pieces of chewing gum stuck to the skin. Not painful.

Hematomas: Collections of blood beneath the skin, especially on the ears. Caused by trauma.

Tender Knots: Frequently found at the site of a shot or vaccination. Resolve spontaneously. Often painful.

Cysts: Smooth lumps beneath the skin. May grow slowly. Can discharge cheesy material and become infected. Otherwise not painful.

Mycetoma: Masses or nodules beneath skin containing blackish granules. Caused by a fungus.

Sporotrichosis: Skin nodule with overlying wet surface of pus. Caused by a fungus.

Grubs *(Cuterebra)*: Inch-long fly larvae that form cystic-like lumps beneath the skin with hole in center to breathe. Often beneath chin or along abdomen.

When a Lump May be a Cancer: Rapid enlargement; appears hard or fixed to surrounding tissue; any lump growing from bone; a lump which starts to bleed; a mole which begins to spread and/or ulcerate; unexplained open sore which does not heal, especially on feet or legs. *Note: Only way to tell for sure is to remove and study under the microscope.* Common surface growths are discussed in the chapter TUMORS AND CANCERS.

INSECT PARASITES

Insect parasites are responsible for the majority of skin ailments encountered by the cat owner. If you groom your cat at regular intervals you can prevent many skin disorders caused by insects. When in spite of adequate care you still find he has acquired fleas, mites, or some other external parasite, you are in a better position to seek consultation or start treatment before the problem becomes advanced.

Bees, wasps, and other insects that sting or bite rather than parasitize the cat, are discussed in the chapter EMERGENCIES (see *Insect Stings*).

Fleas

The flea is the most common parasite found on the cat's skin. Fleas live by feeding on blood. In most cases they cause only a mild itch; but a heavy infestation might cause a severe anemia or even the death of the cat. Fleas also are an intermediate host of the cat tapeworm.

Some cats experience hypersensitivity to flea saliva. This produces an intense itching and localized or even generalized skin reaction. Such cats require special attention (see *Flea Allergy*).

Signs: Flea infestation can be diagnosed by the finding of fleas on your cat; or by seeing salt and pepper-like, black and white grains about the size of sand in the coat. They are flea eggs and flea feces. Fecal material is made up of digested blood. When brushed onto a wet paper, it turns a reddish brown.

Look for fleas on your cat's back and around his tail and hindquarters by running a fine-toothed comb through his fur. Fleas are sometimes seen in the groin where it is warm and there is less hair. Itching is most pronounced in these areas.

The adult flea is a small, dark brown insect which can be seen with the naked eye. Although the flea has no wings and cannot fly, it does have powerful back legs and can jump great distances. Fleas move through the hair rapidly and are difficult to catch. Ticks and lice move slowly and are easy to pick off.

Life Cycle: In order to flourish, fleas need a warm humid environment. They are most common in summer, but can occur all year round in pets living indoors. They mate on the skin of the cat where they lay their eggs. The eggs fall off and incubate on furniture, in carpets, cracks, and cat bedding. After a few days, the eggs hatch into larvae which feed on what debris is available. Then they spin a cocoon. Depending on environmental conditions, the larvae can take three weeks to two years to grow into adult fleas.

Treatment: Because fleas spend most of their life off the cat, treatment of an individual cat is only partly effective. It is most important to eradicate fleas in the environment as well. To learn how to control fleas on the premises, see *Premises Control*. (Insecticide sprays and powders especially effective in the *environmental* control of fleas are Lindane, 0.5% spray or 1.0% dust; Chlorodane, 0.5% solution; DDVP; and Sevin 5% dust).

A variety of products are available for killing fleas on the cat. It is necessary to be certain the product is specifically intended for use on cats. Insecticide preparations for dogs and other livestock are often toxic to cats and irritating to their skins. Mild flea shampoos (such as Fleavol, Fleatol, Sendram) and powders (such as Diryl or SOK), and sprays such as Spectro and Para Bomb-M, are safe to use on cats.

Shampoos provide fair flea control but may be difficult to use if your cat doesn't like to be bathed. Kittens can be shampooed but must be dried quickly to prevent chilling. Prevent reinfestation by using a flea collar, powder, or spray, on a regular basis.

Insecticide dips applied to the cat's coat and allowed to dry are an extremely effective method of ridding your cat of fleas. Paramite is especially active against fleas. Before using an insecticide dip, be sure to read the section on *Insecticides*. Dips should be utilized every two weeks until the cat is free of fleas by direct inspection. Once the fleas have been killed by the dip, prevent reinfestation by applying a flea collar, or using a powder or spray on a regular basis.

Flea powders are easy to apply and last about one week. However, they tend to leave the coat dry and gritty. If your cat licks the powder off, it may make him vomit.

Aerosol sprays are also an effective method of controlling fleas on short-haired cats. Cats who are not used to them may become frightened by the "hissing" sound. You might then spray the product on a wet towel and rub it over the coat against the lay of his fur. In any case, be certain to keep the product away from the cat's face and eyes.

When applying a powder or spray, begin near the cat's head and work toward his tail. This way fleas on the body can't move up onto the face and escape the treatment.

A *flea collar or tag* is a simple and effective method of controlling fleas on the cat when used as directed on the package. They work best on cats who live indoors. These products are impregnated with an organophosphate insecticide *(Dichlorvas)* which acts directly on the parasite causing death. Occasionally a cat is found to be sensitive to the chemicals in flea collars and develops a skin allergy. Flea collar dermatitis sometimes can be prevented by airing the collar for two days before putting it on the cat. The collar should fit loosely enough so that you can get two fingers between it and your cat's neck. Most manufacturers recommend that you do not use their collars on Persians and other long-haired cats.

CAUTION: Do not permit your cat to chew his flea collar. It contains toxic chemicals. Flea collars impregnated with Dichlorvas should be removed before worming with Task (Dichlorvas) and should not be put back on until one week after worming. Otherwise, the additive effect of the insecticide in the flea collar and in the worm medication could be harmful. Flea collars and tags should be removed from sick cats and nursing queens. They should not be used on kittens younger than three months old.

Mites

Mites are microscopic spider-like creatures that live on the cat's skin or within his ear canals. Mites incite a number of skin conditions, from simple dandruff to irregular moth-eaten patches of hair loss complicated by draining sores. Collectively, they are called *mange*. Mange can be classified according to the type of mite that causes it.

Demodectic Mange. This form of mange is common in dogs, but fortunately it is extremely rare in cats. It is caused by a mite which lives deep in the hair pores of the skin. It is spread by direct contact. In cats the infection usually is mild and localized.

In the *localized* form there is first thinning and then loss of hair around the eyes and eyelids, giving them a moth-eaten appearance. After one or two months the hair begins to grow back in. In three months the majority of cases are healed.

Treatment: The diagnosis is made by taking skin scrapings and identifying the characteristic mite under a microscope. A topical preparation such as Canex or Goodwinol can be used to shorten the course in mild cases. Persistent cases should be treated by a veterinarian.

Head Mange (Feline Scabies). Feline scabies is a skin ailment caused by the head mite *Notoedres cati*. It tends to occur in older adult males; or may affect entire litters of kittens. The typical appearance is that of a crusty area on the edge of the ear or face. From here it may spread over the head and neck, or even extend to the feet and perineum.

The predominant sign is *intense* itching along with hair loss and the appearance of bald spots. The severe itching is caused by female mites tunneling a few millimeters under the skin to lay their eggs. Mite eggs hatch in five to ten days. The immature mites develop into adults and begin to lay eggs of their own. The whole cycle takes three to four weeks. The diagnosis is confirmed by skin scrapings, or in difficult cases by skin biopsy (searching for mites).

In severe or untreated cases the skin breaks down to form scabs, crusts, and thickened wrinkled skin on the head which gives the cat an aged-look. With intense scratching, wounds become secondarily infected.

Head mange is highly contagious. It is transmitted primarily by direct animal to animal contact. Dogs and even people can be infested, but only for short periods. The Notoedres mite will reproduce only on cats.

Treatment: Clip scabies-affected areas on long-haired cats and bathe the entire animal in warm water and soap to loosen crusts. Kittens may be dipped or shampooed but must be dried quickly to prevent chilling. Dips active against head mange mites are: Lime-sulphur 2.5% dilution (orchard spray); and Malathion 0.2%. All cats on the premises should be treated once a week for three to four weeks.

Dandruff shampoos such as Seleen are useful. They can be employed between insecticide dips to loosen scales. Apply a topical preparation such as Canex or Goodwinol ointment to areas of localized disease.

Cortisone will help to relieve severe itching. Sores that look infected from self-mutilation should be treated by a soothing topical ointment (Panolog).

Cheyletiella Mange (Walking Dandruff). This type of mange is caused by a large reddish mite that lives on the skin and causes mild itching and a tremendous amount of dry scaly material that looks like dandruff. The dandruff is heaviest over the back, neck and sides. This type of mange is not common in cats.

The life cycle of the Cheyletiella mite is similar to that of the head mange mite. The entire life cycle takes four to five weeks.

Walking dandruff is highly contagious. Humans, too, can become rather easily infested. The signs are itching and the appearance of red, raised bumps on the skin. They look very much like insect bites, which in fact they are. The Cheyletiella mite cannot live off the cat for more than two weeks. The owner's rash should improve as his cat is treated.

Treatment: The diagnosis is confirmed by finding the mite in dandruff scrapings collected on paper and examined under a magnifying glass. All cats on the premises should be treated with an insecticide dip once a week for three to four weeks. Control is achieved by using the same methods as described for *Head Mange.*

The premises should be treated with an insecticide (see *Premises Control*). Dichlorvus (DDVP) fly strips aid in the control of Cheyletiella Mange mites in catteries.

Chiggers (Trombiculid Mites). Chiggers, also called harvest mites and red bugs, live as adults in decaying vegetation. Only their larval forms are parasitic. The cat acquires the infestation while prowling in areas where chiggers are reproducing. The reproductive season of chiggers begins in late spring and may extend throughout the summer.

Larval mites appear as red, yellow, or orange specks barely visible to the naked eye but easily seen with a magnifying glass. They tend to clump in areas where the skin is thin, such as the web spaces between the toes, and about the ears and mouth—but may occur anywhere on the body. The larvae feed by sucking on the skin. The result is severe irritation and the formation of red draining sores with overlying scabs. Patches of raw skin may appear.

Treatment: If the larvae cannot be seen, they usually can be identified by skin scrapings. Chiggers in the ear canals can be eliminated by treating as you would for *Ear Mites.* Those elsewhere on the body will respond to measures described in the treatment of *Head Mange.* When feasible, prevent reinfestation by keeping your cat confined during the chigger season.

Other Mites:

Ear Mites (Ododectes cynotis): These mites are a separate species and should not be confused with *Notoedres cati* causing *Head Mange.* Ear mites are one of the most common problems the cat owner is likely to encounter. These mites live in the ear canals and feed on skin and debris. They are discussed in the chapter EARS.

Sarcoptic Mange Mites: These mites occur frequently in dogs and produce a disease called *Sarcoptic Mange.* Fortunately, they are hardly ever seen in cats. Their effect and treatment is similar to that of *Head Mange.* Veterinary diagnosis is required to make the diagnosis.

Ticks

Most people who live in the country are familiar with ticks. The male tick is a small flat insect about the size of a match head. A "blood" tick is the female tick feeding on the cat. She may swell up to the size of a pea.

Ticks have a complicated life cycle. It involves three hosts including wild and domestic animals and man. The adult tick fastens onto the cat. Males and females mate at this time and the female feeds, on the host. When you see a puffed-up tick (female) on your cat, look for a small male tick nearby.

Ticks are found less frequently on cats than dogs, owing to the fact that cats keep their coats well groomed. When present, ticks usually are found in inaccessible areas such as the ears, neck, head, back, and between the toes.

Treatment: Since cats rarely have more than a few ticks, the easiest thing is to remove them by hand. First kill the tick by applying alcohol, gin, ether, or fingernail polish directly to the tick by means of a cotton-tipped applicator. After a few moments, grasp the dead tick as close to the skin as possible and apply steady traction until it releases its hold. If the head remains fixed to the skin, there is no need for concern. In most cases, this causes only a local reaction which clears up in a few days. Only rarely does a tick bite become infected. To learn how to treat ticks on your cat's ears, see EARS.

For outdoor control of ticks it is advisable to cut tall grass, weeds, and brush. Spray or dust with Toxophene, Chlorodane, or Dieldrin. These products are toxic to pets. Use them with caution.

Lice *(Pediculosis)*

Lice infestation is called pediculosis. Lice are not very common. They occur primarily in cats who are malnourished and run down, and have lost the initiative to keep their coats well-groomed. They are found most often beneath matted hair and around the ears, head, neck, shoulders and perineal area.

The usual picture is itching in a poorly cared for or unkempt cat. Because of constant irritation, bare spots may be seen where the hair has been rubbed off.

Cats are infested only with *biting lice* (Trichodectes felis) which feed on skin scales. Lice are an intermediate host for the common cat tapeworm.

Adult lice are wingless, slow moving, pale-colored insects about two to three millimeters long. They lay eggs called *nits,* which look like white grains of sand and are found attached to hairs. They are difficult to brush off. Nits may look something like dandruff (seborrhea); but cats with seborrhea do not itch as they do with lice. Inspection with a magnifying glass makes the distinction easy as nits are well-formed rounded eggs attached to hair shafts.

Treatment: Lice do not show much resistance to insecticides and do not live long off the cat. They can be killed by giving a thorough bath followed by an insecticide dip which is effective against fleas (see *Fleas).* Three to four dips must be given at ten day intervals. In between, dust the cat with a 5% Sevin powder (see *Insecticides*).

Note: Heavily infested cats who are severely malnourished and debilitated might not be able to withstand the treatment and could go into shock. Begin by reducing the severity of the infestation by using insecticide powders.

Infected bedding should be destroyed and the cat's sleeping quarters disinfected (see *Premises Control*).

Flies

While adult flies do not normally afflict the cat, they may at times deposit their eggs on raw or infected wounds, or in soil where larvae can penetrate the cat's skin. When the eggs hatch, the maggots or grubs emerge to feed on the infected tissue, or to penetrate the epidermis and form lumps beneath the skin which later become infected.

Maggots (Myiasis). This condition, called *myiasis,* is most often caused by the bluebottle or blow fly, which lays its eggs in open wounds, or badly soiled damp matted fur. The eggs hatch in 10 to 12 hours. The larvae grow into large maggots which produce an enzyme in their saliva which digests the skin, causing "punched-out" areas. The maggots then penetrate the skin, enlarge the opening, and set the stage for a bacterial pyoderma. With a severe infestation the cat may go into shock. Signs are due to enzymes and toxins secreted by the maggots.

Treatment: Clip the affected areas to remove soiled and matted hair and apply an insecticide spray such as Spectro; or use a dip such as Paramite. Remove all maggots with blunt-nosed tweezers. Wash infected areas with an antibacterial soap (pHisoHex, Betadine) and dry the cat thoroughly. Then apply a topical antibiotic-steroid ointment (Panolog). Insert the tip of the tube directly into the wound opening.

Repeat the above treatment at intervals. Check closely for remaining maggots. Cats with infected wounds should be treated with an oral antibiotic (Penicillin).

If the cat exhibits signs of shock he should be taken at once to the veterinary clinic.

Grubs (Cuterebriasis). The most frequent cause of grub infestation is the large botfly which has a wide distribution in the United States. This fly lays its eggs near the burrows of rodents and rabbits. The cat acquires the disease by direct contact with infested soil. Newly hatched larvae penetrate the skin to form cystic-like lumps beneath the dermis which have a small opening to the outside to allow the grubs to breathe. From time to time, inch-long grubs protrude from the breathing holes. In about one month, they emerge and drop to the ground.

More than one grub may be found in the same area (usually along the jaw-bone, about the face, under the belly or along the sides). In such cases they form large nodular masses.

Treatment: Clip away hair to expose the breathing holes. Grasp each grub with a fine-tipped forceps and gently draw it out. (*Note:* If unable to grasp, a small incision must be made under an anesthetic to remove the parasite.) A topical antibiotic such as Panolog is used to pack the cavity. Oral antibiotics often are necessary to treat an associated bacterial infection.

Insecticides

Insecticides are used in shampoos, powders, dusts, sprays and dips for the elimination of insects on the cat. They are also used to disinfect bedding, houses, catteries, runs, gardens, garages, and other spots where a cat might infect himself by coming into contact with the adult insect or its intermediate forms.

Insecticides are poisons! *If you decide to use an insecticide preparation, be sure to follow the directions of the manufacturer.* Otherwise, poisonings are likely to occur from improper exposure.

There are four classes of insecticides in current use. They are: *chlorinated hydrocarbons* (Lindane, Chlordane); *organophosphates* (Dichlorvas, also called Task or DDVP; and Ronnel, also called Ectoral); *methylcarbamates* (Diryl, Sevin); and *Pyrethrins* (Fleavol).

Commercial preparations containing insecticides of the classes listed are available through many pet stores and agricultural supply outlets. Preparations for powdering, spraying, shampooing and dipping are discussed above in the paragraphs dealing with the specific parasites.

When you purchase one of these products, be sure that it is made up *especially for cats.* Products manufactured for dogs, sheep and other livestock, can irritate the skin of cats and even cause death through toxic reactions.

Lysol and other household disinfectants are not suitable for washing your cat and should not be used. Like insecticides, they are absorbed through the skin and can cause illness or death.

An *overdose* of an insecticide can cause your cat to twitch at the mouth, foam, collapse, convulse and fall into a coma. Other signs of insecticide toxicity are diarrhea, asthmatic breathing, a staggering gait, and muscular twitching and jerking.

If you suspect that your cat might be suffering from an insecticide reaction, give him a bath in warm soapy water to remove residual compounds from his coat and keep him quiet. Contact your veterinarian.

Dipping. The object of a dip is to rid your cat of surface parasites. Choose a dip which is recommended by your veterinarian or, if you decide to wash your cat with a commercial preparation, check the label to be sure it is effective against the insect in question. Insecticides active against fleas, mites and lice, are listed under the discussion of these parasites.

CAUTION: Some worm medications contain similar chemicals. If your cat has just been wormed, there could be a sudden build-up of chemicals in his system from powdering, shampooing, dipping or spraying with an insecticide. Check with your veterinarian before applying an insecticide dip or a flea collar to a cat who has been wormed within a week.

Dipping is not difficult if you first wash your cat with a gentle commercial cat shampoo or human baby shampoo. Then, while his coat is still wet, rinse him thoroughly with an insecticide dip made up according to the directions on the package. Apply eye ointment or mineral oil to his eyes and plug his ears with cotton so you can treat his head and ears with the dip also.

Most insecticide dips have to be repeated three to four times at intervals of seven to ten days. This varies according to the insect and the severity of the infection.

Premises Control. The object of premises control is to rid the environment of insects, eggs, larvae and other intermediate stages. Otherwise your cat will reinfect himself.

Treat all animals likely to come into contact with your cat or his living quarters.

Destroy infected bedding and scrub down your cat's quarters with a strong household disinfectant. A thorough housecleaning which includes vacuuming of carpets, spraying of furniture, application of insecticides to corners and cracks, will help to eliminate the insect, its eggs and larvae. This usually has to be done more than once. With a heavy infestation, it is sometimes better to enlist the services of a professional exterminator.

Insect bombs such as Vet Fog are suitable for use in homes and catteries and may be used safely in closed spaces. Be sure to remove all pets and read instructions carefully. Some of the insecticide dips can be used as sprays on gardens, lawns and runs. Use according to the method of dilution suggested by the manufacturer.

A cat's sleeping quarters should receive at least two treatments spaced two weeks apart. Eggs and cocoons are resistant to insecticides and can remain dormant for several months.

Sevin is an insecticide powder which can be purchased rather inexpensively from garden and agricultural supply stores. It comes in different concentrations. Be sure to purchase the *five percent* dust. It can be used safely in cat runs and sleeping quarters, on lawns and shrubs; it will not hurt your cat if light powder adheres to his coat. Dust liberally in and around sleeping quarters, runs and cat houses, using a shaker can. Force dust into crevices and cracks. It is effective against fleas, ants and lice. It is partially effective against ticks.

ALLERGIES

General Information

An allergic reaction is an unpleasant side effect caused by the cat's *immune system.* Without an immune system, an animal would not be able to build up resistance to viruses, bacteria, foreign proteins, and other irritating substances that get into his system. In the allergic cat, certain foods, or substances such as pollens, powders, feathers, wool, house dust, and insect bites, trigger a reaction typified by itching and sometimes sneezing, coughing, swelling of the eyelids, tearing, or vomiting and diarrhea.

In order for a cat to be allergic to something in his surroundings, he must be exposed to it at least twice. What he is allergic to is called the *allergen.* The way in which his body responds to that allergen is called a *hypersensitivity reaction* (or allergic reaction).

There are two kinds of hypersensitivity reaction. That of the *immediate* type occurs shortly after exposure and produces hives and itching. Hives in the cat are characterized by sudden swelling of the head, usually around the eyes and mouth, and occasionally the appearance of welts elsewhere on the body. The *delayed* reaction produces itching which occurs hours or days afterward. Flea allergy dermatitis is an example of both types. This explains why a cat may continue to itch even after a successful flea-dipping.

Allergens enter the body via the lungs (pollens, house dust); the digestive tract (eating certain foods); by injection (insect bites and vaccination); or by direct absorption through the skin. While the target area in man usually is the air passages and lungs (producing hay fever and asthma), in the cat it is the skin or gastrointestinal tract. The main sign of skin involvement is *severe itching*.

Food Allergy

Cats may become allergic to certain foods, or to substances in these foods. Fish, cheese and milk, are the most common food allergens. An intensely itchy skin often develops. It may be accompanied by sneezing, swelling of the eyelids, and a runny nose. You may see hair loss and oozing sores from constant scratching. In about half the cases food allergy produces profuse diarrhea.

The diagnosis is made by exposing the cat to a suspected allergen, and then seeing how he reacts to it. Treatment is discussed at greater length in the chapter GASTROINTESTINAL SYSTEM.

Flea Allergy Dermatitis (Miliary Dermatitis)

This skin disease, also called miliary dermatitis, is caused by an allergic reaction to flea saliva. At one time it was believed to be due to a food allergy (fish-eaters eczema); a hormone disorder; and specific nutritional deficiencies.

The affected cat breaks out along the back and around the neck with small crusts and bumps, about the size of a millet-seed. These are the spots where fleas are most common. As the cat licks and scratches frantically, he sometimes produces raw patches of skin which become infected. Lick ulcers may occur.

Miliary dermatitis is the most common seasonal allergy of cats. Symptoms are most prevalent in the middle of summer. However, once the cat is sensitized, if fleas live in the house, itching may persist all year round. Fleas cannot live above 5,000 feet, and as a result are not seen at higher elevations.

The diagnosis is made by seeing the characteristic skin rash and by finding fleas on the cat. You can check your cat for fleas by standing him over a sheet of white paper and brushing his coat. White and black grains of sandy material which drop on the paper are flea eggs and feces.

This is a hypersensitivity reaction of both immediate and delayed type; itching tends to persist long after fleas have been destroyed.

Treatment: Kill fleas with insecticide powders applied twice a week, especially to the areas of crust formation (see *Fleas*). Cortisone tablets or injections block the allergic reaction and relieve the itching. They should be used only with

Allergic contact dermatitis **produced by the insecticide in a** *flea collar.*

veterinary supervision because of potential side effects. Treat sores with a topical antibiotic ointment (Panolog).

Desensitization is not of much value in delayed allergies of this type.

Irritant Contact and Allergic Contact Dermatitis

Irritant contact dermatitis and allergic contact dermatitis are two different conditions discussed together because they produce similar appearing reactions. Both are caused by contact with a chemical. Whereas any cat coming into contact with an irritating chemical will develop a skin reaction, in some cases only cats allergic to a substance show a skin response. A cat does not break out with an allergic contact dermatitis until he has been exposed to the allergen repeatedly. Both irritant and allergic contact dermatitis affect parts of the body where hair is thin or absent (i.e., the feet, chin, nose, abdomen and groin). These areas also are the most likely to come into contact with chemicals. Liquid irritants may affect any part of the body. A contact dermatitis of either type produces red itchy bumps along with inflammation of the skin. Scaliness follows, and the hair falls out. Excessive scratching causes skin injury and infected sores. The rash of an allergic contact dermatitis may spread beyond the area of contact.

Chemicals producing irritant dermatitis are acids and alkalis, detergents, solvents, soaps, and petroleum by-products.

Common substances causing an allergic reaction are flea powders, shampoos (particularly those containing iodine), poison ivy and poison oak, plastic and rubber dishes, and dyes found in carpets. Neomycin, which is found in many topical medications, may produce an allergic reaction.

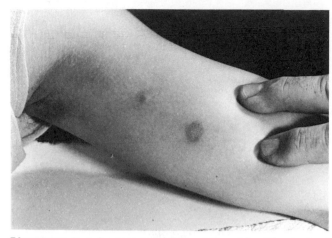

Ringworm is a fungus infection of the skin. The typical appearance is a round patch with scales at the center and an advancing red ring at the margin.

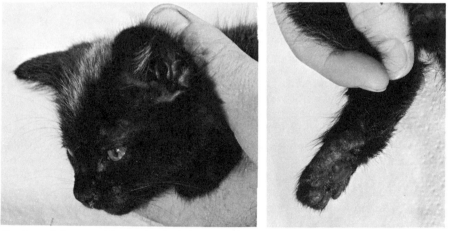

Scaly patches and irregular hair loss on the face and foot of a cat with *ringworm*.

Flea collar dermatitis is a reaction to the insecticide in the collar. It affects the skin around the neck, producing local itching and redness followed by hair loss and crust formation. This condition may spread to other areas.

Litter box dermatitis affects the skin around the tail and anus.

Treatment: Consider the area of exposure and try to identify the skin allergen or chemical causing the problem. Then keep your cat away from it. Treat infected skin as you would for *Cellulitis and Abscess.* Cortisone is of value because it stops the itching, biting and scratching. It should be used only under a veterinarian's supervision.

Remove flea collars at the first sign of skin irritation. Instructions for the safe use of flea collars are given elsewhere (see *Fleas*).

FUNGUS INFECTIONS OF THE SKIN

Ringworm (Dermatomycosis)

Ringworm is not a worm but a plant-like growth which invades the hair and hair follicles. The majority of cases are caused by the fungus *Microsporum canis.* A few are caused by other species.

Ringworm gets its name from its typical appearance, a spreading circle having hair loss and scaly skin at the center and an advancing red ring at the margin. However, the typical form may not be present—especially in cats. Occasionally you will see only scaly patches, irregular hair loss, or just a few broken hairs around the face and ears. (Ringworm of the ear flap is discussed in the EARS chapter.) Although simple ringworm is not an itchy condition, scabs and crusts can form, leading to draining sores which provoke licking and scratching. Cases do occur in which skin involvement is extensive. Ringworm also invades toenails; when the nails grow out they are usually deformed.

The disease is transmitted by contact with spores in the soil, or by contact with the infective hair of other animals (usually dogs and cats). An older cat with an inapparent infection may become a carrier. This represents a source of infection for other pets in the house. Humans can pick up ringworm from cats, and can also transmit the disease to them. Children should avoid handling cats with ringworm, as they are especially likely to catch the disease. Adults seem relatively resistant.

Mild cases of ringworm, with just hair loss and local scaliness, often resemble demodectic mange. A diagnosis of ringworm can be made if the skin glows under ultra-violet light. This test is not positive in all cases. Microscopic examination of skin scrapings, or fungus cultures, are more certain.

Treatment: Clip away the infected hair at the margins of the ringworm patch and bathe the skin with Weldol, Betadine shampoo, or Casteen (an antifungal agent) to remove dead scales. One or two small patches can be treated with a fungistatic creme (Conofite, Tolnaftate). For more extensive involvement, or patches that do not seem to be getting better with topical solutions, your veterinarian can prescribe a drug called Griesofulvin (Fulvicin). It is given by mouth in a daily dose of 10 to 20 milligrams per pound, or at weekly intervals in larger doses. It should not be given to pregnant females as it could be dangerous to unborn kittens. It is also a good idea to give a single large dose (100 milligrams per pound per week) as a preventative to other animals on the premises who are not infected but have been exposed. Infected sores should be treated with a topical antibiotic ointment (Panolog).

Spores should be eliminated from the premises to prevent reinfection. The cat's bedding should be discarded. Vacuum the house to remove infective hair. Boil contaminated clothing and fabrics or wash in Clorox to kill spores. Technical Captan can be used as a spray in 1:200 dilution (in water) to spray a cattery.

Sporotrichosis

This is an uncommon fungus infection of the skin caused by spores in the soil which gain entrance through a break in the skin. It is most common among cats who prowl in sharp underbrush or prairie grass.

A nodule forms at the site of the skin wound. The hair over the nodule falls out, leaving a moist or ulcerated surface. In some cases there is little surface reaction, but you may see several small firm nodules beneath the skin which appear to form a chain.

The diagnosis is made by removing a piece of tissue and examining it under the microscope; or more conclusively, by growing the fungus in culture.

Treatment: The disease is treated by topical and oral iodine. Treatment should be monitored by a professional.

Candidiasis (Thrush)

This yeast-like organism affects the mucous membranes and ear canals. Skin involvement does occur—but almost exclusively among cats who live in moist humid environs.

The infection produces white elevated plaques which form an exudate on the surface of the skin and bleed easily when rubbed.

Treatment: Skin patches are successfully treated by applying an ointment containing Nystatin (i.e. Panolog). Fungus infection of the mouth and ear canals is discussed in chapters dealing with these areas.

Mycetoma

This is a rare fungus disease that produces tumor-like masses or nodules on various parts of the body. Blackish granules are found in these masses. Some species of mycetoma can cause a fatal infection.

Treatment: Professional management is required. A small mass limited to the surface might be cured by complete surgical removal. These infections can be transmitted to people. Use great care in handling a cat who may have this infection.

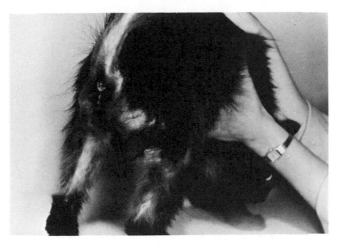

Feline endocrine alopecia, **showing symmetrical hair loss with normal skin.**

HORMONE SKIN DISEASES

Hormone skin diseases are not common. Characteristically they produce a symmetrical loss of hair over the body—one side being the mirror image of the other. They do not cause itching. The rare exception is the cat whose hormone disorder is complicated by an infection of the skin.

Feline Endocrine Alopecia

Alopecia is the name given to balding. It is most common in the neutered male, but intact toms and queens also can be affected.

Older cats may experience lack of hair growth or thinning of the coat because of a deficiency of sex hormones. Loss of hair is first seen on the lower part of the abdomen and insides of the back legs, in a matching or symmetrical distribution. Only in severe cases is the rest of the coat affected. Some cats grow hair back spontaneously only to lose it again later. Itching is not a problem.

Treatment: This is mainly a cosmetic condition. It can be treated by giving an estrogen/testosterone combination; or by Megestral acetate (Ovaban).

Thyroid Deficiency (Hypothyroidism)

Hypothyroidism is rare in cats. Lack of adequate output of thyroid hormone from the thyroid gland impairs new hair growth and prolongs the resting phase. Thus there is a gradual thinning of the coat, which may also appear dull and lifeless. Other signs of hypofunction, including lethargy, weight gain, mental dullness and irregular heat cycles, may or may not be present. You might first suspect hypothyroidism in connection with an infertility problem. Diagnosis requires a thyroid blood test.

Treatment: Hypothyroidism is easy to treat with thyroid hormone given daily. Usually it is permanent and requires lifetime maintenance.

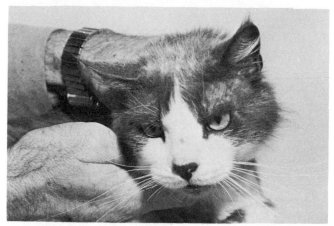

Hair loss over the eyes is common in free roaming males, in whom injuries from cat fights can produce a build-up of scar tissue in these areas.

Pyoderma and *skin abscess.*

Stud tail **is the most common in unaltered males.**

Cortisone Excess (Adrenal Hyperfunction)

This condition is due to overproduction of cortisone by the adrenal glands located on top of the kidneys. This is extremely rare in cats. But if your cat is getting cortisone by mouth or injection, after a time he could get the same effect as if his adrenals were making too much cortisone.

The effect on the coat is to produce loss of hair in a symmetrical pattern over the trunk, with darkening of the underlying skin. There is a pot-bellied look. Such cats gain weight and retain fluid.

Treatment: If your cat is getting cortisone by tablet or injection, your veterinarian may want to reduce the dosage or stop the medication altogether. If it is due to overproduction, treatment might involve drugs to reduce cortisone production by the adrenal glands.

PYODERMA (BACTERIAL INFECTION OF THE SKIN)

Pyoderma is a bacterial infection of the skin. Ninety percent are caused by the staphylococcus. Pyoderma is classified according to the depth of skin involvement.

Impetigo

This is an infection of the dermis of the skin which occurs in newborn kittens. It is discussed in the PEDIATRICS chapter.

Folliculitis

This is a localized infection of hair follicles. It is often associated with more extensive skin involvement, but may occur by itself. Deeper involvement of hair follicles is called *furunculosis*. When numerous hair follicles are affected, a *carbuncle* may form.

Feline Acne

Feline acne develops in the sebaceous glands of the underside of the chin and edges of the lips. Blockage of skin pores by excess sebum or keratin is a predisposing cause. It is more common among cats with oily skin.

Acne is identified by finding blackheads or pimple-like bumps which come to a head and drain pus. Swelling of the entire chin and lower lips may be seen in severe cases.

Treatment: The infection usually responds to twice daily cleansing of the skin with a dilute solution of hydrogen peroxide or surgical soap (pHisoHex), followed by the use of a topical antibiotic (Panolog). When sebum is a problem, the skin should be cleansed with one of the anti-seborrhea shampoos (Seleen, Thiomar, Sebutone, or Selsun Blue). A deep draining infection may require antibiotics. As the underlying condition remains the same, acne often recurs when the treatment is stopped. If this happens, see your veterinarian.

Stud Tail

This condition is similar to acne in that it is caused by over-secretion of sebaceous glands. As you part the hair on top of the tail near its base you may see an accumulation of waxy brown material. In severe cases the hair follicles become infected. The hair becomes matted and greasy, develops a rancid odor, and may fall out.

The condition is most common in tom cats but may occur in females and neutered males.

Treatment: Wash the tail twice weekly with one of the anti-seborrhea shampoos used in treating *Feline Acne* and sprinkle it with corn starch or baby powder. If the skin is infected, treat as you would for *Cellulitis and Abscesses* (below). Neutering may relieve the condition in tom cats.

Cellulitis and Abscesses

Cellulitis is an inflammation which involves the deep layers of the skin. Most cases are caused by animal bites or scratches (i.e., cat fights). These puncture wounds allow skin bacteria to get established beneath the epidermis. Infection can be prevented in many fresh wounds if proper care is taken of them within the first few hours (see *Wounds,* in the chapter EMERGENCIES).

The signs of cellulitis of the skin are *pain* (tenderness to pressure), *warmth* (it feels hotter than normal), *firmness* (it's not as soft as it should be), and change in color (it appears *redder* than it should be). As the infection spreads out from the wound into the subdermal lymphatic system, you may see red streaks in the skin and be able to feel enlarged lymph nodes in the groin, armpit, or neck.

A *skin abscess* is a localized pocket of pus beneath the surface of the skin. Pimples, pustules, furuncles, and boils are examples of small abscesses. The signs are the same as those for cellulitis except that an abscess is fluctuant (it feels like fluid under pressure).

If hot packs are applied to an area of cellulitis, the heat and moisture assist the natural defenses of the body to surround the infection and make it come to a head. The skin over the top of an abscess thins out and ruptures, allowing the pus to be evacuated. Then the pocket heals from below.

Treatment: Localize the infection by clipping away the hair and apply warm soaks three times a day for 15 minutes. Saline soaks, made up to a teaspoonful of salt in a quart of water, make a suitable poultice.

Pimples, pustules, furuncles, boils and other small abscesses which do not drain spontaneously need to be lanced with a sterile needle or scalpel. Flush the cavity with dilute hydrogen peroxide to keep it open and draining until it heals from below.

Antibiotics are indicated in the treatment of wound infections, cellulitis and abscesses. Most skin bacteria respond well to penicillin, Keflex, Tetracycline, or Chloromycetin, but cultures and antibiotic sensitivity tests may be indicated to select the drug of choice.

Foreign bodies (such as splinters) beneath the skin must be removed with forceps as they are a continuous source of infection.

LICK GRANULOMAS

Lick granulomas, also called the *Eosinophilic Granuloma Complex,* are a group of different skin diseases involving ulceration and granulation of the skin. Although the initiating cause is unknown in most cases, they all have in common an association with excessive licking. As the cat begins to lick at his skin the hair is rubbed off. The surface of the skin gets red and shiny-looking and begins to itch. This leads to further maceration of the skin and continues the cycle. Eventually the sore becomes ulcerated.

The *Rodent Ulcer* is a type of lick granuloma that begins on either side of the skin of the upper lip, or in the mouth behind the last upper molar. It is discussed in greater detail in the MOUTH AND THROAT chapter.

The *Linear Granuloma* is a lick sore typically found on the back of the hind legs. In most cases the condition is bilateral, one side being the mirror image of the other. Lick granulomas also occur on other parts of the body, especially the abdomen and feet.

Treatment: Cortisone relieves the itching but will probably be licked off right away. It can also be administered directly into the sore by injection. As with any long-standing skin condition, a squamous (scaly) cell cancer can develop at the site of ulceration. Lick granulomas are difficult to treat and tend to recur.

LUMPS and BUMPS
(Tumors On or Beneath the Skin)

Any sort of lump, bump or growth found on or beneath the skin is by definition a tumor (which means literally "a swelling"). Tumors are classified as *benign* when they are not a cancer - and *malignant* when they are.

Classically, a benign growth is one that grows slowly, is surrounded by a capsule, is not invasive and doesn't spread to other parts. However, there is no good way to tell whether a tumor is benign or malignant without removing it and examining it with a microscope. If the tumor is found to be benign, then it won't come back if it has been completely removed.

Cancers usually enlarge rapidly (a few weeks or months). They are not encapsulated. They appear to infiltrate into surrounding tissue and may ulcerate the skin and bleed. A hard mass which appears fixed to bone (or could be a growth of the bone itself) is a cause for concern. The same is true for pigmented lumps or flat moles which start to enlarge and then spread out and begin to bleed (*Melanomas*).

A hard gray (or pink) open sore which does not heal, especially on the feet and legs, should be regarded with suspicion. This could be a skin cancer.

Any unexplained lump, bump or open sore on your cat should be checked by your veterinarian. Most cancers are not painful. So do not delay because your cat does not seem to be feeling uncomfortable. To learn more about common surface growths, see the chapter TUMORS AND CANCERS.

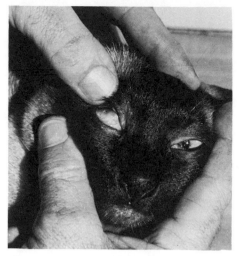

By recessing the eye, you can demonstrate a normal third eyelid.
—J. Clawson.

By constricting his pupil, a cat can see objects close-up in better focus.

When a cat is frightened his pupils dilate.

A white cat with a blue left eye. He was deaf in the left ear.

5

Eyes

SPECIAL CHARACTERISTICS

The eyes of cats have some special characteristics which set them apart from those of most other animals. Whereas dogs use a combination of sight, hearing and smell to orient themselves to their surroundings, cats depend more upon their eyesight, which is uniquely adapted to hunting and stalking.

The eyes of cats are unusually large. In fact, if man had an eye of comparable size, it would measure almost eight inches in diameter.

The eyeball is recessed in a cushion of fat which protects it in its bony socket. Owing to this deep-seated location, eye movements are restricted. But a cat is especially adept at detecting movement out of the corner of his eye and will turn his whole head rapidly to bring the object into focus. He is less skillful at identifying stationary objects and will watch them for long periods with an intense, steady, unblinking stare, in order to detect the slightest movement.

Another interesting fact about a cat's eyesight is that he does not see objects close to his face in good focus. This is because the muscles which change the shape of his lens are relatively weak. His near vision is much like that of a middle-aged person who is becoming presbyopic and needs reading glasses. However, the cat is able to compensate for this to some extent by narrowing his pupils into slit-like openings, which sharpens the image.

The cat's retina is a light sensitive membrane at the back of his eye. It contains two types of photoceptor nerve cells called *rods* and *cones*. Rods react to different intensities of light. They enable a cat to see black, white and shades of gray. Cones respond to different light wave lengths, providing color vision. A cat's retina has many rods and few cones. Thus he is able to see well in dim light, but has poor color vision.

The reason cats' eyes appear to glow in the dark is that they have a special layer of cells behind the retina called the *tapetum lucidum*. These cells act like a mirror, reflecting the light back on to the retina, producing a double exposure of the photoreceptor cells. It is this reflective process, plus the large number of rods in his retina, which is responsible for the cat's exceptional night vision, superior to that of most other animals.

Another special characteristic of the cat's eye is his extra eyelid or *nictitating membrane,* normally not visible but located at the inside corner of the eye, resting on the eyeball. You can demonstrate this extra eyelid by recessing his eye. With your index finger, press gently on the eyeball through the eyelid. The third membrane will immediately slide out across the surface of the eye.

The third eyelid has an important cleansing and lubricating function. It helps to compensate for the fact that a cat seldom blinks. Like a windshield wiper, it sweeps across the surface of the eye, dispersing the tears and removing dust and foreign particles. It also helps to protect the surface of the eye from injury. By partially closing his upper and lower eyelids and protruding his nictitating membrane, a cat can protect his eyes while running through weeds and brush.

STRUCTURE OF THE EYE

The whole clear part of the front of the eye, which you can see when you look at your cat's face, is the cornea. It is covered by a layer of transparent cells. Surrounding it is a white rim called the *sclera.* In the cat, you can see very little of the sclera without drawing back the eyelids. The layer of tissue which covers the white of the eye is called the *conjunctiva.* It reflects back to cover the inner surface of the eyelids and both sides of the nictitating membrane. It does not cover the cornea.

The cat's eyelids are tight folds of skin which support the front of the globe. They do not make direct contact with the surface of the eye because there is a thin layer of tears between them. The edges of the eyelids should meet when the eyes are closed. If this doesn't happen the cornea dries out, causing eye irritation. Normally cats do not have eyelashes, but when present and misdirected, they are a source of irritation to the surface of the eye.

The tears are secreted by glands found in the eyelids, nictitating membrane and conjunctiva. They serve two functions. They cleanse and lubricate the surface of the eye; and they contain immune substances that help prevent bacteria from gaining a foothold and causing an eye infection.

A normal accumulation of tears is removed by evaporation. Excess tears are pooled near the inner corner of the eye and carried via a drainage system to the nose. Excess tearing or watering of the eye indicates an eye ailment (see *The Tearing Mechanism*).

The opening at the center of the eye is the *pupil.* It is surrounded by a circular or elliptical layer of pigmented muscle called the *iris.* The iris changes the size and shape of the pupil. As the iris expands the pupil enlarges and becomes round. As it contracts, the pupil narrows down to a vertical slit-like opening.

Cats' eyes come in a variety of colors. The color is due to pigment present in the iris. The most common eye colors are yellow and green. Some cats have orange, blue, or purplish eyes. Occasionally a cat is born with eyes of different

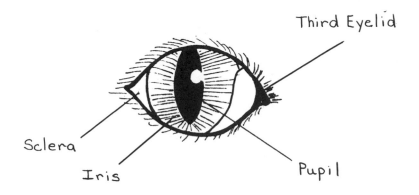

Front View of the Eye.—*Rose Floyd.*

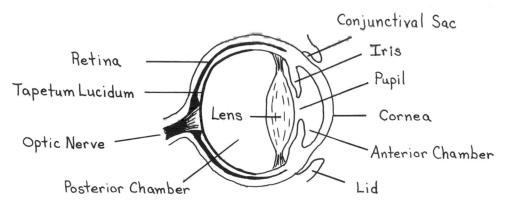

Side View of the Eye.—*Rose Floyd.*

colors. This is seen most often in Persians, in which one iris is orange and the other is blue. It may be associated with congenital deafness on the side having the blue iris. Deafness also occurs in some white-coated cats, especially those with blue irises.

The *inner eye* has two chambers. The *anterior chamber* is found between the cornea and the lens. The *posterior* chamber, containing a clear jelly, is the central cavity of the eye between the lens and the retina.

Light enters the eye by passing first through the cornea and the anterior chamber and then through the pupil and the lens. The *lens* focuses the light, which then passes through the posterior chamber and is received by the retina.

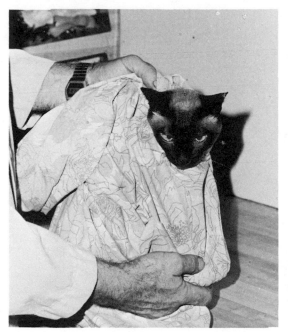

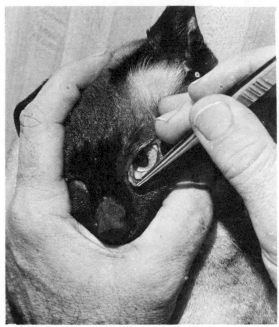

A pillow case is a good restraint for examining the eyes.   —J. Clawson.

A complete eye examination includes looking behind the third eyelid.   —J. Clawson.

WHAT TO DO IF YOUR CAT HAS AN EYE PROBLEM

If your cat has matter in his eye and if his eye waters, if he blinks, squints, paws at his eye and gives evidence that his eye is painful, or if the nictitating membrane is visible, then you are faced with an eye problem. The first thing to do is to examine the eye to see if you can determine the cause.

How to Examine His Eye

The eye examination is best carried out in a dark room using a single light source such as a flashlight. A magnifying glass can be of considerable help. It allows you to see fine details on the surface of the eyelids and the eyeball; and to inspect some of the structures of the inner eye. Most cats should be restrained. Generally they won't remain still and, if frightened, their pupils will dilate. Put the cat in a pillow case and pin it around his neck.

You can often get a clue to the cause of your cat's problem by comparing one eye to the other. Check to see if the eyes are of the same size, shape and color; if they bulge forward or are recessed back into their sockets. There might be an eye discharge; or the third eyelid might be visible over the inside corner of the eye. Does the eye look smoky, hazy or cloudy?

. To examine the outer surface of the eyeball place one thumb against the cheek below the eye, and the other thumb against the bone above the upper lid. Gently draw down on the lower thumb and apply counter traction with the other. The lower lid will sag out and you can look in and see the conjunctival sac and most of the cornea behind it. Reverse the procedure to examine the surface of the eye behind the upper lid.

Flash a light across the surface of the cornea to see whether it is clear and transparent. A dull or dished-out spot is a sign of an injury. The pupils should be equal in size. They should narrow down to vertical slits when light is flashed into the eye.

Push gently on the surface of the eyeball through the eyelid to see if one eye feels unusually hard or soft. If the eye is tender, the cat will give evidence of pain.

To test for vision, cover one eye and touch the other several times with your finger. If the cat has vision, he will blink when he sees your finger approaching.

Signs of Eye Ailment

Disorders of the eye are accompanied by a number of signs and symptoms. Pain is one of the most serious. A cat with a painful eye should receive prompt veterinary attention.

Eye Discharge: The type of discharge helps to define its cause. A clear discharge without *redness* and pain indicates a problem in the tear drainage system (see *The Tearing Mechanism*). Any discharge accompanied by a *painful* eye should alert you to the possibility of CORNEA or INNER EYE involvement. A thick, sticky, mucus or pus-like discharge along with a red (inflamed) eye suggests a conjunctivitis *(Pink Eye).*

Painful Eye: Signs of pain include excessive tearing, squinting (i.e., closing down the eye), tenderness to touch, and avoidance of light. The nictitating membrane may protrude in response to pain. The common causes of painful eye are injuries to the CORNEA (abrasion, foreign body), and disorders affecting the INNER EYE.

Film over the Eye: An opaque or whitish film which moves out over the surface of the eyeball from the inside corner of the eye is a protruded nictitating membrane. Causes are discussed in *The Third Eyelid.*

Cloudy Eye: Loss of clarity or transparency of the eye indicates an inner eye disorder (see *Cloudy Eye*). When it is entirely opaque, the owner might think his cat has a "blind eye," but this is not necessarily correct.

Hard or Soft Eye: Changes in eye pressure are caused by disorders of the INNER EYE. The pupil might become fixed and fail to respond to light. A hard eye with a dilated pupil indicates *Glaucoma*. A soft eye with a small pupil indicates inflammation of the inner structures of the eye *(Uveitis).*

Irritation of the Lids: Conditions which cause swelling, crusting, itching, or hair loss of the eyelids are discussed in *Eyelids.*

Bulging or Sunken Eye: Abnormal contours and positions of the eye are discussed in *The Eyeball.*

Abnormal Eye Movements: Eyes that focus in different directions, or jerk back and forth, are also discussed in *The Eyeball.*

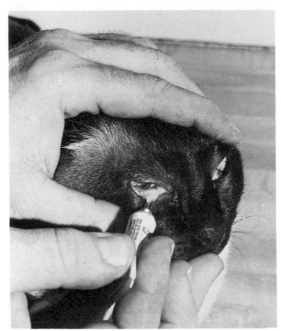 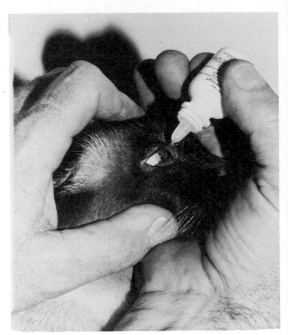

Apply ointment to the inner surface of the lower lid. Drops are applied to the inner corner of the eye.
—*J. Clawson.*

How to Apply Eye Medicine

Steady your cat's head with one hand and draw down on his lower lid to expose the inner surface of the eyelid. Apply ointment to the inside of the lower lid. Direct application to the eyeball is irritating and may cause the cat to jerk his head. Eye injury could result.

Eye drops are applied directly to the eyeball. Steady the heel of the hand in which you are holding the dropper against the side of your cat's head. Tilt his nose upward, then drop the medication into the inner corner of his eye. Rub the eyelids gently to disperse the medicine. Eye drops should be applied frequently since they tend to wash out rapidly with tears.

Use only preparations specifically labeled *for ophthalmic use*. Check to be sure that the preparation is not out of date.

Minor eye ailments should not be neglected. If they do not respond to treatment in 24 hours, consult your veterinarian.

Prolonged administration of antibiotics in the eye can predispose to fungal infection.

THE EYEBALL

Eye out of its Socket (An Emergency)

A hard blow to the head or a forceful strain could push the eyeball out of its socket. The injury tends to occur in breeds with short noses and large prominent eyes. Replacement of the eyeball must be accomplished at once. Shortly after the dislocation takes place, swelling behind the eye makes it extremely difficult to manipulate the eye back to its normal position. To replace the eye, first restrain the cat (see *Handling and Restraint*). Then lubricate his eye with Vaseline and attempt to lift the eyelids out and over the eyeball while gently maintaining pressure on the globe with a wad of cotton. If the eye cannot be easily replaced, cover it with a wet cloth and seek professional assistance. Cold packs will help control swelling.

Caution: Do not make repeated unsuccessful attempts to manipulate a dislocated eye, as this causes further swelling and inevitably leads to greater injury.

Bulging Eye *(Exophthalmos)*

In this condition, swelling of tissue behind the eye pushes the eyeball forward. As seen from above, the affected eye appears to be more prominent. Major protrusion prevents closure of the eyelids. If the nerves to the eye are stretched or damaged, the pupil dilates and won't constrict when a light is flashed in the eye.

Exophthalmos might occur after a blow which fractures the bones of the eye socket and causes a sudden build-up of blood or fluid behind the eye.

Infections that spread to the eyeball from the sinus also might cause the eye to bulge. They are often accompanied by fever and extreme pain when the cat attempts to open his mouth.

A growth behind the eyeball is another cause of eye protrusion. The majority are malignant and respond poorly to treatment. You will notice a *gradual* bulging of the eye which gets worse over a matter of weeks.

Finally, untreated chronic glaucoma can lead to increased size of the eye and protrusion (see *Hard Eye*).

Treatment: All causes of exophthalmos are extremely serious and may cause loss of vision. They require immediate veterinary attention. Drugs can be given to reduce the swelling produced by trauma. Antibiotics are required to treat those caused by infection. Surgery might be advisable to drain an accumulation of blood or pus, either behind the eye or within an infected sinus, or to suture an eyelid over a bulging eyeball to protect it from injury and keep it from drying out.

Sunken Eye *(Enophthalmos)*

Both eyelids may recede when there is loss of substance in the fat pads or cushions behind the eye (i.e., in dehydration or rapid weight loss).

Furthermore, there is a retractor muscle which, when it goes into spasm, can pull the eye back into its socket. This situation might occur with a painful injury

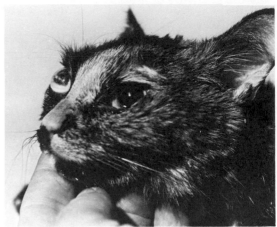

The bulging right eye indicates *exophthalmos.*

A *cross-eyed look* (strabismus) is common among Siamese.
—J. Clawson.

Severe squinting, along with eye discharge and loss of hair, indicates a chronic eye irritation. The cause was *entropion.*

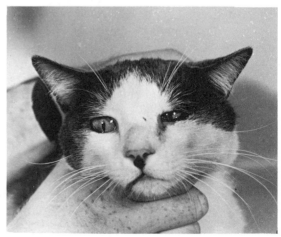

to the cornea. Damage to a nerve trunk in the neck can result in a sunken eyeball and a small pupil (*Horner's Syndrome*). Finally, after a severe injury to the eye, the eye may undergo atrophy. It becomes smaller and sinks into its socket.

As the eye begins to recess, the third eyelid or nictitating membrane becomes visible and there is an accumulation of mucus in the recessed space formed by the sinking of the eye. This gives the eye a peculiar rolled-back look. Owing to the presence of a membrane across the eye, a sunken eye is often mistaken for protrusion of the third eyelid (see *The Third Eyelid*).

Treatment: The treatment of enophthalmos is directed at the underlying cause of the problem.

Cross-Eyed Gaze *(Strabismus)*

A cross-eyed look is extremely common among Siamese cats—so much so that many owners accept it as normal. One eye looks ahead while the other eye turns in. This condition is inherited.

Other types of strabismus are caused by eye muscle paralysis. The eye cannot move in a certain direction. Brain tumors, and injuries to the nerves and muscles of the eye, are predisposing causes. This type of strabismus is rare.

Jerking Eye Movements *(Nystagmus)*

Involuntary movements of the eyes may take the form of irregular side-to-side jerking of the eyeballs, or rhythmic pendulum-like swings having a fast and slow phase. They indicate a disorder of the vestibular system (see *Middle Ear).*

EYELIDS

Severe Squinting *(Blepharospasm)*

Spasm of the muscles around the eye is induced by eye irritants such as foreign materials in the eye. The irritation causes tightening of the muscles of the eyelids, narrowing down the eye and rolling the eyelids in against the cornea. Having once rolled in, the rough margins of the lids rub against the eyeball causing further pain and spasm.

Anesthetic drops can be applied to the eyeball to relieve the pain and break the cycle. The relief is temporary if the underlying irritant is not found and removed.

Irritated Eyelids *(Blepharitis)*

Blepharitis, or inflammation of the eyelids, occurs often—primarily because the eyelids are frequently injured during a cat fight. Scratches and surface injuries can easily become infected. This leads to itching and scratching, crust formation, and the accumulation of pus and debris on the eyelids.

Blepharitis also can be caused by head mange mites (*Notoedres cati*), demodectic mange mites, and ringworm infection. Head mange causes intense itching. Owing to persistent scratching there is hair loss, redness, and scab formation. Ringworm affects the hair on the eyelid, causing it to become brittle and break off next to the skin. This is not an itchy condition. The skin may look scaly and crusted, but it is seldom red or irritated.

Treatment: Apply warm soaks to the eyelids to loosen scabs. Protect the eye by instilling mineral oil and then remove the scabs with a cotton-tipped applicator soaked in hydrogen peroxide solution. Afterwards, apply Panolog cream twice daily to the eyelids. The treatment of ringworm and mange is discussed in the SKIN chapter.

Sudden Swelling *(Chemosis)*

Sudden swelling of the eyelids may be due to allergic reactions such as insect bites, hives, allergens in medications (Neomycin); or it may be seen in certain skin allergies. The lids are fluid-filled, puffy and soft. Water has passed out of the circulation into the tissues in response to the allergen.

This is not a serious problem. It is of short duration and improves when the allergic agent is removed. Simple cases may be treated with drops or eye ointments containing a corticosteroid (Neocortef).

Foreign Bodies in the Eye

Foreign material such as dust, grass seed, dirt and specks of vegetable matter can become trapped behind the eyelids and nictitating membranes. The first indication is tearing and watering of the eye, along with signs of eye irritation such as blinking and squinting. The third membrane may protrude to protect the irritated eye.

Treatment: First examine the eye as described above (see *How to Examine His Eye*). You might be able to see a foreign body on the surface of the eye or behind the upper or lower eyelid. If not, the foreign body may be caught behind the third eyelid, in which case the cat will need to be given an anesthetic before you can lift up the eyelid and remove it.

If the foreign body can be seen, you can gently remove it with blunt-nose tweezers, such as women use to pluck their eyebrows. Or you can moisten a cotton-tipped applicator and use it to swab the eye. The foreign body may adhere to it. When there is dirt in the eye, irrigate the eye with a salt-water solution (one teaspoon of salt to a pint of water). Soak a wad of cotton and squeeze it into the eye. Thorns which cling to the surface of the eyelids can be removed with tweezers; but those which penetrate the surface of the eye should be removed by a veterinarian.

After you have removed a foreign object, apply an antibiotic ophthalmic ointment (Neosporin).

The cat may persist in rubbing his eye after treatment. In this case the foreign body may still be in the eye or a corneal abrasion may have occurred (see *Cornea*). Obtain professional assistance.

Eye Irritation from Lashes *(Trichiais)*

Normally cats do not have eyelashes, but there are exceptions. When present, they may grow in from the eyelid and rub against the cornea, producing eye

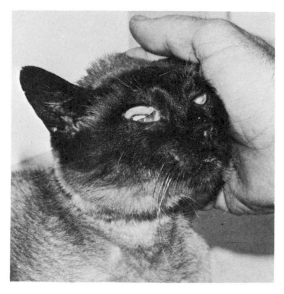

Sudden swelling of the conjunctiva (*chemosis*).

Foreign bodies can be removed with blunt-nosed tweezers.
—*J. Clawson.*

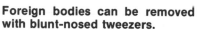

Protrusion of both nictitating membranes, due to chronic illness and weight loss.

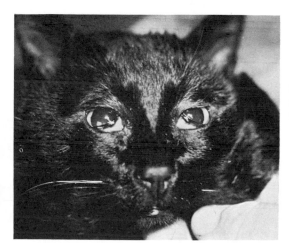

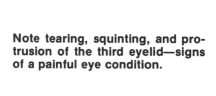

Note tearing, squinting, and protrusion of the third eyelid—signs of a painful eye condition.

irritation and injury. In such cases the hairs should be removed by surgery or burned out with an electric needle. Plucking them with blunt-nosed tweezers provides temporary relief.

Eyelid Rolled Inward *(Entropion)*

This condition occurs sporadically as an hereditary defect in the Persian cat, but can occur in all cats as a result of scarring of the lower lid following a bout of purulent conjunctivitis or a laceration of the eyelid.

The rolled-in lid produces eye irritation including tearing and severe squinting. The defect in the adult cat can be corrected by an operation.

Eyelid Rolled Outward *(Ectropion)*

In this situation the lower eyelid rolls out from the face exposing the eye to irritation. It may be due to a birth defect but most cases are due to an improperly healed laceration involving the lid. Plastic surgery might be necessary to tighten the lid and protect the eye.

Tumors

Benign and malignant tumors occur on the eyelids. Some have a cauliflower-like appearance while others are ulcerated. Usually they occur in the older cat. Malignant tumors grow rapidly and spread to lymph nodes in the neck. Squamous cell cancers characteristically affect cats with white coats. All growths of the eyelids should be removed.

THE THIRD EYELID

Film over the Eye (Protrusion of the Nictitating Membrane)

An opaque third eyelid, normally not seen, may come out to protect an injured eye. It can vary in extent from time to time (as if blinking); or remain fixed. When the nictitating membrane is visible over the inside corner of the eye it is said to be protruding.

When one eye is involved the most likely cause is a painful eye condition such as corneal injury, foreign body in the eye, or a cloudy eye problem. Other signs of a painful eye usually are present. They include excessive tearing, squinting, and pawing at the eye.

When both eyes are involved the condition is most likely caused by a feline viral respiratory infection. However, any chronic illness or disease which causes your cat to lose weight or become dehydrated can be associated with the appearance of this film across his eyes. In such cases, veterinary examination is warranted.

Conditions which cause the eyeball to recede into the eye socket also can cause the nictitating membrane to protrude (see *Sunken Eye*).

Protrusions of the third eyelid frequently occur in cats for no apparent reason. One theory is that there is a loss of function of the sympathetic nerve fibers going to the nictitating membrane. If so, the condition tends to clear up in a few weeks. Meanwhile if your cat has trouble seeing, your veterinarian can provide you with an eyedrop solution such as 1% or 2% Pilocarpine, which reduces the severity of the protrusion.

THE TEARING MECHANISM

The Watery Eye *(Epiphora)*

There are a number of conditions in which a watery or mucus-like discharge overflows the eyelids and runs down the sides of the face, staining the hair.

First it is important to determine whether the eye is *red* (irritated). Irritative eye disorders are characterized by excessive tearing along with a red and/or painful eye. They are discussed above. However if the eye is *not* red, then a blockage in the tear drainage system is at fault.

Keep in mind that excessive tearing, and/or a sticky pus-like discharge from the eyes or nose, is frequently associated with feline respiratory infections. This possibility should be investigated before the eye alone is treated (see INFECTIOUS DISEASES). These illnesses are accompanied by a red eye.

Cats do not experience emotional tearing. They do not cry as people do, so this is not a factor to be considered as one of the causes. In all cats having a runny eye problem, the cause should be determined so that proper treatment can be given.

Inadequate Tear Drainage *(Nasolacrimal Occlusion).* This is a factor to be considered in the cat who has a persistent discharge from the eye without redness or an obvious cause. The problem here is that while his tears are secreted in normal amounts they are not adequately drained away. Overflow is due to an obstruction in the tear drainage system.

A cat may be born with this condition or acquire it later in life. When it is acquired, there is a predisposing cause. Some of them are: scarring from lacerations (e.g. cat fights); infection somewhere in the ductal system; and plugging of the ducts by thick secretions, dirt or grass seeds.

The drainage system is first tested to see if it is open by staining the tears with Fluorescein dye. If the dye appears at the nostril, the tear duct is open on that side. Nasolacrimal probes are inserted into the ductal opening and various flushing techniques used to show the point of obstruction. The flushing often opens the duct and removes the problem.

Treatment: An infection in the ductal system is treated with antibiotics. Antibiotics also are used to flush out the system. The dosage, type, and route of administration should be determined by your veterinarian.

Tear Stains in Persians. This problem is seen most often in Persians, but other cats also can be affected. The breed standard for Persians calls for large prominent eyes and a flat face. In consequence the pooling space at the inner corner of the eye might be too small—or the duct might not be in the proper location for effective drainage. Narrowing of the nasolacrimal duct is another possibility. The result is an overflow of tears with unsightly staining of the hair below the eyes.

Treatment: When no underlying disease is found, symptomatic improvement often results from giving a course of broad spectrum antibiotic (Tetracycline, Lincocin). When a chronic infection does in fact exist, the antibiotic treats it.

Tetracycline, which is secreted in the tears after oral administration, also binds that part of the tears which cause them to stain the fur. If improvement is due just to the binding action of the drug, the face remains wet but not discolored. Tetracycline is given by mouth for three weeks. If the stain returns after treatment, then long-term administration might be considered. Some owners prefer to add Tetracycline in low dose to the cat's food for long-term control. When cosmetic considerations are important, you can improve your cat's appearance by clipping the hair close to his face.

THE OUTER EYE

Pink Eye *(Conjunctivitis)*

Conjunctivitis is an inflammation of the lining membrane that covers the inner sides of the eyelids, and surface of the eyeball up to the cornea. It is one of the most common eye problems of cats.

Signs of conjunctivitis are a red eye, discharge, and pawing at the eye (itching). There is a tendency to classify any eye discharge as a conjunctivitis. Unless the discharge is accompanied by a red or inflamed eye, this could be a mistake and might lead to improper treatment.

Conjunctivitis usually is not painful. When there are signs of pain such as squinting, tenderness to touch, and protrusion of the third eyelid, you should suspect a more serious eye ailment involving the CORNEA or INNER EYE.

Types of conjunctivitis seen in cats are:

Serous Conjunctivitis. This is a mild condition in which the membrane looks pink and somewhat swollen. The discharge is clear and watery. It is usually caused by physical irritants to the eye such as wind, cold weather, dust, and various allergens. Serous conjunctivitis may be the first sign of a feline viral respiratory disease.

Purulent Conjunctivitis. It often begins as a serous conjunctivitis which becomes secondarily infected by bacteria. Thick tenacious secretions crust the lids. The eye discharge contains mucus or pus.

When purulent conjunctivitis involves both eyes your cat may be suffering from a feline viral respiratory illness. The *Chlamydia* and *Mycoplasma* are two bacteria-like microorganisms that can cause a purulent conjunctivitis. They can be detected under a microscope by taking scrapings from the conjunctival membrane. Specific antibiotics are required.

Conjunctivitis due to fungal infection is rare and requires special laboratory aid for diagnosis.

A *purulent conjunctivitis* associated with feline upper respiratory disease.

Chronic conjunctivitis — thick mucus discharge from the eyes.

Follicular Conjunctivitis. In this condition the backsides of the nictitating membrane and upper and lower eyelids enlarge to form a rough, cobblestoned surface. This gives an irritated look to the lining membrane. The eye discharge is mucoid.

This type of conjunctivitis frequently is caused by an allergy or infection. Occasionally, after the initiating factor has been removed, the follicles remain enlarged. The roughened surface of the conjunctiva then acts as a persistent irritant to the eye. It can be removed by a process in which copper sulphate crystals are used to cauterize the conjunctiva. A smooth membrane regenerates. This treatment must be undertaken by a veterinarian.

Treatment of Conjunctivitis: Mild irritative forms of conjunctivitis can be treated at home. The eye should be cleansed with a dilute solution of boric acid made up for ophthalmic use. This can be purchased over-the-counter and used as directed for people. You should expect definite improvement within 24 hours. If not, have your cat examined by a veterinarian.

Purulent conjunctivitis requires the application of antibiotics several times a day. An ointment containing a combination of neomycin, bacitracin and polymyxin works well (Neosporin Ophthalmic Ointment).

Deep-seated infections are difficult to clear up. In such cases you should suspect that the tear ducts may have been affected. Repeated cleansing of the eye, correction of any underlying problem, and specific antibiotics tailored to cultures and sensitivities, form the primary approach to this problem.

Conjunctivitis in Newborn Kittens *(Ophthalmia Neonatorium)*

The eyelids of newborn kittens do not open until they are 10 to 12 days old. Before this there is a closed space behind the lids which can become infected if bacteria or other infectious agents gain entrance to it via the blood stream, or through small scratches about the eye.

The closed eyelids bulge out. A partially opened eye may develop a dry crusty covering. Any discharge from the eye of a kitten is abnormal. Neonatal conjunctivitis usually affects several kittens in the litter.

Treatment: The eyelids must be teased open with a toothpick to allow the pus to drain out. Otherwise there may be permanent damage to the forepart of the eye. Once the eyelids have been separated, pus will drain out in large drops. The eyes should be flushed with boric acid eyewash and medicated with antibiotic drops (Neomycin, Gentamycin) four times a day. Crusted eyelids must be cleansed several times a day so they don't paste shut again. It is often necessary to treat the entire litter.

Eye Worms

Cats can be afflicted by an eyeworm transmitted by flies feeding on eye secretions. The adult worms, about 1½ inches long, can be seen in the conjunctival sac. They can be removed with blunt-nosed tweezers. If left unattended, they can damage the eye.

This disease affects cats living on the West Coast of the United States.

CLOUDY EYE

There are certain diseases which change the clarity of the eye, turning it cloudy or making it seem as if the cat has a "blind eye." This cloudiness can vary in extent from a small localized haziness to complete opacification of the eye—in which case none of the inner eye structures are visible.

Disorders that can cause a cloudy eye are *Keratitis, Glaucoma* and *Cataract.* They are discussed in the sections below.

A cloudy eye is beyond the scope of home veterinary care. It should receive immediate professional attention.

CORNEA

The cornea, or clear part of the eye, is covered by a protective layer of epithelial cells. Most destructive processes affecting the cornea begin with an injury to the epithelial layer. Any irritative process, such as a foreign body or cat scratch, can cause an epithelial injury. Cats with prominent eyes are especially susceptible to corneal injury. Once the continuity of the epithelium has been destroyed, the injury either heals spontaneously or progresses to a more serious problem. The outcome depends upon the magnitude of the injury, how quickly it is recognized, and whether or not the initiating factor has been identified and removed.

Corneal Abrasion

This is defined as an injury to the eye caused by a scratch. Corneal injuries are extremely painful. The cat squints, waters, paws at his eye; and light may hurt his eyes. Often the third eyelid comes out to protect the injured eye.

With an extensive injury the surface of the cornea immediately surrounding the injury becomes swollen, giving it a cloudy or hazy look.

The cause of a corneal abrasion often can be suspected from its location. Those in the upper part of the cornea may be caused by misdirected eyelashes on the upper lid. Lower corneal opacities suggest a foreign body imbedded in the cornea. Abrasions near the inner corner of the eye suggest a foreign body beneath the third eyelid.

Healing of a corneal abrasion usually takes place in 24 to 48 hours by a process in which the epithelium thins and slides over a small defect. Larger and deeper abrasions require more time.

A corneal abrasion will not heal if a foreign body is imbedded in the cornea or beneath one of the eyelids. Accordingly, in all but mild cases, examination for foreign bodies under the eyelids should be performed. Delay leads to persistent corneal defect (*Ulcer*); or inflammation of the cornea (*Keratitis*). Removal of foreign bodies is discussed above (*see Eyelids*).

Corneal Ulcers

Corneal ulcers are dangerous and must receive prompt attention. Most of them are caused by an injury to the cornea. Others are associated with an infection (virus, bacteria, fungus); or a nutritional deficiency. In some cases the cause is unknown.

Large ulcers may be visible to the naked eye. They appear as dull spots or dished-out depressions on the surface of the cornea. Smaller ones are best seen after the eye has been stained with Fluorescein. Early treatment is vital to avoid serious complications or even loss of the eye. Cortisones, which are incorporated into many eye preparations used for treating conjunctivitis, should not be put into an eye suspected of having a corneal injury. They delay healing and may lead to rupture of the eye.

Keratitis

Keratitis is defined as inflammation of the cornea or clear part of the front of the eye. There are many different kinds of keratitis and several causes. All result in loss of transparency of the cornea which at first appears dull, later hazy, then cloudy, and finally is covered by a whitish-blue film. In late stages there is a deposit of black pigment on the cornea which blocks out light. Keratitis always is considered serious because it may lead to partial or complete blindness in the eye. All forms of keratitis should be managed by a professional.

Superficial (surface) Keratitis. This condition is a sequel to an eye injury such as a corneal abrasion. Because the initial injury (perhaps a cat scratch) is often slight and easily overlooked, there might be a temptation to treat the tearing and discharge as conjunctivitis. Since this would be a mistake, every effort should be made to distinguish between keratitis and conjunctivitis. Keratitis is an extremely painful condition accompanied by excessive tearing, squinting and sensitivity to light. The third eyelid comes out to protect the eye. This is not usual with a simple conjunctivitis. Conjunctivitis, on the other hand, is characterized by a chronic discharge with very little pain.

Infectious Keratitis. This occurs when a corneal injury becomes complicated by an infection. A pus or mucus-like discharge runs from the eye. The lids are swollen and mattered. There are several kinds of bacteria which cause infectious keratitis. Cultures and appropriate antibiotics are indicated.

Chronic Degenerative Keratitis. This condition, which is unique to cats, occurs in the Persian, Siamese and domestic short-haired breeds. Although the exact cause is unknown, injuries and infections of the cornea have been suspected. The signs are similar to those of superficial keratitis. Characteristically, devitalized tissue forms a brown or black plaque on the surface of the cornea (sequestrum). Treatment involves removal of the sequestrum.

INNER EYE

The Blind Cat

Any condition which prevents light from getting into the eye will impair a cat's vision. Disease of the cornea (*Keratitis*) and of the lens (*Cataract*) fall into this category. Inflammations of the deep structures of the eye (*Glaucoma, Uveitis*) also lead to blindness. Finally, any disease which reduces the sensitivity of the retina to light impulses (*Retinal Atrophy*), or any other disease which affects the optic nerves or the sight center of the brain (*trauma*), can produce various forms of visual disturbance including blindness.

Most cases of blindness will not be evident on general observation of the eye itself. Ophthalmological studies are required to make an exact diagnosis.

Shining a bright light into a cat's eyes to test for pupillary constriction is not an exact method of determining whether or not he sees. The pupil may become smaller simply because of a light reflex. This won't tell you whether he has the ability to form a visual image in his brain. But there are other indications which might suggest your cat is not seeing as well as he should. For example, activities which require eye and body coordination, such as pouncing on a ball or jumping from a sofa to a chair, might be impaired. In a dimly lighted room the cat may bump into furniture. He may carry his nose close to the ground and feel with his whiskers.

Quite often an older cat's eyesight begins to fail shortly after the onset of deafness. He then relies more and more upon his memory to find his way around the house. Many totally blind cats get along surprisingly well when kept in familiar surroundings. However, one thing he should not do is run free. He must be kept indoors, or in an enclosed area, and taken out only under supervision to protect him from dangers.

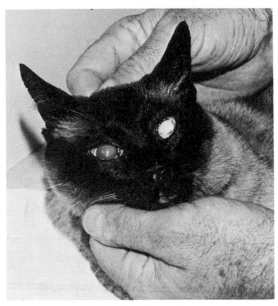

A *cataract* in the left eye.

Cataracts

A cataract is defined as any opacity on the lens which interferes with transmission of light to the retina. A spot on the lens which blocks out light, regardless of its size, technically is a cataract.

Cataracts are rare in cats. Usually they are a sequel to conjunctivitis of the newborn kitten, an old eye injury, or an eye infection. Infrequently they are inherited and associated with other eye defects.

Cataracts may develop later in life in cats who are diabetic. It is most important to recognize this possibility in any adult cat who forms a cataract.

As a cat gets older, there is a normal process of aging of his eye. New fibers, continually forming on the surface of the lens throughout life, push toward the center. The lens also loses water as it ages. These changes lead to the formation of a bluish haze seen on the lens behind the cornea in older cats. Usually this does not interfere with vision and does not need to be treated. This condition, called *nuclear sclerosis,* should be distinguished from a cataract.

A cataract is important only when it impairs vision. Blindness can be corrected by removing the lens (cataract extraction). While this restores vision, there is loss of visual acuity because the lens is not present to focus light on the retina. Accordingly, this operation is reserved for individuals with cataracts in both eyes who are having problems getting around.

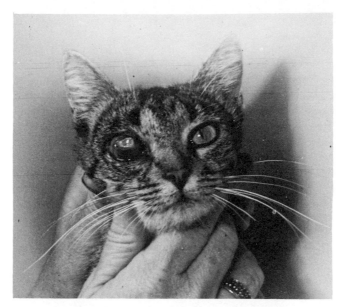

A *corneal ulcer* complicated by *glaucoma*.

Hard Eye *(Glaucoma)*

Glaucoma is due to an increase in fluid pressure within the eyeball. There is a continuous (although very slow) exchange of fluid between the eyeball and the venous circulation. Anything which upsets this delicate balance can cause a build-up of pressure and produce a hard painful eye. When eye pressure reaches a point at which it is greater than the arterial blood pressure, arterial blood cannot enter the eye to nourish the retina.

An eye suffering from *acute* glaucoma is exquisitely tender and has a fixed blank look which is due to the hazy and steamy appearance of the cornea and the *dilated* pupil. When you gently press against the eye with your index finger through the eyelid, the affected eye feels harder than the normal one. Excessive tearing and squinting is a response to pain.

Untreated *chronic* glaucoma may result in increased size of the eye and protrusion.

Glaucoma may occur as a complication of diseases of the lens or the anterior chamber. This is called *secondary* glaucoma. It is distinguished from *primary* (congenital) glaucoma which is rare but has been observed in the Persian, Siamese, and domestic short-haired breeds.

Measurement of intraocular pressure using an instrument placed on the surface of the eye, and inspection of the interior of the eye, are needed to make the diagnosis. Some permanent vision may be lost before the disease is discovered.

Chronic glaucoma may be managed for a time with drops and medications.

Soft Eye *(Uveitis)*

This disorder is caused by an inflammation of the inner pigmented structures of the eye. One of the distinguishing signs of uveitis is increased softness of the eye and a small pupil. When you push against the eye through the eyelid with your index finger, the eye is tender and feels like a soft grape. Uveitis is a painful eye condition. The cat squints, his eye waters, and there may be clouding of the eye.

Uveitis is one of the most common inner eye conditions of cats. There are three illnesses causing it. They are Feline Leukemia, Feline Infectious Peritonitis, and Toxoplasmosis. Uveitis also may be caused by a penetrating eye injury or infection.

Treatment: It is directed at correcting the underlying cause as well as treating the uveitis. This requires the care of a professional.

Retinal Diseases

The retina is a thin delicate membrane which lines the back of the eye and actually is an extension of the optic nerve. In retinal disease the eye loses its ability to interpret the light which gets to it. The visual image may be blurred; part or all of the visual field may be blacked out.

The inheritance patterns of retinal disease in cats are not well known. More will be learned in the future. At present, the following retinal diseases are recognized:

Retinitis. This condition is defined as inflammation of the retina leading to destruction of the light receptors. It can occur in association with feline Toxoplasmosis, Feline Infectious Peritonitis, Cryptococcosis and Lymphoma. It can also occur for reasons unknown.

Progressive Retinal Atrophy. This disease has been linked to a nutritional deficiency. In some cats the disease appears to have a genetic basis. In others (e.g. Persians, Siamese, domestic short-hairs) it occurs spontaneously for reasons unknown.

Progressive retinal atrophy begins with loss of night vision. At this point the cat hesitates to go out at night. He won't jump on or off furniture in a darkened room. Since the disease affects the retina in a generalized fashion, it leads in time to blindness.

Central Retinal Atrophy. This disease has been seen in all breeds and is not related to sex, coat color, or diet. Because it is the central part of the retina (where the cat sees best) that is first destroyed, the cat retains some peripheral vision but is unable to see stationary objects well. He is able to detect moving objects because motion is seen at the periphery.

Treatment of Retinal Diseases: There is no effective treatment for most retinal diseases. Nutritional deficiencies and infectious diseases known to be associated with retinal degeneration should be treated in the hope that further progression of the retinal disease can be stopped. These disorders eventually lead to blindness. However, many totally blind cats get along surprisingly well when kept in familiar surroundings.

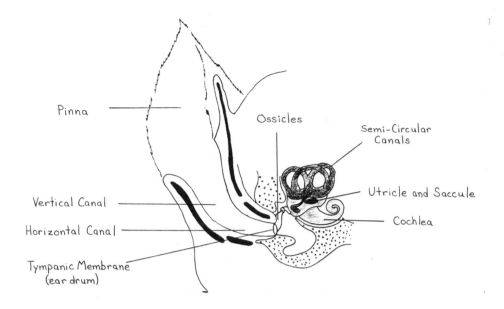

Anatomy of the Ear.—*Rose Floyd.*

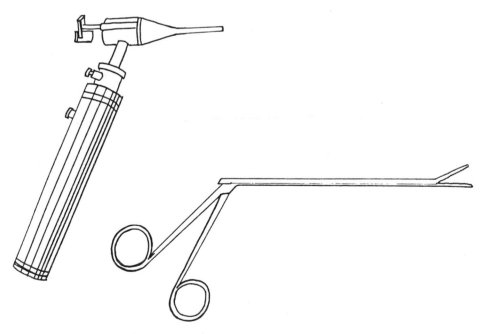

An otoscope (left) is used to examine the ear canal. Foreign bodies in the ear canal are removed with alligator forceps (right). —*Rose Floyd.*

6

Ears

SPECIAL CHARACTERISTICS

A cat's hearing is one of his best developed senses. He can hear sounds too faint for us to detect. He can also hear noises pitched at a much higher frequency—even beyond the acute range of the dog. When a cat hears a noise he turns his whole head toward the source of the sound and cocks it from side to side. His ears move forward and backward, or in a half circle, to locate the angle of direction. His eyes also focus in the same direction.

A cat also has a remarkable sense of equilibrium. This is due to a mechanism in his inner ear which allows him to adjust his body with great speed and agility. When dropped from a height in an upside-down position, he will land on his paws in less than two seconds. He does this by rotating his forequarters ahead of his hindquarters. Then, with the aid of his strong tail, he twists his body to bring all four feet down together for the landing. The fact that he can land on all four feet does not mean he can fall from a great height without sustaining an injury. If you live in an apartment above the ground floor, be sure to keep screens on your windows. Cats may jump with little or no regard to heights.

STRUCTURE OF THE EARS

The ear is divided into three parts. The OUTER EAR is composed of the ear flap (*pinna*) and ear canal (*external auditory canal*). The MIDDLE EAR is made up of the ear drum (*tympanic membrane*) and the auditory bones or *ossicles*. The INNER EAR contains the *cochlea, bony labyrinth* and *auditory nerves.*

Sound, which is really air vibrations, is collected by the ear flap and directed down the ear canal to the ear drum. Movements of the ear drum are transmitted via a chain of small bones, the ossicles, to the bony canals of the inner ear.

The cochlea is a system of fluid-filled tubes in which waves are created by movements of the ossicles. Here the waves are transformed into nerve impulses and carried via the auditory nerve to the brain.

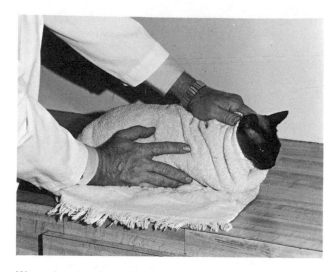

Wrapping in a towel is a good way to restrain a cat for ear treatment. —*J. Clawson.*

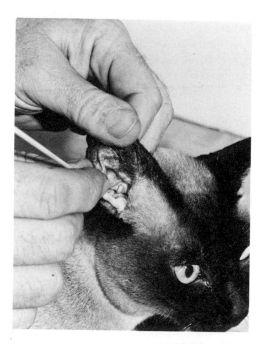

Folds and creases are cleaned with a cotton-tipped applicator moistened with mineral oil. —*J. Clawson.*

A cat's ears are carried erect. The skin on the outside is covered by hair and, like the rest of the body, is susceptible to the same diseases. The skin on the inside is light pink in color, occasionally with spots of pigment. A small amount of brown waxy secretion in the ear canals is normal.

When a kitten is born, his ear canals are closed. They begin to open at five to eight days. Kittens become oriented to sound at 13 to 16 days. They learn to recognize or distinguish between different sounds at three to four weeks. Knowing this sequence can help you to judge whether your kitten's hearing is developing at a normal rate.

The signs of a disorder of the OUTER EAR are discharge, head-shaking, ear-scratching and tenderness about the ear. Diseases causing these symptoms frequently can be treated at home.

Diseases of the MIDDLE EAR produce head-tilt and loss of hearing. When the INNER EAR is affected, you will note that your cat has a problem with his balance (he wobbles, circles, falls and rolls over, or has trouble righting himself). He may show rapid jerking eye movements (nystagmus); or he may tilt his head down on the affected side. Middle and inner ear disorders should receive prompt veterinary attention.

BASIC EAR CARE

How to Avoid Ear Problems

When you bathe your cat see that no water gets into his ears. Prevent this by inserting cotton wadding into his ear canals before bathing. Water in the ear predisposes to an ear infection.

DO NOT swab out or irrigate your cat's ears with ether, alcohol, or other irritating solvents. They are painful and cause swelling of the tissues. Use mineral or olive oil instead.

If your cat has been in a fight, check his ears for any cuts or bites which might need to be treated (see *The Ear Flap*).

Cleaning the Ears

Cleaning the ears as a routine is not necessary. Excessive cleaning may induce trauma to the delicate surface of the ear canal. Also, a certain amount of wax is necessary to maintain health of the tissues. Cats are naturally fastidious. They don't need to have their ears cleaned unless there is an excess amount of wax, dirt or debris in the ears. This usually indicates an ear infection.

To clean a dirty ear, moisten a cloth or cotton wad with mineral oil and wrap it around your little finger. Then insert your finger into the ear canal as far as it will go and gently wipe the surface to remove dirt, excess wax and debris.

Folds and creases which cannot be reached with a cloth can be cleaned with a cotton-tipped applicator moistened with mineral oil. The ear canal descends vertically for a considerable distance before turning horizontally and ending at the ear drum. The vertical canal can be swabbed without danger of damaging the ear drum as long as the applicator is held vertically and directed downwards.

Many cats object to having their ears cleaned and should be gently restrained as described in the chapter EMERGENCIES: *Handling and Restraint*. Should the cat jerk his head, the tip of the applicator might injure the delicate skin lining the sides of the narrow passage.

How to Apply Ear Medicines

Some ear preparations come in tubes with long nozzles; others with medicine droppers. Restrain your cat so that the tip of the applicator doesn't accidentally lacerate the skin of his ear canal. Fold his ear flap over the top of his head. Insert the end of the applicator as far as you can see into the ear canal. Squeeze in a small amount of ointment, or instill three to four drops of liquid.

As most infections also involve the horizontal ear canal, it is important that the medicine reaches this area too. With your fingers, squeeze the cartilage at the base of his ear to disperse the medicine, which makes a squishy sound.

Antibiotic Ear Preparations: Antibiotic preparations commonly used in the treatment of external ear infections are Panolog, Fulvidex, and Liquichlor. Others are available. They should be applied to *clean* ear canals twice daily. You should expect to see improvement in two to three days. If not, then consult your veterinarian, as further delay can cause harm.

Canex is a miticide (destructive to mites) preparation. It should be applied twice weekly for three to four weeks, or as directed by your veterinarian.

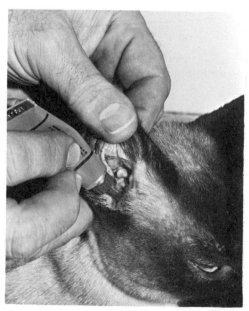

Insert the tip of the nozzle as far in as you can see and squeeze in a small amount of ointment.

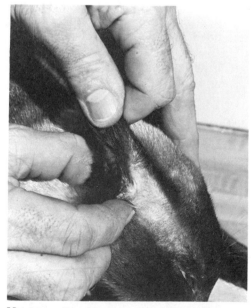

Massage the base of the ear to disperse the medication.   —J. Clawson.

OUTER EAR DISEASES

If your cat scratches at his ear and shakes his head repeatedly, if his ear has a bad odor or you notice large amounts of waxy discharge or pus draining from his ear, then you are faced with an ear problem. The most likely cause is ear mites—but other diseases do occur.

A cat with an itchy ear ailment often scratches at himself so vigorously that the skin behind his ear becomes severely traumatized. This is a form of "auto-mutilization". The abraded skin may become secondarily infected by bacteria, leading to an abscess. Attempts to treat the traumatized ear flap may not be successful until the basic cause, usually an ear canal infection caused by ear mites, is also recognized and treated (see *The Ear Canal*).

Disorders affecting the ear flap and canal are discussed below.

The Ear Flap (Pinna)

The pinna is an erect flap of cartilage covered on both sides by a layer of skin. It is very fragile and easily damaged.

Bites and Lacerations. Cats give and receive painful bites and scratches which are prone to severe infection. The ear flap is a frequent site for such injuries. Some of them occur at mating. One has only to look at an old tom to witness evidence of this.

Treatment: All cat bite wounds should be thoroughly cleaned and inspected. First trim away the hair from the edges of the wound to prevent it from sticking to the surface. Bathe the wound with half-strength hydrogen peroxide solution (one part to two parts of water) to remove dried blood and foreign debris. (*Note:* Omit this if there is fresh bleeding.) Then apply an antibiotic ointment such as Furacin or Panolog. Because claws and teeth produce deep wounds and punctures, injuries caused by cat fights are often complicated by abscesses. Some of them can be prevented by giving your cat a course of antibiotics by mouth (e.g., Penicillin).

Large lacerations, and those which involve the margin of the ear or the cartilage, should receive veterinary attention. Surgical repair will help to prevent scarring and deformity.

Swollen Ear Flap. A sudden swelling about the ear is due to an *abscess* or a *hematoma*. Abscesses are the most common. They are caused by an infection of the ear and frequently occur after a fight or some other ear injury; or after an irritative process such as scratching at the ear. Abscesses are found below the ear and hematomas involve the flap. Abscesses are discussed in the SKIN chapter.

A hematoma is a blood clot under the skin. It, too, can be caused by trauma or by violent head-shaking and scratching at the ear. Look for some underlying itchy ear disorder, such as ear mites or an infection involving the ear canal—which should be treated along with the hematoma.

Treatment: Blood should be released from a hematoma to prevent ultimate scarring and deformity of the ear. Removing it with a needle and syringe usually

An ear bandage may be required to protect an injured ear after treatment of a bite or laceration. *—J. Clawson.*

Abscess below the ear.

is not effective as serum accumulates in the space formerly occupied by the blood clot. Surgery, the treatment of choice, involves the removal of a window of skin to provide open and continuous drainage. Sutures are then taken through both sides of the ear to pull the skin down and eliminate the pocket between.

Ear Allergies. Allergies are typified by the sudden onset of itching and redness of the skin without drainage. They respond well to steroids (1% Hydrocortisone cream). Because of intense scratching the cat may traumatize his ears and set the stage for a secondary bacterial infection.

Allergies can affect the skin of the ear canals as well as the ear flap.

Frostbite. Frostbite affects the ears of cats left outdoors in severe winter weather, particularly under conditions of high wind and humidity. The ears are especially susceptible because they are openly exposed and only lightly protected by fur, particularly at the tips. The treatment of frostbite is discussed in the chapter EMERGENCIES.

Having been frozen, the ear tips of dark-coated or Siamese cats may become rounded and develop white hairs at their tips. Drooping of the ear pinna is another condition which occurs as a consequence of prolonged exposure to wind and cold.

Sunburn (Solar Dermatitis). This condition affects white cats and cats with white ears. At first the hair is lost from the tips and edges; then the underlying skin becomes reddened. Next, because of scratching at the ear, the skin becomes traumatized and eventually breaks down and forms an open sore or ulcer. The condition grows worse with each passing summer. In time a squamous cell skin cancer can develop in an ulcerated area.

Treatment: The cat should be permitted outdoors only at night. Keeping him inside only on sunny days does not answer the whole problem because the ultra-violet rays which are responsible for skin damage can penetrate clouds.

Surgery is indicated if an open sore does not heal. Usually ulcerated ear tips are rounded off. A small ulcer can be excised. Large ulcers, which are often malignant, may require removal of the entire ear-flap.

Head Mange. This disease is caused by a head mite called *Notoedres cati* which lives on the skin about the head and ears of cats. Itching is the predominant symptom. The presence of clean ear canals helps to tell this condition apart from ear mite infection caused by *Otodectes cynotis.* Treatment is discussed in the SKIN chapter.

Ringworm. This is a fungus infection which affects the ear flap as well as other parts of the body. The typical appearance is that of a dry, scaly, hairless patch of skin. Hair is broken off at the skin surface. Ringworm can be told apart from ear mite infection because ringworm does not cause itching—and in the majority of cases only one ear is involved. Treatment is discussed in the SKIN chapter.

Flea Infestation. Fleas frequently feed on the skin of the ear flap. You may be able to see the actual flea on the ears or elsewhere on the body; or you might see only black, crumbly crusts, which are dried blood. Treatment is discussed in the SKIN chapter.

Tumors. Squamous cell cancers can occur on the ears after prolonged exposure to sunlight (see *Sunburn*). Other tumors also can grow on the skin of the ears. Most of them are malignant. Any growth on the ear is a cause for concern. Have it examined by your veterinarian.

The Ear Canal

Signs of irritation or infection of the ear canals are ear discharge, head-shaking, scratching and pawing at the ear. Common causes are listed below.

Ear Mites (Otodectes cynotis). Ear mite infection is one of the most common health problems seen in cats. Ear mites are tiny parasites which live on the surface of the skin of the ear canal and feed by piercing the skin. Mites are very prolific. Most kittens are infected by their mothers while still in the nest. Suspect ear mites when *both* of your cat's ears are infected.

The most frequent sign is *intense itching* characterized by scratching and violent head-shaking. When you look into the ears you will see a typical dry, crumbly, dark brown, waxy discharge, which looks like coffee-ground material and may be foul smelling. Constant scratching at the ears may cause raw areas to develop, along with scabs and loss of hair around the ears. The initial problem might become complicated by a chronic bacterial infection of the ear canals.

Ear mites often can be identified by removing some ear wax with a cotton-tipped applicator and looking at it under a magnifying glass against a black background. Mites are white specks, about the size of the head of a pin, which move.

At times ear mites leave the ear canals and travel out over the body. They are highly contagious to cats and dogs. If there are other pets in the household, they should be treated.

Treatment: Do not begin treatment until you have identified the cause of the problem. Other ear ailments can be complicated by using an ear-mite preparation.

First clean the ears as described above (see *Cleaning the Ears*). This is an important step. If the ear stays dirty the mites remain sheltered by wax and cellular debris. This would make it difficult for the ear medication to reach and destroy them. Next medicate the ears, as described earlier in this chapter, with a miticide preparation (Canex) twice weekly for *three to four weeks*. The medication does not destroy eggs; so a new crop of mites can re-infect your cat if you stop too soon.

Finally dust your cat thoroughly with a flea powder or mite insecticide made up especially for use on cats. This kills mites on the surface of the body. Since most cats sleep with their tails curled up next to their ears, don't forget to dust the tail too.

An antibiotic is given when the ear mite problem is complicated by bacterial infection. An ear preparation such as Mitox, which combines a miticide with an antibiotic and a steroid (to reduce itching), is especially useful in this circumstance.

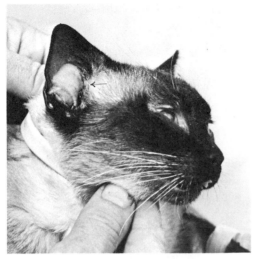

A *hematoma* is often associated with ear mites or some other itchy ear disorder.

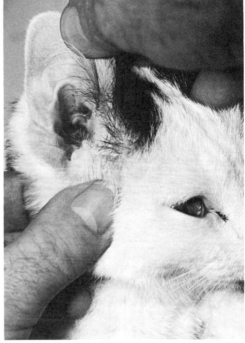

A dark brown waxy discharge is typical of *ear mites.*

Bacterial Infections (Otitis Externa). Bacterial infections frequently are the result of infected scratches and bites. Some infections begin in an ear canal that contains an excessive amount of wax, cellular debris or foreign material. Ear mite infections are often complicated by a bacterial otitis.

The most common sign of an infected ear canal is head-shaking and scratching at an itchy ear. A cat may tilt his head down on the affected side and exhibit pain when his ear is touched. An examination will reveal redness and swelling of the skin folds of the ear canal. There may be an excess amount of wax or even a discharge of pus.

An otoscope is often needed to examine the deep portions of the ear canal for foreign bodies and other unsuspected causes of chronic infection. This is best left to a qualified professional.

Bacterial infections which have been allowed to progress over a long period produce extreme reddening and thickening of the ear canal and considerable discomfort and pain. Treatment is prolonged. Inflammatory polyps and tumor-like masses can build-up and block the ear passages. Surgical intervention may be necessary to open the ear and promote drainage.

Treatment: The first step in the treatment of an external ear infection is to determine the cause. Mild cases in which the discharge is not excessive but perhaps associated with a dirty ear or the build-up of wax, may be treated at home. Clean the ears as described above (see *Cleaning the Ears*). Remove crusts and serum with a cotton-tipped applicator soaked in half-strength hydrogen peroxide solution (one part to one part water), or a surgical soap (Weldol, pHisoHex). When there is extreme wax build-up, a wax dissolving agent such as Squaline may be needed. Afterwards, dry the ear canals with a cloth or applicator and apply an antibiotic ear preparation as described earlier in this chapter. Clip the toenails to minimize injuries produced by scratching at the ear.

Fungus Infections. The presence of excess wax and moisture in the ear canal predisposes to fungus infection. It is much less common in the cat than the dog, owing to the fact that a cat's ears are erect and get plenty of air to keep them dry. It may occur when long-standing infections have been treated with antibiotics.

Signs and symptoms are not nearly so pronounced as when the infection is caused by bacteria. The ear is less inflamed and less painful. The discharge usually is dark and waxy—but not purulent. A rancid odor is characteristic.

Treatment is similar to bacterial otitis except that an antifungal agent (Nystatin) is used to medicate the ears. Panolog, which contains Nystatin, can be used. Yeast and fungus infections tend to recur. Their treatment is often prolonged.

Foreign Bodies and Ticks. Foreign bodies in the ear canal cause irritation and later infection. They are less common in the cat than the dog. Usually they are due to plant material (i.e., grass seeds, awns) which first cling to hair surrounding the ear opening and then drop down into the canal. Ears should be examined after a cat has been prowling in tall grass, weeds and brush. When a foreign body can be seen it can be removed with blunt-nosed tweezers or a cotton-tipped applicator moistened in mineral oil. Foreign bodies deep in the ear canal next to the drum should be removed with special instruments. This is a sensitive area and requires an anesthetic.

Ticks can adhere to the skin of a cat's ear. If the tick is easily accessible it can be removed. First kill the tick by applying an insecticide or a substance such as nail polish directly to it by means of a cotton-tipped applicator. In a few moments, grasp the dead tick as close to the skin as possible and apply steady traction until it releases its hold. The tick can be grasped with long fingernails or tweezers.

Ticks deep in the ear canal may require veterinary removal.

THE MIDDLE EAR

Infection *(Otitis media)*

Middle ear infections are not common. At times an outer ear infection can extend to the middle ear; or bacteria can gain entrance to the middle ear through a perforated ear drum. Another pathway by which the middle ear can become infected is via the Eustachian tube, a passage which connects the middle ear to the back of the throat. Tonsillitis or some other nasopharyngeal infection can ascend to the middle ear through the Eustachian tube.

Initially the signs of a middle ear infection may be masked by the ear canal infection which precedes it.

As infection advances to involve the middle ear, pain increases. The cat crouches low and tilts his head down on the affected side. To minimize pain, he holds it as still as possible. His gait is unsteady.

An otoscopic examination may show perforation or loss of the ear drum. X-rays may show bone involvement. The face might droop on the affected side if the nerve which crosses the surface of the ear drum is injured.

Middle ear infections can extend to involve the inner ear. All infections of the middle and inner ear should be treated by a veterinarian.

INNER EAR

Infection *(Otitis interna)*

An inner ear infection usually is preceded by a middle ear infection. Extension to the inner ear should be suspected if the cat vomits, staggers or falls toward the affected side, circles toward that side, or shows rhythmic jerking movements of his eyeballs (rapid eye movements). These are signs of *labyrinthitis.*

Infections of the inner ear should be managed by a professional.

There are other disorders which produce signs similar to those of an inner ear infection. They include brain tumor, drug intoxication, poisoning, and a condition called *Idiopathic Vestibular Syndrome* of cats (see *Vestibular Disorders* in NERVOUS SYSTEM). The Idiopathic Syndrome is the most common. It often corrects itself spontaneously.

You should suspect that one of these disorders might be at fault when a cat shows signs of labyrinthitis without having had a prior infection of his outer or middle ear.

Deafness

Some cats are born without the ability to hear owing to developmental defects in their hearing apparatus. In most cases this occurs in white cats with blue eyes. In addition, loss of hearing can be caused by senile changes (old age), middle ear infections, head injury, blockage of the ear canals by wax and debris, and by certain drugs and poisons. In particular, the antibiotics Streptomycin,

Congenital deafness **often occurs in white cats with blue eyes.**

Neomycin and Kanamycin, if used for long periods, can cause damage to the auditory nerves, leading to deafness and signs of labyrinthitis.

It is sometimes quite difficult to tell if a cat is going deaf. His ability to hear must be judged by his actions and how he uses his ears. The cat who hears well cocks his head and looks in the direction of a noise. He moves his ears back and forth to pin-point the sound. Therefore lack of attentiveness is one of the first indications you may have that your cat is not hearing as well as he should. One way to test this is to speak loudly to him when he's asleep. The cat who doesn't wake up is probably deaf.

Gradual loss of hearing can occur in cats after ten years of age—but not as often as in dogs. Senile deaf cats often retain some hearing for high-pitched sounds such as a dog whistle. Stamping on the floor also attracts their attention as they can feel the vibrations.

Older deaf cats usually get along quite well because they are able to use their other senses (those of sight, smell, and the tactile sensations transmitted through their whiskers) to compensate for their hearing loss.

Congenitally deaf cats should not be used for breeding.

7

Nose

GENERAL INFORMATION

A cat's nose is made up of his nostrils (nares) and the nasal cavity, which runs the length of the muzzle. The cat has large frontal sinuses which communicate with the nasal passages. The nasal cavity is divided by a midline partition into two passages, one for each nostril. These passages open into the throat behind the soft palate.

The nasal cavity is lined by a mucous membrane richly supplied with blood vessels and nerves. On the surface of this membrane is a layer of mucus which is moved by cilia towards the throat and the nose (the *muco-ciliary* blanket). This blanket traps bacteria and foreign irritants, acting as a first line of defense against infection. Exposure to prolonged cold, or to dehydration, stops the motion of the cilia and thickens the layer of mucus. This reduces the effectiveness of the muco-ciliary blanket.

The nasal cavity is extremely sensitive to trauma and bleeds easily when irritated. Instruments or packs should never be poked into the noses of cats. Because of their small size and sensitivity, the nasal passages usually have to be examined under sedation or anesthesia. An otoscope and special forceps are used to remove foreign bodies.

Other functions of the nose are to warm, humidify, and clean the inhaled air, and to enable the cat to detect and react to odors. Although both the cat and the dog have an extremely keen sense of smell, only the dog uses it for tracking. In the cat the sense of smell is used primarily for self-orientation (which includes recognition of threatening odors), and for appetite stimulation. This last is so important that nasal obstruction is almost always accompanied by complete loss of appetite.

Cats also rely upon their sense of smell to identify one another. This is why cats greet each other by first smelling each other's faces, and then their anal areas.

The cat also has an additional odor sensing mechanism man does not have. It is composed of two small air passages, called the *nasopalatine ducts,* located in the roof of the mouth just behind the incisors. These ducts permit air in the

151

mouth to pass up into the nose. When using this accessory scent mechanism, the cat raises his upper lip as if baring his teeth, wrinkles his nose, partially opens his mouth, and then draws air up into his nose through these ducts. This behavior, which is called "flehman", can be seen in kittens as early as two months of age. It is most common in adult toms.

Certain odors are uniquely attractive to cats. Catnip, frequently incorporated into toy mice and other cat playthings, is the one most people have heard about. It is a variety of mint that acts as a nerve stimulant and seems to cast a spell over the cat. He will approach it, sniff at it, then usually lick or chew it. Afterwards he seems dazed, rolls on the floor, or rubs against furniture. The immediate effect last but a few minutes, but repeated exposure can result in long term side effects including confusion and loss of awareness. Catnip sensitivity is hereditary. It affects about two out of three domestic cats.

Cats also are attracted to the odors of garlic and onion. These flavorings are frequently added to pet foods, to enhance their appeal. On the other hand, the smell of mothballs and orange peels is repugnant to cats, a fact which can be used to keep them away from certain spots.

The color of a cat's nose can vary from light pink (or salmon-colored) to blue, brown, black or even freckled. Some breed standards call for a nose of a certain color (e.g., blue for a "Blue Point" Siamese; black for a "Seal Point's"). In showing, points may be subtracted for a mottled or off-colored nose.

A cat with a normally pink nose might develop a white nose after being out in cold weather, or when excited. These changes are temporary. However, a nose which is white for no obvious reason could indicate an anemia.

A warm dry nose could mean that a cat is dehydrated or has a fever. This is not always the case. Occasionally the reverse is true; a sick cat has a runny nose which is cool because of evaporation.

A cat's whiskers are sensitive tactile organs which transmit complex information about its prey and surroundings to nerve bundles beneath the skin. A cat knows that if his whiskers can pass through a small opening, then his body can pass through too. For these reasons, a cat's whiskers should never be clipped or trimmed.

SIGNS OF NASAL IRRITATION

A cat with nasal irritation could be suffering from a generalized illness in which nasal discharge is but one symptom; or he could have a problem localized to the nose itself.

A discharge through both nostrils accompanied by fever, loss of appetitie, eye discharge, drooling, cough, or sores in the mouth, suggests a feline viral upper respiratory infection. It is important to recognize the early signs of viral respiratory illness as professional attention may be required (see INFECTIOUS DISEASES). In addition, infected cats should be isolated to prevent them from spreading the disease to other cats in the household.

When just one nostril is involved, your cat may have a foreign body in his nose, an injury to the nose, a nasal polyp or tumor. By holding the back of your hand in front of his nose, you can tell if air is coming from both sides. Alternately, cover one nostril and note his ease of breathing through the other. When unilateral nasal symptoms come on suddenly, think of a foreign body or an injury to the nose. Polyps and tumors present symptoms which come on gradually.

Signs of nasal irritation are discussed below.

Runny Nose (Nasal Discharge)

A discharge from the nose which persists for several hours indicates a nasal irritation. Possible causes include infections, foreign bodies, allergies and tumors.

Often you can tell whether a discharge is serious by observing its appearance. A *watery* discharge with sneezing might be due to local irritation or allergic rhinitis. A *mucoid* discharge is characteristic of feline viral respiratory infections. A thick yellow *mucopurulent* (containing both mucus and pus) or *purulent* (containing pus) discharge indicates that the muco-ciliary blanket has been penetrated by bacteria. This suggests the need for antibiotics.

Tumors and fungal infections cause erosion of the nasal membrane. The discharge is purulent but also contains blood. Veterinary examination is indicated.

A cat with an eye discharge often has a nasal discharge. This is because the nasolacrimal ducts drain into the nose.

Colds. Cats don't catch colds as people do. Human cold virus does not affect the cat. However, cats are afflicted by a number of viruses which produce symptoms much like those of the human cold. The important point is that these illnesses vary in severity. Some are mild. Others are quite serious or even life-threatening. Should your cat develop a runny nose along with a discharge from his eyes—and if he coughs, sneezes, and runs a slight fever—he may have an infection produced by one of the feline respiratory viruses. Consult your veterinarian.

Noisy Breathing

A cat who has trouble breathing may be suffering from nasal congestion; or he may have a blockage somewhere in the back of his throat, voice box or lower airway. The exact location is important. Airway obstructions below the nasal passages become emergencies (see RESPIRATORY SYSTEM).

When *both* nasal passages are blocked by swollen membranes the cat will sniffle and sneeze. This is *noisy breathing*. It may be accompanied by *mouth breathing*. But since cats avoid breathing through their mouths whenever possible, mouth breathing may be seen only after exercise, or at times when the demand for air is increased.

With a blockage in the back of the *throat,* noisy breathing is accompanied by snoring and swallowing. Cough, when present, is high-pitched and throat-clearing in nature.

Blockages in the *voice box* produce wheezing which is heard both on inspiration and expiration.

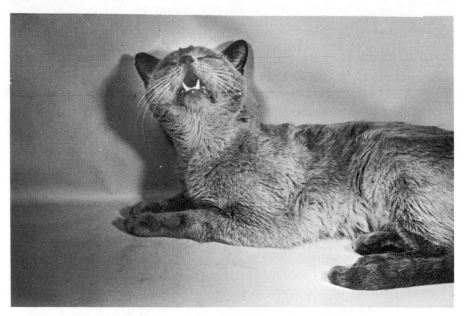

Sneezing **is one of the chief signs of nasal infection.**

Sneezing

This is one of the chief signs of nasal irritation in cats. Sneezing is a reflex which results from stimulation of the lining of the nose. When the cat sneezes off and on for a few hours, but shows no other signs of illness, his symptoms may be due to a minor nasal irritation or allergy. Sneezing which persists all day long may be the first sign of a viral upper respiratory illness.

A foreign body in the nasal cavity produces bouts of *violent* sneezing along with head-shaking and pawing at the nose. The foreign body may be sneezed out, yet the irritation caused by it could continue to cause sneezing.

Bacterial infections in the nasal passages and frontal sinuses also produce bouts of sneezing and sniffling, usually accompanied by a nasal discharge. These diseases tend to become chronic.

Reverse Sneezing

This uncommon condition is a cause of alarm because it sounds as though the cat has something caught in his air passages. It is believed to be due to a temporary spasm of the throat muscles. An accumulation of mucus or an irritation at the back of the throat may be the initiating factor.

During an attack the cat violently pulls air in through his nose, producing a loud snorting noise as if something were caught in his nose and he was trying to draw it in. He is perfectly normal before and after these attacks.

Rarely, reverse sneezing indicates a foreign body trapped at the back of the nasal cavity (see *Foreign Bodies in the Nose*).

THE NASAL CAVITY

Trauma and Nose-bleeds *(Epistaxis)*

Nose-bleeds do not occur spontaneously in cats as they do in children. The majority are associated with a blow to the face which damages the nose. Others are due to erosion of the nasal membrane by a foreign body, infection, tumor or parasite.

Rarely a nose-bleed may be one manifestation of a generalized clotting disorder, such as that produced by liver disease or Warfarin poisoning. In such cases veterinary examination is warranted.

A cat who receives a blow to the nose sufficient to cause bleeding may have sustained a midline fracture of the roof of his mouth. Suspect this if he opens his mouth to breathe (which suggests that his nasal passages are obstructed). The fracture can cause malposition of his teeth, in which case it should be adjusted and his teeth should be wired together to maintain the position of the upper jaw until healing is complete.

Treatment: Nose-bleeds frequently are accompanied by spasmotic sneezing which aggravates the bleeding. Keep the cat quiet. Confine or sedate him if possible. Apply ice cubes or packs to the bridge of his nose to reduce blood flow and aid in clotting. Do not poke about in his nostrils with nasal packs or instruments as this only induces sneezing and will be resisted. Minimal bleeding usually subsides rather quickly of its own accord, especially when interference is kept to a minimum. Profuse bleeding may cause the cat to choke. This becomes an emergency. Veterinary attention is required.

Foreign Bodies in the Nose

They include pieces of straw, grass seeds and awns, fish bones, string, and wood splinters. Occasionally an insect becomes wedged between the nasal turbinates.

The most striking sign is the sudden appearance of *violent* sneezing—at first continuous and later intermittent—along with pawing at the nose. Reverse sneezing, and repeated attempts to clear the throat, suggest a foreign object trapped at the back of the nasal cavity.

A cat with a foreign body in his nose may tilt his head to the affected side and also squint his eye on that side. Or he may drop his nose to the floor, extend his neck, and make deep inspiratory efforts.

Foreign objects which have been allowed to remain for a day or longer are associated with secondary bacterial infection (see *Nasal Infections*).

Treatment: A foreign body may be visible close to the opening of the nostril, in which case it can be removed with tweezers. More often it is lodged farther back. If you look down the throat you may see a piece of string or grass bent over the soft palate and projecting into the pharynx. If the foreign object is not visible it will be necessary to give the cat an anesthetic to locate and remove it. Do not poke about in your cat's nose. His membranes are easily damaged.

After removing a foreign body, an antibiotic should be given to prevent infection (Chloromycetin, Tetracycline).

Allergic Rhinitis (Nasal Allergies)

This condition is characterized by periodic bouts of sneezing which last a short time. Sometimes they are accompanied by a clear watery discharge from the nose. They tend to occur on a day to day basis. In most cases they are caused by contact with an environmental irritant or allergen (see *Allergy*). This type of rhinitis responds well to medications containing a steroid and antihistamine.

Nasal Infections

Nasal infections can be recognized by the symptoms they produce—notably sneezing, nasal discharge, noisy breathing and mouth breathing. When nasal congestion interferes with the ability to smell, the cat loses his appetite and refuses to eat.

The most common cause of nasal infection in the cat is a feline viral respiratory illness. Suspect this when both nostrils are involved and when other cats in the household exhibit the same symptoms. The nasal discharge is at first watery but soon becomes mucoid, yellow and thick. Viral respiratory infections also are accompanied by fever, tearing, redness and discharge from the eyes; ulcerations of the tongue; cough and lethargy. These illnesses are discussed in greater detail in the chapter INFECTIOUS DISEASES.

Bacterial infections become established when the lining of the nose has been injured by a foreign body or a blow to the nose; or by a prior viral upper respiratory disease. On occasion infection spreads to the nasal cavity from the frontal sinus (see *Sinusitis*).

The most common sign of bacterial involvement of the nose is a nasal discharge which is mucoid, creamy yellow or purulent. A bloody discharge indicates ulceration of the lining membrane.

Treatment: The objectives are to restore normal breathing, prevent or treat infection, and make the cat as comfortable as possible. Gently wipe his nostrils to remove dried crusts and secretions, using a moist cotton ball or linen cloth. Rub in baby oil or Vaseline to keep the nostrils from cracking and drying out. Vaporizers loosen exudates and help to restore the integrity of the muco-ciliary blanket. Encourage eating by feeding aromatic foods such as canned fish.

Shrink swollen nasal membranes by administering Afrin Pediatric Nose Drops (0.25%), or Neo-Synephrine Pediatric Strength Nose Drops (0.25%), three times daily.

A purulent discharge signifies a bacterial infection and indicates the need for an antibiotic (Tetracycline, Ampicillin). When the discharge persists in spite of treatment it should be cultured. An appropriate antibiotic can be selected on the basis of sensitivity testing. In long-standing cases suspect a fungus.

To prevent subsequent infection, it is advisable to treat all nasal cavity injuries (such as those caused by a foreign body) with an antibiotic.

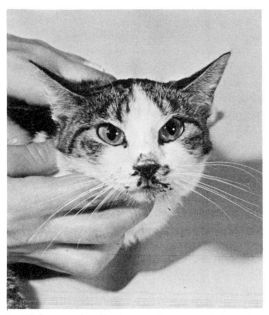

A thick, crusty discharge from both nostrils indicates nasal infection.

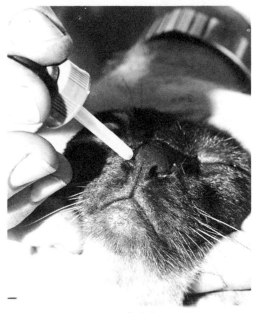

Nose drops help to shrink swollen membranes. This eases breathing and restores appetite.

Sinusitis

The cat has two frontal and sphenoid sinuses. The major sinuses are the frontals. The small sphenoid sinuses are of little importance.

Since respiratory infections are quite common in the cat, secondary infections of the frontal sinuses occur with some frequency. The signs of a chronic bacterial infection are a persistent purulent nasal discharge—often just on one side—accompanied by frequent sneezing and sniffling. X-rays may show increased density of one sinus. The cat may appear to have a headache and sit with his eyes partially closed and his head hanging. Diminished appetite might lead to rapid weight loss.

An abscessed tooth (usually the root of the top premolar) can lead to an abscessed frontal sinus. This produces a painful rising below the eye. It is not common in the cat.

Yeast infection (Cryptococcus) can be an uncommon cause of sinus infection in the cat. The discharge is mucoid. If the infection erodes into the frontal bone, the bone becomes soft and bulging.

Treatment: Sinusitis can be suspected from the clinical signs. Usually it is confirmed by X-rays. Trial with an appropriate antibiotic is indicated. Sometimes this is not successful. Then a surgical procedure, which involves making an opening into the sinus through the skin to facilitate drainage, may be undertaken.

Nasal Polyps and Tumors

Benign and malignant tumors are found in the nasal cavity and sinuses, usually on just one side. Early signs are sneezing and sniffling. They are followed by obstructed breathing. Bleeding can occur through the affected nostril.

A polyp is a growth which begins as an enlargement of one of the mucous glands. It is not a cancer. It looks like a cherry on a stalk. Polyps can cause symptoms by bleeding and by blocking the flow of air through the nostril. Polyps and small tumors should be removed by your veterinarian.

Large tumors can make one side of the face protrude more than the other. When they extend behind the eye, the eye will bulge. These tumors are far advanced. Treatment is generally not possible.

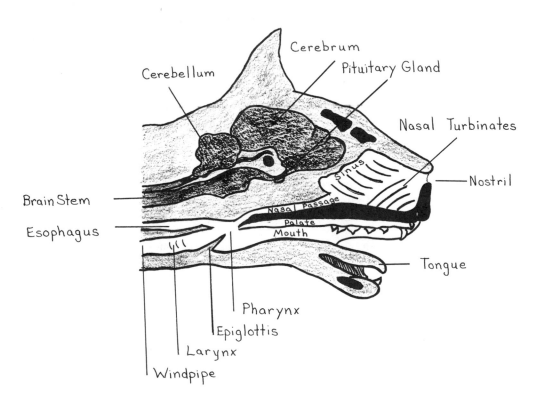

Anatomy of the Head.—*Sydney Wiley.*

8

Mouth and Throat (Oropharynx)

GENERAL INFORMATION

The oral cavity or mouth of cats is subdivided into the *vestibule,* the space between the lips and the teeth, and the *oral cavity* itself, which is contained within the dental arches. The mouth is bounded on the front and sides by the lips and cheeks, above by the soft and hard palate; and below by the tongue and muscles of the floor of the mouth. Four pairs of salivary glands drain into the mouth.

The *pharynx,* or throat, is a space formed by the joining of the nasal passages with the back of the mouth. Food is kept from going down the wrong way by the epiglottis, a flap-like valve which closes off the larynx and windpipe when the cat swallows.

The average adult cat has thirty teeth. This is two less than man and twelve less than the average dog.

A cat's teeth are designed for grasping, cutting, tearing and shredding. As a cat grasps a piece of meat with his front claws, he bites down on it with his four canine teeth, scissors the meat between his back teeth, and tears off a mouthful which he swallows without chewing. His back teeth, like those in the front, are pointed and sharp. They are not designed to grind up food.

The peculiar structure of the surface of the cat's tongue, with its sharp inwardly directed spikes, makes it an ideal comb for self-grooming. However, one disadvantage is that hair clings to the tongue. The only way the cat can get rid of it is to swallow it. This is one of the chief reasons why hairballs are such a big problem in cats.

The saliva of cats is alkaline. It contains antibacterial enzymes which help to prevent infections. While a dog licks his wounds repeatedly to keep them clean, a cat is much less likely to do so because the rough surface of his tongue hurts the wound. This might account in part for the fact that cat wounds are quite likely to become infected.

Cats have sensitive whiskers on their lips, cheeks, and above their eyes. These tactile organs help them to detect and avoid objects in the dark.

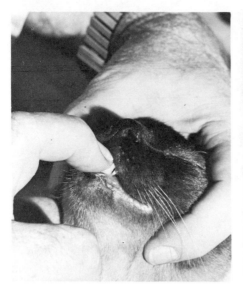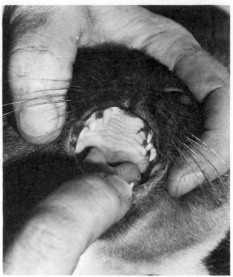

To open your cat's mouth, steady the top of his head with one hand. Press down on his jaw with the index finger of your other hand as he begins to open his mouth.
—*J. Clawson.*

How to Examine the Mouth

Most mouth disorders will be evident by a careful examination of the lips, teeth, palate, throat, and soft tissues of the chin and neck.

Small movable nodules beneath the chin, at the angle of the jaw bone and below the ear, are lymph nodes. When swollen and tender, they indicate a mouth or throat infection.

To examine your cat's bite, close his mouth and raise his upper lip while drawing down on his lower one with your thumb. The bite is determined by seeing how the upper and lower incisors meet (see *Incorrect Bite*). This also allows you to examine his gums and teeth. Many cats have pigmented or black-spotted gums. Healthy gums are firm. In non-pigmented areas the color is pink. Pale gums are a sign of ill-health (parasites, chronic blood loss, anemia). Bluish-gray gums indicate shock or dehydration.

To open a cat's mouth, place the palm of one hand over the top of his head and press inward against his upper lip with your finger and thumb. As he begins to open his mouth, press down on his lower jaw with the index finger of your other hand. To see the tonsillar area and the back of the throat, push down on the back of his tongue with your finger.

Many cats are reluctant to have their mouths examined. In such cases they should be restrained (see *Handling and Restraint*). Struggling with them can lead to a painful scratch or bite.

Signs of Mouth Disease

One of the first signs of mouth disease is *failure to eat*. This is caused by pain in the mouth rather than loss of appetite. The cat often will sit beside his food dish and give every indication of wanting to eat. He might even take food into his mouth but quickly drop it. When you attempt to examine his mouth, he usually draws back and struggles to get away.

Since a cat uses his mouth for self-grooming, something else you might notice rather quickly about a cat with a sore mouth is his *unkempt appearance*. The hair on his chin and chest may be dirty and wet from constant drooling. A sore mouth is one of the main causes for drooling; however, other causes also should be considered (see *Drooling*).

A further indication of mouth disease is *bad breath*. When accompanied by drooling, the most likely causes are *Stomatitis* and *Gingivitis*. Excess tartar on the teeth is another leading cause of bad breath (see *Tooth Decay*). Garlic and onion are added to some pet foods to enhance their appeal. Of course, this too can cause a characteristic odor to the breath. But a persistent disagreeable odor from the mouth is not normal. Its cause should be determined so that proper treatment can be given.

Gagging, choking, drooling and difficulty in swallowing suggest a foreign object in the mouth, tongue or throat.

Difficulty opening the mouth (or swallowing) accompanies head and neck abscesses and injuries to the jaws. Rabies should be considered if the mouth sags open and the cat drools or foams at the mouth.

Diseases of the mouth and throat are discussed below.

LIPS

Inflammation of the Lips *(Cheilitis)*

Cheilitis is recognized by serum crusts which form at the junction of the haired parts with the smooth parts of the lips. As the crusts peel off, the area beneath looks raw and denuded. It is sensitive to touch. Inflamed lips are often caused by an infection within the mouth which extends to involve the lips. Other causes are contact with weeds and brush which irritate the lips, giving them a chapped look.

Treatment: Clean the lips with a surgical soap (pHisoHex, Weldol) and apply an antibiotic-steroid cream (Panolog) twice daily. When the infection subsides, apply Vaseline to keep the lips soft and pliable until healing is complete.

Rodent Ulcer (Lip Granuloma)

This unsightly condition is found in cats nine months to nine years of age. It is unique to the cat. Typically it begins as a yellow or pink shiny spot on either side of the center of the upper lip, where the tongue makes contact as the cat licks his nose. Less commonly, it occurs at the back of the jaw behind the last upper molar.

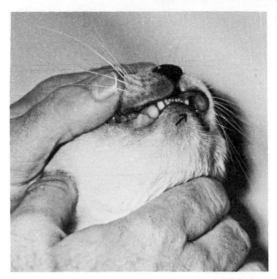

A *rodent ulcer* typically begins near the center of the upper lip.

Lip granulomas seem to cause little pain or discomfort; but granulomas in the mouth may cause symptoms like those of *Gingivitis.* As a rodent ulcer advances, the cat's lip may be partly destroyed by a large ulcerated swelling that exposes his teeth and gums.

The exact cause of rodent ulcer is unknown. It has been found in cats exposed to the leukemia virus, suggesting that impaired immunity may play a role in its onset. However, not all cats with a rodent ulcer have a positive blood test for the leukemia virus, nor does a rodent ulcer necessarily mean that a cat has leukemia.

A similar process involving ulceration and granulation occurs in other parts of the body. In all such cases it is associated with excessive licking (see SKIN: *Lick Granulomas*).

Treatment: Cortisone injected directly into the ulcer, followed by oral cortisone two times a day for two to four weeks, is the most effective treatment. Recently the use of progesterone (Ovaban) has been advocated. The pill is given every other day until the ulcer begins to disappear. Thereafter it is given once a week.

Direct application of a steroid cream to the lip ulcer, as described in the treatment of cheilitis, may be of aid. The medication should be applied frequently as the cat will lick it off.

Rodent ulcers tend to recur, especially when treatment is stopped too soon. As with any long-standing skin condition, a squamous cell skin cancer can develop at the site of ulceration.

Lacerations of the Lips, Mouth and Tongue

The soft tissues of the mouth are common sites for cuts. Most are caused by animal bites. Some are due to picking up or licking sharp objects, such as the top of a food can. An unusual cause of tongue trauma is freezing to metal in extremely cold weather. When pulled free, the surface of the tongue strips off, leaving a raw bleeding patch.

Treatment: Bleeding can be controlled by applying pressure to the cut for five minutes. Use a clean gauze dressing or a piece of linen. A cat with a painful mouth usually must be restrained before he can be successfully handled (see *Handling and Restraint*).

Cuts on the upper lip are covered with a gauze which is held in position between the fingers. On the lower lip, bleeding is controlled by pressing the gauze directly against the wound. Bleeding from the tongue requires opening the mouth as described above. You may need to pull the tongue forward to see the bleeding site.

Minor cuts which have stopped bleeding do not need to be sutured. Stitching should be considered when the edges of the cut gape open; when lip lacerations involve the borders of the mouth; and when bleeding recurs after the pressure dressing is removed.

Puncture wounds are prone to infection. Proper early treatment of these wounds as described in the chapter EMERGENCIES is important.

During healing of the wound, cleanse the cat's mouth twice daily with a mild mouth wash such as Scope. Feed him a bland diet and avoid kibble, milk bones, and other foods which require chewing.

Burns of the Lips, Mouth and Tongue

Electrical Burns. These burns usually are caused by chewing on an electric cord. They can be quite painful but most heal spontaneously. In some cases a gray-appearing membrane appears on the surface of the burn and an ulcer develops. Surgical removal of the dead tissue back to healthy tissue will be necessary.

An electric burn may be associated with a shock to the cat's body. If he has difficulty breathing or is found unconscious, see treatment of *Electric Shocks* in the chapter EMERGENCIES.

Chemical Burns. They are caused by a variety of substances including lye, phenol, phosphorus, household cleaners, alkalis, and other corrosive agents. Should the substance be swallowed, there is a possibility the throat will be burned—leading to a more serious problem (see *Esophagus: Stricture*).

Treatment: Immediately flush the poison from his mouth using copious amounts of water while sponging and rinsing. If the poison is an alkali, sponge his mouth with vinegar or fruit juice. If an acid, use baking soda in water.

The aftercare for burns of the mouth is the same as for lacerations.

GUMS

Sore Gums *(Gingivitis)*

Gum infection, the first sign of impending tooth decay, should not be ignored. The signs of gum disease are loss of appetite, ungroomed appearance, difficulty chewing, sometimes drooling, and an unpleasant odor to the breath.

Healthy gums are firm and their edges are closely applied to the teeth. If a cat has gingivitis you will notice that his gums appear red, swollen, and may bleed when rubbed. Next the edges of his gums begin to recede from the sides of his teeth. This allows little pockets or crevices to develop. They trap food and bacteria and cause infection at the gum line (see *Tooth Decay*). When you press on the sides of the gums, pus may come from below.

The only form of gingivitis not related to tooth decay is the eosinophilic granuloma which occurs on the gums behind the last molars (see *Rodent Ulcer*).

Treatment: Brush your cat's teeth and gums once a day using a 3% hydrogen peroxide solution. Then massage his gums with your fingers or a piece of linen, using a gentle circular motion, while pressing on the outside surface of the gums. Continue the program until his gums are healthy-looking.

Dental deposits and diseased teeth should be treated as described in the section *Teeth*. Treatment of all associated conditions is a necessary part of restoring a healthy mouth.

Growths on the Gums

Tumors of the gum are rare. They tend to occur in elderly cats. Most of them are malignant, the most common being a squamous cell cancer. Cancers often spread to other structures in the mouth. Therefore treatment is difficult.

A benign tumor of the gum, called an *epulis,* can be seen in older cats. It is a form of localized gum enlargement in which a mass of tissue develops on a flaplike base. It can interfere with locking of the teeth when the cat closes his mouth. It should be removed.

TEETH

Dental problems in domestic cats are due in part to their diets. Some cats who live predominantly on soft canned foods are prone to excess tartar formation, with subsequent periodontal disease and tooth loss.

Teeth can be chipped, broken, and lost—usually after a fight with another animal.

A cat's teeth should be inspected at regular intervals. A program of good oral hygiene will prevent many dental problems which could otherwise lead to a poor state of health and nutrition.

Baby Teeth

The average kitten has 26 deciduous (baby) teeth. They are the incisors, canines and premolars. Kittens do not have molars.

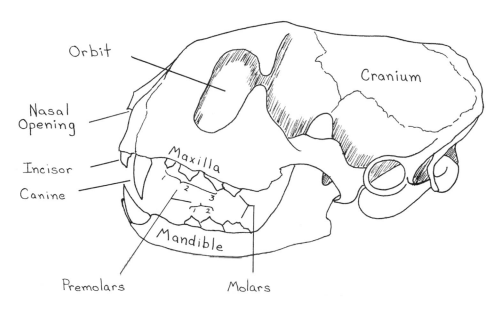

TEETH — Side View.—*Rose Floyd.*

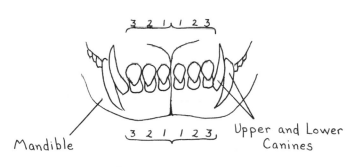

Upper Incisors

Lower Incisors

TEETH — Front View.—*Rose Floyd.*

With rare exceptions, kittens are born without teeth. The incisors are the first deciduous teeth to appear, usually at three to four weeks. They are followed by the canines and premolars. The last premolar arrives at about six weeks of age. This sequence can be used to determine the approximate age of young kittens.

Teething in Kittens

The baby teeth are replaced in a gradual fashion by the permanent teeth. At three to four months of age the incisors erupt, followed in turn by the molars, canines and premolars. By seven months the cat's adult teeth are fully developed. Knowing this sequence can give you an idea of the approximate age of the older kitten.

During teething, which lasts two to three months, a kitten may exhibit some soreness of his mouth. He may be off his feed from time to time, but usually not enough to affect his growth and development.

Aging a Cat by his Teeth

The method of aging an adult by the amount of wear on the cusps of his teeth is relatively reliable for the dog and some other domestic animals, but not so for the cat whose teeth are not used for grinding. The general condition of the teeth and gums may allow a guess as to the approximate age of the cat, but accurate determinations are possible only for very young cats. They are based upon the time of eruption of the deciduous and permanent teeth as described above.

The dental formulae for the cat are:

Deciduous (Baby) *Teeth:* $2 \, (I \frac{3}{3} \ C \frac{1}{1} \ P \frac{3}{2}) = 26$

Permanent (Adult) *Teeth:* $2 \, (I \frac{3}{3} \ C \frac{1}{1} \ P \frac{3}{2} \ M \frac{1}{1}) = 30$

For example, there are 3 upper and 3 lower incisors; the first number (2) indicates that this is true for both the right and left sides of the mouth.

Retained Baby Teeth

In the normal situation, roots of baby teeth are re-absorbed as adult teeth grow in to take their place. When this fails to happen you will see what appears to be a double set of teeth. The permanent teeth are then pushed out of line. This leads to malocclusion or a bad bite.

Kittens at two to three months should be watched carefully to see that their adult teeth are coming in normally. Whenever a baby tooth stays in place while an adult tooth is coming in, the baby tooth should be pulled.

Abnormal Number of Teeth

It is not uncommon to see adult cats with fewer teeth than normal. Some cats are born with missing tooth buds. This hereditary defect can influence a cat's chances in the show ring, but it has little or no effect on his health.

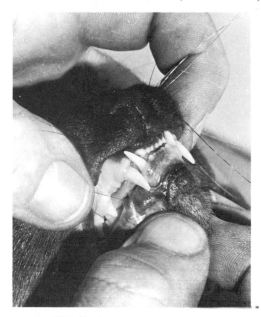

To examine your cat's bite, raise his upper lip while drawing down on his lower one with your thumb. This is a correct or *even* bite—the incisors meeting edge to edge.
—*J. Clawson.*

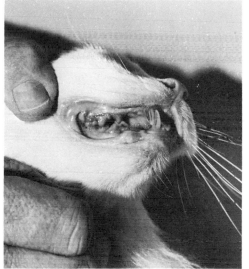

Dental tartar predisposes to gum disease and tooth decay.

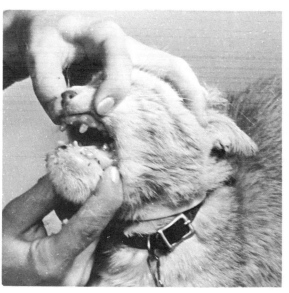

Advanced *periodontal disease* and *gingivitis*. Note also swelling of the lower jaw due to bone infection (osteomyelitis).

Rarely you may find that your kitten has more than the average number of teeth. This can cause his teeth to twist or overlap. One or more of the extra teeth will need to be extracted to make room for the rest.

Incorrect Bite

A cat's bite is determined by how his upper and lower incisor teeth meet when his mouth is closed. In the *even* or *level* bite, the incisors meet edge to edge. In the *scissors* bite, the upper incisors just overlap but still touch the lower incisors. Bites other than these may be associated with malocclusion.

An *overshot* bite is one in which the upper jaw is longer than the lower jaw, so that the teeth overlap without touching. The *undershot* bite is the reverse of the above with the lower jaw projecting beyond the upper (like the Bulldog's). The *wry* mouth is the worst of the malocclusion problems. In this situation one side of the jaw grows faster than the other, twisting the mouth so as to give it a wry look. Incorrect bites interfere with the ability to grasp and chew food; while malpositioned teeth may cause injuries to the soft parts of the mouth.

Incorrect bites are much less common in cats than dogs because the shape of the cat's head is quite similar despite other breed differences. Bite problems are caused by genes which control the length of the jaws, so that one grows at a different rate than the other; and by retained baby teeth which interlock in such a way as to block normal development. Most bite problems have an hereditary basis. Short-nosed breeds such as the Persian are most often affected.

Treatment: The overshot bite may correct itself if the gap is no greater than the head of a match.

Teeth which interfere with the growth of the jaw should be extracted. This is most successful when it is done early (i.e. by four to five months of age), before the jaw has stopped growing. Bites are "set" by the time a kitten is eight months old.

Tooth Decay

The *crown* or top of the tooth is covered by a hard substance called enamel. Enamel is impervious to bacteria and acids. Beneath the enamel is a softer material called dentin, and beneath the dentin is the pulp or center of the tooth. It contains blood vessels and nerves. When the pulp is exposed to bacteria, it decays rapidly and results in death of the tooth.

The *root* of the tooth, however, is not covered by a protective layer of enamel. Instead it is covered by a substance called *cementum,* which serves to fix the tooth to the periodontal membrane. The periodontal membrane, in turn, attaches the tooth to the bony socket. The point at which the cementum and periodontal membrane meet at the gum line is the point most susceptible to tooth decay. Accordingly, gum disease, which exposes cementum and periodontal membrane, is the leading cause of tooth decay in the cat.

Periodontal Disease

This is the most common disease in the cat's mouth. All cats living in hard water areas eventually develop tartar stains on their teeth. Tartar is a dark brown or tan stain, a mixture of calcium phosphate and carbonate with organic material. When allowed to accumulate it becomes mineralized and forms a hard rough surface near the gum line called plaque or calculus. Little pockets form between the calculus and gum, in which bacteria grow and feed on trapped food. As these pockets become infected, the gums become soft and mushy and begin to recede, allowing infection to attack the weakest point of the tooth where the cementum joins the periodontal membrane. In time the bone recedes, the roots are exposed, and the stability of the tooth is lost. But as long as 50% of the root is anchored in bone, good oral hygiene may still save the tooth.

Normal chewing on hard material cleans the teeth and reduces the chances of calculus formation. It also stimulates the flow of saliva which contains antibacterial enzymes. This is why cats who eat primarily soft canned food are more likely to develop dental calculus and subsequent tooth decay, usually after five years of age.

It has been suggested that some cats are naturally more susceptible to periodontal disease than others. Increased susceptibility seems to occur among cats who suffer from repeated viral respiratory infections; and among those who have been exposed to the leukemia virus.

One of the first signs of periodontal disease is an offensive mouth odor. It may have been present for some time—perhaps even accepted as normal.

Another sign is a change in the cat's eating habits. Since it hurts to chew, he may sit by his food dish but refuse to eat. Weight loss, and an ungroomed appearance, are common.

If you look closely you can see tartar deposits on the premolars, molars and canine teeth. Pressure against the gums nearly always causes pus to exude from pockets alongside the teeth. This is an indication of *Gingivitis.*

Many dental problems go undetected until they cause major symptoms. Cats resist examination, particularly when suffering from a painful mouth. Furthermore, they often withdraw and seek seclusion when in pain.

Treatment: The mouth must be thoroughly cleansed and restored to a near normal condition. This involves the removal of dental tartar and calculus, drainage of pus pockets, and polishing the teeth. This can be carried out by your veterinarian. Afterwards the cat should be placed on an antibiotic.

Initial treatment is then followed by a home program of good oral hygiene in which the teeth are cleaned daily and brushed weekly (see *Care of Your Cat's Teeth*). Feed dry cat food which encourages chewing and stimulates the flow of saliva. Saliva contains substances which fight mouth bacteria.

Loose teeth, those in which less than 50% of the root is firmly anchored in bone, should be extracted.

Cavities (Dental Caries): Cavities are not common, primarily because a cat's diet is quite low in carbohydrates and sugars. Cavities account for only 20 percent of lost teeth. They develop along the gum line in association with periodontal disease and not the crown. However, the crown can be injured by trauma (*fractured tooth*). When a tooth is fractured infection can erode into the pulp. The broken tooth should be pulled, or the pulp sealed, to prevent an abscess.

Care of Your Cat's Teeth (Oral Hygiene)

Cats' teeth need special attention to prevent gum disease and tooth decay. A program of good oral hygiene is important:

1. Give your cat something to chew on at least once or twice a week. A cat can be encouraged to chew on a large knuckle bone, especially if a little meat is left on. Avoid long bones such as ribs or chicken bones that splinter.

2. Remove calculus. It is not normal and should be removed as soon as it appears. Heavy deposits are found on the outside on the canines and the incisors. Dental tartar or calculus is a good media for bacterial growth (see *Periodontal Disease*).

Tartar stains can be removed by brushing the teeth with a 3% hydrogen peroxide solution, or a solution of 1% hydrochloric acid. Moisten a rough cloth with the solution and then scrub the teeth vigorously, particularly on the outside and next to the gums where stains are heaviest. In advanced cases the teeth will have to be scaled and polished. Special dental instruments are needed to break loose particularly thick deposits.

Dry cat food is recommended to keep tartar stains from forming. However, if your cat is prone to the plugged penis syndrome, you may need to take special precautions as outlined in the chapter FEEDING AND NUTRITION (see *Types of Cat Food*).

3. Brush your cat's teeth and gums at regular intervals. Twice a month may be sufficient. Older cats will need to have their teeth brushed more frequently. In general, cats object to toothbrushes and the taste of toothpaste. Use a solution made up by adding a teaspoon of salt and a teaspoon of baking soda to a cup of water. Moisten a rough cloth and wrap it around your finger. Slip your finger inside his cheek and scrub his teeth and gums vigorously, paying special attention to the outside surfaces.

A program of good oral hygiene will increase the life of your cat's teeth, and help to keep him in good health during his later years.

TONGUE

Sore Tongue *(Glossitis)*

A sore tongue is usually associated with the *Feline Viral Respiratory Disease Complex,* in which case other signs of illness will be present (see INFECTIOUS DISEASES).

Burns of the tongue can be caused by licking caustic material off the feet, or by licking a metal surface in freezing weather. Cats can irritate their tongues while removing burrs or other abrasive substances from their coats. Glossitis occurs when a tongue wound becomes infected.

A cat with a sore tongue has an ungroomed appearance. The fur on his neck may be dirty and wet from saliva. Frothing at the mouth can be alarming. As the surface layer is shed, the rough spikes are lost, causing the tongue to appear red and shiny. Ulcers may be present.

Treatment: Flush out the cat's mouth twice daily with a weak solution of hydrogen peroxide and water. Ulcers should be cauterized with a silver nitrate stick. Antibiotics are given twice daily (Amoxicillin). A cat with a painful mouth may refuse to eat. Liquid meals are more easily accepted.

Foreign Bodies in the Tongue

Small plant awns, burrs, splinters and needles can become imbedded on the surface of the tongue. When visible, they can be removed with tweezers. A thread attached to a needle should not be pulled out, as it can be used to trace the needle.

The signs of a foreign body in the tongue are the same as for *Foreign Bodies in the Mouth.*

One common place for a foreign body is the underside of the tongue. Confirm this by looking. You may see a grape-like swelling or a draining tract, which means that the foreign body has been present for some time. Most of them will need to be removed under anesthesia. A follow-up course of broad-spectrum antibiotic is recommended.

Glossitis. The tip of the tongue appears smooth and shiny. This condition is most often associated with feline upper respiratory disease.

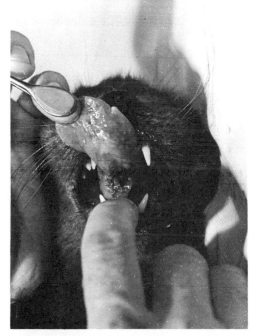

An abscess beneath the tongue, produced by a *foreign body.*

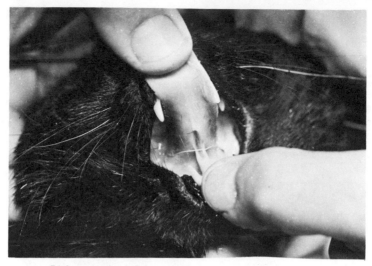

String around the tongue, cutting into the base.

String Around the Tongue (Strangulation)

In this condition as the cat swallows one end of a piece of string the other loops around his tongue. The more he swallows, the harder the string cuts onto the base of his tongue. Eventually it might cut off the blood supply, producing strangulation.

It may be difficult to locate the cause of this problem. The cat will be hard to examine, and the string could be as small as a thread. Close inspection is necessary to find and remove the cause of the constriction.

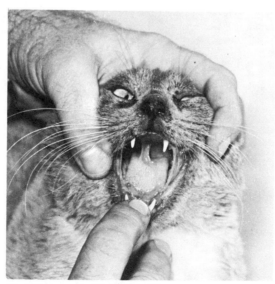

Trench mouth. **Note the thick tenacious saliva.**

MOUTH

Sore Mouth *(Stomatitis)*

Stomatitis should be suspected when a cat drools, refuses to eat, has diffi-culty chewing, shakes his head, paws at his mouth, and shys away when you attempt to look inside.

The inside of the mouth looks reddened, inflamed, swollen and tender. The gums may bleed when rubbed. There is a bad odor to the breath. Lack of self-grooming is evident.

Many cases are associated with an underlying or predisposing cause. They include foreign objects in the mouth (sometimes caught between the teeth or em-bedded in the tongue); feline leukemia; kidney failure; periodontal disease; and fracture of the joint where the jaw bones meet.

Those cases caused by a specific infection are listed below:

Trench Mouth (Vincent's Stomatitis): This extremely painful stomatitis is caused by a bacteria-like germ. There is a characteristic, offensive mouth odor, usually accompanied by a brown, purulent, slimy saliva which stains the teeth and the front of the legs. The gums have a beefy-red raw look and bleed easily. Trench mouth tends to occur in cats with severe periodontal disease and those who are run-down owing to a chronic illness or dietary deficiency. Infections of the frontal sinus can occur as a complication of trench mouth (see *Sinusitis*).

Treatment: Your veterinarian may want to thoroughly cleanse the cat's mouth under anesthesia. This affords the opportunity to treat decayed roots, loose teeth, and dental calculus when present. Ulcers are cauterized with silver nitrate. The cat is placed on Penicillin and a liquid diet. The after-care involves daily mouth washes using dilute hydrogen peroxide solution, accompanied by a home program of good oral hygiene (see *Care of Your Cat's Teeth*).

Ulcerative (Viral) Stomatitis: This is an extremely painful stomatitis in which ulcers form on the tip of the tongue and hard palate. The flow of saliva is at first clear, then becomes blood-tinged and foul smelling. A yellow pus-like ex-udate forms on the surface of the ulcers. Ulcerative stomatitis is seen most fre-quently with feline viral respiratory infections (see INFECTIOUS DISEASES).

Treatment: It is the same as for trench mouth, except that antibiotics are not recommended unless the problem is complicated by secondary bacterial infec-tion. Cats with this condition should be examined by a veterinarian.

Thrush (Yeast Stomatitis): This is an uncommon stomatitis seen chiefly when a cat has been on a prolonged course of broad-spectrum antibiotic. The mucous membranes of the gums and tongue are covered with soft white patches which coalesce to form a whitish film. Painful ulcers appear as the disease progresses.

Treatment: Nystatin is the drug of choice. Frequently it is supplemented with Penicillin to prevent secondary infection. Large doses of B-Complex vita-min are recommended.

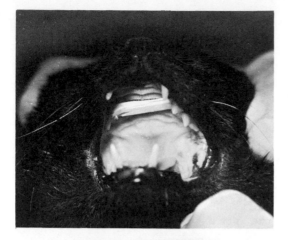

A *foreign body* wedged across the roof of the mouth.

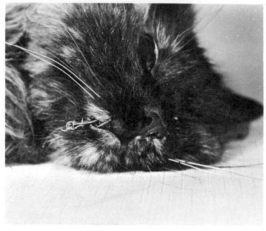

Push the barbed-end through the lip. Cut off the shank and remove the hook in two pieces.

Foreign Bodies in the Mouth

Foreign bodies lodged in the mouth include splinters of bone, gristle, slivers of wood, sewing needles, pins, porcupine quills, fish hooks, and plant awns. They can penetrate the lips, gums, and palate; get caught between the teeth; or get wedged across the roof of the mouth. Pieces of string may become wrapped around the teeth and tongue.

Suspect a foreign body if your cat paws at his mouth, rubs his mouth along the floor, drools, gags, licks his lips, or holds his mouth open. Sometimes the only signs are loss of pep, bad breath, refusal to eat, and general unthriftness.

Foreign bodies in the tongue, and back of the throat, are discussed elsewhere in this chapter.

Treatment: Obtain a good light and gently open your cat's mouth as described earlier in this chapter. A good look may show the cause of the problem. Direct removal of some foreign bodies if possible. If not, then a sedative or anesthetic will be required.

To remove a fish hook, determine which way the barb is pointing and then push it through the soft tissue until it is free. Cut the shank next to the barb with wire cutters and remove the fish hook in two pieces.

Foreign bodies left in place for a day or longer may cause infection. A broad-spectrum antibiotic is recommended.

Porcupine Quills. Porcupine quills can penetrate the face, nose, lips, oral cavity, feet and skin of the cat. To remove the quills, sedate or tranquilize the cat. With adequate restraint, clip the quill next to the skin to relieve the pressure in the hollow shaft. Using pliers, remove each quill by drawing it straight out. If the quill breaks off, a fragment will be left behind to work in further, causing a deep-seated infection. Veterinary attention is required.

Quills inside the mouth are difficult to remove without first giving the cat an anesthetic.

Growths in the Mouth

Any solid tumor growing in the mouth is a cause for concern. The majority are cancers. They require immediate professional attention.

Growths of the gums and salivary glands are discussed elsewhere.

THROAT

Sore Throat *(Pharyngitis)*

Isolated sore throats are not common in the cat. Most sore throats are associated with viral illness or mouth infection. Therefore veterinary attention is desirable.

The signs of sore throat are fever, coughing, gagging, vomiting, pain in the throat when attempting to swallow, and loss of appetite.

Foreign bodies in the throat give symptoms much like those of sore throat and tonsillitis. This possibility should be considered.

Treatment: Place your cat on a liquid diet and administer a Penicillin antibiotic for one week.

Tonsillitis

This also is rare in cats. The tonsils are aggregates of lymphoid tissue, much like lymph nodes, located at the back of the throat as they are in people. Usually they are not visible unless they are inflamed. Infected tonsils cause symptoms much like those of a sore throat, except that fever is more pronounced (over 103 degrees F), and the cat appears more ill. Most cases are caused by a bacteria.

Treatment: The treatment is the same as for sore throat. Removal of chronically inflamed tonsils is seldom necessary.

Foreign Bodies in the Throat (Choking and Gagging)

Cats choke on stones, string, cloth, and other small objects that lodge in the back of their throats and block their windpipes. Pieces of bone that lodge sideways in the throat are another cause of choking and gagging.

(*Note:* If the signs are *coughing* and the cat is having difficulty taking in air, the foreign body may be in his larynx—see RESPIRATORY SYSTEM: *Object in the Voice Box*).

Treatment: If your cat is getting enough air, try to soothe and quiet him down. Should he panic, the need for air is greater and the situation becomes more of an emergency. Hold the cat securely. Wrap him in a heavy blanket for effective handling. Open his mouth and see if you can find the cause of the problem. If the foreign body cannot be removed easily, take your cat to the veterinarian at once. Attempts to remove a stubbornly situated foreign object frequently cause further damage, or push it further back.

If the cat has fainted, the foreign body will have to be removed at once to re-establish the airway. Open his mouth. This is now easily accomplished because the cat is unconscious. Take hold of his neck in back of the object and apply enough pressure to his throat to keep the object from passing down while you hook it with your fingers. Work it loose as quickly as possible. Then administer artificial respiration.

Prevention: Watch your cat carefully and don't let him play with any small, easily torn toys. Don't feed him chicken bones or long bones that can splinter.

SALIVARY GLANDS

There are four main salivary glands which drain into the cat's mouth. Only the parotid gland, located below the cat's ear at the back of the cheek, may be felt from the outside. The salivary glands secrete an alkaline fluid which lubricates the food and aids in digestion.

Drooling (Hypersalivation)

Healthy cats do not drool, as do some dogs. However, it is common for cats to drool when they know they are going to be given an unpleasant-tasting medicine, or receive a shot. This is psychological.

Keep in mind that an animal who drools excessively and acts irrationally may have rabies. Exercise great caution in handling such an animal.

Drooling accompanied by signs of ill-health, such as watering of the eyes, is quite likely to be due to a feline viral respiratory infection.

Most mouth infections are accompanied by drooling. They include stomatitis, gingivitis, and foreign bodies in the mouth. Heat stroke can cause excess salivation, as can certain poisons (e.g. insecticides, arsenic).

Treatment depends upon finding the cause and correcting it.

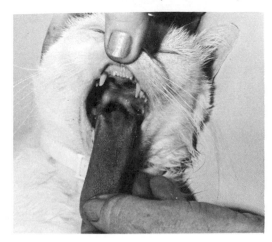

Pull the tongue out to inspect the back of the throat for an obstructing foreign body.

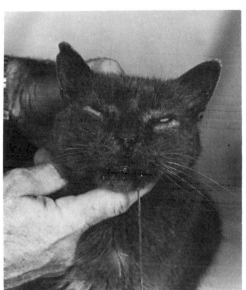

Drooling associated with severe stomatitis.

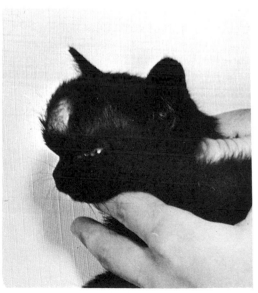

Swollen head due to an abscess.

Salivary Gland Infections and Cysts

Disorders of the salivary glands are rare in cats. A swelling might be due to extension of a mouth infection, or an infected bite on the face. When fluid backs up in an obstructed duct, a fluid-filled cyst develops in the gland. *Ranula* is the name given to a cyst in the floor of the mouth to one side of the tongue. It is treated by opening the cyst so that saliva can drain into the floor of the mouth.

SWOLLEN HEAD

Allergic Reaction

Sudden swelling of the skin of the face, lips, and eyelids, may be due to an allergic reaction. The cat's head can appear grotesquely distorted and much too large for his body. Possible causes are food allergy, contact and inhalation allergy, and the bites and stings of insects.

Treatment: Most cases subside in about three hours. Your veterinarian may want to administer adrenalin or an antihistamine. You should try to find out what caused the allergic reaction, so you can prevent your cat from coming into contact with it in the future. Allergies are discussed in the SKIN chapter.

Head and Neck Abscesses

Head and neck swellings which appear suddenly and are accompanied by fever and pain are abscesses.

Common causes in the head and neck region are infected animal bites; mouth infections which spread into the frontal sinus, or the space behind the tonsils; and foreign bodies such as wood splinters and quills which work back into the soft tissue.

Head and neck abscesses are extremely tender and may give a lop-sided look to the head, face or neck. Opening the mouth to eat may cause pain.

Retrobulbar abscesses behind the eye cause tearing and protrusion of the eye. *Submandibular* abscesses cause swelling beneath the chin. An abscess in the *frontal sinus* causes swelling beneath the eye. Ear flap abscesses are discussed in the chapter EARS.

Treatment: Incision and drainage will be necessary after the abscess becomes fluctuant (soft-feeling). Your veterinarian may first suggest applying warm salt-water packs for fifteen minutes four times a day. Antibiotics are prescribed.

After incision and drainage, a wick of gauze frequently is used to keep the edges apart so that the wound can heal from the bottom. You may be required to change the dressing and care for the wound at home.

9

Digestive System

GENERAL INFORMATION

The digestive tract is a complex system that begins at the mouth and ends at the anus. Mouth and throat structures are considered in the preceding chapter. The organs considered in this chapter are the esophagus, stomach, duodenum, small intestine, colon, rectum and anus. Organs which aid in the digestion and absorption of foodstuffs are the pancreas, gallbladder and liver.

The esophagus is a muscular tube which carries food down to the stomach. This is accomplished by rhythmic contractions. At the lower end of the esophagus is a muscular ring which helps to keep food and liquids from refluxing back up into the mouth.

Food remains in the stomach three to six hours. Here it is acted upon by acid and pepsin. Pepsin breaks down proteins into chains of amino acids.

Most bacteria are unable to live in the acid environment of the stomach.

As food enters the duodenum and upper small intestine, it is acted upon by the pancreatic enzymes *amylase* and *lipase,* and by the *succus entericus,* a mixture of enzymes secreted by the small bowel. The gallbladder contracts in the presence of a meal, emptying stored bile into the duodenum, which aids in the absorption of fats.

Lipase acts on dietary fats, forming fatty acids. Amylase converts starches into short-chained sugars. The final stage of digestion is accomplished by the succus entericus. The end products of digestion are then passed through the wall of the bowel and into the bloodstream.

Blood from the intestines flows to the liver. The liver has numerous functions connected with metabolism. Here the materials of the cat's meal are converted into stored energy.

Because of the relatively relaxed abdominal wall, it is possible to feel many of the organs in the cat's abdomen. Your veterinarian may be able to tell whether the liver and spleen are enlarged. He may be able to feel other swellings which could indicate a problem in the gastrointestinal or genitourinary system.

179

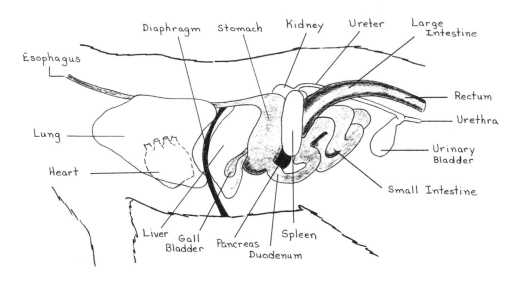

Anatomy of the Gastrointestinal System.—*Rose Floyd.*

ESOPHAGUS

The purpose of the esophagus is to transport nutrients from the mouth to the stomach. When a cat has a disease affecting his swallowing tube he may drool, have difficulty swallowing, swallow painfully, or regurgitate.

Regurgitation is the *passive* expulsion of undigested food without apparent effort. It is due to blockage or malfunction of the swallowing mechanism.

When the blockage is located at the back of the throat or in the *upper* esophagus the food comes back almost immediately. Attempts to eat or drink frequently produce gagging. Food regurgitated from the upper esophagus may be sausage-shaped and coated with saliva. With a complete blockage, the cat is unable to swallow liquids.

Lower esophageal disorders are associated with regurgitation of undigested food hours after eating. Usually the cat can drink water and retain liquids. Dry food is the most difficult to swallow and usually causes pain. The cat makes repeated swallowing attempts while stretching out his neck.

Regurgitation should not be confused with vomiting and coughing. Vomiting, which is preceded by drooling, repeated swallowing motions and retching, is the *forceful* expulsion of stomach and/or intestinal contents. The material vomited usually is sour-smelling, partly digested, and stained with yellow bile.

The retching which precedes vomiting can be mistaken for coughing. However, coughing is a dramatic act in which the cat gets down next to the floor, stretches out his neck, gives several short hacks followed by one loud final cough—and then brings up phlegm which is usually swallowed. Occasionally a cat coughs so frequently that he causes himself to vomit. Therefore these two conditions are often confused.

(*Note:* When a cat drools, makes repeated efforts to swallow—and especially if his jaw sags open—it is of extreme importance to be sure he does not have rabies. This disease causes paralysis of the throat and swallowing muscles. DO NOT handle such a cat until you are positive his condition is not due to this cause.)

Foreign Body in the Esophagus

When a cat becomes suddenly distressed, drools, swallows painfully or regurgitates food, suspect a foreign body such as a needle or bone splinter lodged in his esophagus. A history of regurgitation and difficulty swallowing for several days or longer does not rule out a foreign body.

Treatment: Removal requires an instrument called an *endoscope*. The cat is first given an anesthetic. Then the instrument is passed through his mouth and into his esophagus. The object is visualized through the endoscope and removed with long forceps.

Perforations of the esophagus can occur with sharp objects such as bone splinters, needles and fish hooks. Surgical removal is often required. Early diagnosis and treatment is important.

Strictures

A stricture is a narrowing of the esophagus produced by scar formation after an injury. Common causes are foreign bodies, caustic liquids, and reflux of stomach acid into the lower esophagus. Acid reflux can occur when a cat is under anesthesia.

Treatment: Most early strictures can be treated by stretching the wall of the esophagus with endoscopic dilators. Following dilation, some cats swallow normally. Others don't. The esophagus above the stricture remains enlarged, capable only of weak contractions. These cats require surgical removal of the strictured segment.

When a cat has a stricture, overloading his esophagus with large meals aggravates the problem. Feed him several small semi-solid meals instead.

Growths

Cancers (usually lymphosarcomas) which invade the lymph nodes around the esophagus can produce pressure on the esophagus. This narrows the passage and makes swallowing difficult. Tumors of the esophagus itself are not common but when present are often malignant. They generally occur in older cats.

Swallowing Problems in Kittens

These are not common. The symptoms are difficulty in swallowing, usually accompanied by regurgitation.

Achalasia is a condition related to spasm of the lower esophageal ring. As a result, food is unable to pass into the stomach. The esophagus above the constriction enlarges and balloons out. Food from the esophagus may be regurgitated into the windpipe. This can produce repeated bouts of pneumonia.

Kittens begin to show signs of achalasia shortly after they start to eat solid food. They begin to eat eagerly but, after a few bites, back away from the food dish. They frequently regurgitate small amounts of food which they eat again. After repeatedly eating the food, it becomes quite liquid and often passes into the stomach.

Achalasia appears to have an hereditary basis. Many kittens in the litter can be affected.

Treatment: A problem can be suspected by the symptoms, but its exact nature can be confirmed only by special studies. Surgery and dietary measures may be of aid.

STOMACH

Vomiting

A number of diseases and upsets in the cat are associated with vomiting. It is one of the most common non-specific symptoms you are likely to encounter.

Cats vomit more easily than most other animals. Some cats seem to do so almost at will, at times for no apparent reason. A cat may vomit undigested food immediately after eating, and then eat it again. A mother will vomit her food so that her kitten will have a soft, predigested meal.

All vomiting is the result of stimulation of the vomiting center in the brain, by numerous receptors located in the digestive tract and elsewhere. As the need to vomit is perceived, the cat appears anxious and/or depressed. He may seek attention and reassurance, or conversely, want to be left alone. He begins to salivate and makes repeated efforts to swallow.

As the cat starts to vomit there is a simultaneous contraction of the muscles of the stomach and abdominal wall. This produces a sudden build-up in intra-abdominal pressure. At the same time the lower esophageal ring relaxes which allows the stomach contents to travel up the esophagus. As the cat vomits he extends his neck and usually makes a harsh, gagging sound. This sequence should be distinguished from regurgitation which is discussed above.

As a general rule, the longer the interval between eating and vomiting, the lower in the digestive tract is the problem. Vomiting which is not related to eating frequently is associated with an infectious disease or central nervous system disorder.

The most common cause of vomiting is eating grass or some other indigestible material such as hair which is irritating to the stomach. Most cats experience this at one time or another.

Another common cause is overeating—or eating too fast. Kittens who gobble their food and immediately exercise are likely to vomit. This after-meal vomiting is not serious. It may be due to feeding kittens from a common food pan (which encourages rapid eating). Separating kittens, or feeding small meals more often, usually eliminates the problem.

If your cat vomits once or twice, but appears perfectly normal and shows no signs of illness, his condition is probably not serious and can be treated at home (see *Gastritis*).

Infectious diseases frequently associated with vomiting include feline panleukopenia, tonsillitis, sore throat, and acute metritis. Other signs of illness will be present. In young cats, sudden vomiting with fever is suspicious of panleukopenia. The white blood count will be below 5,000.

Another serious cause of vomiting is the ingestion of poisons such as antifreeze, or drugs such as aspirin. Poisons are discussed in the chapter EMERGENCIES.

A most serious cause of vomiting is that associated with peritonitis. This is an emergency situation. Common causes are also discussed in the chapter EMERGENCIES: see *Painful Abdomen*.

Often it is possible to get a clue to your cat's problem by noticing *how* he vomits, and *what* he vomits. Types of vomiting that may be serious are discussed below.

Repeated Vomiting. The cat first vomits his food. Then, as he continues to retch, he brings up a frothy clear fluid. This type of vomiting suggests a stomach irritant. Spoiled food, grass, hairballs, other indigestibles, and certain infectious diseases, all cause irritation of the stomach lining (see *Gastritis*). If the vomiting is accompanied by diarrhea, consult the paragraphs on diarrhea elsewhere in this chapter.

Sporadic Vomiting. The cat vomits off and on but not continuously. There is no relation to meals. Appetite is poor. The cat has a haggard look and displays loss of pep. Suspect a disorder of one of his internal organs, such as the liver or kidneys. Or he may have an illness such as chronic gastritis, a heavy worm infestation, or diabetes. A thorough check-up is in order.

Vomiting Blood. Fresh blood indicates a break in the mucous lining somewhere between the mouth and the upper small bowel. The most common cause is a foreign body. Other causes are tumors and ulcers. Material which looks like *coffee grounds* is old blood which is partly digested. This usually indicates that the bleeding point lies in the stomach or duodenum. Some cases may be due to swallowed blood. If a cat vomits blood his condition is serious and warrants a trip to the veterinarian.

Fecal Vomiting. If a cat vomits material that looks and smells like stool, he probably has an obstruction low in his intestinal tract. Severe or penetrating abdominal wounds are another cause of fecal vomiting. A cat with this condition becomes markedly dehydrated due to losses of fluids and salts. The problem cannot be managed without professional aid.

Projectile Vomiting. This is a forceful type of vomiting in which the stomach content is ejected suddenly, often a considerable distance. It usually indicates a complete blockage in the upper gastrointestinal tract. Foreign bodies, hairballs, tumors and strictures are possible causes. Conditions which cause an increase in intracranial pressure also produce projectile vomiting. They include brain tumor, encephalitis, and blood clots.

Vomiting Foreign Objects. Hairballs may form tubular, brownish, cast-like wads, too large to pass out of the stomach. Other material may be incorporated into them. They are called *bezoars.* Usually they are vomited by themselves or along with a clear frothy fluid. They are discussed in the section *Intestinal Foreign Bodies.* Other foreign objects which might be vomited include pieces of cloth, bone splinters, sticks and stones. Kittens with a heavy roundworm infestation may vomit adult worms. These kittens should be treated.

Emotional Vomiting. Highly sensitive cats may vomit when upset, excited, jealous, or wanting attention. *Treatment:* Remove your cat from the cause of his anxiety and tranquilize him with Acepromazine.

Motion Sickness. Cats can suffer from car sickness. The usual signs are restlessness followed by salivation, yawning, nausea and vomiting. This is a form of sea-sickness. It is due to a disturbance in the balance center. Most cats get over it once they get used to traveling. *Treatment:* If from past experience you suspect your cat is going to be sick, give him Dramamine (12.5 mg) by mouth three times a day. Give the first dose about an hour before traveling. Don't feed your cat before taking a trip. Cats travel best on an empty stomach.

Vomiting in kittens is discussed in the PEDIATRICS chapter.

Gastritis (Upset Stomach)

Gastritis is an inflammation of the lining of the stomach. The principal sign is vomiting. Gastritis may be of sudden onset (*acute*); or it may come on insidiously and be protracted (*chronic*).

Acute Gastritis. Severe and continuous vomiting which comes on suddenly most likely is caused by ingestion of an irritant or poison. Gastroenteritis and feline panleukopenia are other possibilities. Usually they are accompanied by diarrhea.

Common stomach irritants are grass, hair, bones, spoiled food and garbage. Chemical irritants include toxic plants, fertilizers, cleaning agents and antifreeze. Certain drugs (notably *aspirin,* but also cortisone, butazolidine and some antibiotics) frequently produce gastric irritation.

Characteristically, a cat with an upset stomach vomits shortly after eating. Later he may stop eating altogether and appear lethargic, sitting with his head hanging over the water bowl. His temperature remains normal, unless he has an infectious disease process.

Treatment: It is important to put the stomach at rest. Withhold food and water for 24 hours. Should the cat appear thirsty, give him some ice cubes to lick. Administer a dose of Kaopectate (one teaspoonful per five pounds body weight) each time he vomits—but not until after he relaxes.

After 24 hours start him off on a bland diet of boiled rice mixed two parts to one of hamburger. Boil the hamburger to remove the fat (fat delays gastric emptying). Other bland foods which you can substitute are cottage cheese, macaroni, baby food, and chicken-rice soup. Offer several small feedings. If well tolerated, advance to a normal diet.

Vomiting which persists for more than 24 hours suggests a serious disorder. Consult your veterinarian.

Chronic Gastritis: Cats with a chronically upset stomach show signs of impaired nutrition. They vomit sporadically (not always after meals), appear lethargic, carry a dull hair coat, and lose weight. The vomitus sometimes consists of food eaten the day before.

A common cause of chronic gastritis is a steady diet of poor quality (or spoiled) food. Consider also the possibility of hairballs in the stomach. Other causes are persistent grass-eating and the ingestion of cellulose, plastic, paper, rubber and other irritating products.

Aspirin, when given to cats on a regular basis, can produce thickening and peptic ulceration of the stomach, a condition which may be complicated by gastrointestinal bleeding. Cats do not tolerate aspirin in the usual dosages (see DRUGS AND MEDICATIONS). It should be given only under veterinary supervision.

If there is no obvious explanation for the cat's sporadic vomiting he might be suffering from an internal disorder such as liver disease, kidney failure, diabetes, tonsillitis, infected uterus, or a stricture at the outlet of his stomach.

Treatment: This depends upon finding and correcting the underlying cause. Special diagnostic studies are often required.

Put your cat on a soft bland diet as described above. As he begins to improve, advance to a high quality dry cat food. Cats with kidney disease require a special diet such as Hill's Feline K/D.

Other Causes of Upset Stomach:

Some cats are unable to tolerate certain foods, or brands of commercial cat food (see *Food Intolerance*). This is determined by trial and error. Special diets can be prescribed by a veterinarian.

If your cat vomits about two hours after eating, the problem could be *Food Allergy*. This is often accompanied by a watery, mucus-like, or even bloody diarrhea (see *Common Causes of Diarrhea*).

A swallowed *foreign body* or hair bezoar in the stomach might be the focus of a chronic irritation. The prevention of hairballs is discussed in the section *Intestinal Foreign Bodies*.

Should your cat swallow a smooth object which you suspect is too large to pass through his lower tract, make him vomit it as described in the section *How To Induce Vomiting* (see EMERGENCIES).

BLOATING (ABDOMINAL DISTENSION)

There are several disorders that cause the abdomen to appear bloated or swollen. Over-eating, eating fermentable foods, and constipation, can give a cat a somewhat bloated or pot-bellied look. Worm infestation can produce this in kittens.

Sudden swelling, accompanied by pain and signs of distress in the abdomen, always indicates an urgent condition such as a bowel obstruction, bladder outlet obstruction, abscessed uterus or peritonitis (see *Painful Abdomen* in the EMERGENCIES chapter, and *Intestinal Obstruction* below).

Acute gastric dilitation or volvulus, which occurs in dogs, is extremely rare in cats. The signs are sudden abdominal swelling, a shock-like state and peritonitis. Rush your cat to the veterinary hospital.

An abdominal swelling which comes on slowly, perhaps over several days or weeks, is most likely due to *ascites,* a condition in which fluid accumulates in the abdomen. Feline infectious peritonitis should be suspected. Other causes are right-sided heart failure and liver disease.

Keep in mind that pregnancy and false pregnancy are common causes of abdominal enlargement in queens.

Treatment depends upon determining the exact cause. Veterinary consultation is often required.

INTESTINES

Cats have a relatively short intestinal tract. They derive most of their nutrients from meat, which requires less length and surface area for digestion.

Problems in the intestinal tract (small and large bowel) are associated with three common symptoms: *diarrhea, constipation,* and the *passage of blood.* Vomiting also may occur with certain intestinal disorders.

Diarrhea in kittens is discussed in the PEDIATRICS chapter.

Diarrhea

Diarrhea is the passage of loose, unformed stool. In most cases there is a large volume of stool and an increased number of bowel movements.

Food in the small intestine takes about eight hours to get to the colon. During this time the bulk of it is absorbed. Eighty percent of water is absorbed in the small bowel. The colon concentrates and stores the waste. At the end, a well-formed stool is evacuated. A normal stool contains no mucus, blood, or undigested food.

Transit time in the intestinal tract can be speeded up under a number of circumstances. When this happens a large volume of feces in a semi-solid or liquid state arrives at the rectum. This results in a large, loose, unformed bowel movement. A common cause of this is overfeeding. Dietary overload presents the colon with more volume than it can easily handle.

Some adult cats (and occasionally kittens) are unable to handle milk and some milk by-products. This is because they lack sufficient amounts of the enzyme *lactase* which aids in the digestion of milk sugars. The unabsorbed sugar, called *lactose,* keeps water from being absorbed in the small intestine, which produces increased motility and a large volume of stool.

Other foods which some cats are unable to tolerate or can be allergic to are fish, eggs, spices, horsemeat, people food (table scraps), and some commercial cat foods. At times, even a minor deviation from the customary diet can cause diarrhea, with or without vomiting.

Cats can have emotional diarrhea when they are excited or upset—for example, when going to the veterinary hospital or a cat show.

In attempting to narrow the search for the cause of a diarrhea, begin by examining the *color, consistency, odor* and *frequency of stools:*

Color (A normal stool is brown).
> *Yellow or greenish stool*—indicates rapid transit.
> *Black tarry stool*—indicates bleeding in the upper digestive tract.
> *Bloody stool*—red blood or clots indicates lower bowel (colon) bleeding.
> *Pasty, light-colored stool*—indicates lack of bile (liver disease).
> *Large gray rancid-smelling stool*—indicates inadequate digestion.

Consistency
> *Soft bulky stool*—often seen when cats are overfed; or receive poor quality food high in fiber.
> *Watery stool*—indicates bowel wall irritation (i.e., severe infections, toxins), and impaired absorption.
> *Foamy stool*—suggests a bacterial infection.
> *Greasy stool* (often with oil on the hair around the anus)—indicates malabsorption.

Odor (The more watery the stool, the greater the odor).
> *Food-like, or smelling like sour milk*—suggests both incomplete digestion and inadequate absorption (for example, overfeeding, especially in kittens).
> *Putrid smelling*—suggests intestinal infection and/or blood in the stool (i.e., feline panleukopenia).

Frequency
> *Several in an hour, each small with straining*—suggests colitis.
> *Three to four times a day, each large*—suggests malabsorption or some small bowel disorder.

Diarrhea which persists for a week or longer suggests a chronic ailment such as colitis, parasite infestation, or malabsorption syndrome.

Some specific disorders of the small and large intestine associated with diarrhea are:

Enteritis: The small intestine contains a normal flora of bacteria which is not harmful to the cat. However, when this balance is upset by stress, illness, change in diet, the administration of antibiotics, or for reasons unknown, growth of harmful bacteria can lead to *enteritis* or inflammation of the lining of the small bowel. Symptoms can be mild or severe, depending upon the extent of the illness.

The ingestion of toxins and irritants is another cause of enteritis. Irritating substances that cats are liable to eat include:
> —dead animals, rodents and birds
> —garbage and decayed food
> —rich foods, gravies, salts, spices and fats
> —sticks, cloth, grass, paper, plastic, etc.
> —parts of flea collars

Some toxic substances causing enteritis are:
   —gasoline, kerosene, oil or coal tar derivatives
   —cleaning fluid, refrigerants
   —insecticides
   —bleaches, often in toilet bowls
   —wild and ornamental plants, toadstools
   —building materials (cement, lime, paints, caulks)
   —fireworks containing phosphorus

Toxic enteritis is not common in the cat. Cats are quite careful of what they eat, and tend to eat slowly. However, these substances could be ingested when a cat cleans his feet or grooms his coat. Many of these substances are equally toxic to the stomach and cause vomiting.

Infectious Enteritis. A number of agents can be responsible for infectious diarrhea. One of these, feline infectious enteritis (or *Panleukopenia*), is a viral disease which attacks many parts of the body including the gastrointestinal tract. Signs include fever, vomiting, diarrhea, loss of appetite and extreme depression. Secondary infection of the bowel wall by opportunistic bacteria may be responsible for diarrhea in some cases. Feline panleukopenia is discussed in the chapter INFECTIOUS DISEASES.

Protozoa which can produce an infectious enteritis are coccidia, giardia and toxoplasma. Coccidia, in particular, is a consideration in young cats. However, the finding of protozoa in the stool does not necessarily mean they are the cause of the problem. This subject is also discussed in INFECTIOUS DISEASES.

Intestinal parasites (e.g., roundworms, tapeworms, hookworms) also can cause a diarrhea. They are discussed in the chapter WORMS (INTESTINAL PARASITES).

Colitis. This is an inflammatory disease of the lower bowel, often of unknown cause. The signs are straining, pain on defecation, flatulence, and the passage of many small stools sometimes mixed with mucus and blood. Because nutrients are absorbed in the upper intestine, colitis has little effect on the cat's appearance or well-being.

Malabsorption Syndrome. Malabsorption syndromes are characterized by the inability to absorb nutrients from the intestine. Such cats are unthrifty and malnourished. There is a great deal of fat in the stool, giving it a rancid odor. The hair around the anus is oily or greasy.

Malabsorption disorders are not common. They can be due to pancreatic disease (causing lack of digestive enzymes); liver disease (causing lack of bile); injury to the wall of the intestine caused by a prior infection; a growth such as lymphosarcoma; and circulatory problems in which there is insufficient blood flow to the wall of the bowel (i.e., right-sided heart failure).

The cause of the malabsorption can usually be determined, but this requires special diagnostic studies. Afterwards, the cat can be given the missing enzyme with his meals.

Treatment of Diarrhea

Diarrhea is a symptom—not a disease. The first step is to find and remove the underlying cause.

When milk is a problem it can be removed from the diet without causing a nutrient deficiency as it is not a necessary part of the adult cat's diet.

Diarrhea caused by *overeating* (characterized by several large, bulky, unformed stools) is controlled by cutting back the overall food intake and feeding three small meals a day. When unfamiliar drinking water is the problem, carry an extra supply. When irritating or *toxic substances* have been ingested, an effort should be made to identify the agent, as specific antidotes may be required (see *Poisoning* in the chapter EMERGENCIES).

Food allergies or intolerances respond to the removal of the specific food causing the problem. Non-allergenic prescription diets are available through veterinarians. They contain mutton and rice, two ingredients your cat is not likely to be allergic to. They are used as a base to which other foods are added gradually, to test their effect on the animal's digestive tract.

An acute diarrhea which persists for more than 24 hours can be a serious problem. A cat dehydrates quickly when his fluid losses go unchecked. This leads to shock and collapse, a life-threatening situation. Consult your veterinarian without delay. Other indications to consult your veterinarian are bloody diarrhea and diarrhea accompanied by vomiting, fever and signs of toxicity.

Diarrhea of short duration not associated with excessive fluid loss can often be treated at home. Withhold all food for 24 hours. If your cat appears thirsty give him small amounts of water, or ice cubes to lick. As he begins to respond, start him off on an easily digestible diet which contains no fats. Diets containing boiled hamburger (one part to two parts of cooked rice—discard the broth), cottage cheese, cooked macaroni, or soft-boiled eggs, are suitable in small amounts. Special prescription diets (Hill's I/D) are available through your veterinarian. Continue the bland diet for three days, even though your cat seems well.

The cause of a chronic diarrhea (over a week's duration) is difficult to diagnose and treat. It requires laboratory analysis and close professional monitoring.

Intestinal Obstruction (Blocked Bowel)

Intestinal blockages occur as a result of swallowed foreign objects, tumors and strictures of the small and large intestine, adhesions following abdominal surgery, navel and groin hernias, and *intussusception*—a condition in which the bowel telescopes in upon itself, much as a sock pulled inside out. On occasion, obstruction of the colon may be caused by a fecal impaction.

An intestinal blockage can be partial or complete.

The signs of a *complete* blockage are vomiting, dehydration, and swelling of the abdomen. When the blockage is high, projectile vomiting occurs shortly after eating. When low, there is progressive distention of the abdomen followed by vomiting of dark brown material having a fecal odor. A cat with a complete obstruction passes no gas or stool per rectum.

A *partial* or intermittent obstruction, such as that caused by a tumor or stricture, may cause signs which come and go. These signs include weight loss, intermittent vomiting and/or diarrhea. Tumors tend to occur in older cats. Most of them are malignant. They often attain large size before being discovered, usually by feeling a mass in the abdomen.

Intestinal obstruction leads to death of the animal unless treatment is instituted. The cat's condition is most urgent when there are signs of *strangulation* or interference with the blood supply to the bowel. This is characterized by sudden distress, an extremely tender "board-like" abdomen to touch, shock and prostration. Strangulation requires immediate surgical relief, A dead segment of bowel must be removed and the bowel restored by an end-to-end hook-up.

Intestinal Foreign Bodies

Foreign objects in the small and large bowel may cause obstruction, perforation, or constipation. The cat who swallows foreign material also may suffer from an irritant gastritis (see *Vomiting Foreign Objects*).

Hairballs are common causes of gastric and intestinal upset. As the cat grooms his coat, he picks up and swallows hair in the process. The hair then forms a thick wad of material called a *bezoar*. Some cats have an affinity for tearing and chewing up wool. This also contributes to bezoar formation. If you find that your cat vomits hairballs, or if his stool has quite a bit of hair in it, you should anticipate a problem and take measures to prevent it as described below.

Other objects sometimes swallowed by cats include pins and needles, wood splinters, nylon stockings, rubber bands, feathers, cloth, plastic and string. A sharp object can perforate the bowel. Fortunately this is not common, even when a pin is swallowed. Should perforation occur, however, it leads to peritonitis. Then immediate surgical intervention is necessary.

Surgery is also indicated to remove string. One end of the string often knots up while the other gets caught in food. Tension on the string then causes it to cut through the wall of the bowel.

Prevention: Don't let your cat play with string, cloth or plastic toys he might tear up and swallow. Brush his coat to remove loose hair, especially at shedding-time.

Prevent hairballs by administering a commercial hairball preparation (cat laxative) which you can acquire at pet stores or through your veterinarian. A safe and effective home remedy for hairballs is Petroleum jelly (one teaspoonful twice a week).

Note: Mineral oil might be effective but should be used with caution. It should not be given by mouth to an uncooperative cat who could accidentally inhale it while struggling to keep from swallowing. If using mineral oil, add it to the cat's food once or twice a week at a dose of one teaspoonful per five pounds body weight.

Should your cat swallow a sharp object such as a pin, you might be able to coat it by feeding him either bread soaked in milk or a flour paste. This affords the possibility that the object will pass through without causing harm.

An operation may be necessary to remove swallowed string.
—*Sydney Wiley.*

Constipation

Constipation is defined as difficulty in the passage of stool. Usually it is associated with increased hardness of the stool or an obstructed passage. Often there is an element of pain during defecation. A cat who strains repeatedly but is unable to pass stool is probably constipated. However, keep in mind that straining occurs with colitis and the feline urinary syndrome (FUS). The distinction must be made before treating the cat for constipation. An overlooked bladder outlet obstruction is especially serious, particularly since it can produce permanent damage to the kidneys. FUS is discussed in the chapter URINARY SYSTEM.

Chronic Constipation

Incorrect diet and lack of exercise are the most common causes of chronic constipation. Most cats have one to two stools a day. However, some cats have a bowel movement every two or three days. These stools may be quite hard and difficult to pass.

A frequent cause of dietary constipation is eating undigestible parts of birds and rodents. This slows movement through the bowel and produces hard feces held together by hair, bones and feathers. Such fecal concretions may have to be broken down with forceps and removed by enemas.

Concentrated high meat diets produce dark, tenacious, small gummy stools. Owing to their lack of volume and consistency, they are difficult to pass. Furthermore, the intake of water among cats is generally low in comparison to most other animals. This can add to the problem. Cats eating canned food, which is 75 percent water, may not feel the need to drink for one or two days.

Diets low in fiber also cause the stools to be of small caliber.

Older less active cats experience reduced bowel activity and have weakness of their abdominal wall muscles. Either condition can lead to prolonged retention and an increase in the hardness of the stool.

Hairballs are another common cause of hard stools, particularly in long-coated breeds. You should suspect this if your cat vomits hair or if you see hair in his stool. The prevention of hairballs is discussed above. Other non-digestible substances such as grass, cellulose, paper and cloth, can lead to constipation or a fecal impaction.

An occasional case of chronic constipation is due to an enlarged, sluggish, poorly-contracting colon. This condition is called *megacolon*. These cats require life-long treatment with stool softeners and special diets. Veterinary supervision is necessary.

A chronically constipated cat may have a bloated look, seem lethargic and pick at his food. Cats with impactions often pass blood-tinged or watery-brown stool. This might be taken for diarrhea, but what is actually happening is that liquid stool is being forced around the blockage. If you suspect a fecal impaction, confirm this by digital examination using a well-lubricated glove.

Treatment: Attempt to determine the cause of a chronic constipation. Remove any predisposing factors to assure long-term success.

A change in diet may relieve the problem, particularly if you are using canned food as a major part of the diet. Dry kibble has a higher fiber content and adds more bulk to the stool. If already feeding a kibble, switch to another product to see if it makes the stools softer. In the older cat with an inactive bowel, soaking the kibble with equal parts of water can aid him greatly. Let the mixture stand for 20 minutes before feeding. If you are able to increase his exercise and activity, this too will assist him.

Small hard stools can be made softer by adding residue to the diet. High residue foods are bran cereal, whole wheat bread, pumpkin, squash or celery. Alternately, you can add Miller's bran to his food bowl at a dose of two teaspoons a day. In some cats it may be simpler to use a stool softener such as Colace. This medication comes in drops or syrup and is added directly to the meal. Use the pediatric-size dose.

An episode of mild constipation can be treated with a laxative such as Milk of Magnesia. The usual dose is two to three teaspoons a day. Do not use laxatives on a regular basis unless instructed to do so by your veterinarian. Instead, use liver or milk which has a laxative effect.

A fecal impaction requires an enema. Enemas are given at the rate of one ounce per ten pounds body weight. Several kinds are available. Pediatric Fleet Oil Retention enemas can be purchased over the counter. They come in plastic bottles with attached nozzles. Lubricate the nozzle well and insert it into the anal canal.

Tap water enemas are given through a rubber catheter connected to an enema bag. Lubricate the tip and insert it far enough into the anal canal so the rectum retains the fluid. One to two inches is enough. Otherwise, if the cat struggles, the catheter could injure the wall of his rectum.

Passing Gas (*Flatus*)

Cats who continually pass gas can embarrass or distress their owners. This condition, called flatus, is caused by undigested carbohydrates in the diet which, when fermented by bacteria in the colon, produce gas. Highly fermentable foods, such as onions, beans, cauliflower, cabbage and soybeans, are prone to cause flatus. Large quantities of milk, and high meat diets, also predispose to it.

Treatment: If a change in diet fails to control the problem, you may want to suppress undesirable gas-forming bacteria by giving your cat an antibiotic by mouth (Tetracycline, Chloromycetin) for five days. Afterwards, repopulate his bowel with more desirable non-gas-forming bacteria by giving him cultured buttermilk or yogurt for a week.

Loss of Bowel Control

Fecal incontinence follows injuries to the spinal cord. In most cases it is accompanied by paralysis of the bladder and urinary retention. This injury may occur when a car runs over a cat's tail. The sacral and/or coccygeal vertebrae are pulled apart, damaging the nerves to the rectum and bladder. An injured cat with a limp tail should be x-rayed to see if a spinal injury exists.

Loss of function may be temporary or permanent, depending on the severity of the nerve injury (see NERVOUS SYSTEM: *Spinal Cord Diseases*). Loss of the ability to void is particularly serious. If untreated, it leads to kidney failure.

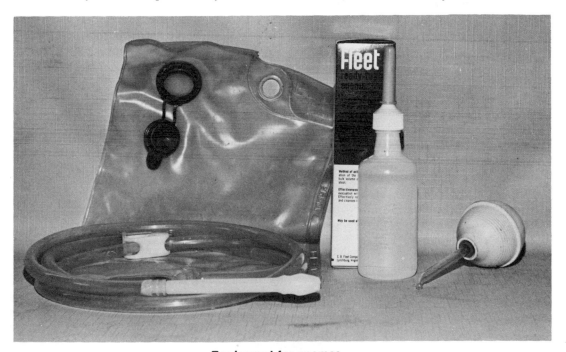

Equipment for enemas.

ANUS AND RECTUM

The signs of anal and rectal disease are pain on defecation, severe straining, scooting, the passage of bright red blood, and repeated licking at the rear.

Cats with anal and rectal pain often try to defecate from a standing position.

Bleeding from the anus or rectum is recognized by finding blood on the outside of the stool rather than mixed in with it.

Scooting along the ground is a sign of anal itching. It can be caused by flea bites, inflammation of the anus, anal sac disease, roundworms, and tapeworm segments.

Inflamed Anus and Rectum *(Proctitis)*

Maceration of the anal skin frequently is caused by feces adhering to the hair over the anus.

Irritation of the anorectal canal is produced by passage of bone chips, sharp objects, and hard dry stools. Repeated bouts of diarrhea, especially in kittens, can cause an inflamed anus and rectum. Other causes are insect bites and worms.

Straining is the most common sign of proctitis. Other signs are scooting, biting and licking at the rear. The rough surface of the cat's tongue may aggravate the problem, causing further ulceration and extreme discomfort.

Treatment: Clip away matted stool if present to let air get to the skin. An irritated anus can be soothed by applying an ointment such as Vaseline or one of the hemorrhoidal preparations used by people. If the skin about the anus is weepy-looking, apply a topical antibiotic ointment (Polysporin). Put your cat on a bland diet and feed him small amounts more often.

You can try to keep the cat from licking his rear by applying bad-tasting repellent medication which you can obtain from your veterinarian, or by using an Elizabethan Collar.

Protrusion of Anal Tissue (Anal and Rectal Prolapse)

With forceful and prolonged straining, a cat could protrude the lining of his anal canal. A *partial* prolapse is confined to the surface membrane. In severe cases a *complete* segment, several inches long, may protrude. This difference is quite evident on examination. Protrusion of anal tissue could be taken for hemorrhoids, but for all practical purposes hemorrhoids do not occur in cats.

A partial anal prolapse can be treated at home by correcting the cause of the straining (see *Constipation* and *Diarrhea*). Apply a topical anesthetic to relieve pain (Benzocaine Ointment). Treat as you would for inflamed anus and rectum.

A complete rectal prolapse should be replaced manually. Clean the tissue and lubricate it with Vaseline. Then gently push it back through the anus. To prevent recurrence, it is usually necessary for your veterinarian to take a temporary purse-string suture around the anus to hold it in place until healed.

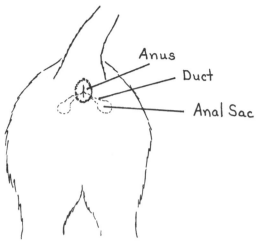

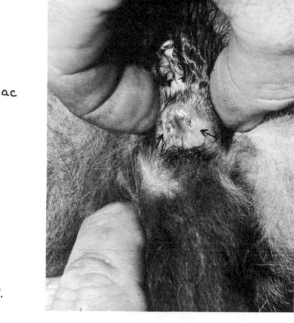

**Position of the *anal sacs*
and openings.** —*Rose Floyd.*

ANAL GLANDS OR SACS

The cat has two anal glands or sacs located at about 4 and 8 o'clock in reference to the circumference of the anus. A cat's anal glands are about the size of peas. They are smaller than the dog's, and therefore less likely to cause problems.

The openings of the anal sacs are found by lifting up the cat's tail and looking for the openings in the described locations.

The anal sacs are sometimes referred to as "scent" glands. In the skunk they serve a protective purpose. In the cat they mark the stool with an odor which identifies that particular individual and establishes his territory.

Normally the anal sacs are emptied by rectal pressure during defecation. The secretions are liquid, malodorous, and light gray to brown in color. At times they may be thick, creamy, or yellow-looking.

In most cats it is not necessary to express the anal glands unless there is some medical reason to do so. However, when frequent odor poses a problem, such as a cat who has overactive anal sacs, you can express the sacs yourself.

How to Empty the Anal Sacs

Raise the cat's tail and locate the openings as shown in the illustration. You can feel the sacs as small pea-sized lumps in the perianal areas at the 4 and 8

Proctitis. **Infection of the skin around the anus.**

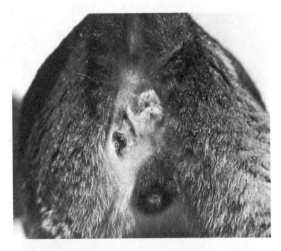

Recurrent anal sac infection with draining abscess.

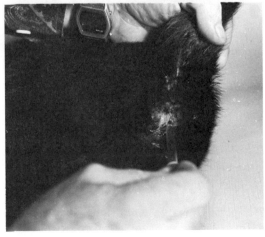

Instill an antibiotic into the anal sac through the duct opening.

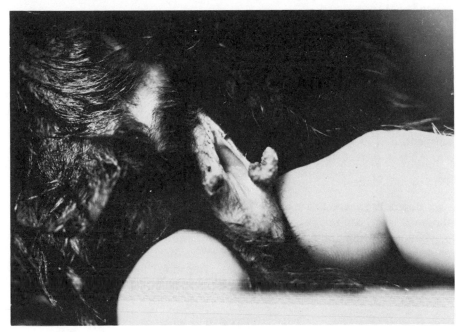

The anal sacs can be emptied by pinching the anal skin between your fingers.

o'clock positions. Grasp the skin surrounding the sac with your thumb and forefinger and squeeze together. As the sac empties, you will note a pungent odor. Wipe the secretions away with a damp cloth. If the discharge is bloody or purulent, anal sac infection is present and you should treat it as described below.

Impaction of Anal Sacs

Impaction is not common in cats. It occurs when the sacs fail to empty normally. It might be caused by plugging of one of the small ducts by their pasty secretions. Often it is not recognized until infection ensues.

Uncomplicated anal sac impaction is treated by manual emptying.

Anal Sac Infection *(Anal Sacculitis)*

This condition complicates impaction. It is recognized by seeing blood or pus in the secretions, swelling on one or both sides of the anus; and by the presence of anal pain and scooting. Abscesses may exist (see below).

Treatment: Empty the anal sacs and instill an antibiotic preparation into the sacs through the duct openings. Panolog, which comes in a tube with a small rounded tip at the end, can be used to pack the anal sacs. Insert the tip of the tube into the opening and squeeze. Repeat the packing process in two days. Administer a broad spectrum antibiotic (Chloromycetin or Tetracycline).

Anal Sac Abscess

An abscess is recognized by the signs of infection and swelling at the site of the gland. The swelling is at first red, then turns a deep purple.

Treatment: An abscess is ready to drain when it becomes fluctuant (soft and fluid-like). At this point it should be lanced. Pus and blood will drain out. The abscess cavity must heal from the bottom up. Keep the edges apart by flushing the cavity twice daily with a dilute hydrogen peroxide solution followed by an application of Panolog. Administer an antibiotic by mouth. Healing usually is uneventful.

Cats with recurrent anal gland infections can have their glands removed.

Polyps and Cancer

Polyps are grape-like growths which occur in the rectum and protrude from the anus. They are not common. They should be removed.

Cancer of the anorectal canal is not common. Cancer appears as a fleshy growth which ulcerates and bleeds. Signs are like those of a prolonged proctitis—straining being one of the most common symptoms. The diagnosis is made by obtaining a fragment of tissue for microscopic examination.

LIVER

The liver has many vital metabolic functions. They include synthesis of proteins and sugars, removal of wastes from the bloodstream, manufacture of enzymes (including those which cause the blood to clot), and detoxification of many drugs and poisons.

Signs of liver disease are quite variable. The two that are most specific are *jaundice* and *ascites*.

Jaundice is a condition in which bile accumulates in the circulation, turning the skin and whites of the eyes yellow and the urine tea-colored.

Ascites is the accumulation of fluid in the abdomen. It is caused by increased venous pressure in the portal veins which drain into the liver. A cat with ascites has a swollen or bloated look to his abdomen.

Spontaneous bleeding can be a sign of advanced liver disease. Common sites of bleeding are the stomach, intestine, and urinary tract. Small areas of hemorrhage, the size of the head of a pin, occur in the mouth—particularly on the gums.

A cat with impaired liver function appears weak and lethargic and exhibits loss of appetite and weight. He may also suffer from vomiting and diarrhea, drink excessively, and experience pain in the abdomen. Signs of central nervous system involvement in the form of seizure and coma are late manifestations.

Causes of Liver Insufficiency

A number of diseases, drugs and toxins, can adversely affect the liver causing death of liver cells. Liver involvement frequently is just one aspect of a generalized disease.

Infectious diseases which often involve the liver are feline infectious peritonitis and toxoplasmosis. Feline leukemia, and cancers which begin in the liver or spread to it from other locations, are further causes of liver insufficiency.

A blockage of one or more of the bile ducts by gall stones or parasites (liver flukes) is not common but becomes a consideration when a cat has jaundice of unexplained cause.

Chemicals known to induce liver toxicity are carbon tetrachloride, insecticides (chlorinated hydrocarbons such as Chlordane or Dieldin), and toxic amounts of copper, lead, phosphorus, selenium and iron.

Drugs adversely affecting the liver include inhaled anesthetic gases, antibiotics, diuretics, sulfa preparations, anticonvulsants, arsenicals, and some steroid preparations. Most of them cause problems only if the recommended dosage is exceeded, or when administered over long periods.

Treatment of liver insufficiency depends upon making the diagnosis. Special laboratory studies (at times liver biopsy) are needed to determine the exact cause. This requires hospitalization and a complete work-up. Prognosis for recovery is related to the extent of damage; and to whether the cause can be removed.

PANCREAS

The pancreas has two main functions. The first is to provide digestive enzymes; and the second is to make insulin for sugar metabolism.

Pancreatic enzymes are secreted into the small intestine through the pancreatic duct. Lack of these enzymes is one cause of a digestive disturbance called the malabsorption syndrome.

Insulin is secreted directly into the circulation. It acts upon cell membranes, enabling blood sugar to enter the cells where it can be metabolized to form energy.

Sugar Diabetes *(Diabetes Mellitus)*

Diabetes is not as common in the cat as it is in many other animals.

Sugar diabetes affects all organs. It is due to inadequate production of insulin by the pancreas. Without insulin, the body cannot utilize sugar. Sugar builds up in the blood. Soon there is an excess which the kidneys must get rid of. This results in excessive urination. There is a need to compensate for fluid losses by drinking lots of water.

Glycosuria is the name given to sugar in the urine. When a urine sugar test is positive, diabetes should be suspected.

Acids (ketones) are formed in the blood of diabetics because of inability to metabolize sugar. High levels lead to a condition called *ketoacidosis*. It is characterized by acetone on the breath (a sweetish odor that smells like nailpolish remover); labored rapid breathing; diabetic coma; and finally death.

In the early stages an animal will try to compensate for his inability to metabolize sugar by eating more food. Later, as he suffers the effects of malnourishment, there is a drop in appetite.

Accordingly, the signs of early diabetes are frequent urination, drinking lots of water, a large appetite, and unexplained loss of weight. The laboratory findings are sugar and acetone in the urine and a high blood sugar.

In more advanced cases there is loss of appetite, vomiting, weakness, ketone breath, dehydration, labored breathing, lethargy, and finally coma. Cataracts are more common in diabetic cats.

Treatment: It involves careful dietary control. Daily injections of insulin may be required in some cats but the dosage level is very difficult to adjust. The amount of insulin cannot be predicted on the basis of weight. It must be established for each individual. Small increases can produce coma or seizures. For success of initial therapy it is important that each cat be hospitalized to determine his daily insulin requirement.

As insulin requirements vary with the diet, it is important that the number of calories taken in by the cat be kept constant from day to day. Accomplish this by feeding him a balanced high quality cat food. His diet may have to be changed from time to time for periods of stress, illness, and loss of appetite. Follow your veterinarian's instructions.

Insulin substitutes by mouth (such as those used for people) have not been successful in treating diabetic cats.

Insulin Overdose. When an overdose of insulin is given, it causes a drop in blood sugar below normal levels. The condition is called *hypoglycemia.* Suspect this if your cat appears confused, disoriented, drowsy, shivers, staggers about, collapses, or has a seizure. *Treatment:* If the cat remains conscious and is able to swallow, give him sugar in water, candy, syrup, or orange juice. If unable to treat, seek professional help.

10

Respiratory System

GENERAL REMARKS

The cat's respiratory system is made up of the nasal passages, throat, voice box, windpipe, bronchial tubes and lungs. The bronchial tubes branch and become progressively smaller until they open into the air sacs. It is here that air exchanges with the blood.

The lungs are composed of the breathing tubes, air sacs and blood vessels. The ribs and muscles of the chest, along with the diaphragm, function as a bellows, moving air into and out of the lungs.

A cat at rest takes about 25 to 30 breaths per minute, about twice as many as a resting human. It takes about twice as long for a cat to exhale as it does to inhale. His respiratory motion should be smooth, even, unrestrained.

In evaluating a cat's ease of breathing, you should count the rate—and also see if he has any difficulty breathing in or out—in which case his breathing usually will be noisy and perhaps accompanied by forced effort. The presence of wheezing, rasping, coughing, and bubbling in the chest, indicates an abnormal state.

Causes of abnormal breathing are discussed below.

ABNORMAL BREATHING

Rapid Breathing

Rapid breathing can be caused by *pain,* emotional stress, fever, and overheating. Other conditions to consider are shock (reduced circulation, hemorrhage), lung and heart disease (not enough oxygen in the blood), and acid build-up (diabetes, kidney disease). Dehydration and various toxic states will cause the cat to breathe rapidly.

The cat who is excited or out of breath after exercise breathes rapidly, sometimes sixty to ninety breaths per minute. This is normal.

An increased rate of breathing at rest suggests a disease state and veterinary examination is necessary. *Normal 20-30 rest*

Slow Breathing

A very slow rate of breathing is found in narcotic poisoning, encephalitis, a blood clot pressing on the brain, and in the late stages of shock or collapse—in which case it usually signifies a terminal condition.

Panting

Panting is a normal process after exercise. It is one of the chief means by which a cat lowers his body temperature. This is accomplished by the evaporation of water from the mouth, tongue and lungs, and by the exchange of cooler air for the warm air in his lungs.

Cats also cool themselves by licking their fur, and by perspiring through the pads of their feet.

When panting is rapid, labored, and accompanied by an anxious look, heat stroke should be considered.

Noisy Breathing

Noisy breathing indicates obstructed breathing and is a cardinal sign of upper respiratory disease.

Croupy Breathing

This refers to the high harsh sound caused by air passing through a narrowed voice box. When the onset is sudden, the most likely diagnosis is a foreign body in the voice box or swelling in the throat.

Wheezing

A wheeze is a whistling sound which occurs during inspiration or expiration. It indicates narrowing or spasm in the windpipe or bronchial tubes. Tight deep-seated wheezes are best heard with a stethoscope. Causes of wheezing are asthma, lung worms, congestive heart failure, and tumors or growths in the airways.

Shallow Breathing

Shallow breathing is seen with conditions which restrict the motion of the rib cage. In most cases shallow breathing is associated with splinting. To avoid the pain of a deep breath, a cat breathes rapidly but less deeply. Pain of pleurisy and rib fracture causes splinting.

Fluid in the chest (blood, pus, serum) produces restricted breathing—but without pain.

Meowing (Crying)

A cat who suddenly begins to meow continuously most likely is in pain. You should determine the cause of his anxiety. Seek veterinary attention.

Excessive meowing can lead to voice strain (laryngitis).

Purring

A cat's purr is one of his most unique characteristics. Exactly how a cat produces the sound is a matter of conjecture. One theory is that the sound is caused by turbulence in major blood vessels during inhalation and exhalation. Another is that it is produced by vibrations of the soft palate. The most likely explanation is that the sound arises in the voice box from tensing of the vocal cords which vibrate as the cat breathes in and out.

Purring is an instinctual act. Kittens purr as early as two days of age.

A common misconception about purring is that it always indicates a state of pleasure. In fact, cats also purr when they are hungry, upset, or in pain. Cats have been known to purr just before dying.

COUGH

A cough is a reflex produced by an irritation of the air passages. Coughs are caused by infectious agents (viruses, bacteria, fungi) inhaled irritants such as smoke or chemicals, foreign objects in the airway (grass seeds, food particles), and by pressure on the larynx (tight collars, growths). Parasites in the respiratory tree, such as hookworm and roundworm larvae, or lung worms, also produce bouts of coughing. Some coughs are due to allergies.

The type of cough often suggests its location and probable cause: A cough accompanied by fever, sneezing, noisy breathing ("snuffles"), nasal and/or eye discharge, should alert you to the possibility of a feline viral respiratory disease. A high, weak, gagging cough associated with swallowing or licking of the lips is characteristic of tonsillitis and sore throat. Harsh dry hacking coughs, which follow exercise, are characteristic of acute bronchitis. A moist bubbling cough indicates fluid or phlegm in the bronchial tubes. A deep, tight, wheezing cough associated with difficulty in breathing, is typical of asthma.

Intermittent bouts of deep, low-pitched, moist-sounding coughs are seen with chronic and allergic bronchitis. The cat often hunches up his shoulders, gets down next to the floor, stretches out his neck and gives several short hacks followed by one loud final cough—then gags up frothy phlegm which is usually swallowed.

Bouts of severe coughing associated with the production of phlegm may at times be mistaken for *regurgitation* or *vomiting*.

Coughs are self-perpetuating. Coughing itself irritates the airways, dries out the mucous lining, and lowers resistance to infection—leading to further coughing.

Treatment: Only minor coughs of brief duration should be treated without professional assistance. Coughs accompanied by fever, difficulty breathing, discharge from the eyes and nose, or other signs of a serious illness require veterinary attention.

It is important to identify and correct any other contributing problem. Air pollutants such as cigarette smoke, aerosol insecticides, house dust and perfumes should be eliminated from the atmosphere. Nose, throat, lung and heart disorders should be treated if present.

A variety of children's cough suppressants are available at drug stores for the treatment of mild coughs. Most of them are suitable, but preparations containing codeine or some other narcotic substance should not be given to cats. The dose for an adult cat is the same as that for an infant. Administer every four to six hours.

The purpose of cough suppressants is to decrease the frequency and severity of the cough. They do not treat the disease or condition causing it. Therefore, over-use may delay diagnosis and treatment. Cough suppressants should not be given to cats in whom phlegm is being brought up or swallowed. These coughs are clearing unwanted material from the airway.

VOICE BOX *(Larynx)*

The larynx is a short oblong box located in the throat above the windpipe. It is composed of cartilage and contains the vocal cords. In the domestic cat the voice box is connected directly to the base of the skull by the hyoid bone. In lions, tigers, leopards, and other members of the large cat family, the hyoid bone is partly replaced by cartilage. As a result, the vocal apparatus of large cats is able to move freely and produce the characteristic full-throated roar. In contrast, small cats can make only weak cries.

The larynx is the most sensitive cough area in the body. At the top of the larynx is the epiglottis, a leaf-like flap that covers it during swallowing, keeping food from going down the windpipe.

Disorders of the larynx give rise to coughing, croupy breathing, and loss of voice.

Loss of Voice *(Laryngitis)*

Laryngitis is an inflammation of the mucous membrane of the voice box. Signs of laryngitis include hoarseness and loss of voice. The most common causes of loss of voice are excessive meowing and a chronic cough. Both produce vocal cord strain.

Laryngitis can be associated with tonsillitis, throat infections, tracheobronchitis, pneumonia, inhalent allergies, and (rarely) tumors in the throat. The lining of the larynx is not coated with cilia. Therefore, mucus frequently accumulates in the larynx. Exaggerated throat-clearing efforts are needed to dislodge it. This further irritates the larynx and lowers resistance to infection.

Top View of the Larynx

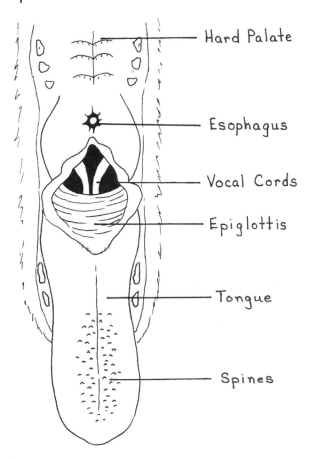

— Hard Palate

— Esophagus

— Vocal Cords

— Epiglottis

— Tongue

— Spines

THE LARYNX—*Rose Floyd.*

To determine if your cat has laryngitis, you can exert pressure with your thumb and index finger over his voice box. This produces a spasm of coughing. Or you can look into his throat by depressing his tongue and noting the bright red appearance of the mucous membrane of his larynx. Veterinary examination is necessary to determine the cause.

Treatment: Laryngitis due to excessive meowing usually responds to removing the cause of the cat's anxiety or distress. Tranquilizers may be of aid. When due to prolonged coughing, administer a cough suppressant and treat as described above (see *Cough*). Antibiotics (Penicillin, Tetracycline) might be indicated.

Foreign Object in the Voice Box

The sudden onset of severe coughing and respiratory distress in a healthy cat suggests a foreign body caught in the larynx. This is an emergency. Get your cat to the veterinarian as soon as possible.

If he collapses, he is not getting enough air. Immediately perform the *Heimlich Maneuver.* Lay him on his side with his head and chest down. Place your palm just behind the last rib and give four quick thrusts directed slightly upward. The maneuver thrusts the diaphragm up and produces a forceful exhalation of air. Usually this dislodges the object (commonly a large piece of meat). Check his mouth to see if the object has been dislodged; if not, repeat the thrusts.

Foreign bodies caught in the larynx are not common. Most food particles are of little consequence because the resulting cough expels them.

(Note: If your cat is *choking, gagging* and *retching,* probably he has a foreign body such as a bone, splinter or rubber ball caught in his throat. Open his mouth and see if you can find the cause of the trouble—see MOUTH AND THROAT).

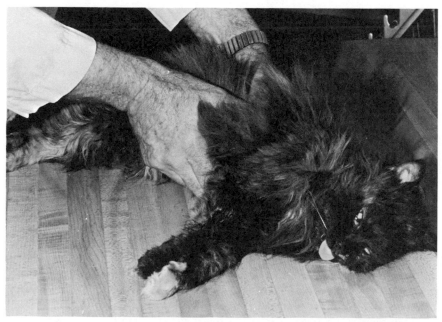

The *Heimlich maneuver.* Place your hand just behind the last rib and give four quick thrusts.
—*J. Clawson.*

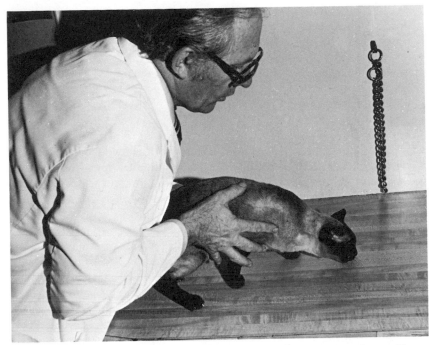

The cough of *acute* or *chronic bronchitis.* Note the typical posture with hunched-up shoulders, lowered head, and stretched-out neck.
—*J. Clawson.*

BREATHING TUBES *(Trachea and Bronchi)*

Foreign Bodies in the Windpipe

Grass seeds and food particles are the most common foreign material of sufficient size to lodge in the windpipe or bronchus when inhaled by the cat. Most of these are quickly coughed up. If an object becomes lodged in the airway it causes intense irritation and swelling of the passage.

Sudden attacks of coughing after a cat has been prowling in weeds or long grass, or immediately after vomiting, suggest aspiration of a foreign body.

Treatment: Give your cat a mild sedative or tranquilizer to settle his nerves and have him seen by your veterinarian. Cough medicines should be avoided since they serve no purpose and delay treatment. Foreign objects can be located by chest x-ray or by direct inspection via a bronchoscope.

Bronchitis

Inflammation of the smaller breathing tubes is called bronchitis. It is characterized by repeated coughing. The coughing further irritates the lining of the breathing tubes and spreads infection up into the trachea. For this reason the term *tracheobronchitis* may be more accurate in most cases.

Spread of secretions up into the throat often elicits a gagging reflex and/or repeated swallowing movements. If bronchitis is present, you can produce a coughing spasm by pinching the trachea just above the inlet to the chest. It is important to distinguish coughing from conditions producing gagging and retching (which are discussed in the chapter DIGESTIVE SYSTEM: *Esophagus*) because the treatment is quite different.

The trachea and bronchi have a protective layer of mucus which traps foreign material and infectious agents. Along with hair-like cilia which move foreign material toward the mouth, it serves as a major defense system against infection. Thus conditions which interfere with the function of the mucociliary blanket—such as chilling, breathing cold dry air, and dehydration—predispose to bronchial infection.

The major cause of bronchitis is an acute viral upper respiratory illness (see *Feline Viral Respiratory Disease Complex* in the chapter INFECTIOUS DISEASES). Following a break-down of local resistance, secondary bacterial infections are common and frequently lead to persistent cough and chronic bronchitis. Other causes of bronchitis include inhaled irritant fumes, foreign materials such as grass seeds, and pollens to which the cat might be allergic.

The cough of acute bronchitis at first is harsh, dry and hacking. It is aggravated by cold dry air, which is particularly irritating to the respiratory tract.

Vigorous exercise, followed by rapid breathing or a sudden deep inhalation, produces a bout of coughing. The cough itself is irritating and tends to perpetuate itself. Thus warm humid air and restricted exercise is of great therapeutic value.

Later in the illness the cough is moist or bubbling and often ends with retching and expectoration of foamy saliva. This type of cough is associated with chronic bronchitis and secondary bacterial infections.

Chronic Bronchitis. Bronchitis that persists for several weeks is referred to as chronic. All cases begin as acute bronchitis. In consequence of failure to cure or remove the inciting cause, secondary bacterial infection becomes established. Chronic bronchitis can lead to severe damage to the breathing tubes and the accumulation of infected mucus and pus in partially destroyed bronchi. This condition is called *bronchiectasis*. Chronic coughing can lead to break-down and enlargement of the air sacs, a condition called *emphysema*. These conditions are not reversible. For these reasons, chronic coughs require veterinary examination and professional management.

Treatment: Rest and proper humidification of the atmosphere are important items in the treatment of bronchitis. Confine your cat in a warm room and use a home vaporizer. Dry hacking coughs should be suppressed as described in the treatment of *Cough*. Antihistamines (e.g., Benadryl) are of assistance. They relax the breathing passage and also sedate. Expectorants may be of aid. Do not suppress moist bubbling coughs which produce phlegm. In addition, narcotic cough suppressants should not be used in cats.

A broad-spectrum antibiotic such as Tetracycline is indicated in the treatment of bronchitis. It is used to prevent or treat secondary bacterial infections. A cortisone preparation is of value if infection is not present. It reduces the inflammatory response which tends to perpetuate the cough. It should be used only under professional supervision.

Asthma (Allergic Bronchitis)

An acute respiratory disease occurs in cats which in many ways resembles bronchial asthma in humans. Attacks might be brought on by exposure to pollens, or some other allergen. In many cases the cause is not identified. Recurrent attacks can be anticipated.

An asthmatic attack is characterized by the sudden onset of difficulty in breathing accompanied by wheezing and coughing. The wheezing is heard as the cat exhales and usually it is loud enough to be heard by the naked ear. With a severe attack the cat may sit with his shoulders hunched up, or lie on his chest with his mouth open, and strain to breathe. His mucous membranes show a bluish color due to lack of oxygen (cyanosis).

Treatment: Immediate veterinary attention is often needed to relieve bronchial spasm and ease respiratory distress. Bronchodilators, adrenalin, and cortisone are effective in the acute attack. Antihistamines and cough suppressants are not helpful and should not be used as they interfere with the cat's ability to clear his secretions.

Asthmatic cats may have to be hospitalized for sedation and to remove them from an allergenic environment.

Attacks which are due to exposure to a known allergen can be prevented by eliminating the allergen. When this cannot be accomplished, cortisone may be recommended to stop repeated attacks. To prevent dependency on the drug, usually it is given every other day.

LUNGS

Pneumonia

Pneumonia is an infection of the lung tissue. Usually it is classified according to its cause: viral, bacterial, fungal, parasitic or inhalation in type.

Pneumonia might occur as a sequel to one of the feline viral respiratory illnesses where the natural defenses of the host are weakened by the primary infection. This allows secondary bacterial invaders to gain a foothold. Individuals most likely to be affected are kittens, old cats, and cats who are malnourished or debilitated.

Occasionally pneumonia is caused by a primary viral, bacterial, or parasitic infection—but this is not common in the healthy, well-cared for cat.

Aspiration of foreign material during vomiting (perhaps while the cat is under anesthesia), and the unskilled administration of medications or supplemental feedings, might account for the occasional case.

Tuberculosis and systemic fungus infections are infrequent causes of pneumonia. These illnesses are discussed in the chapter INFECTIOUS DISEASES.

Treatment: Pneumonia is a serious illness which requires urgent veterinary attention. The diagnosis is confirmed by laboratory tests and x-ray.

Until veterinary help is available, move your cat to warm dry quarters and humidify the air. Give him plenty of water to drink. Do not use cough medications. Coughing in pneumonia helps to clear the airways.

Pneumonia usually responds to an antibiotic specific for the causative agent. Your veterinarian can select an appropriate one.

Fluid in the Chest Cavity *(Pleural Effusion)*

A common cause of difficult breathing in cats is fluid accumulation in the pleural space surrounding the lungs. The fluid compresses the lungs and keeps them from filling with air.

This condition is much more common in cats than other animals. The reason is that cats suffer from two species specific diseases which can produce pleural effusion. They are *Feline Infectious Peritonitis* and *Feline Leukemia* (see INFECTIOUS DISEASES). Pleural-space infections from bacteria also are more common, perhaps because of puncture wounds of the chest produced by cat fights. The subsequent infection leads to pus formation (*empyema*). A severe blow to the abdomen might rupture a cat's diaphragm, allowing abdominal organs to press on the lung. This is another cause of difficulty in breathing.

Other causes of pleural effusion are congestive heart failure and liver disease. Bleeding into the chest usually follows a severe chest injury. The cat frequently shows evidence of shock.

The signs of fluid in the chest are primarily those of respiratory insufficiency. The cat often sits or stands with his elbows out, his chest fully expanded and his head and neck extended to draw in more air. He may not be able to lie down. The least degree of effort produces sudden distress or collapse. His breathing is open-mouthed. His lips, gums and tongue may look pale or appear gray or blue. The blue color, called *cyanosis,* is due to insufficient oxygen in the blood.

Depending upon the cause of the fluid accumulation, other signs of illness may be present. They include weight loss, fever, anemia, signs of heart or liver disease; and a history of trauma.

Treatment: When fluid builds up rapidly in the chest, urgent veterinary attention is required to prevent acute respiratory insufficiency and sudden death. The fluid may need to be drained. The cat should be hospitalized for further studies.

11

Circulatory System

The circulatory system is composed of the heart, the blood and the blood vessels.

HEART

The heart is a pump made up of four chambers: the right atrium and right ventricle, and the left atrium and the left ventricle. In cats, the heart is relatively small and slightly more rounded than in humans. The two sides of the heart are separated by a muscular wall. In the normal heart blood cannot get from one side to the other without first going through the general circulation or the pulmonary circulation. Four valves are present. Their function is to keep blood flowing in one direction. When the valves are diseased, blood can leak backwards creating difficulties.

Physiology

Blood, which is pumped out of the left ventricle into the aorta, passes through arteries of progressively smaller caliber until it reaches the capillary beds of the skin, muscle, brain and internal organs. Here oxygen and nutrients are exchanged for carbon dioxide and water. The blood is conducted back to the heart through veins of progressively larger diameter, finally reaching the right atrium via two large veins called the superior and inferior *vena cavae*.

The blood then passes into the right ventricle and out into the pulmonary circulation through the pulmonary artery. The pulmonary artery branches into smaller vessels and finally into capillaries (around the air sac), where gas exchange occurs. From here the blood returns via the pulmonary vein to the ventricles, thus completing the circle.

The beating of the heart is controlled by its own internal nervous system. The force and rate of the heartbeat is influenced by outside nervous and hormonal factors, too. Thus the rate speeds up when the cat exercises, becomes excited, runs fever, is overheated, is in shock—or in any circumstance in which more blood flow to the tissues is needed.

211

Heart rhythms follow a fixed pattern which can be seen on an electro-cardiogram. Whether the heart beats fast or slow, the sequence in which the various muscle fibers contract remains the same. This sequence causes a synchronized beat, allowing both ventricles to empty at the same time. Heart disease can upset this normal pattern, causing arrhythmias (variations from the normal rhythm).

The arteries and veins also are under nervous and hormonal influences. They can expand or contract to maintain a correct blood pressure.

The amount of blood within the entire circulatory system of the cat is about one-half pint (or 35 cc/lb. body weight).

There are outward physical signs which help to determine whether a cat's heart and circulation are working properly. Familiarize yourself with the normal findings so you can recognize the abnormal signs if they appear.

Pulse. The pulse, which is a reflection of the heartbeat, is easily detected by feeling the femoral artery located in the groin. With your cat standing or lying on his back, feel along the inside of his thigh where his leg joins his body. Press with your fingers until you locate the pulsations. Alternately, take the pulse by pressing against the rib cage over the heart. With the cat standing, feel the chest pulse just behind the elbow joint. If the heart is enlarged or diseased, you may be able to detect a buzzing, or vibration, over the chest wall.

The pulse rate, which is the same as the heart rate, can be determined by counting the number of beats in a minute. Most cats run a rate of 110 to 140 beats per minute at rest.

The pulse should be strong, steady and regular. An exceedingly fast pulse indicates fever, anemia, blood loss, dehydration, shock, infection, heat stroke, or heart (and lung) disease. A very slow pulse can indicate heart disease, pressure on the brain or an advanced morbid condition causing collapse of the circulation.

An erratic, irregular or disordered pulse suggests an arrhythmia which is a serious condition. When untreated, it can cause the heart to fail.

Various drugs your cat may be taking can affect the rate and rhythm of the heart.

Heart Sounds. Veterinarians use a stethoscope to listen to the heart. You can listen to the heart by placing your ear against the chest. Or you can hold an ordinary drinking glass over the heart and listen through the open end.

The normal heartbeat is divided into two separate sounds. The first is a LUB, followed by a slight pause; and then a DUB. Put together, the sound is LUB-DUB . . . in a steady, regular manner.

When the heart sounds can be heard all over the chest, the heart probably is enlarged. A running-together of the sounds, and interrupted rhythm, is abnormal.

Murmurs. Murmurs are caused by a turbulence in the flow of blood through the heart. Serious ones might be due to feline cardiomyopathy or birth defects. Anemia is a common cause of heart murmurs in the cat.

Not all murmurs are serious. Some are called functional—that is, there is no disease, just a normal degree of turbulence. Your veterinarian can determine whether a murmur is serious or of little consequence.

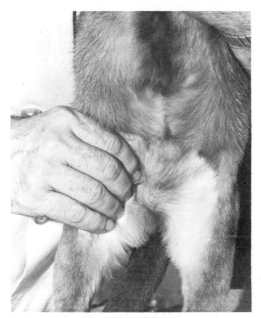

To take your cat's *femoral pulse*, feel along the inside of his thigh where his leg joins his body. Press with your fingers to locate the pulsation. —*J. Clawson.*

Taking the pulse with the cat standing. —*J. Clawson.*

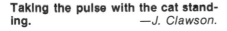

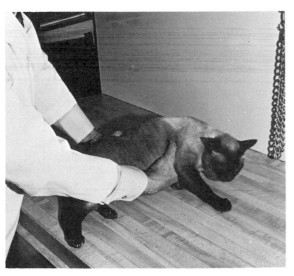

Another way to take the pulse is to feel for the heart beat just in back of the elbow. —*J. Clawson.*

Thrills. A thrill is caused by turbulence of such a degree that you can feel a buzzing or vibration over the heart. It suggests an obstruction to the flow of blood—for example, a narrowed valve or a hole in the heart. A thrill indicates a heart condition.

Circulation. If you examine the gums and tongue of your cat's mouth, you can gain a clue to the adequacy of his circulation. A deep pink color is a sign of adequate circulation.

The quality of the circulation can be tested by noting the time it takes for the tissue to pink-up after the gums have been pressed firmly with a finger. With normal circulation the response is immediate (one second or less). More than two seconds suggests poor circulation. When the finger impression remains pale for three seconds or longer, the cat is in shock.

A grey or bluish tinge to the mucous membranes of the gums, lips and tongue, is a sign of insufficient oxygen in the blood (*cyanosis*). This can be seen in heart and lung failure.

HEART FAILURE

Heart failure may be defined as the inability of the heart to provide adequate circulation to meet the body's needs. It is the end result of a weakened heart muscle. It is not a simple condition. The liver, kidneys, lungs and other organs are affected, too, causing a multiple organ-system problem. Keep in mind that a diseased heart can compensate for many years before symptoms of failure begin to appear. Accordingly, most cases represent long-standing conditions which have stressed or damaged the heart.

When a diseased heart begins to weaken, signs of right or left-sided failure occur. Symptoms differ. The treatment of heart disease is directed at preventing and treating the symptoms of failure.

Left Heart Failure

When the left ventricle starts to fail, pressure builds up in the pulmonary circulation. This results in lung congestion and accumulation of fluid in the air sacs (*pulmonary edema*). In the late stages of pulmonary edema the cat coughs up a bubble red fluid and can't get enough oxygen. Pulmonary edema is likely to be precipitated by exercise, excitement, or any stress that causes the heart to accelerate. Fluid also may accumulate around the lung in the chest space, pressing on the lungs and causing further breathing difficulties.

The early signs of left-sided heart failure are impaired exercise ability and shortness of breath. They are less apparent in the sedentary individual. Following moderate exercise, the cat begins to cough. In advanced cases breathing is labored and the cat assumes a characteristic sitting position with his elbows apart and his head extended to take in more air. His pulse is rapid, weak, sometimes irregular. Murmurs or thrills may be detected over the chest. Anxiety and fainting, occurring late in the disease, might be mistaken for a seizure disorder.

Right Heart Failure

Signs of right heart failure are less common than those of left-sided failure. As the right heart muscle begins to weaken, pressure backs up in the veins, causing congestive heart failure. In advanced cases the gums are gray and the limbs are swollen (dropsy).

The early signs of right-sided heart failure in the cat are lethargy, loss of appetite, shortness of breath, rapid pulse. In late stages you will observe weight loss, enlargement of the liver and spleen, and accumulation of fluid in the abdomen (ascites), giving a pot-bellied look. This condition may resemble lymphosarcoma or the wet form of feline infectious peritonitis. Fluid retention is augmented by the kidneys which respond to the slowed blood flow by retaining salt and water. You may be able to detect a murmur or thrill.

The treatment of heart failure is discussed below (see *Feline Cardiomyopathy*).

FELINE CARDIOVASCULAR DISEASE

Heart disease is much less common in cats than it is in man or dog. Coronary artery disease, for all intents and purposes, does not occur in cats.

The major cause of heart disease in cats is *cardiomyopathy,* or degeneration of the heart muscle. Congenital heart defects account for about 15 percent of cases of heart disease. Valvular disease and heartworm infestation do occur in the cat, but not very often.

Congenital heart defects are detectable in the young cat. They usually produce heart failure by 10 months of age. In most cases death occurs before the cat is one year old. In contrast, heart muscle disease is seldom noted in a cat younger than two to three years—but there are exceptions.

Congenital Heart Disease (Birth Defects of the Heart)

Almost all forms of congenital heart disease found in people occur in the cat. The most common ones are developmental malformations of the heart valves; and septal defects or holes which connect one or more of the heart chambers. Another defect is a marked narrowing of one or more of the major arteries carrying blood from the heart (aortic or pulmonic stenosis). Several defects may exist at the same time.

The extent and severity of the symptoms depends on the type and location of the defect. Thrills and murmurs may exist. The first indication often is the appearance of right-sided or left-sided congestive heart failure (see *Heart Failure*). Most cats with significant congenital heart defects die in less than a year.

Early detection in some cases might allow medical or surgical care which can prolong life.

Feline Cardiomyopathy (Heart Muscle Disease)

This is a disease of uncertain cause which affects cats of all ages. It can occur in young cats without warning, in which case congenital heart disease might be suspected.

In the *early* stage of heart muscle disease the heart swells and becomes inflamed. Bleeding into the muscle may occur. These abrupt changes could throw a strain on the heart and produce acute heart failure or sudden death. This stage usually affects cats two to three years of age.

In the *intermediate* stage, muscle swelling still exists but scar and elastic tissue replace part of the heart muscle. The heart becomes less efficient as a pump and begins to compensate by becoming larger. This stage is most common in six to seven year old cats.

In the *final* stages the heart muscle begins to deteriorate. Signs of left-sided congestive heart failure appear, usually before those of right heart failure. The final stage commonly affects cats nine to 10 years of age, but there is considerable variation.

The early signs of cardiomyopathy are vague and indefinite—perhaps loss of appetite and reduced activity. It is unusual to detect heart disease before signs of failure. Cats are unique in their ability to recognize their limitations and restrict their activities accordingly. Coughing is rarely a sign of heart disease in cats, although it is in dogs. A chronic cough is much more likely to indicate a problem in the respiratory system.

The usual picture is that of a rapid illness which progresses over two or three days as the heart begins to fail. The most frequest sign is difficult labored breathing, even at rest. The cat often sits with his head and neck extended, elbows out, straining to take in air. Coolness of the feet and ears, and a below normal body temperature, are signs of poor circulation. Heart murmurs are heard when muscle disease has produced incompetent valves. The pulse usually is rapid and thready. It may be irregular; or at times it may be slow.

Loss of appetite, rapid weight loss, weakness, fainting attacks, crying out spells, frequently accompany the above signs of illness.

The appearance of a blood clot in an artery, discussed below, might be the first indication of heart muscle disease.

Treatment: An accurate diagnosis as to the stage or type of cardiomyopathy is necessary to provide the most appropriate therapy. Special laboratory tests, x-rays and electrocardiograms, might be required.

A low salt diet is essential in treating a cat suffering from congestive heart failure. Fluid build-up is best managed by the use of diuretics and diets low in salt. Digoxin is a drug which increases the force of heart muscle contraction and slows the heart rate. It should be used under veterinary supervision; cats are particularly sensitive to its dangerous side effects. Other drugs are available to stabilize heart rhythm. They are indicated in the management of various arrhythmias.

Feline cardiomyopathy, showing the typical appearance of heart failure with the head and neck extended, straining to breathe.

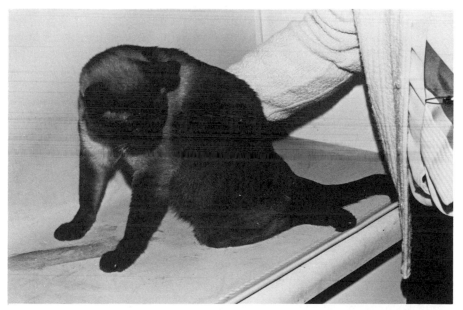

Sudden onset of paralysis in the rear legs. Conditions to consider are *arterial thromboembolism* and ruptured disc.

Restricting a cat to activities well within his exercise tolerance is of prime importance. This reduces the strain on his heart. Your veterinarian may prescribe a period of cage rest.

As arterial thromboembolism is a common complication of cardiomyopathy, a drug such as heparin might be prescribed to try and prevent it.

These measures can yield substantial results in terms of a longer, more comfortable, and more active life for your cat.

Arterial Thomboembolism (Blood Clot in an Artery)

This condition is characterized by the passage of a blood clot (called an *embolus*) out of the left side of the heart into the general circulation where it becomes lodged in an artery. The resulting obstruction to the flow of blood leads to clotting of the artery (called *thrombosis*).

The most common site of blockage is the point at which the abdominal aorta branches into the main arteries to the legs. Arteries elsewhere in the body can be affected. Diagnosis is difficult and requires special techniques, usually not available to the practitioner.

Arterial thromboembolism occurs in about half of all cats suffering from feline cardiomyopathy; it might be the first indication of heart muscle disease. You should suspect the possibility of thromboembolism if your cat experiences the sudden onset of weakness in his rear legs without a history of trauma or injury. Look for the following signs: cold legs; bluish skin (from lack of oxygen); reduced or absent pulses at the groin (see how to take the pulse earlier in this chapter). On occasion, one leg may be more severely blocked than the other. The colder leg with the weakest pulse is the more severely affected.

Treatment: This depends upon the severity of the blockage. Medications can be given to try to dissolve the clot. In some cases, surgery might be required.

Acquired Valvular Disease

This condition is rare in the cat, although it is the most common form of heart disease in the dog. In the cat, valvular disease is nearly always due to blood-bone infection. Bacteria lodge on the heart valves, forming clumps of infective material containing fibrin and debris. Infected valves become damaged. In cats who recover from the primary infection, congestive heart failure occurs later as a consequence of impaired valve function.

The disease can be prevented by treating skin abscesses and other infections likely to invade the blood stream.

Heartworms

Heartworm disease, so-named because the adult worms live in the right side of the heart, is common in dogs. It has also been found to infect the cat, although rarely. In fact, cats may only be accidental hosts. The heartworm, *Dirofilaria immitis* is spread by the bite of a mosquito which harbors infective larvae in its saliva. The larvae burrow into the cat's tissues and undergo several changes in form which lead to the developments of small adult worms. The worms then make their way to a vein and move to the heart. This process takes about six months. Mature heartworms produce microfilariae which circulate in the blood stream and can be identified by a blood test.

Because of the small size of the cat's heart, one or two worms may be enough to cause serious heart trouble, or even sudden death.

Signs of heartworm infestation include a cough made worse by exercise; lethargy; anemia; loss of weight and condition; and the production of bloody sputum. Labored breathing and congestive heart failure appear as the disease advances. At times, the worms are discovered at autopsy following a sudden unexplained death.

Treatment: Because treatment is complex and potentially dangerous, it should be undertaken only under veterinary supervision. Drugs are available to kill both the adult worms and larval stages.

Areas of most frequent heartworm infestations are along coastal regions where swamps or other brackish water provide ideal conditions for mosquitos to breed. Since mosquitos have a flight range of ¼ mile, in many cases spraying around catteries can be partially effective.

In theory, the best way to prevent heartworms is to keep your cat from being bitten by a mosquito. Cats can get reasonable protection if kept indoors in the late afternoons and evenings, when mosquitos are feeding.

ANEMIA

Anemia can be defined as a deficiency of red blood cells in the circulation. The average life span of red cells in the cat's circulatory system is 66 to 78 days, considerably shorter than that of the dog's. The purpose of these cells is to carry oxygen to the tissues. Thus the signs of anemia are due to insufficient oxygen in the blood and tissues.

Anemia exists when there are fewer than five million red cells in one milliliter of blood; or when the percentage of red cells in whole blood is less than 25 percent by volume. Once anemia is identified, its cause can be determined by other blood tests.

Causes of Anemia: Anemia can be caused by excessive loss of red blood cells, or by inadequate production. In some cases the body produces red cells rapidly, but not fast enough to keep up with the losses. In addition, it may take three to five days for the bone marrow to respond to the challenge of blood loss by producing new red blood cells.

Excessive Blood Loss. Sudden blood loss might be due to a major hemorrhage. In such cases shock will ensue. Treatment of shock is directed at control of bleeding and restoring fluid volume and red blood cells—by intravenous salt solutions and transfusions. The treatment of shock is discussed in the EMERGENCIES chapter.

A more insidious loss of blood could take place through the gastro-intestinal tract as a result of hookworm or coccidia infestation, tumor or ulceration. External parasites such as fleas and lice which feed on the skin can produce surprising amounts of blood loss in the poorly cared-for unkempt cat.

Rat poisons containing anticoagulants can produce spontaneous bleeding into the tissues. The cat might be found dead without apparent cause.

Blood loss can occur through destruction of red blood cells in the circulation. This condition is called *hemolysis.* It might be caused by an autoimmune hemolytic anemia, a toxic drug, or an infectious microorganism. Feline Infectious Anemia and Feline Cytauxzoon are two diseases that produce red cell hemolysis (see INFECTIOUS DISEASES).

Inadequate Production. The majority of feline anemias (70 to 80%) are due to inadequate red cell production. Red blood cell production is under the influence of certain hormones which cause the bone marrow to produce more red blood cells when the amount of oxygen in the blood falls below a critical level. Conditions which depress the bone marrow lead to insufficient red cell production.

Iron, trace minerals, vitamins, and essential fatty acids are incorporated into red blood cells. Thus a deficiency in building materials can result in failure to manufacture the final product.

Conditions which produce bone marrow depression include viruses (especially feline leukemia, feline infectious peritonitis); drugs (e.g., Chloromycetin); chronic kidney disease; and toxins and poisons.

Iron deficiency is especially prominent as a cause of anemia, but any chronic illness in which the cat loses weight and eats poorly can be a cause of nutrient deficiency. Some cases are caused by feeding an unbalanced diet.

Signs of Anemia: Signs vary considerably, depending upon the cause. Often they are overshadowed by the signs of the acute or chronic illness, of which anemia is but one of the associated symptoms. In general, anemic cats lack appetite, lose weight, sleep a great deal, and show generalized weakness. The mucous membranes of the gums and tongue are pale instead of bright pink as they should be. Temperature might be subnormal. With severe anemia, heart murmurs are common. The pulse is rapid, and so is the breathing rate. The cat may faint when he over-exerts. Most of these signs are those of poor circulation. As they also occur with heart disease, these two conditions might be easily confused.

Treatment: Uncomplicated nutritional anemias respond well to replacement of the missing substances in adequate amounts; and to restoring the cat to a nutritionally complete diet.

Iron deficiency anemia should alert you to the possibility of chronic blood loss (especially since each milliliter of blood contains 0.5 mg iron). Have your cat investigated for internal parasites. A stool check will show whether there are ova or traces of blood in the feces. Treat external parasites, especially fleas.

Complicated anemias require professional diagnosis and management.

12

Nervous System

GENERAL REMARKS

The *central nervous system* of the cat is composed of the cerebrum, cerebellum, mid-brain (which includes the brain stem), and spinal cord.

The spinal cord passes down a bony canal formed by the arches of the vertebral bodies. The cord sends out nerve roots which combine with one another to form the *peripheral nerves*. They carry motor impulses to the muscles and receive sensory input from the skin and deeper structures.

The **cerebrum** is the largest part of the brain. It is composed of two hemispheres. It is the area of learning, memory, reasoning and judgment. It initiates voluntary action on the part of the cat. Diseases affecting the cerebrum are characterized by changes in personality and learned behavior. A well socialized cat may begin to make mistakes in the house; perhaps grow irritable or become aggressive; exhibit compulsive pacing, circling, or various degrees of blindness. *Seizures are frequently associated with cerebral disease.* Trauma to the cerebrum produces a characteristic set of signs and symptoms. They are discussed in the section *Brain Injuries*.

The **cerebellum** is extremely large and well developed in the cat. It, too, is a bilobed structure. Its main function is to integrate the motor pathways of the brain. Injuries or diseases of the cerebellum result in *uncoordinated body movements* such as jerking, stumbling, falling, over-reaching with the paws, and various degrees of spasticity.

In the **mid-brain** are found centers which control the respiratory rate, heart rate, blood pressure, and other activities essential to life. At the base of the brain and closely connected to the mid-brain and brain stem are the hypothalamus and pituitary gland. These structures are vitally important in regulating the cat's body temperature and hormone systems. They are also the centers for primitive responses such as hunger, rage, thirst.

Injury to this part of the brain is particularly serious because of its effect on vital functions. *Coma* is a characteristic finding. Usually it is preceded by a depressed level of consciousness.

A special set of 12 nerve pairs, called the *cranial* nerves, pass directly out from the mid-brain into the head and neck region through special holes in the skull. The optic nerves to the eyes, auditory nerves to the ears, and olfactory nerves to the scent organs, are examples of such nerves.

Spinal cord injuries produce pain at the site of trauma, with paralysis and loss of feeling at or below the level of the injury. Both sides of the body are affected. This is in distinction to localized brain injuries in which paralysis and loss of feeling are likely to involve just one side of the body. Exceptions do occur. Special diagnostic studies are used to tell one condition apart from the other.

In the assessment of neurological illnesses, history is of the greatest importance. Your veterinarian will want to know if your cat has been in an accident. Did he receive a blow to his head? Was there a history of poisoning? Is he taking any drugs? Has he been exposed to other cats exhibiting signs of illness? When did you first notice his symptoms? Have they progressed? If so, has the progression been rapid or gradual? These are all important points to consider.

To further evaluate a neurological disorder, special tests may be of assistance. They include x-rays, electroencephalography (the EEG), and the spinal tap—a procedure in which fluid is removed from the spinal canal and submitted for laboratory analysis.

BRAIN DISEASES

Central nervous system disorders affect less than one percent of cats. The most frequent cause of brain disorder is injury due to trauma, primarily from automobile accidents and falls. Next in frequency is drug intoxication and poisoning, followed by cerebrovascular disease and brain infection. Other conditions which occur less frequently are vestibular disease, tumors, vitamin deficiencies and congenital malformations. These conditions are discussed below.

Brain Injuries

Forty percent of cats hit by a car suffer a head injury. Since the brain is not only encased in bone but surrounded by a layer of fluid and suspended from the skull by a layer of tough ligaments, it takes a major blow to the skull to injure the brain. Injuries of sufficient magnitude to fracture the skull often are associated with brain lacerations or bleeding into the brain from ruptured blood vessels. At times, even head injuries without skull fracture can cause severe or irreversible brain damage.

Brain injuries are classified according to the severity of damage they produce to the brain:

Contusion (Bruising). This is a mild sort of injury in which there is no loss of consciousness. After a blow to the head the cat remains dazed, wobbly, disoriented—and then clears in a gradual fashion.

Concussion. By definition, a concussion means the cat was knocked out, or experienced a *brief* loss of consciousness. Upon returning to consciousness, the cat exhibits the same signs as contusion.

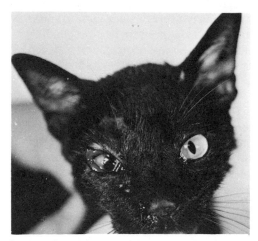

Severe head injury with unequal pupils. The right pupil is dilated and fails to react to light.

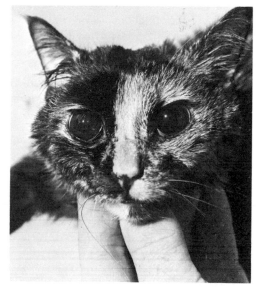

Dilated pupils, indicative of brain injury.

Coma. One of the most important things to observe is the level of consciousness. This cat can't be aroused.

Blood Clot or Brain Swelling. This is the most severe degree of brain injury. Since the brain is encased in a bony skull, pressure on the brain by an expanding blood clot, or by swelling of the brain itself—a condition technically called *cerebral edema*—produces pressure on the brain stem. This leads to herniation of the base of the brain through the large opening at the base of the skull, and quickly interferes with vital functions.

Cerebral edema also can occur when the brain is deprived of oxygen. Complete interruption of the oxygen circulation for as short a time as five minutes can produce fatal brain swelling. This could happen with suffocation, drowning, and cardiac arrest. Chronic causes of brain swelling are severe anemia, brain infection, heat stroke, heart failure, and respiratory insufficiency.

Hemorrhage into the brain (stroke) is a non-traumatic cause of blood clot. Toxic causes of brain injury are various drugs and poisons. Poisoning is discussed in the chapter EMERGENCIES.

Signs of Brain Injury (Increased Intracranial Pressure).

Following a blow to the head, or a period of oxygen deprivation, you should observe your cat for signs of brain swelling or the development of a blood clot. These signs can occur anytime during the first 24 hours after injury.

One of the most important things to observe is the level of the cat's consciousness. An alert cat is in no danger. A stuperous cat is sleepy but still responds to his owner. A semi-comatose cat is somnolent but can still be aroused. A comatose cat cannot be aroused. After a physical or emotional stress, cats tend to sleep after the excitement wears off. It is important to awaken the cat every two hours for the first 24 hours to check on his level of consciousness.

Depending on the severity of the injury, other signs to look for are:

Slight Pressure on the Brain. The cat is alert. He may show weakness on one side. Breathing is normal. The pupils remain small and constrict when a light is flashed in his eyes.

Mild Increase in Pressure. The cat may be difficult to arouse. His breathing is irregular. There is generalized weakness. Eye movements and pupils are normal.

Moderately Severe Pressure. The cat is in coma. All four legs are rigid. Breathing is rapid and shallow. Pupils are dilated and don't react to light. Eye movement is slight or absent.

Severe Pressure. The cat is in coma. Respirations are gasping or irregular. The heart rate is slowed. Pupils are dilated and there is no eye or leg movement.

Treatment of Brain Injury

Consider that the cat also may have internal injuries with bleeding, shock, and unstable limb fractures. Treatment of these takes precedence over management of the head injury. If possible, stabilize all fractures before transporting the cat (see MUSCULOSKELETAL SYSTEM: *Broken Bones*).

Handle an injured cat with great care and gentleness. Pain and fright deepen the level of shock in cats. Wrap the cat in a blanket to keep him warm. This also helps to restrain a cat who is unconscious but may wake up. Carry him with his head lower than his feet in case he vomits. Transport him to the nearest veterinary clinic.

With severe brain injury the cat may exhibit few if any signs of life. Signs of death are no pulse; no effort to breathe; dilated pupils and a soft eye. Usually it is impossible to tell whether sudden "death" is caused by head injury or a state of shock from internal bleeding. It is wise to administer cardiopulmonary resuscitation immediately upon suspicion of death (see EMERGENCIES: *Artificial Respiration and Heart Massage*).

The outlook following brain trauma depends upon the severity of the injury and whether treatment is successful. Steroids are employed to reduce brain swelling. An operation on the skull to release a blood clot may lead to a cure.

When coma persists for more than 24 hours the outlook is poor. But if the cat shows steady improvement throughout the first week, the outlook is good.

Cats who recover from brain injuries may exhibit permanent affection that includes seizures, head-tilt, and partial blindness.

Brain Infections *(Encephalitis)*

Encephalitis is the name given to inflammation of the brain. Signs produced by encephalitis can be caused by the destructive effect of the infectious agent, or by secondary brain swelling. They include fever, behavioral and personality changes (especially aggression), loss of coordination, unstable gait, seizures and coma. Encephalitis can be associated with signs of brain swelling, as discussed above.

Brain infection is not common. Viruses that produce encephalitis include those of feline infectious peritonitis, panleukopenia, rabies and pseudo-rabies. Rabies is of the greatest concern to cat owners. Fortunately this is an uncommon cause of behavioral change in the cat. Signs of rabies are discussed in the chapter INFECTIOUS DISEASES. Panleukopenia is a problem in the fetus or newborn where it produces cerebellar hypoplasia.

Bacteria also can produce encephalitis. Most of them gain entrance to the brain via the bloodstream; or by direct extension from an infection of the sinus, nasal passage, eye, or head and neck region. Fungal brain infection (*Cryptococcus*) is a rare cause of encephalitis, as is protozoan infection (*Toxoplasmosis*).

Treatment of encephalitis is directed at the cause of the primary disease. Steroids are used to reduce swelling of the brain.

Feline Cerebrovascular Disease *(Stroke)*

Strokes do occur in cats, perhaps more often than generally recognized. A stroke is caused by an interruption in the blood supply to a small part of the brain. This produces an area of cerebral damage. Signs, frequently of sudden onset, include seizures which involve the face and limb muscles; paralysis; loss of coordination; and blindness. Usually just one side of the body is affected. Residual signs appear a few days later. They include behavioral changes, pacing and circling, and seizures.

The diagnosis of stroke can be suspected from the history and physical findings. However, it can be confirmed only by special studies which are not generally available to most practitioners.

In most cases the cause of a stroke will be unknown. An association with a recent upper respiratory infection, or an illness which produced fever, has been observed in some cases.

Tumors

Brain tumors are rare. *Lymphosarcoma* is the most common tumor of the central nervous system. It affects the spaces around the brain and the spinal cord. Signs of brain tumor are like those of *Cerebrovascular Disease,* except they tend to come on gradually as the tumor grows.

Other Causes of Central Nervous System Disease

There are a number of other conditions which can produce signs of a central nervous system disorder.

Hypoglycemia, or low blood sugar, can produce seizures, depressed level of consciousness, and coma. It is sometimes associated with prolonged chilling. Insulin overdose is another cause (see *Sugar Diabetes*).

Hypocalcemia causes signs and symptoms much like those of hypoglycemia. It is discussed in the chapter PREGNANCY AND KITTENING (see *Milk Fever*).

Drugs and poisons associated with seizures and coma are discussed below (see *Seizure Disorders*).

Thiamine deficiency can occur when a cat fails to eat regularly or is fed an unbalanced diet containing large amounts of raw fish. Raw fish contains an enzyme which destroys Vitamins B-1. Signs of central nervous system involvement include loss of coordination, staggering gait, bizarre behavior, rigid extension of the neck, seizures and coma. In some cases the bizarre behavior may suggest rabies.

When the deficiency is discovered and treated before the cat becomes comatose, injections of thiamine and the establishment of a balanced diet usually lead to recovery.

Inherited Metabolic Diseases are a group of genetically determined feline disorders which produce degenerative changes in the central nervous system. In each case, a specific enzyme required for nerve cell metabolism is missing. Although these diseases are quite rare, the cat breeder should recognize that such progressive neurological diseases do exist.

Signs first appear at weaning time or shortly thereafter. They include muscle tremors and loss of coordination. The kitten's gait may be wobbly or unstable. As the disease progresses the kitten develops late signs which may include weakness, paralysis of the back limbs, blindness, and seizures.

Inherited metabolic diseases should be distinguished from *cerebellar hypoplasia* which follows intrauterine exposure to the virus of feline panleukopenia. It is discussed in the chapter INFECTIOUS DISEASES.

Metabolic nervous system diseases are inherited as homozygous recessive traits. Siamese and Domestic Short-haired cats are most often affected. Both parents must carry the gene and each must pass it on to an affected kitten. Littermates who do not show signs of the disease may carry the trait. Accordingly, when one of these diseases is discovered in a family or blood line, carriers should be identified by special enzyme tests so that steps can be taken to eliminate the trait.

Other congenital malformations do occur. They are rare. *Hyrdocephalus* is an enlargement of the dome of the skull due to a blockage in the flow of cerebral spinal fluid. *Lipodystrophy* is due to an enzyme deficiency that allows accumulation of fatty material in several body organs, notably the brain. These conditions produce a variety of central nervous system symptoms.

SEIZURE DISORDERS (FITS)

A seizure is a sudden and uncontrolled burst of activity which begins in a bizarre fashion with champing and chewing, foaming at the mouth, collapse, jerking of the legs, loss of urine and stool. There is a brief loss of consciousness followed by a gradual return to normal.

Some fits are atypical. Instead of the classical convulsion, the cat might exhibit strange and inappropriate behavior such as a sudden rage or hysteria. The cat may turn and lick or chew at himself, or bite his owner.

Seizures are caused by a burst of electrical activity within the brain, commonly one of the cerebral hemispheres. The electrical focus spreads out and involves other parts, including the mid-brain.

Seizures commonly are associated with those brain diseases which affect the cerebral hemispheres. Most of them have been discussed. Seizures sometimes can occur at the time of a brain injury but in most cases do not appear for several weeks. In most cases it will be found that the cat was knocked unconscious.

Common poisons which induce seizures are strychnine, antifreeze (ethylene glycol), lead, insecticides (chlorinated hydrocarbons, organophosphates), and rat poisons. They are discussed in the chapter EMERGENCIES. Organophosphates characteristically produce seizures which are preceded by drooling and muscle twitching. History of exposure to an insecticide (i.e., a dip) suggests the diagnosis (see *Insecticides*).

There are a number of conditions which, while actually not true seizures, can easily be mistaken for them. *Insect stings,* for example, can cause shock with fainting or collapse. Similarly, a cat with a foreign object in his larynx, who is unable to get air and turns blue at the mouth and collapses, might look like a cat having a convulsion. This condition is discussed in the chapter RESPIRATORY SYSTEM (see *Foreign Object in the Voice Box).*

Heart arrhythmias (any variations from the normal rhythm of the heart beat), accompanied by fainting, are often thought to be seizures.

Epilepsy is a recurrent seizure disorder of cerebral origin. It is far less common in cats than it is in dogs. Most seizures in cats are the sequella of a head injury or are caused by acute poisoning.

To establish a diagnosis of epilepsy, the attacks must be *recurrent* and *similar*. Toward this purpose your veterinarian will ask you to provide him with a complete description of your cat's behavior—before, during and after the seizures.

Treatment. If your cat starts to have a seizure, cover him with a blanket and stand aside until he quiets down. (Don't put your fingers in his mouth or try to wedge something between his teeth.) Then call your veterinarian. He may want to examine the cat to determine the cause of the seizure.

Seizures lasting over five minutes (continuous seizures) are dangerous. They must be stopped to prevent permanent brain damage. Valium is given intravenously to stop a continuous seizure.

Recurrent seizure disorders often can be prevented by using certain drugs. Those used in treating seizures in dogs and people can be quite toxic when given to cats. Close veterinary supervision is required.

COMA

Coma is a depressed level of consciousness. It begins with mental depression and confusion, progresses through stupor, and ends in complete loss of consciousness. Following a blow to the head, coma can occur without progressing through the earlier stages. Unconscious cats are not responsive to pain. For the signs and symptoms associated with coma, see *Signs of Brain Injury*.

Coma is associated with a number of brain diseases, most of which have been discussed earlier in this chapter. Central nervous system disorders which cause convulsions also can cause coma. What happens depends upon whether the brain is made more or less excitable.

Coma which appears with high fever or heat stroke is a grave sign. Vigorous efforts to bring down the fever are needed to prevent permanent brain damage (see *Heat Stroke*). Likewise, coma is ominous when it is associated with severe brain injury and the late stages of kidney and liver disease. Coma associated with low blood sugar is discussed in the GASTROINTESTINAL SYSTEM (see *Sugar Diabetes*).

If your cat is found in a coma for which there is no apparent explanation, he may have been poisoned. Common poisons which cause coma are ethylene glycol, barbiturates, turpentine, kerosene, arsenic, cyanide, dinitrophenol, hexachlorophene, amphetamines, and lead salts. A cat transported in the trunk of a car can develop carbon monoxide poisoning from the exhaust fumes. Poisoning is discussed in the chapter EMERGENCIES.

Treatment. First determine the cat's level of consciousness and whether he is alive. An unconscious cat can inhale his own secretions and strangle on his tongue. Pull out his tongue and clear his airway with your fingers. Lift him by his rear legs and set him on a table with his head hanging over the side. If alive, wrap him in a blanket and take him at once to a veterinarian.

If he shows no signs of life, begin artificial respiration and heart massage (see EMERGENCIES).

If you think your cat might have a piece of food caught in his airway, administer the Heimlich Maneuver as described in the chapter on the RESPIRATORY SYSTEM: *Foreign Object in the Voice Box.*

VESTIBULAR DISORDERS

The vestibular apparatus (*labyrinth*) is a complex sense organ composed of three semi-circular canals, the utricle and saccule (see *Structure of the Ears*). The labyrinth is stimulated by gravity and rotation movements. It plays an important role in balance and normal attitude of the body.

Disorders of the vestibular system are common in cats. An affected cat has a problem with his balance. He wobbles, circles, falls and rolls over, or has trouble righting himself. He may lean against the wall for balance or crouch low to the floor when walking. He often shows rapid jerking eye movements (*nystagmus*) and will usually tilt his head down on the affected side. When picked up and turned in a circle he may seem to be dizzy.

A common cause of labyrinthitis is inner ear infection (see EARS).

Other causes are feline cerebrovascular disease, encephalitis (especially Toxoplasmosis), drug toxicity (streptomycin), and thiamine deficiency. These conditions are discussed elsewhere in this chapter.

The *Idiopathic Vestibular Syndrome* is a condition which occurs rather commonly in cats for reasons unknown. The onset is sudden. The cat exhibits head-tilt and nystagmus. He may have difficulty walking. In two to three days he begins to recover. In most cases he is well in three weeks, although some cats retain their head-tilt permanently.

SPINAL CORD DISEASES

Injuries and diseases of the spinal cord produce a variety of neurological findings.

With injury, there is usually pain or tenderness at the site of trauma. There may be weakness, loss of feeling, paralysis of both rear legs or even all four extremities. Spinal cord disorders usually produce bilateral symptoms, while localized brain disorders often produce symptoms on just one side of the body— perhaps the front and rear legs on that side.

Spinal cord injuries can be told apart from injuries to peripheral nerves because the latter usually affect just one limb.

Other conditions producing limb weakness or paralysis that might be mistaken for a spinal cord problem are aortic thromboembolism, acute abdomen, bone fracture, muscle contusion, and arthritis.

Aortic embolus can be distinguished by absent or reduced pulses in the groin (see CIRCULATORY SYSTEM). Acute abdominal pain (peritonitis, FUS, kidney or liver infection) produces a peculiar hunched-up appearance which might be taken for a back problem. The acute abdomen will show signs of pain when pressure is applied to the abdominal wall (see *Painful Abdomen* in EMERGEN-CIES).

Spinal Cord Injuries

Spinal cord injuries occur following automobile accidents and falls. Not infrequently a cat is caught in the blades of an automobile fan when a car is started. Solitary cats frequently will huddle up next to a warm radiator in cold weather to keep warm.

A characteristic injury occurs when a car runs over a cat's tail, pulling apart the sacro-lumbar and/or coccygeal vertebrae. This could damage the nerves to the rectum and bladder. The signs are fecal and urinary incontinence, and a tail that hangs like a limp rope. The urinary incontinence is due to an overloaded hypotonic bladder that "overflows" continuously. A stretch of the nerves might result in temporary urinary retention, but if the condition is not recognized and treated shortly after the accident, bladder paralysis remains even though nerve function is restored. For this reason it is important that any cat with a limp tail be seen by a veterinarian and x-rayed for a sacral injury.

Another condition which is frequently mistaken for a broken back is a pelvic fracture. In both injuries the cat is unable to use his back legs and will exhibit pain when handled in the area of the injury. Thus it might appear that the outlook is poor, even though a cat with a broken pelvis usually recovers completely.

A cat who has received a severe blow to his back might suffer a bruise or contusion of his spinal cord and lie paralyzed for days. As the effects subside, the cat may begin to recover. However, if the cord has been torn or disrupted, it cannot regenerate and paralysis will be permanent.

Ruptured discs are common in older cats but seldom produce weakness or paralysis as they do in dogs. Most of them are the result of trauma. Spinal arthritis, called *spondylitis,* is a condition in which spurs of calcium develop on the backbones. They, too, can exert pressure on the spinal cord, or roots of the spinal nerves, occasionally causing pain and rarely weakness of a limb.

Infections

Spinal cord infections are not common. Most of them are due to a neighboring abscess, caused by a penetrating wound such as a bite or laceration. *Meningitis* is an infection of the lining of the spinal canal and brain. On rare occasions it may be caused by a blood borne microorganism.

Malformations

Spina bifida is a developmental defect in the closure of the bones in the lower back. It is common in the Manx breed. Signs include lack of bladder and bowel control. These cats exhibit weakness of the hind legs and a peculiar gait that resembles a "bunny hop".

Spinal cord injury with paralysis of both rear legs.

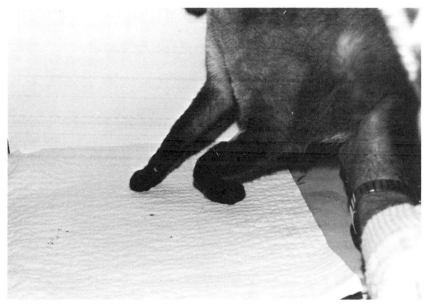

Paralysis of the front leg due to nerve injury.

NERVE INJURIES

An injury to one of the peripheral nerves results in loss of sensation and motor function in the distribution of that nerve. Common injuries are stretches, tears and lacerations.

Brachial and radial nerve palsies involve one of the front legs. Usually they are caused by an auto accident, during which the leg is jerked backwards away from the trunk, which stretches the nerves. The leg hangs limp. When paralysis is partial, the cat may be able to stand but stumbles when he takes a step.

Lacerated nerves must be repaired. Stretched nerves often return to normal.

Another cause of temporary nerve paralysis is the injection of an irritating medication into the tissue surrounding a nerve. This problem is infrequent but can be a source of concern. The majority heal spontaneously. The correct procedure for giving injections is described in the chapter DRUGS AND MEDICATIONS.

13

Musculoskeletal System

GENERAL INFORMATION

The cat's skeleton is made up of an average of 244 individual bones, connected by ligaments and surrounded by muscles. This is about 40 more than man. Nearly half the difference is made up by the cat's tail which contains 19-28 small vertebrae—except for the Japanese Bobtail and Manx breeds.

The outside of the bone is called the *cortex*. It is composed of minerals and protein. The cortex gives the bone its rigidity. Nutritional deficiencies can cause poor bone development, or can result in bone demineralization, making fractures more likely.

Inside is the *marrow* cavity. Bone marrow is important in red blood cell production.

Bones are held together by specialized connective tissue called *ligaments*. The union of two bones is called an *articulation* or joint. Bones in a joint would grate against each other and cause considerable wear if it were not for a protective layer of *cartilage* over their ends. In some joints a pad of cartilage is interposed between the two surfaces, giving a cushion effect.

Even though cartilage is tough and resilient, it can be damaged by joint stress and trauma. It is not easily mended or replaced. Once damaged it may deteriorate and become calcified, acting as a foreign body or irritant to the joint surfaces.

Joint position is maintained by ligaments, tendons, and a tough fibrous capsule surrounding the joint. These combine to provide stability or tightness to the joint. Joint *laxity* is due to loose ligaments and/or a stretched capsule. It can cause slippage of the articulating surfaces, leading to cartilage injury and arthritis.

Joints of the hip and shoulder are called *ball and socket*. They move forward and backward, from side to side, or in a circle; but the bone should remain firmly seated in the socket.

The rest of the limb joints are of the "hinge" type. They flex and extend in a plane from front to back. They must be stable to prevent the bones from slipping to the sides.

Cats owe much of their flexibility to their extremely mobile back bones. While the degree of movement between individual vertebrae is small, these bones are less tightly connected than in many other animals. When taken together, the overall flexibility of the vertebral column is considerable. For example, a cat can arch his back into an inverted U shape, bend himself in half, or rotate the front part of his body 180 degrees relatively to the back. When dropped on his back, a cat can turn right side up and land on his feet in less than two seconds.

The skeletal anatomy of man and cat have much in common, including similar terminology. Due to the fact that man evolved into a two-legged creature, there are some significant differences in terms of angles, lengths, and the position of bones.

The hock, so prominent on the cat, is actually the heel-bone in a person. Whereas we walk on the soles of our feet, the cat actually walks on his toes.

The clavicle, which in man stabilizes the shoulder joint, is only slightly developed in the cat or may even be absent. Each shoulder blade moves with the corresponding foreleg. This narrows the cat's chest and enables him to keep his legs and feet close together—thereby providing for speed, flexibility, and the ability to squeeze through tight openings.

Cat breeders, judges, and veterinarians use certain terms to describe a cat's overall structure and conformation.

Conformation is the degree with which the various angles and parts of an animal's body agree or harmonize with one another. Standards for purebred cats describe the ideal conformation for each particular breed. At one end of the scale is the strong sturdily-built, short-bodied or "cobby" variety, typified by the American Shorthair, Persian and Himalayan. At the other end is the sleek, lithe, fine-boned type with tapering lines, exemplified by foreign or Oriental breeds such as the Siamese. Other breeds, such as the Abyssinian, may embody characteristics of these two extremes. Standards for cats also describe head features, length of coat, color and points, balance, and personality of the breed. To some extent they are based upon esthetic considerations, but they do take into account the breed's utility and working purposes as well.

Another term used to assess the physical attributes of an animal is *soundness*. When applied to the composition of the musculoskeletal system, it means that a sound cat is one in whom all the bones and joints are in correct alignment and functioning properly.

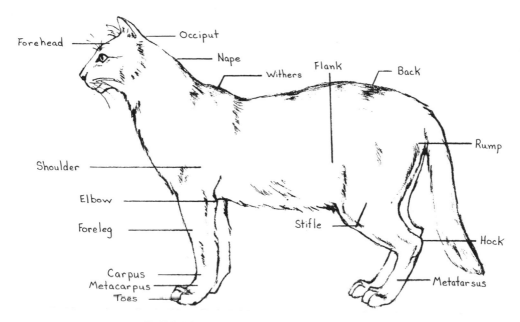

TYPOGRAPHICAL ANATOMY.—*Sydney Wiley.*

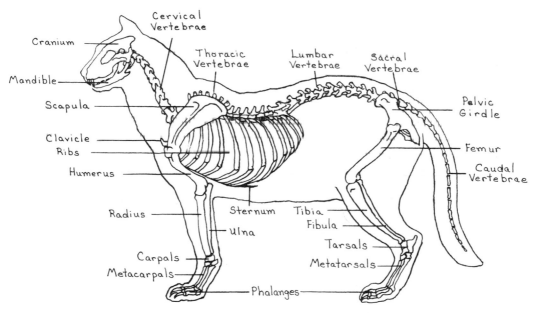

SKELETAL ANATOMY.—*Sydney Wiley.*

LIMPING (LAMENESS)

The limp is the most common sign of bone or joint disease. However, muscle or nerve damage can produce lameness. It indicates pain or weakness in the involved leg.

Locating which leg is affected can be difficult. A cat will take weight off a painful leg when standing. When he is moving, usually he will take a shorter step on a painful or weak leg and you may notice that his head "bobs" or drops as weight comes down on the affected leg.

Having identified which leg is involved, you should attempt to identify the site and possible cause. First flex and extend all joints to their maximum to ascertain if joint or tendons are involved. Next carefully feel the leg from the toes up. Attempt to locate a point of tenderness by applying pressure. Having located an area of pain, see if it is produced by movement of a joint, or by local tenderness in a muscle (such as might be caused by a puncture wound or a bruise). Check for swelling and discoloration of the area. With this information consider the following:

Infected areas are tender, reddened, warm to touch, and often associated with a break in the skin. Infections produced by cat fight wounds are the most common cause of lameness. The limp usually grows steadily worse. Fever is often present.

Sprains and strains (of joints, tendons and muscles) are of sudden onset; frequently they show local swelling and discoloration; they gradually improve. Ordinarily the cat has limited use of his leg. Pain is mild. There is no fever.

Fractures and dislocations are associated with severe pain and inability to put weight on the leg. Deformity often is present. Movement of the involved part produces a gritty sound. Tissues are swollen and discolored from bleeding.

Spinal cord injuries and diseases usually produce paralysis or weakness of both rear legs. *Ruptured discs* do occur, especially in older cats, but seldom produce weakness or paralysis as they do in dogs. Peripheral *nerve injuries* are caused by accidents in which the leg is jerked backwards from the trunk. The leg hangs limp. These conditions are discussed in the NERVOUS SYSTEM chapter.

Arthritis is a joint disease. Pain in the joint sometimes produces lameness which gets better as the day wears on.

Metabolic bone diseases come on gradually. The most common one is Paper Bone Disease (*Nutritional Secondary Hyperparathyroidism*). Bone fractures are frequent in this disorder.

Congenital Hip Dysplasia, which is common in some breeds of dog, is seldom a consideration in cats. Congenital bone disorders that do occur with some frequency include absent or kinked tail, extra toes and cleft foot. They seldom produce a physical handicap.

INJURIES TO BONES AND JOINTS

A cat who is injured or in pain should be handled gently as described in the chapter EMERGENCIES: *Handling and Restraint.* Do not struggle unsuccessfully with a seriously injured cat as this could tire him out and produce further shock and collapse. Take precautions to avoid a painful scratch or bite.

Sprains

A sprain is an injury to a joint caused by sudden stretching or tearing of the joint capsule or ligaments. The signs are pain over the joint, swelling of the tissues, and limitation of motion leading to a temporary lameness.

Cases with severe swelling and/or pain (in which the cat refuses to put weight on the leg) should be examined by a veterinarian to rule out a fracture or dislocation. If the problem does not begin to improve within four days, x-rays should be taken.

Treatment: The primary treatment is to *rest the part.* When torn ligaments are suspected, the joint should be immobilized by splinting as described below under *Broken Bones.* Ice packs help to keep the swelling down. Add crushed ice to a plastic bag and wrap the limb to hold the bag in place over the injured joint. Apply ice for 20 minutes every hour for the first three hours. Analgesics should not be given to a cat without veterinary approval (see DRUGS AND MEDICATIONS). In addition, the limp is important in protecting the part from further injury.

Tendon Injuries

A tendon may be stretched, partly torn, or completely ruptured. An irritated or inflamed tendon is called a *tendonitis.* Strained tendons sometimes follows sudden wrenching or twisting injuries to the limb.

The signs of tendonitis are temporary lameness, pain on bearing weight, pain and swelling over the course of the tendon. Tendons of the paws (front and back) are affected most often.

Rupture of the *Achilles* (Heel) tendon, which attaches to the hock joint, can be caused by sudden and extreme flexion. This tendon is most often injured during auto accidents and cat fights.

Treatment: It is the same as for *Sprains.* A ruptured tendon might require surgical repair.

Muscle Strain

An injured or torn muscle is caused by: (a) sudden stretching of its fibers; (b) prolonged stress or overexertion; and (c) a blow to the muscle. The symptoms are lameness, a knotting-up of the muscle, and swelling with tenderness over the injured part.

Treatment: Rest and cold packs are recommended (see *Sprains*).

Dislocated Joint (Luxation)

A strong force is necessary to rupture a joint and displace the bone. Such injuries usually are the result of falls, a fight with a dog, or car accidents. The signs are sudden onset of pain with inability to use the limb. There is an observable deformity (or shortening) when compared to the opposite side.

The hip is the most commonly dislocated joint in the cat. It can be recognized by signs of pain on movement of the hip, a "gritting" sensation, and shortening of the leg by about one inch.

Other joints sometimes dislocated are the kneecap, hock, and jaw. A dislocated kneecap occurs with some frequency in the Devon Rex, in whom there may be an hereditary predisposition.

Treatment: Veterinary examination is necessary to rule out an associated fracture and to replace the joint in its socket. These injuries frequently involve shock and internal bleeding.

Broken Bones (Fractures)

In cats the majority of fractures are caused by automobile accidents and falls from apartment windows—especially in cities during hot weather.

Fractures of the femur and pelvis are the most common. The jaw is next. Skull, vertebral and other fractures also occur.

A rather common type of fracture is one which occurs when a car runs over a cat's tail, pulling apart the sacro-lumbar or coccygeal vertebrae. This could damage the nerves to the rectum and bladder. Urinary retention might be a serious complication. For this reason it is important that any cat with a limp tail be seen by a veterinarian. This condition is discussed in more detail in the NERVOUS SYSTEM.

Bone fractures are classified by type and whether the injury involves a break in the skin. Incomplete (*greenstick*) fractures tend to affect young cats, whereas the bones of elderly cats are brittle and more likely to break completely. Complete breaks are divided into *simple* and *compound*. A simple fracture does not break through the skin. In a compound (open) fracture the bone has made contact with the outside, either because of an open wound which exposes it, or because the point has thrust through the skin from the inside. Compound fractures may be associated with bone infection.

Treatment: Many of these injuries are associated with shock, blood loss, and injuries to other organs. Control of the shock takes precedence over treatment of the fracture.

When possible, suspected fractures should be immobilized to prevent further damage during movement of the cat to a veterinary hospital. Accomplish this by splinting the involved limb. A satisfactory splint is one which crosses the joint above and below the injury. This assures non-movement of the fractured part.

When a fracture is below the knee or the elbow, immobilize it by folding a magazine or piece of thick cardboard around the leg. Then wrap it with roller

With a *ruptured achilles tendon*, the cat walks on the back of his leg.

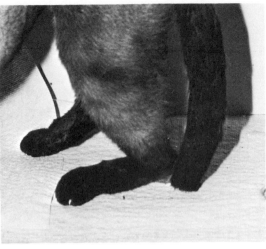

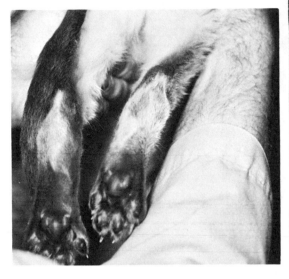

A dislocated hip, showing the affected right leg shorter than the left.

  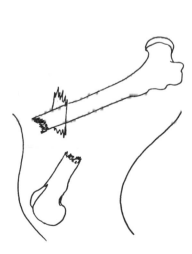 

Greenstick fracture.

Oblique fracture.

Open or Compound fracture.

Chip or avulsion fracture.

—Rose Floyd.

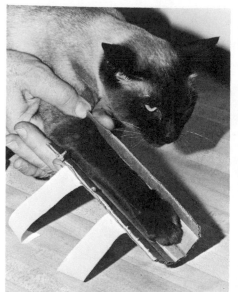 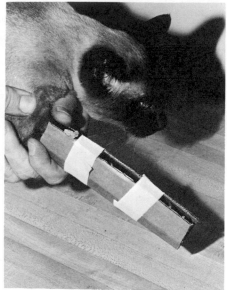

A piece of cardboard makes a good temporary splint for fractures of the front leg below the elbow.   —*J. Clawson.*

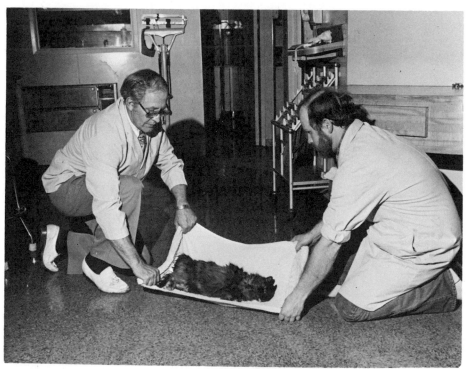

Use a blanket or towel to transport a severely injured cat.   —*J. Clawson.*

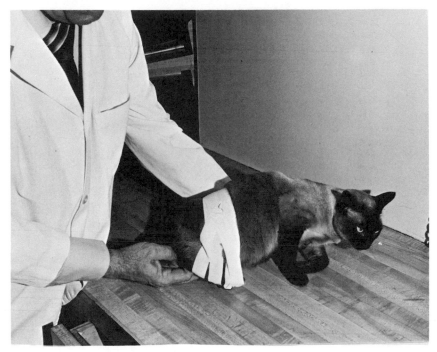

Fractures above the knee joint can be immobilized by taping the leg to the body. —*J. Clawson.*

gauze, a necktie, or anything handy. Higher fractures can be immobilized by binding the limb to the body.

If the fracture is a complete break, your veterinarian may need to reduce the fracture and return the ends of the bones to their original position. Reduction is accomplished by pulling on the limb to overcome muscle spasm (which causes shortening). Usually this requires an anesthetic. Once reduced, the position of the bones must be maintained. In general, fractures above the knee or elbow require stabilization with pins or metallic plates, while those below can be immobilized by plaster splints or casts.

Jaw fractures associated with displacement can cause malposition of the teeth. They should be adjusted and the teeth wired together to maintain the position until healing is complete.

Skull fractures pressing on the brain require surgery to elevate the depressed fragment. Cats with head injuries should be observed carefully during the first 24 hours for signs of brain swelling or intra-cranial hemorrhage (see *Brain Injury* in the chapter NERVOUS SYSTEM).

Sacrococcygeal injuries, in which the nerves to the tail are stretched rather than torn, may improve. However, if after six weeks the tail is still paralyzed it should be removed. It tends to remain soiled, gets caught in doors, and presents a significant handicap to the cat.

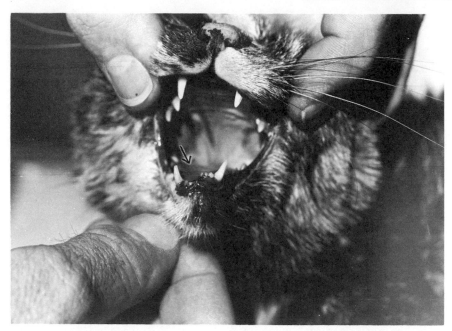

Fractured lower jaw, showing separation of the junction and malalignment of teeth.

Pelvic fractures are common. The cat is unable to bear weight on his hind limbs. This might be confused with a spinal cord injury or aortic thrombo-embolism.

Bone Infection *(Osteomyelitis)*

This problem is more common in the cat than the dog, owing to the fact that cat bites are puncture wounds which are prone to infection. An infected deep wound often progresses to involve the bone. Other causes of osteomyelitis are open fractures and surgical operations on bones.

The signs of osteomyelitis are lameness, fever, pain, swelling, and discharge through a sinus tract connecting the bone to the skin. The diagnosis is confirmed by x-ray.

Treatment: Bone infection is difficult to eliminate. Bacterial cultures aid in the selection of an appropriate antibiotic combination. Surgical cleansing with removal of devitalized bone and overlying tissue, and wide open drainage, are indicated in some cases. Treatment is prolonged.

Torn Knee Ligaments (Ruptured Cruciates)

The knee joint is stabilized by two internal ligaments called the *cruciates* which cross in the middle of the joint. They are sometimes ruptured after a fall from a building, or following an automobile accident.

Signs of injury are pain on flexing and extending the knee along with looseness of the joint. You may be able to detect a "click" in the joint, which is a slipping cartilage.

Treatment: Surgical repair of the torn ligaments is the treatment of choice. When allowed to heal spontaneously, the leg develops scar tissue around the joint which lessens its degree of mobility. Arthritis occurs later in life.

Rubber Band Around the Leg

Children occasionally put rubber bands around a cat's leg and then forget to remove them. In time, the rubber band cuts through the skin. This condition may not be noticed until the cat exhibits pain at the site of injury and has trouble putting weight on his leg.

Treatment: Surgical removal of devitalized tissue and repair of the wound, which might involve muscle and tendon, is required.

ARTHRITIS (DEGENERATIVE JOINT DISEASE)

Arthritis is a condition which can affect one or more joints in the cat. There are several different kinds of arthritis.

Osteoarthritis is the most common variety. It usually occurs in older cats as a process of aging, but can occur in younger animals as a sequel to a joint injury. Although it can begin in the first half of life, symptoms usually don't appear until much later.

Osteoarthritis is called a "degenerative" joint disease. The cartilage covering the articulating surfaces of the joints wears out and the underlying bone develops a roughened surface. This irritates the lining of joints—or in the case of the spinal column can create pressure points on the nerve roots.

Osteoarthritis is less common in cats than in dogs, and produces milder symptoms. Signs mainly are those of stiffness and lameness. Lameness usually is worse on arising but gets better as the day wears on. Spinal column involvement is called *Spondylitis*. It is the most frequent cause of significant arthritic symptoms in the cat. It is discussed in the NERVOUS SYSTEM.

Treatment: Aspirin and related drugs used to relieve pain and joint inflammation in people are toxic to cats and should not be given without veterinary approval (see DRUGS AND MEDICATIONS). Fortunately, in cats pain and/or severe lameness is infrequent and seldom produces significant disability.

Polyarthritis is an uncommon inflammatory condition that involves a number of joints. One or more viruses have been found in some cats. The feline leukemia virus has been isolated most often.

Rheumatoid arthritis is part of a generalized disease of body connective tissue. It is rare in the cat.

Septic arthritis is more common in cats than in dogs. Cats are more likely to acquire infected bite wounds which penetrate the joint. The treatment of a septic joint is like that of *Bone Infection*.

METABOLIC BONE DISORDERS

Parathyroid Bone Diseases

There are four small glands in the neck of the cat, located in proximity to the thyroid. They are called the *parathyroids*. They secrete a substance called parathyroid hormone which is essential to bone metabolism.

As the calcium level in the blood starts to fall, the parathyroid glands begin to compensate by releasing more parathyroid hormone which, in turn, raises the serum calcium level by drawing calcium out of the bones. Another stimulant to parathyroid secretion is a high serum phosphorus level. Accordingly, either a low serum calcium or a high serum phosphorus will cause an excess of parathyroid hormone in the blood. When this situation goes unchecked, the bones become demineralized, brittle, soft and cystic—and may break with even minor stress.

The following conditions are related to abnormal parathyroid gland metabolism:

Primary Hyperparathyroidism. This rare condition is due to a parathyroid gland tumor which produces excess hormone. Surgical removal of the affected gland is the only possible treatment.

Renal Secondary Hyperparathyroidism. This condition is the result of long-standing kidney disease which leads to the retention of phosphorus. The high serum phosphorus stimulates the parathyroid glands to produce excessive amounts of hormone.

Effects on bone are the same as those of Nutritional Secondary Hyperparathyroidism (discussed below). However, the symptoms are usually dominated by the kidney picture (uremia). Treatment is directed at correcting the kidney problem.

Nutritional Secondary Hyperparathyroidism (Paper Bone Disease). The cause of this nutritional bone disease is a diet which consists primarily of meat products such as beef heart, liver or kidney. Such a diet is too high in phosphorus and too low in calcium and vitamin D. (Vitamin D is necessary for calcium to be absorbed from the intestinal tract).

Kittens are especially at risk because they require large amounts of calcium for growth and development. The daily calcium, phosphorus, and Vitamin D requirements for *growing kittens* up to six months of age are:

Vitamin D: 100 I.U.; Calcium: 400 mg; Phosphorus: 320 mg.

The requirements for adult cats are one-half of the above.

If a kitten receives as his sole source of nourishment eight ounces of meat a day, he would receive only 20 mg of calcium, but 800 mg of phosphorus. This would result in overactivity of his parathyroid glands. Symptoms begin in about four weeks.

Affected kittens are reluctant to move, develop an uncoordinated gait, and sometimes lameness in the back legs. The front stance is often bowed. The thin, paper-like bones are easily fractured. These fractures, often multiple, tend to heal rapidly and may not even be recognized. Because the meat diet supplies adequate calories, kittens often appear well-nourished and have a healthy hair coat despite their metabolic bone disease.

The adult form of the disease is called *osteoporosis*. It occurs in older cats who receive large quantities of meat at the expense of other nutrients. As adult calcium requirements are lower than those from kittens, bone demineralization takes longer to occur. The first sign of demineralization often is thinning of the jaw bones with exposure of the roots of the teeth. The teeth loosen and are expelled.

Other feeding practices that can lead to osteoporosis include all vegetable diets; cornbread diets; and feeding left-over table scraps (which are frequently just vegetables).

Treatment: Dietary correction is required. Diets which meet all the nutritional requirements for growing kittens and adult cats are discussed in the chapter FEEDING AND NUTRITION.

A calcium supplement should be given when, due to advanced periodontal disease or fixed eating habits, the cat will not consume adequate amounts of the balanced ration. However, excess calcium should be avoided. Overdosing could make the situation worse, as discussed below. Vitamins A and D (and trace minerals) should be added to meet normal requirements.

Rickets (Osteomalacia)

Rickets (called *osteomalacia* in the adult) is due to a deficiency of Vitamin D. Since this vitamin is active in the absorption of calcium and phosphorus from the intestine, these minerals may be deficient also. Disease in the cat is rare because only small amounts of Vitamin D (50 to 100 I.U.) are required as a daily allowance. Many cases classified as rickets are probably due to nutritional secondary hyperparathyroidism.

Signs: There is a characteristic enlargement of the joints where the ribs meet the cartilages of the sternum (richettic rosary). Bowing of the legs and other growth deformities in the kitten, along with fractures in the adult, are common in severe cases.

Treatment: It is the same as for nutritional secondary hyperparathyroidism.

OTHER NUTRITIONAL DISORDERS

Overdosing with Vitamins

Many people believe that a rapidly growing kitten needs to have supplemental vitamins and minerals for correct health and development. Modern name-brand commercial cat rations, made up for kitten growth and development, supply all the needed vitamins and minerals to sustain normal growth, provided the kitten or young cat eats it well. Vitamins and minerals in excess of those required will not add more coat and substance to the growing animal.

When calcium, phosphorus and Vitamin D are given to a cat beyond his capacity to use them normally, his growth and development can be adversely affected. Overdosing with vitamin D causes bones to be calcified in an uneven fashion. In addition, calcium may be deposited in the lungs, heart and blood vessels.

High levels of Vitamin A produce swollen, painful joints. Growth of bone can be impaired. Knob-like deposits may develop. Lameness is common.

Vitamin and mineral supplements are most efficacious when given to queens in late pregnancy and during lactation (see PREGNANCY AND KITTENING); or to the elderly individual. They might be indicated for the occasional growing kitten who is a poor eater. In such cases, discuss this with your veterinarian.

Pansteatitis (Yellow Fat Disease)

This disease is due to a deficiency of Vitamin E. It is one of the most important vitamin deficiency diseases of cats. It occurs among cats who are fed an overabundance of unsaturated fatty acids (found especially in red meat tuna). The fatty acids oxidize and destroy Vitamin E. Moreover, canned tuna intended for human consumption is not supplemented with this vitamin.

Vitamin E deficiency produces inflammation of body fat, due to the deposit of a pigment in fat which acts like a foreign body. The fat assumes a yellow appearance and becomes tender to touch. Affected cats run fever, lose their appetite, are reluctant to move, and exhibit signs of pain when handled or stroked. Digestive disturbances, caused by inflammation and degeneration of fat in the abdomen, occasionally dominate the picture. The disease is difficult to diagnose but can be suspected by the feeding history. A fat biopsy might be needed to confirm the diagnosis.

Treatment: The disorder is corrected with a daily dose of Vitamin E. Full recovery may take weeks. It can be prevented by feeding a complete cat ration; and by feeding fish products only as occasional treats.

14

Urinary System

GENERAL INFORMATION

The urinary system is composed of the kidneys and ureters, bladder, prostate and urethra.

The kidneys are paired organs located on each side of the backbone just behind and below the last rib. Each kidney has a renal pelvis or funnel that siphons the urine into a ureter. The ureters pass on down to the pelvic brim and empty into the bladder. The passageway that connects the neck of the bladder to the outside is called the urethra. The opening of the urethra is found at the tip of the penis in the male and between the folds of the vulva in the female. In the male, the urethra also serves as a channel for semen.

The chief function of the kidneys is to maintain water and mineral balance and excrete the wastes of metabolism. This is accomplished by *nephrons,* the basic working units of the kidneys. Damage to nephrons leads to renal insufficiency (kidney failure).

Normal urine is yellow and clear. Its color can be altered by the state of hydration of the cat, and by various drugs and diseases.

The act of voiding is under the control of the central nervous system. A cat can decide when he wants to void. This is the basis for successful litter box training. But once the decision to void is reached, the actual mechanism of bladder emptying is carried out by a complicated spinal cord reflex.

Urinary Tract Infections

Bacterial urinary tract infections are not nearly as common in cats as they are in dogs, yet *urinary tract inflammation is one of the most frequent problems encountered in cats.* The reason for this is that the Feline Urologic Syndrome accounts for the great majority of feline urinary tract symptoms and, although the signs of FUS might suggest a bladder or urethral infection, recent studies have shown that in most cases a bacterial component is not a part of this disease—at least not initially. Therefore, veterinarians have had to revise their thinking

247

about the association of bacterial infections with urinary tract symptoms in the cat. Points to consider in this regard are:

1. There is a normal bacterial flora limited to the terminal portion of the cat's urethra. Accordingly, cultures taken from voided urine specimens could be contaminated and show growth of bacteria even though the bladder urine is sterile. This could lead to a misdiagnosis of bladder infection. Cultures taken by catheter or bladder puncture are more accurate.
2. The lining of the cat's urethra and bladder contains antibodies and immune substances which tend to destroy harmful bacteria. The process of emptying the bladder "flushes" out the lower system and keeps the channel clean.
3. Valves at the junction of the ureters with the bladder prevent reflux of infected urine up into the kidney.
4. The concentrated urine of cats contains acids, urea, and other substances which create an unfavorable living environment for most bacteria. Dilute urine is more supportive of bacterial growth. However, heavily concentrated urine which contains sediment is not desirable and may predispose to FUS.

Accordingly, for a cat to develop a bacterial urinary tract infection there must be some breakdown—either in local bacterial immunity or normal bladder function—which allows harmful invaders to gain a foothold, such as:

1. Repeated attacks of obstruction, which produce scarring of the urethra and further bladder outlet obstruction. The primary cause of this is FUS.
2. Repeated catheterizations of the male, which produce injury to the lining of the urethra and afford the opportunity to introduce bacteria into the bladder.
3. Tumors or growths in the bladder, and strictures of the urethra—which impair the flushing effect of urination and leave a residual pool of urine for bacterial growth.
4. Conditions in which the flow of urine is reduced, such as dehydration, kidney insufficiency, inadequate fluid intake. Occasionally a housebroken cat becomes unwilling to use his litter tray and voluntarily retains his urine.
5. A prior urinary tract infection, which leads to tissue injury and reduced local resistance. A cat who has had one urinary tract infection is at increased risk for subsequent ones.

In summary, keep in mind that signs of bladder and urethral inflammation do not always mean infection. Bacterial infections usually are preceded by some process which damages the cat's normal defense mechanisms and sets the stage for bacterial invasion. Once established, recurrent infections are common. Failure to promptly correct the initial problem makes repeated infections almost a certainty.

SIGNS OF URINARY TRACT DISEASE

Signs of urinary tract disease can be divided into two categories: those which affect the kidneys and ureters, and those which involve the bladder and urethra. In general, *any disturbance in the normal pattern of voiding suggests a problem somewhere in the urinary system.*

You should suspect a KIDNEY disorder if your cat appears to drink and/or urinate a lot more than usual; if he has fever, pain in the mid-back, and seems to move with a stiff, arched gait; if he passes bloody or cloudy urine; and if he shows signs of uremic poisoning (see *Kidney Failure*).

Signs that point toward involvement of the BLADDER or URETHRA are: obvious distress during urination (straining, dribbling, licking at the penis or vulva, crying out in pain); squatting but not passing urine (even after many tries); passing a weak, splattery stream; sudden urges to void (bladder spasms); pain and swelling in the lower abdomen (an over-distended bladder); the passage of mucus, gravel, blood clots or bloody urine; and loss of urinary control.

Due to overlapping symptoms and the fact that more than one organ may be involved at the same time, it is difficult to make an exact diagnosis on the basis of symptoms alone.

In the diagnosis of urinary tract disease, the laboratory can be of considerable help. Routine tests are a urinalysis, which tells your veterinarian whether your cat has a urinary tract inflammation, and blood chemistries, which provide information about the function of the kidneys.

Additional studies are often indicated. They include urine cultures and x-ray examinations of the abdomen. The intravenous pyelogram is an x-ray examination in which a dye is injected into the circulation. It is excreted by the kidneys and outlines much of the urinary tract.

Cystoscopy is an examination of the interior of the bladder using a lighted instrument. Other selective studies may be performed when indicated. They include surgical exploration and/or biopsy.

KIDNEY DISEASES

Infection of the Kidney and Renal Pelvis *(Pyelonephritis)*

One or both kidneys may be involved by a bacterial infection. Usually this is preceded by an infection lower in the system. There may be a blockage or congenital malformation of the urinary tract. In some cases bacteria gain entrance to the kidney via the bloodstream.

Acute pyelonephritis begins with fever and pain in the kidney area. A stiff-legged gait and a hunched-up posture are characteristic signs. Pus may appear in the urine. It is often bloody.

Chronic pyelonephritis is an insidious disease. It may be preceded by signs of acute infection but often these are lacking. When the disease is of long duration, you will see weight loss and signs of kidney failure. If chronic pyelonephritis is found before irreversible changes occur in the kidneys (for example, during a periodic health check-up) treatment may prevent complications.

Treatment: The urine should be cultured. Appropriate antibiotics are selected on the basis of bacterial sensitivity. Prolonged treatment is required.

Nephritis and Nephrosis

There are a number of uncommon diseases which produce inflammation and scarring of the kidneys with loss of functioning tissue. Most of them are progressive and lead to kidney failure. A condition called *chronic interstitial nephritis* is perhaps the most common; but even this may not be a single disease but the result of various toxins, drugs, poisons or viruses. The term "nephritis" is sometimes used to describe kidney disease, irrespective of the cause.)

Glomerulonephritis is an inflammatory disease which affects the filtering mechanism of the kidneys. The disease appears to be related to a malfunction of the cat's immune system.

Amyloidosis is a rare disorder in which a substance called amyloid is deposited in the cat's kidneys and other organs.

The *nephrotic syndrome* is a condition in which a large amount of protein leaks through the kidney filtering system and is lost in the urine. This results in abnormally low serum proteins. Protein in the serum produces a certain osmotic pressure which keeps fluid from passing out of the bloodstream into the cat's tissues. In consequence of low serum protein, there is generalized swelling of the body. The signs are similar to those of right-sided congestive heart failure. However, absence of heart disease along with low serum and high urine proteins makes it easy to distinguish these two conditions.

Treatment: These diseases usually are not recognized until the cat develops signs of uremia. A kidney biopsy usually is required to make an exact diagnosis. Steroids and special diets may be of temporary help in some cats (see treatment of *Kidney Failure*).

Kidney Failure (Uremic Poisoning)

Kidney failure is defined as inability of the kidneys to remove waste products from the blood. The build-up of toxic amounts produces signs and symptoms of uremic poisoning.

Kidney failure can come on suddenly; or it can occur gradually, perhaps over weeks or months.

Causes of *acute* kidney failure include:

1. A complete blockage in the lower urinary tract (especially *Feline Urologic Syndrome*).
2. Trauma, especially a ruptured bladder or urethra.
3. Shock, when due to sudden blood loss or rapid dehydration.
4. Arterial thromboembolism, particularly when both renal arteries are obstructed.
5. Congestive heart failure, when associated with a persistently low blood pressure (reduced circulation).

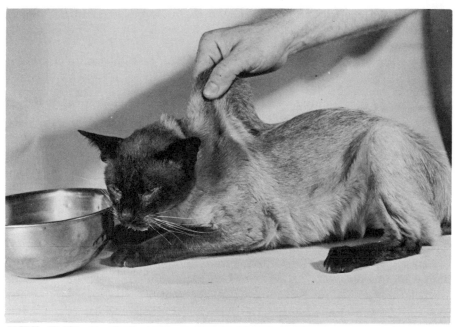

Kidney failure, **showing weight loss, dehydration, depressed sensorium, and ulcerations of the mouth.**

Causes of *chronic* renal failure include:

1. Nephritis and the nephrotic syndrome.
2. Infectious diseases (especially Feline Infectious Peritonitis and Feline Leukemia).
3. Toxins, particularly certain antibiotics which have toxic side effects when given for prolonged periods or in high doses, such as Polymyxin B, Gentamicin, Amphotericin B, and Kanamycin. Antifreeze is another poison which produces renal damage, as do some of the heavy metals (mercury, lead, thallium).
4. The aging process. Most elderly cats, if they live long enough, will have some degree of kidney insufficiency.

Cats with kidney diseases do not begin to show signs of uremia until 70 percent of their nephrons are destroyed. Thus, a considerable amount of damage can occur to the kidneys before you will begin to see signs of kidney failure.

One of the first signs of kidney failure is an increase in frequency of urination. Because the cat is voiding frequently, it might be assumed that his kidneys are functioning properly. What is actually happening is his kidneys can no longer conserve water and so he has an obligate urine output much greater than normal. He will want to go to the litter box several times a day to relieve himself, or he will begin to make mistakes in the house, especially at night. This large obligate urine output must be compensated for by increased fluid intake. Accordingly, he will need to drink a lot more than usual. A constant supply of clean fresh water should be made available at all times. This step is important in helping the cat adjust to his reduced kidney function.

As his renal function continues to deteriorate, he will begin to retain ammonia, nitrogen, acids and other waste products in his bloodstream and tissues (uremic poisoning). Signs of uremia are apathy and depression, refusal to eat, loss of weight and condition, dry hair-coat, a brownish discoloration to the surface of the tongue, ulcers on the gums and tongue, and an ammonia-like odor to the breath. Vomiting, diarrhea, anemia, and episodes of gastrointestinal bleeding can occur. Terminally, the cat falls into a coma.

The outlook for a cat with kidney failure depends upon a number of factors. They include the extent of permanent damage to his kidneys; the rate of progress of the underlying disease; and whether the underlying disease can be improved by treatment. Acute failure of sudden onset often can be reversed. Chronic progressive disease, over months or years, has a poor outlook. The goal of treatment here is to lessen the work load on the kidneys.

Treatment: A cat suffering from chronic kidney failure still can have many happy months or years of life ahead of him with proper treatment. Your veterinarian may want to make an exact diagnosis by ordering special tests, or by exploratory surgery and biopsy. This helps to determine whether the ailment is reversible.

Most cases of chronic renal insufficiency occur in cats who have sustained irreversible damage to their kidneys. It is extremely important in these individuals to be sure they take in enough water to compensate for their large urine outputs. Fresh clean water should be available at all times. Your veterinarian may recommend adding salt to your cat's food each day to stimulate thirst. The amount depends upon the size of the individual and the response.

The diet of a uremic cat should be of high quality but rather low in protein to minimize the nitrogen load. Special diets (such as *Hill's Feline K/D*) are available through your veterinarian. Large amounts of B Vitamins are lost in the urine of uremic cats. These losses should be met by giving Vitamin B supplements. Sodium bicarbonate tablets may be required to maintain correct acid/base balance. They also provide additional salt.

A uremic cat who becomes ill, dehydrated, or fails to drink enough water may suddenly decompensate (*uremic crisis*). He should be hospitalized and rehydrated with appropriate intravenous fluids. Excessive amounts of acid in the blood should be neutralized with intravenous sodium bicarbonate.

Some exercise is good for a uremic cat, but stressful activity should be avoided.

Tumors

Kidney tumors are rare in cats. However, the kidney is involved in 20 to 30 percent of cases of feline lymphosarcoma. Therefore, when a growth or mass occurs in the kidney, the prime consideration is lymphosarcoma. This disease is discussed in the chapter INFECTIOUS DISEASES.

Congenital Defects

Cats may be born with malformations of the kidneys. They include cystic kidneys, malpositions, and incomplete developments. Such defects often are accompanied by abnormalities in the reproductive system.

Severe defects produce neonatal death. Others do not produce symptoms until later in life, when kidney damage has progressed to the point of failure.

Obstructions in the urinary tract also can cause cystic kidneys. It might be difficult to tell whether the condition is congenital or acquired. This could make a difference in treatment. Veterinary evaluation is desirable.

DISEASES OF THE BLADDER AND URETHRA

In the lower urinary tract there are two basic problems: the feline urologic syndrome and urinary tract infections, primarily cystitis. One other problem is loss of voluntary control over the act of voiding—which leads to *dribbling*.

Feline Urologic Syndrome (FUS)

This is the most common disorder affecting the lower urinary tract in male cats. It is by far the major health concern of cat owners despite the fact that it affects only about 1% of all cats. One reason for this is that FUS has a 50 to 70 percent rate of recurrence.

FUS, also called the "blocked cat", or "plugged penis" syndrome, can include any or all of the following: (1) cystitis; (2) urethritis; (3) urethral plugs containing little mineral content; and (4) urinary stones. Young, inactive males are most often affected. The disease is most common in the winter months.

FUS is caused by plugging of the urethra by a paste-like, gritty or sandy material, composed primarily of mucus and struvite crystals (magnesium - ammonium - phosphate) which are about the size of salt. The chief signs of FUS are frequent voiding, straining with partial or complete urethral obstruction, and the passage of blood in the urine.

Straining to urinate could be mistaken for constipation. However, the behavior of the cat makes this difference obvious. A cat who is unable to pass urine wanders about the house restlessly, turns and repeatedly licks at his penis, and often attempts to pass urine in places other than his litter box. Instead of squatting close to the ground in the usual fashion, he often adopts a characteristic attitude in which he attempts to void from a standing position.

Major obstructions can occur with the first episode or during subsequent attacks. With back-pressure on the kidneys, toxic wastes build up in the bloodstream, leading to uremia. Loss of functioning kidney tissue could be irreversible. Thus, it is of vital importance to relieve the obstruction as soon as this condition is suspected. Keep in mind that cats will often seek seclusion when ill or in pain. Therefore, a cat with an obstructed bladder should not be allowed outdoors.

Feline Urologic Syndrome. Note the mucus plug at the tip of the penis.

By massaging the penis, the plug can sometimes be expelled.

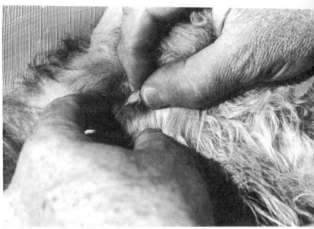

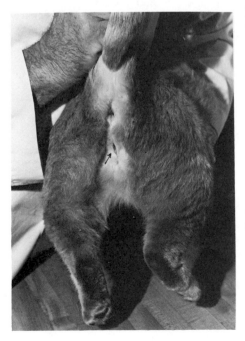

In *perineal urethrostomy,* the penis is removed to enlarge the urethral opening. The cat is able to control his urine.

Causes of FUS. The exact cause of FUS is unknown. A number of theories have been advanced:

1. Three viruses have been isolated and found experimentally to produce symptoms of the disease in some cats. Not all investigators have been able to confirm these findings.
2. Castration of the male has been advanced as a cause. Early castration, before sexual maturity, is believed to interfere with growth of the adult male urethra. One survey revealed no difference in the size of the penile urethra among castrated and non-castrated males.
3. Bacterial cystitis and urethritis have long been accepted as a basic cause. Current research indicates that bacteria are not involved in most cases, at least not initially. However, bacterial cystitis may be a very important cause of recurrent attacks. Keep in mind that the potential for infection increases with obstruction.
4. Urinary sediment has received a great deal of attention. Struvite crystals constitute a major part of some plugs; but other crystals are sometimes found. Some plugs are composed primarily of mucus, blood and white cells. FUS has been produced by feeding high levels of magnesium and phosphorus. However, the amounts are many times those found in commercial cat foods.

   On the other hand, in one study taking just those cats who had had at least one episode of FUS, feeding a diet low in magnesium led to a significant reduction in the recurrence rate.
5. The acidity of the urine is another consideration. Struvite crystals form more readily in an alkaline urine. Acid urine is theoretically protective, and also has antibacterial properties. However, many cases of FUS occur in cats with acid urine.
6. Diet and water intake have been proposed as contributing factors. Cats who eat dry food take in less water with their meals, and also lose more water in their stools. Presumably dry cat food leads to a more concentrated urine and a greater amount of sediment. Another theory is that twice as much dry food is needed to meet caloric requirements, therefore twice as much magnesium is taken in each day.

In summary, no one theory accounts for all cases. It seems likely that any inflammatory condition of the lower urinary tract is partially obstructive in male cats. Therefore viruses, bacteria, urinary retention, reduced water intake, dietary administration of sediment precursors, and perhaps other factors could all be contributory. The higher incidence among inactive males in winter might be due to decreased water intake, reduced frequency of urination, increased concentration of urine, and the subsequent higher rates of sediment formation.

As a result of one or more bouts of FUS, some cats develop scarring which narrows their urethra. This predisposes them to further attacks, and to bacterial cystitis.

Treatment of FUS. A cat with a plugged penis is in need of immediate veterinary attention. An obstructed male often protrudes his penis. You can massage the penis by rolling it between your thumb and index finger. This might crush the plug and allow the material to be expelled. If this is not successful, immediate veterinary attention is required. In most cases a small soft rubber or flexible polyethylene catheter can be inserted through the urethra into the bladder to relieve the obstruction, usually under sedation or anesthesia. Intravenous fluids are frequently given to rehydrate the cat and encourage the flow of urine. Antibiotics are prescribed to prevent or treat an associated bladder infection.

Prevention. Recurrent attacks are common. This suggests that (a) the initial attack produced scarring which potentiates further attacks; or (b) factors which caused the initial attack have not been corrected. The following steps should be taken to eliminate excessive urinary sediment and/or infection:

1. Keep the litter box clean. It should be changed every day. Some cats refuse to use a dirty litter box. This could result in voluntary retention.
2. Encourage water consumption by keeping clean fresh water available at all times.
3. Feed a restricted magnesium diet. Based on currently available research data, the optimum dietary magnesium level for prevention of recurrence of FUS is less than 0.1% dry weight basis (DWB). Few commercial cat foods meet these requirements. Hill's C/D is a prescription diet low in sediment precursors and high in water content. It is available through veterinarians.
4. Prevent obesity. Maintain normal body weight by restricting food intake as discussed in the chapter FEEDING AND NUTRITION.
5. If urinary tract infection is present, treat with an appropriate antibiotic for three or more weeks. Wait one week and then reculture. If the culture is positive, administer a second course of antibiotic. Your veterinarian may prescribe a long-term urinary antiseptic such as Methenamine to prevent recurrences. It is given on a daily basis.
6. The use of supplemental salt and urinary acidifiers may be recommended in certain cases. Mix thoroughly into the daily ration ½ teaspoon of table salt and ¼ teaspoon of ammonium chloride. Salt increases water intake and therefore urinary excretion. Ammonium chloride acidifies the urine, which increases the solubility of struvite crystals. (*Caution:* Avoid urinary acidifiers if the cat is uremic. This could predispose to the development of an acid-base imbalance and lead to uremic crisis.)

Cats with repeated attacks who fail to respond to the preventive measures listed above should undergo a complete urologic work-up, searching for bladder stones or other abnormalities in the urinary tract. In some cases no correctable condition is found. In such cases your veterinarian may suggest an operation in which part of the penis is removed to enlarge the urethral opening. The operation is called *perineal urethrostomy*. It is usually quite successful, especially when FUS is complicated by an overdistended, poorly contracting bladder. When the cat recovers, he will still be able to control his urine and use the litter pan.

Finally, should all adult male cats be placed on a magnesium restricted diet as a prophylactic measure to prevent FUS?

Considering that 99 percent of cats are not affected by FUS no matter what they eat, and that there are other factors besides diet which may be important in the etiology of this syndrome, feeding a severely restricted magnesium diet such as Hill's C/D to all cats is probably not justified. If you are concerned about FUS and want to do everything possible to prevent it, you could choose to feed, as a cost-effective alternative, a moderately restricted magnesium diet such as *Science Diet Feline*.

Cystitis

Cystitis is the name given to an infection of the bladder. It is the most common urinary tract disorder in female cats. The majority of cases are caused by bacteria which ascend upward from the vagina and urethra. For bacterial growth to occur, there must be a break in the defense mechanism of the lower urinary tract. The reasons for this are discussed above (see *Urinary Tract Infections*). In males, most cases of cystitis are associated with or preceded by a bout of FUS.

A female with cystitis may have a discharge from her vagina and lick at her vulva. Other characteristic signs of cystitis are frequent urination, straining to void, and the passage of blood or traces of blood in the urine.

In the male, these signs should make you think of FUS. Palpate the lower abdomen and feel for a swollen, distended bladder just in front of the pubic bone. It is important not to overlook this possibility as an obstructed bladder requires urgent veterinary attention.

Treatment: Cystitis should be treated promptly to prevent ascending infection and damage to the kidneys. An appropriate antibiotic combination can be determined by your veterinarian. An initial attack should be treated for ten days and a recurrent attack for at least three weeks.

Cystitis, like FUS, can be a recurrent problem. Prevent further attacks by using the methods described under *Feline Urologic Syndrome*.

Bladder Stones

True bladder stones, as distinguished from the very small crystalline material that produces the plugged penis syndrome, do occur in cats occasionally—especially queens. Stone formation is one aftermath of recurrent urinary tract infections.

Stones irritate the bladder wall, prolong infection, and produce symptoms much like those of cystitis. They are treated by surgical removal.

Kidney stones, which are common in people, are almost unknown in the cat.

Urinary Incontinence

Incontinence is defined as loss of voluntary control over the act of voiding. It should be distinguished from lapses in house-training and psychological causes, which are discussed in the chapter FELINE BEHAVIOR AND TRAINING (see *Soiling in the House*).

In cats, a common cause of incontinence is loss of bladder tone as a result of recurrent attacks of urinary retention associated with FUS. Having been repeatedly over-distended, the bladder loses its power of contraction. A more or less constant dribbling of urine occurs from the inert, overloaded bladder. Perineal uretherostomy is most beneficial when used in the treatment of this complication (see *Feline Urologic Syndrome*).

Another cause of incontinence is cystitis, especially when associated with an irritated bladder. The irritable bladder goes into spasm, producing a voiding urge which comes on suddenly before the cat can get to the litter box. This type of incontinence improves with treatment of cystitis. However, after many attacks, the bladder sometimes becomes shrunken and scarred. This is accompanied by loss of urethral outlet control. This condition is difficult to improve.

Damage to the nerves of the bladder (spinal cord diseases, trauma, brain tumor) also can lead to loss of bladder (and bowel) control.

Treatment of incontinence is directed at finding the underlying cause and correcting it if possible. Drugs which act on the bladder muscle may be useful in selected cases.

15

Sex and Reproduction

BREEDING

Pedigreed Cats

The majority of cats living as household pets are not purebreds. They are born of parents who are themselves unregistered, and in most cases are of mixed ancestry. Such cats are called *freebreds*. But certainly for intelligence, hardiness, utility and charm, a freebred kitten is every bit as likely to be a pleasing companion as one with a blue-ribbon ancestry.

For pedigreed owners there is the distinction of owning a cat that has a very distinguished family background and conforms to a set standard, which is essential if serious breeding is anticipated. Then too there are those who are attracted to the body, form, expression, coat-coloring, or some other characteristic of a particular breed.

What constitutes a "breed" of cat can be a matter of interpretation. In a practical sense it is a group of cats having in common a unique body conformation and structure, color and/or pattern of coat, hair type, and geographic place of origin.

Whereas the selective breeding of dogs for many centuries has resulted in the establishment of well-defined breeds based upon similarities of head type, size and body structure, the physical differences among cats are not so pronounced. One reason for this is that up until the middle of the last century cats were kept primarily as companions and for general utility. Little regard was given to selecting for features that would set one cat breed apart from another.

But with the advent of cat exhibitions in Great Britain and North America, interest began in breeding cats to meet certain physical and aesthetic requirements. As the merits of one individual were judged against another of the same general type, the need to develop new standards to describe the "ideal" for each breed was realized. Afterwards, cat fanciers became dedicated to maintaining these standards.

There are at least 36 recognized breeds of cat and as many color varieties. Features which distinguish one breed from another can be found in the shape of

The *Persian,* with his long fine-textured coat, full mane and tail, massive rounded head with short nose and small wide-set ears, gives one the overall impression of strength and dignity. —*Sydney Wiley.*

The *Siamese* is an elegant individual with his long wedge-shaped head, slanted vivid blue eyes, and large pointed ears. —*Sydney Wiley.*

The *Himalayan* is a man-made breeding having the head type and full coat of the Persian, but with the pale coloring and darker parts of the Siamese. —*Sydney Wiley.*

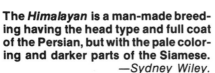

the face and ears; the length and character of the coat; the color and distribution of markings; and differences in body length, size and bone structure.

The Persian is currently the most popular breed—as determined by the number of kittens registered each year. Next is the Himalayan, followed by the Siamese, Burmese and Abyssinian. There are many other breeds from which to choose; but specimens are more difficult to come by, owing to their relative scarcity.

Registration. While the American Kennel Club serves as an official registering body for dogs in the United States, in the cat fancy there are a number of such organizations, both here and abroad, which recognize and register various breeds of cat. Many countries, such as Great Britain, have a single official organization (the *Governing Council of the Cat Fancy*)—but other countries have several, sometimes formed on regional lines or by fanciers who disagree with the policies of a particular organization. In the United States there are several such organizations. They are listed in the APPENDIX. *The Cat Fanciers' Association* (CFA) is the largest and oldest in the U.S. The *Cat Fanciers Federation* has a large membership on the East Coast.

Each organization has its own registering procedures. Cross-recognition of pedigrees, and standards for particular breeds, may vary from one organization to another. In addition, the organizations do not always agree with each other as to what constitutes a distinct breed as opposed to a color variety within an existing breed. You can write to these organizations to receive further information. Cat clubs, breeders, and veterinarians also can provide advice.

If you wish to register your cat with the CFA or some other organization, the individual must be *purebred.* This means that the cat will need to have a pedigree, usually containing at least four generations, showing that all his ancestors are representative specimens of the breed. When you purchase a purebred kitten, your breeder should be able to provide such a pedigree. He or she may even have pre-registered the entire litter. In that case you should receive a form which must be filled out and sent to the registering agency, a step that is necessary to enroll your individual kitten.

Genetics and Planned Breeding

Heredity is subject to the random combination of countless genes. The smallest combination of genes that can determine an inherited trait is a pair. A pair is called an *allele.* One gene is inherited from each parent. When they combine to form the allele, the *dominant* gene is the one that determines the expression of the trait. The other gene is called a *recessive.*

For example, if a kitten inherits a dominant gene for black coat and a recessive gene for blue, his coat will be black. Recessive genes can determine a trait too, but only when paired together. A kitten who inherits two recessive genes for a blue coat will be blue. Still other genes are *additive,* the trait being expressed by the combined effects of two or more of them.

The domestic cat has 38 chromosomes and each chromosome contains more than 25,000 genes. Although this permits a vast array of potential combinations, only a small number are actually concerned with the bodily features that together define a breed or variety. The great majority are simply responsible for the smooth functioning of the many aspects of the cat's physiology.

When both genes in an allele are identical, the cat is said to be *homozygous* for the physical trait the allele determines. When they are different, the cat is *heterozygous*.

The stud and queen are equally responsible for determining the inheritance of their kittens. When both parents have identical homozygous alleles (either dominant or recessive), it doesn't matter how the genes assort, as in any case all their kittens will inherit the same allele and all will express the same physical trait as did their parents.

In essence, this is the strategy behind most planned breeding programs. The relationship between the various breeding individuals is kept rather close, so as to concentrate the desired genes in the breeding stock. The method is called *inbreeding*. It is discussed below.

A number of different breeds and varieties of the domestic cat have arisen through the accidental or "spontaneous" appearance of *mutant* genes. Mutant genes occur rarely, perhaps once in a million offspring. Accordingly, it is not surprising that cat breeders have adopted only about 20 such mutations, despite the large number of cats bred each year. When they do occur, mutant genes are passed along like any others and follow the same rules. Most, but not all of them, are recessives.

The most important mutant genes for breeders are those producing distinctive coat colors. There are only 12 of these, but in various combinations they are responsible for a wide range of cat breeds and varieties. The length and texture of the coat is also an essential feature of many breeds. There are at least five such coat mutants which have been adopted.

A few breeds are based upon a bodily characteristic caused by a single mutant gene. Best known is the Manx breed, in which a dominant gene causes the tail to be deformed or absent.

Desirable and undesirable traits can be caused by both dominant and recessive genes. The Scottish Fold breed, for example, is based upon the expression of a single dominant gene that causes the tip of the ear to bend forward, giving the breed its characteristic look.

A completely unrelated dominant gene affecting all breeds is the gene for extra toes (*polydactyly*). Extra toes, sometimes as many as seven, are found usually on the front feet (see PEDIATRICS).

Another dominant gene which may be associated with deleterious side effects is the gene for the completely white coat. This gene also predisposes to a form of deafness which affects one or both ears. Although deafness is more common in white cats with blue eyes, it also occurs in white cats with orange ones.

In a typical short-coated cat, the length of the guard hair is about 5 centimeters. In contrast, the silky abundant coat of a long-haired exhibition specimen may exceed twice that length. This difference is due to a recessive gene which appears to prolong the period of growth in hair follicles, so that the hair reaches a greater length before entering the dormant phase. Selective breeding

The *Burmese* also is a man-made breed, derived from Siamese and Asiatic crosses. The short rounded head, wide-set ears, and rounded almond-shaped eyes give the breed its distinctive expression.
—*Sydney Wiley.*

The tailless *Manx* has a distinctive appearance. The breed originated on the Isle of Man in the Irish Sea, as the result of a spontaneous mutation. Lack of a tail is no handicap. The Manx is known as a fast runner and agile climber. —*Sydney Wiley.*

Scottish Folds first appeared in Scotland as the result of a spontaneous mutation in the 1960's. The uniquely folded ears, short nose and large round eyes, give to the head an almost completely round look. —*Sydney Wiley.*

over many generations for this long-haired homozygous recessive coat trait has resulted in the fuller and more silky coat seen in Persians and some other long-coated breeds.

An example of the *additive* effect of multiple genes is seen in the wide range of eye colors typical of many cats. The colors orange, yellow, hazel and green are determined by additive genes. In the Siamese and white breeds, however, eye color is determined by major genes.

Body structure and conformation is another multiple-gene effect. In various combinations, polygenes influence the rate of bone growth, the development of muscle, and deposition of fat.

Breeding cats to a high degree of excellence demands careful attention to detail and great patience. The modern breeder has far more information on cat genetics than existed in the past, and he or she also has the product of many generations of selective breeding upon which to base a successful program.

The object of any breeding program is to preserve the essential qualities and attributes of the breed. Accordingly, a thorough understanding of the breed standard is a basic requirement.

Pedigrees are important because they are the means to study the bloodlines and learn the relationships between the various individuals. They are of the greatest value when the individual cats are known, or actually have been seen. A pedigree only assures that the animals in the breeding program are registered specimens of the breed. It does not necessarily testify as to the actual quality of the cats in question.

Championships do indicate merit and do give some indication of quality. However, they are not always completely informative as to the overall superiority of the individuals listed. Some championships are won through the accident of less than normal quality in the competition. The opposite is also true, some cats do not win their medals because of lack of exposure.

A subject that concerns many breeders is the matter of inbreeding. Close inbreeding involves the mating of parent to offspring and brother to sister. Less close is the mating of half-blood relations, such as half-brother and sister, grandparent and grandchild, and cousins.

As mentioned above, the consequence of repeated inbreeding is to make the strain increasingly homozygous. By always selecting kittens showing the physical attributes in question, the "purity" of the strain is increased. This strategy is the one most often used by cat breeders to increase the frequency with which desired traits are expressed, while eliminating unwanted ones from the bloodline.

Inbreeding by itself is neither good nor bad. It is a process which exposes both good and bad qualities in the stock. If the strain does carry a recessive mutant gene (which in the nature of things is more likely to be harmful than beneficial), then this is more likely to become quickly apparent with inbreeding. This might be a disaster in the short-term, but exposure is in the long-term best interests of the breed.

Since it is the genetic potential of the individuals in the background which determines success, they should possess outstanding qualities worthy of being passed on to their offspring. The breeder should possess a knowledge of the virtues and faults of all the common cats in the pedigree for at least three generations. He or she should have the judgment and experience to pick the best kittens, and the willingness to eliminate (as breeding animals) all defective or substandard specimens.

Close inbreeding for three to four generations generally leads to fixation of type, after which further improvement becomes more difficult. At this point the vitality of the strain may begin to suffer. There could be an increased incidence of reproductive failure and/or a lessened resistance to disease. Most breeders have found from experience that it is wise to bring in new blood. The use of a stud from a different bloodline may be considered. This produces an *outcross* litter and "reshuffles" the genes that have tended to become fixed in a more or less predictable manner through previous inbreeding. An improvement in the health and vigor of the resulting kittens may be apparent from the time they are born. These kittens are then bred back into the original strain.

A single outcross can be advantageous—but the continuous use of outcrosses, or the mating of animals who are not related with the hope of finding complimentary qualities, is rarely rewarding. It merely breaks up a carefully built-up genetic constitution and nullifies any progress that has been made in improving the strain.

The Queen

Queen is the name given to a breeding female.

If you are planning to breed pedigreed cats, it is best to start with a good female kitten with an outstanding pedigree. It is not a good idea to start with a stud. The management of a stud requires considerable experience and expertise; and if he does not have a reputation and at least a championship, it is not likely that he will attract many good queens for breeding. It is equally unwise to buy unrelated male and female kittens in the hope that when they grow up they will be suitable breeding partners.

Before you make the decision to breed your female, give careful thought to the effort and expense which goes into producing a litter of healthy and active kittens. It can be both time-consuming and expensive. Many purebred kittens cannot be sold locally. This means advertising and the added cost and effort of finding the right sort of home in which to place them.

If you decide not to breed your queen, she should be spayed (see *Birth Control*).

It is safe to mate a queen on her second heat, usually after she is ten to twelve months old. At this age she is physically and emotionally mature and able to adjust well to motherhood.

The frequency with which a queen can be mated depends on the size of her litters, her general health and nutrition, the adequacy of her quarters, and the ease with which the kittens can be sold. A valuable queen in a cattery, if properly cared for and in the prime of life, may be permitted to have two or three litters a year. Overweight queens, and those who are metabolically depleted by improper diet, excessive breeding, and unsanitary living conditions, are unsuitable brood matrons. Often they do not come into season regularly, are difficult to breed, experience problems during delivery, and are unable to properly care for their kittens.

Once you decide to mate your queen, take her to your veterinarian for a physical check-up. She should be examined to see that her vaginal opening is of normal size and that there are no obstructions to successful intromission. She should be vaccinated against Feline Panleukopenia, Feline Viral Rhinotracheitis, and Feline Calcivirus (see *Vaccinations* in the chapter INFECTIOUS DISEASES.) A stool test will show whether she has roundworms, tapeworms, or some other intestinal parasite. If found, they should be vigorously treated. A queen with an active worm infestation is less likely to give birth to healthy kittens.

Part of the breeding preparation is to choose the stud well in advance. The show record of a prospective stud may include a Championship or a Grand Championship. If he has had a career as a producer, his record becomes a matter of considerable importance. If he has sired outstanding kittens, particularly if several different queens were used, you have strong evidence of his potency. The number of show winners he has produced is also of importance. However, as there can be a lapse of several years before a mating and a championship, some of the best producers are often recognized well after they have stopped producing.

If your queen came from a breeding establishment, it is a good idea to talk to your breeder before making a final selection. Your breeder will be familiar with the strengths and weakness which lie behind your queen. This knowledge can be vitally important in choosing a compatible mate.

Some breeding catteries offer stud services. If you have an outstanding queen from that bloodline, you may give serious thought to using a stud from that same strain to reinforce the best qualities of your queen.

It is the responsibility of the *breeder* (who is the owner of the queen) to come to a clear understanding with the owner of the stud concerning breeding terms. Usually a stud fee is paid at the time of the mating, or the stud's owner may agree to take "pick of the litter", which is a kitten of his own choosing. The age of the kitten should be agreed upon. If the queen does not conceive, the stud's owner may offer a return service at no extra charge. However, this is not obligatory in any way. Terms vary with the circumstances and the policies of the owner of the stud. If these are in writing, there will be no misunderstandings at a later date.

The Stud

Stud (or *Tom*) is the name given to a breeding male.

The age at which a male cat reaches sexual maturity and begins to produce sperm varies from six to 18 months but the average is about nine months. Two months later, sperm are present in the collecting tubules. He has reached sexual maturity and can now fertilize a queen. Ordinarily a stud should not be used for breeding before he is a year old. If he is to be shown, it may be two years before he is available.

An active tom has a natural instinct to spray his surroundings with strong-smelling urine. A pen with a house and spacious run is therefore highly desirable.

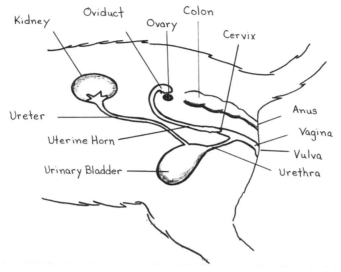

Female Genitourinary System.—*Rose Floyd.*

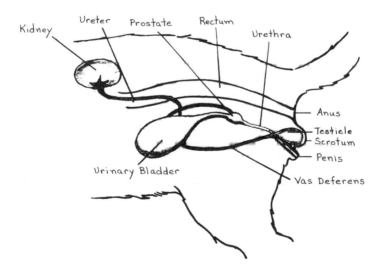

Male Genitourinary System.—*Rose Floyd.*

A stud should be given frequent human contact. He should be maintained in top physical condition with regular exercise, routine health check-ups and a sound diet. A young healthy stud in top condition can service two queens a week.

His first matings should be with queens who have already had a litter. The mating of two inexperienced animals can be fraught with difficulty and frustration.

If you own a male cat and do not plan to use him at stud he should be neutered (see *Birth Control*).

The Estrus Cycle (Heat Cycle)

Queens vary in the age at which they first "call" or go into heat. Some breeds (such as the Siamese) may call as early as five months of age. Others, particularly the long-haired breeds of Persian type, are not sexually mature until ten months or older.

Mating Seasons. The mating seasons of cats are determined by a number of factors, among them the length of daylight, temperature, and presence of other cats. When conditions are optimal, a hormonal system is activated and the queen begins her reproductive cycle. The usual mating seasons are early spring and again in late summer and fall; but queens who live indoors in controlled lighting or in warm climates may cycle all year round. Cats in the southern hemisphere cycle opposite to those in the northern.

During the mating season a queen will go into and out of heat several times. During each heat cycle she is sexually receptive and able to conceive.

Signs of Heat. The estrus or reproductive cycle of cats is divided into four distinct phases. There is great individual variation in length of phases from one queen to another. Furthermore, the signs of one often overlap those of the next. Accordingly, it is not always possible to be certain when a queen is most likely to conceive. Vaginal cytology, in the hands of one who is experienced in the technique, can be of aid in predicting the moment of peak fertility in the difficult queen (see *Shy Breeders—Cats That Won't Mate*).

The four phases of the heat cycle are:

Proestrus. This is the first stage of heat. It lasts from one to three days. You may notice that the vulva enlarges slightly and appears somewhat moist, but this is easily missed. The queen shows increased appetite and restlessness, utters short low calls, and displays more than usual affection for her owner. At this time she begins to attract toms—but refuses to mate.

Proestrus has been thought of as a period of courtship, during which exposure to the male acts as a hormonal stimulus which brings on full heat rapidly. This belief stems from the fact that in street matings, where male companionship is common, there is a higher conception rate than in catteries, where courtship is less frequent and spontaneous.

Estrus. The second phase of the reproductive cycle is the period of sexual receptivity. It is what breeders refer to as *heat,* or the *call.* It lasts from four to six

Estrus. **The characteristic stance of a queen in heat.**

days if the queen is mated, and ten to 14 days if she is not. The queen begins to make more noise and her meow is louder and more frequent. There is an obvious change in her behavior. She becomes much more affectionate toward people, weaves in and out and rubs against their legs, shakes her pelvis and rolls about on the floor. As the urge to mate becomes pronounced, her cries grow stronger and stronger, sounding much more like that of an animal in pain. This is the call, which attracts toms from near and far. It can be quite frightening to the un-initiated cat owner.

To tell if your queen is receptive to mating, hold her by the scruff of her neck with one hand and stroke her down her back near the base of her tail with the other (or stroke her vulvar area). If in heat, she will raise her hindquarters, switch her tail to the side, and tread up and down with her hind feet.

As soon as you suspect your queen is in heat, take steps to prevent an un-wanted pregnancy (see *Accidental Pregnancy*).

During the breeding season most females experience a new heat phase every two to three weeks, but there are many exceptions. Some queens go into heat once a month and others, more rarely, just once or twice during the season. Each queen establishes her own normal rhythm and, once established, it tends to repeat itself. Abnormal heat cycles are discussed in the section *Infertility*.

Metestrus. The third phase of the reproductive cycle is the least distinct. Some people include it in the estrus phase because it is of short duration (24 hours). During this phase the queen aggressively rejects the stud if intercourse is attempted.

What happens now depends upon what happened during estrus:

If the queen was successfully bred and becomes pregnant, gestation lasts from 58 to 70 days. See PREGNANCY AND KITTENING.

If the mating was sterile, she enters a period of false pregnancy lasting 30 to 45 days. See *False Pregnancy*.

If a mating did not take place, she enters a period of sexual inactivity lasting 14 to 28 days (with an average of 21 days), and afterwards begins a new cycle.

Anestrus. The fourth stage of the sexual cycle is a period of reproductive rest. It lasts until the beginning of the next breeding season (about 90 days).

Hormonal Influences During Estrus

Pituitary Influence. Proestrus begins when the brain (hypothalmus) signals the pituitary gland to release FSH (follicle stimulating hormone) which causes the ovaries to grow the egg follicles and begin to make estrogen.

Physical stimulation of the queen's vagina by the male's penis during sexual intercourse again signals the pituitary gland, this time to release a hormone called LH (leutinizing hormone), which serves two functions. It stimulates the ovaries to release the eggs (ovulation); and it causes the egg follicles to become corpus leuteal cysts and manufacture progesterone.

Ovarian Influence. Under the influence of FSH, the ovaries produce the female hormone estrogen, which prepares the queen's reproductive tract for mating and fertilization. It also accounts for the physical and behavioral changes of the queen in heat.

After ovulation, the egg follicles make less estrogen and begin to produce progesterone (the pregnancy hormone). An important function of progesterone is to prepare the lining of the uterus to receive the fertilized eggs. This function can be blocked by giving an injection of estrogen within two days of mating (see *Accidental Pregnancy*).

The egg follicles now become small cystic structures (corpus lutea) whose purpose is to continue to make progesterone and support the pregnancy. Removal of the ovaries in the first 50 days of pregnancy, or inadequate output of progesterone from the ovaries during this period, will result in abortion (see *Fetal Loss During Pregnancy*).

Ovulation. Cats are unusual in that they are *induced* ovulators. This means that unlike the dog, and most other mammals including women, they do not ovulate spontaneously. Instead, ovulation is induced by the act (or multiple acts) of sexual intercourse, during which the female's vagina is stimulated by barb-like projections on the male's penis.

Usually four eggs are released from the ovaries. This is variable. Up to 18 kittens have been reported in a single litter.

Ovulation takes place about 24 to 30 hours after intercourse. This too is variable. Some queens ovulate as early as 12 hours after intercourse. Once a queen has ovulated, she loses her interest in sex and will refuse to mate.

It is possible to artifically induce ovulation by stimulating the queen's vagina with a plastic rod. This simulates a mating and induces a false pregnancy which lasts 35 to 44 days. It is a method of bringing the queen out of heat (see *Birth Control*).

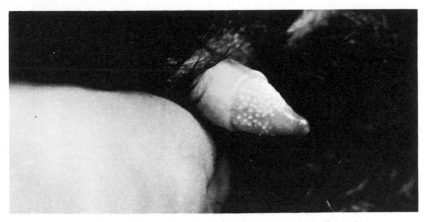

A protruded male penis, showing the characteristic spines.

Fertilization

Fertilization occurs in the fallopian tubes which lead from the ovaries to the uterus. Fertilized eggs implant in the wall of the uterus some 14 days after mating.

While only one sperm can fertilize each egg, a queen who has mated with a number of different toms could produce a litter of kittens having different fathers. This phenomenon is called *superfecundity*.

Although ovulation and pregnancy normally suppress the estrus cycle, about ten percent of queens go back into heat and may even be willing to breed. In such circumstances the act of mating again induces ovulation, with the result that a second litter is conceived. The two litters can subsequently be born at the same time (in which cases the second is premature and seldom survives), or the second litter can be born alive a few weeks after the first. This phenomenon is known as *superfetation*.

MATING

Getting Ready

Once the signs of estrus are confirmed, the owner of the stud should be notified. He may want the queen at once. This has the advantage of letting her settle into her new surroundings before the mating.

If at all possible you should take the queen to the stud yourself, transporting her in a suitable container or cage. If the distance is too great, you might have to ship her by air. However, such a trip can be nerve-racking and may upset the queen and put her off her call.

The stud's owner may require a certificate showing that she is free of Feline Leukemia.

Normal Mating Procedure

Ideally, the queen's container is placed in a pen next to the stud's. The door of her cage is opened to allow her to come out as she chooses and explore her surroundings. Once the queen approaches the dividing wire and begins to make overtures to the stud, a gate is opened to allow the queen to enter his pen.

If adjoining pens are not available and the mating is to be carried out in the house instead, the method of introducing the cats can be modified to suit the circumstances.

It is most important that the stud's owner (or someone familiar with the mating of cats) be present to observe the mating. Even when both cats are experienced, their courtship and mating can become quite violent. Some cats will refuse to mate when a person is present. The owner should stay out of sight but be in a position where he or she can observe the mating and still step in quickly if it becomes apparent that the stud or queen may be injured.

A sexually receptive queen will allow the stud to approach her, touch noses, lick her face and investigate her genital area. This necessary ceremony of greeting and foreplay helps to initiate sexual arousal. In most cases it provides sufficient stimulus for a mature queen to adopt a characteristic position in which she crouches down, raises her pelvis, and switches her tail to the side.

If the queen is insufficiently aroused or not far enough along in estrus to be willing to breed, she will growl at the male and try to bite him. The stud, on the other hand, may become quite aggressive if he finds it difficult to get the queen into position for mounting. At this point the pair should be separated. A frightening experience can be a serious setback to future mating attempts.

Once the female assumes the receptive position, the stud will approach her from the rear and mount her, clasping her by the sides with his front legs. He then seizes her neck with his teeth and treads up and down with his back feet. Intromission occurs with a few deep pelvic thrusts. Ejaculation takes place within five to 15 seconds. At the moment of ejaculation the male utters a low growl and the queen screams piercingly. This dramatic sequence is followed by an almost explosive separation, in which the queen may turn and strike out at the stud with her teeth and claws as he jumps back and to the side.

The aggressive behavior of the queen at the end of ejaculation may be caused by the withdrawal of the male's penis which contains numerous barb-like projections. They produce an intense and possibly painful stimulation of the queen's vagina. The same reaction, however, occurs when the queen's vagina is stimulated with a smooth object such as a plastic rod. In any case, the stimulation is essential to induce ovulation 24 hours later (see *Ovulation*).

After mating, the queen exhibits the so-called "after-reaction". She rolls over a few times, relaxes, and then begins to groom herself, paying special attention to her genital area.

(Among free-roaming cats, this pattern of courtship and mating might be repeated many times over the course of several hours for up to three days.)

The mating sequence, showing the position of the receptive queen. The male mounts and seizes her by the nape of her neck. At the moment of ejaculation, the queen screams piercingly. The cats separate and the queen strikes out with her claws.   —*Sydney Wiley.*

The queen should now be returned to her container or placed in a separate pen, but not until she has passed through the rolling-over and self-grooming stage. If disturbed too soon, she may inflict a painful scratch or bite. At this time you should check the stud to be sure that his penis has returned to its sheath (see *Penis That Can't Retract*).

Most breeders agree that two to three matings are needed to ensure the success of ovulation and conception. The second mating should be attempted later the same day.

Shy Breeders—Cats That Won't Mate

The most common cause of sexual reluctance is breeding at the wrong time in the estrus cycle (usually during proestrus). If a queen has to be sent to the stud, the resulting stress may send her off her call. Most will call again in one or two days, but some take much longer. If breeding is attempted too early in the cycle, the queen will growl at the male and attempt to bite him. This is normal proestrus behavior, but some breeders may see it as a sign that the mating isn't going to take place.

When you are certain that the queen is in the correct stage of her breeding cycle (estrus) and still refuses to mate, then the problem is most likely a psychological block. A physical disorder or hormone deficiency must also be considered.

A pampered female raised as a house pet could be a shy breeder because of inadequate prior social contact with members of her own species. Mate preference, too, can be a determining factor. Some females will not mate with a timid stud. Others prefer studs of a certain breed, or even a specific color.

Sexual aggressiveness in the male fluctuates at different times of the year, usually in association with the breeding seasons of the female.

A gentle and friendly tom, often selected by breeders who want to produce kittens well socialized to human company, may lack the sexual aggressiveness to mate a dominant queen. Less commonly, a tom with a low libido may be suffering from a hormone imbalance (see *Impotence*).

When a stud is unwilling to mate it is important to examine his external genitalia. The penis should be capable of full protrusion. Intromission could be prevented by hair caught in the spines and wrapped around the shaft of the penis. Small or soft testicles suggest a hormone deficiency and/or a reduced sperm count. These subjects are discussed in the section *Diseases of the Male Genital Tract.*

Treatment: When the queen refuses to accept the stud, she should be tried again in 24 hours. A successful mating may yet take place. If not, a hormonal or psychological problem may exist.

Vaginal cytology is an effective means of determining this difference and staging the estrus phase. Taking the smear may induce ovulation—but only if the queen is in estrus. When the smear is positive, mating should be attempted at once. If the mating takes place, then a pregnancy should result. However, if the queen still won't mate, a psychological block can be inferred. One then needs to decide whether to proceed with a forced mating or turn instead to AI (see *Artificial Insemination*).

A forced mating can still take place if the queen is held by her owner and *well tranquilized.* However, successful forced matings do not always result in kittens. The necessary sedation may depress the stimulus to ovulate. Forced matings, and those accomplished by AI, must be timed to coincide with the estrus phase. Vaginal cytology is essential.

In cats it is important that at least one of the partners have prior sexual experience. For example, if an inexperienced male grasps the skin of the female too far back (i.e., not by the nape of her neck), intromission is not possible. Accordingly, virgin queens should be bred only to experienced studs. Conversely, an experienced brood matron who is a willing breeder can help a bashful tom build up his ego. Once having bred a female successfully, generally his problems are over.

INFERTILITY

When a queen fails to conceive after successful matings, you are faced with an infertility problem. Either the stud or the queen can be at fault.

Fertility Problems in the Male

A common cause of reduced fertility in the male is excessive use. Most virile toms can be bred three times a week. When bred more often they should be rested for a week. When a stud is much in demand, a single mating and low fertility may be the cause of a missed pregnancy. A stud used at regular intervals should receive a balanced diet high in protein.

High fertility tends to be inherited. Some strains produce studs who for generations are known to sire large healthy litters.

Toms that have not been used at stud for some time may have a low sperm count due to sexual inactivity. During a second mating, 48 hours after the first, the quality of semen is often improved.

It is better to use a stud at regular intervals. Infrequent matings, instead of saving up sperm, often lead to decreased production. If a stud is known to have a low sperm count, it may be better to use him twice a week.

As a stud grows older (beyond eight years) his fertility may diminish owing to a reduction in sperm number and quality. This may result in smaller litters, but the quality of the kittens will not be affected. After 12 years of age, testicular atrophy is common.

A male whose testicles fail to descend into the scrotum, or in whom descent was delayed, will have an absent or reduced sperm count (see *Undescended Testicles*).

Prolonged elevation of body temperature depresses sperm production. Some cats are less fertile in summer, especially when the weather is hot. A tom recovering from a serious illness may take several months to regain his normal sperm count.

An excess or deficiency of Vitamin A can induce sterility. Signs of deficiency are weight loss, loss of hair, and night-blindness. An excess can occur among cats fed large amounts of raw liver.

Other causes of reduced fertility are close confinement, boredom, improper diet, and lack of exercise.

Treatment: A semen analysis will determine if the sperm are of normal number and quality. In many males it is difficult to obtain a semen specimen in the office. The sample is then obtained from a female right after mating. When sperm are present, often the stud's potency can be improved by treating the underlying problem.

Infertility can be caused by diseases of the male reproductive tract. Treatment is discussed elsewhere in this chapter.

Genetic and chromosomal abnormalities are rare causes of infertility. Male tortoise shell cats and white blue-eyed cats are nearly always sterile. Other abnormalities are difficult to diagnose. Such investigations are best carried out at a school of veterinary medicine.

Impotence. In most cases impotence, the lack of male sex drive or libido, is caused by psychological factors (see *Shy Breeders—Cats That Won't Mate*).

Many toms who live as household pets and receive lots of human affection lose interest in breeding. This is one reason why pedigreed-cat breeders prepare special living quarters for their breeding animals apart from the house.

Hypothyroidism is a treatable condition that causes lack of vitality and sex drive; it can also lower a cat's sperm count. It is managed by thyroid replacement and male hormone.

The male sex drive is under the influence of testosterone which is produced by the testicles. Rarely, impotence is caused by failure of the testicles to produce enough hormone. One explanation for this is that just before or after birth male kittens normally receive a surge of testosterone which conditions or "masculanizes" the brain. When this process fails to occur, a male kitten develops a female behavior pattern. He responds primarily to the female hormone and not the male.

Semen analysis is not a test for the male hormone because the cells that make the sperm are not the ones that make testosterone. Thus a fertile male can be impotent, and a sterile male can be quite willing and able to mate with a queen.

Treatment: Impotency due to hormonal rather than behavioral causes is difficult to diagnose and treat. Some cats may respond to the administration of testosterone when given before breeding. Unfortunately, the dose which activates the male libido also depresses sperm production. It must be used with caution.

Catnip may increase the sexual aggressiveness of some males.

Fertility Problems in the Female

Infertility in the female can be caused by failure to ovulate or conceive; or by fetal loss during pregnancy. Infection in the reproductive tract is a chief cause of conceptual failure. It is discussed in the section *Diseases of the Female Genital Tract.*

Irregular heat cycles also present problems, and for this reason are discussed below.

Abnormal Heat Cycles. Heat cycles of queens are quite variable. In general, each queen establishes her own normal rhythm and, once established, it tends to repeat itself.

As a queen grows older, her heat periods become less regular and in some cases will not be accompanied by ovulation. Other factors which adversely affect a queen's estrus cycle and her fertility are improper diet, environmental stress, and ill-health.

A queen low in the social hierarchy of a group of cats may fail to call until she is taken out and placed near a stud.

Hormonal causes of an abnormal heat cycle are:

Hypothyroidism. This is not common. When present, other indications of thyroid deficiency may or may not be observed. The diagnosis is established by a blood test. It is treated by giving thyroid hormone.

Hypoestrinism. A low estrogen level is caused by failure of the ovaries to develop to sexual maturity. The vulva and vagina remain small and undeveloped. Heat does not occur owing to the low estrogen level. This too is an uncommon condition.

Hyperestrinism (Cystic Ovaries). This condition is caused by excess output of estrogen from the ovaries. A queen who is allowed to call repeatedly but is never mated can, after several heat cycles, develop cysts on her ovaries. These cysts produce an abnormally high estrogen level which suppresses ovulation and prevents implantation. The queen enters a continuous or prolonged heat. She becomes irritable, inclined to fight other cats (both male and female), and refuses to mate—or conversely, will mate frequently (nymphomania) but be unable to conceive.

Treatment of Abnormal Heat Cycles: A female who is slow to come into heat may do so if exposed to light for 14 hours a day; or when placed with another queen in estrus. In such cases the estrus of one may cause the other to call. Their heat cycles may even become synchronized.

Failure to come into heat, from psychological or hormonal cause, may at times be treated successfully by giving injections of follicle stimulating hormone. If heat develops, this indicates that the ovaries are able to respond. An injection of leutinizing hormone is then given to induce ovulation.

Ovarian cysts are treated by removing the ovaries or cysts. When kittens are desired, removing the cysts may be sufficient to correct the problem. The queen might then become pregnant. If breeding is not desired, both ovaries and the uterus should be removed (see *Spaying*).

Failure to Ovulate. A single act of mating may not be sufficient to induce the queen to ovulate. This is why most breeders prefer to mate a queen two or three times during her period of receptivity.

Other causes of anovulation are related to abnormal heat cycles, as discussed above.

Treatment: Ovulation is followed by a rise in the serum progesterone level. This test is positive at five days. If no rise occurs, then ovulation has not taken place. It may be possible to induce ovulation during the next estrus cycle by giving an injection of LH soon after mating.

Fetal Loss During Pregnancy. Fetal loss may take place even before implantation of the fertilized egg in the wall of the uterus, owing to unfavorable environmental conditions (i.e. infection), or a genetic defect in the fertilized egg.

It is easier to recognize the situation in which a queen becomes pregnant but fails to carry her kittens to term. Pregnancy can be detected at three to four weeks by palpating the queen's abdomen (see *Determining Pregnancy*). A blood or urine test, commonly used to diagnose early pregnancy in women, is not available for cats.

If the queen is found to be pregnant and subsequently does not deliver kittens, one of two things must have happened: either she miscarried (aborted), or her kittens were reabsorbed.

Signs of *abortion* are vaginal bleeding and the passage of tissue. These signs may not be observed if the queen is fastidious. Her owner will then be unaware for some time that she has lost her litter.

Fetal reabsorption occurs before the seventh week of gestation. The developing kittens are absorbed back into the mother's body through the wall of her uterus and are no longer felt in the abdomen. Occasionally you may notice a slight pinkish vaginal discharge.

Death of kittens in utero can be due to inadequate output of progesterone from the placenta. During the first half of pregnancy, developing kittens are supported by progesterone made in the ovaries. At about the fortieth day of gestation this function is taken over by the placenta. Should this transition fail to occur, there is insufficient progesterone to support the pregnancy. Placental insufficiency can be a frequent cause of *habitual* fetal losses in some queens.

Another well recognized cause of habitual fetal loss is the feline leukemia virus. This is a particularly important consideration when an entire breeding colony is affected. Reproductive failure in a cattery could be the first indication of such infection. Most stud owners will not accept a queen for breeding unless she has a certificate showing she has been tested and found free of the disease.

Recently the virus of feline infectious peritonitis (FIP) has been implicated as the cause of an entire syndrome of reproductive failure which includes repeated abortions, fetal reabsorption, still births, and kittens who sicken and die shortly after birth. This syndrome, known as the *Kitten Mortality Complex,* is discussed in the PEDIATRICS chapter.

Another prominent cause of habitual fetal loss is chronic endometritis, or infection of the lining of the uterus (see *Diseases of the Female Genital Tract*).

Causes of *sporadic* miscarriages include emotional upsets, violent exercise (such as jumping from heights), a blow to the abdomen, and improper diet and/or prenatal care. Care and feeding of the pregnant queen is discussed in the chapter PREGNANCY AND KITTENING.

Treatment of Habitual Fetal Loss: Unsuccessful pregnancy always is a cause for concern. It should be investigated by a veterinarian. It may represent a health hazard to the queen or other cats in the breeding colony or household.

Queens with progesterone induced placental insufficiency can be treated during the next pregnancy by giving a weekly injection of long-acting progesterone, beginning a week before the anticipated abortion.

Diseases of the Male Genital Tract

There are several disorders of the male genital tract that can lead to mating problems and, on rare occasions, can cause infertility. Among them are orchitis, balanoposthitis, phimosis, paraphimosis, and undescended testicles.

Examination of the penis is best carried out from in back by raising the tail to expose the perineum below the anus. A cat's penis points toward the rear. The glans or head of the penis can be exposed by retracting the sheath which covers it. Grasp it between your thumb and forefinger and slide it forward (toward the cat's head). The tip will begin to protrude.

In a fully mature tom, the shaft of the penis has barb-like projections which slant toward the base. After ejaculation, as the stud begins to withdraw his penis, these barbs cause intense stimulation of the queen's vagina. This initiates the release of a hormone causing the queen to ovulate (see *Ovulation*).

In the young tom and the neutered male the penis is smooth.

Infection of the Prepuce and Head of the Penis (Balanoposthitis). Irritation of the foreskin and head of the penis can be caused by hair caught in the spines during mating. Other causes are excess sexual activity, and awns or pieces of straw caught beneath the sheath. The irritation may be complicated by infection and abscess of the sheath. This makes intromission painful or impossible.

On occasion flies lay eggs in the infected tissue. The eggs hatch in a few days producing maggots.

A cat suffering from balanoposthitis licks himself excessively and has a purulent, foul-smelling discharge from his prepuce.

Treatment: First, clip away hair near the foreskin. Push back the foreskin to expose the tip of the penis. Wash the area thoroughly with surgical soap and apply an antibiotic ointment. If your cat won't allow you to retract his foreskin, use a syringe and flush the sheath with a dilute solution of hydrogen peroxide twice daily. Then infuse Panolog or Furacin ointment. Repeat until all signs of discharge and inflammation are gone.

For persistent cases, flush the sheath with an astringent solution made up of 5% salicylic acid mixed with two parts of propylene glycol and continue the treatment for four days.

Cats with balanoposthitis should not be used at stud. The infection can be transmitted to the female during mating.

Strictured Foreskin—Penis Can't Protrude (Phimosis). In this condition the opening in the foreskin is too small to let the penis extend. It may be so small that urine can escape only in small drops. Some cases are due to infection or a birth defect.

When the problem is related to an infection of the sheath, treatment of the infection, as previously described, also may correct the phimosis. If not, a surgical operation is required.

Penis That Can't Retract (Paraphimosis). In this condition the penis is unable to return to its former position inside the sheath. When there is long hair on the skin around the sheath it could cause the foreskin to roll under when the penis is partly retracted. Another predisposing cause is a ring of hair formed around

A ring of hair around the penis may prevent it from retracting back into the sheath.

the shaft of the penis by the barbs which collect hair from the queen during the mating process.

Paraphimosis can be prevented by cutting long hair around the prepuce prior to mating. After intercourse, a stud usually licks the tip of his penis and removes any attached hair. If not, it should be removed. Check your male after mating to be sure his penis has returned to its sheath.

Treatment: The penis should be returned to its normal position as quickly as possible in order to prevent permanent damage. Push the prepuce back on the shaft of the penis toward the cat's head, while rolling it out so the hairs are not caught. Lubricate the surface of the penis with mineral oil or olive oil. With one hand, gently draw the head of the penis toward you. With the other hand, slide the prepuce back in place. If these measures are not immediately successful, notify your veterinarian.

In most cases the skin of the penis is irritated and it will be necessary to flush the sheath twice daily with an antiseptic solution as described under the treatment of infection of the head of the penis.

Undescended Testicles. The testicles descend into the scrotum at birth, or shortly thereafter. Usually they can be felt by six weeks of age. If a testicle can be felt one time but not another, there is no need for concern. Testicles can retract back up into the groin when the kitten is cold, excited, or actively playing. Both testicles should be fully descended before six months of age. Consult your veterinarian if they have not come down by that time.

The testicles should be of similar size and feel rather firm. Since much of the testicle's size is due to its sperm-producing tissue, soft or small testicles in the sexually mature cat are likely to be deficient in sperm.

Monorchid cats, those with only one testicle in the scrotum, may be fertile. However, they should not be used at stud because the condition may be inherited. *Cryptorchid* cats, those with no testicles in the scrotum, are sterile.

Although a retained testicle does not produce sperm, it continues to make testosterone, which is the male hormone responsible for the sexual behavior of toms.

Monorchid and cryptorchid cats should be neutered. An abdominal operation may be necessary to find and remove the testicles.

Orchitis (Inflammation of the Testicle). The most frequent cause of orchitis is an infected cat bite of the scrotum or testicle. Other causes include trauma to the testicle (shotgun wounds, blows). Scrotal infections produced by frostbite, chemical and thermal burns, can spread to the testicles, as can infections of the bladder, urethra, and sheath of the penis.

The signs of orchitis are swelling and pain in the testicle. The testicle becomes enlarged, hard, and tender to touch. The cat assumes a spread-legged stance with his belly tucked up. Later the diseased testicle shrinks and becomes small and firm.

As most cat bites are puncture wounds and quite likely to become infected, even relatively minor-appearing injuries should be examined and treated by a veterinarian.

Diseases of the Female Genital Tract

Infections of the female genital system affect fertility and the health of the queen.

Vaginal Infection. This is a cause for concern because it can lead to a subsequent uterine infection. The most easily recognized sign is excessive licking at the vulva. A discharge is usually present and might contain an odor attractive to the male, thereby giving the impression that the female is in heat. As female cats are fastidious, this discharge may not be seen.

Bacterial infection of the vagina often spreads to the urinary tract causing pain on urination and increased frequency. A veterinary examination is necessary to confirm the diagnosis and determine whether there is an associated uterine infection.

Juvenile vaginitis is seen in kittens six to twelve weeks of age. The only sign is a slight vaginal discharge. In most cases this disappears when the kitten goes into heat for the first time.

A queen with vaginitis should not be bred until her infection has been successfully treated. Infected vaginal secretions are spermacidal. More important, there is danger of infecting the male.

Treatment: Administer a betadine vaginal douche twice daily for seven days and accompany it with an oral antibiotic. An appropriate antibiotic can be selected on the basis of cultures and sensitivities. Treat urinary tract infection if present.

282 SEX AND REPRODUCTION

Uterine Infection. In cats, excessive production of the hormone progesterone appears to contribute in an important way to the development of most uterine infections. One cause of prolonged progesterone production is false pregnancy. It occurs when a queen ovulates but does not become pregnant. Usually this is associated with a sterile mating, but in some cases it may occur spontaneously, or for reasons that are unknown.

The effect of progesterone is to thicken the lining of the uterus and make it fluid-filled and cystic. A fluid-filled uteris is called a *hydrometra,* while one containing a lot of cystic material is called a *mucometra.* Either provides an ideal media for bacterial growth, sometimes leading to the formation of an abscess in the uterus (*pyometra*).

Abscess of the Uterus (Pyometra). This is a life-threatening disease which occurs most often in queens over five years of age who have never become pregnant. It appears two to eight weeks after the queen goes out of heat.

A queen with pyometra refuses to eat, appears depressed and lethargic, usually runs a fever (but may have a normal or even subnormal temperature), drinks a great deal and urinates frequently. The abdomen is quite markedly distended and firm. This may suggest the possibility of feline infectious peritonitis (the wet form of FIP), but the combination of a *severe illness* with a *distended abdomen* in a *non-breeding queen* after a *heat period* will suggest the correct diagnosis.

In the *open* type the cervix relaxes, releasing a large amount of pus which is often cream-colored, pink or brown. In the *closed* type there is no vaginal discharge. As pus collects in the uterus the cat becomes quite toxic, often vomits, runs a high fever, and quickly dehydrates.

Treatment: In order to save the life of the queen, a veterinarian should be called at once. Hysterectomy is the treatment of choice. It is much better to do this operation early before the cat becomes toxic.

A disease similar to pyometra, *acute metritis,* occurs in the post partum queen (see *Post Partum Problems* in the chapter PREGNANCY AND KITTENING).

Endometritis. This is a low grade infection which occurs in queens two years and older. Its principal concern is that it is a cause of infertility in the female. When it persists for two or more cycles, it is called *chronic endometritis.* Vaginitis is a predisposing cause.

A queen with endometritis may appear to be in excellent health, have a normal heat period and be mated successfully—yet fail to conceive, or lose her kittens during pregnancy. Suspect this possibility when the queen is bred at the right time but doesn't conceive on two or more cycles; when she delivers stillborn kittens or kittens who sicken and die within the first few days; and when litters are uniformly small.

Endometritis is difficult to diagnose and requires the use of appropriate smears and cultures taken from the cervix during estrus.

Treatment: Do not breed a queen with infection. Instead, culture the cervix and treat her for three weeks with antibiotics selected on the basis of sensitivity testing. During the next estrus, re-culture the cervix. If negative, she can be bred.

ARTIFICIAL INSEMINATION

Artificial insemination is a technique whereby semen is collected from the male and introduced into the reproductive tract of the female. When properly performed, it can be as successful as actual mating. When used as a last resort, it may be too late in the heat cycle for the queen to conceive.

AI has its widest application when natural mating is contraindicated or impossible. Usually this is for psychological reasons, anatomical reasons, or fear of transmitting a disease.

The queen's behavior usually will indicate when she is in estrus and receptive to successful fertilization. When for psychological reasons she does not display signs of sexual receptivity, vaginal cytology must be used to stage the heat cycle (see *Shy Breeders—Cats That Won't Mate*).

The best results with AI will be obtained by inseminating the queen two to four times over an interval of 24 hours.

After AI, the queen should be confined until she goes out of heat. If she mates with another male, a mixed litter may result.

The techniques of AI are well standardized in the dog and many domestic livestock animals. However, AI is just beginning to be used in the cat. In the matter of selecting equipment, collecting semen, and inseminating the queen, great care in handling is important to insure a successful pregnancy. For this reason, the procedure is best left to a veterinarian, or one who has had experience with it.

Techniques to freeze and preserve feline semen are just beginning to be explored. It is entirely possible that these techniques will alter the future of pedigreed cat breeding.

FALSE PREGNANCY (Pseudocyesis)

If ovulation occurs but the eggs remain unfertilized, a pseudopregnancy or false pregnancy results. The signs are caused by progesterone, the pregnancy hormone, which is manufactured by corpus luteal cysts in the ovaries (see *Hormonal Influences During Estrus*).

A false-pregnant queen exhibits all the physical and behavioral signs of a true pregnancy. The signs usually disappear at about five weeks, but in some cases may continue up to 45 days. Some of them are increased appetite, weight gain, reddening of the nipples, and breast enlargement. Rarely a queen will exhibit nesting behavior, carry small toys (kitten substitutes) around in her mouth, and even attempt to adopt a puppy or the kittens of another queen.

Milk production, caking of the breasts, uterine cramps and labor pains can occur. This is not common.

False pregnancy can easily be confused with a true pregnancy in which the kittens have been aborted or reabsorbed (see *Fetal Loss During Pregnancy*).

Treatment: Mild cases require no treatment. Your veterinarian may wish to prescribe testosterone and/or diethylstilbesterol to relieve uterine cramps. For caked breasts, see PREGNANCY AND KITTENING: *Post Partum Problems*.

A false-pregnant queen is likely to have other false pregnancies. They tend to get worse with each episode. Such queens are more likely to develop uterine abscesses and breast tumors. If breeding is no longer desired, the queen should be spayed. This is best done after the false pregnancy is over.

ACCIDENTAL PREGNANCY

Accidental pregnancies are common. A queen in heat will go to any lengths to get to a tom. Her vocal call, and the potent chemical substances in her urine (pheromones), attract toms from miles around. If left outdoors for just a few minutes, an unwanted pregnancy can occur.

Once your are certain that your queen is in heat, keep her indoors. *Do not let her out of your sight.* Queens must be isolated throughout the entire estrus cycle which begins with the signs of proestrus and may continue for ten to 14 days.

If a valuable breeding queen has been mismated, it may be safest to let her go through with the pregnancy. She will be perfectly able to breed true to type the next time.

If the queen's owner does not have the time and facilities to take care of a litter of kittens, there are two alternatives to the unwanted litter. One is spaying. This operation can be performed during the first half of pregnancy without added risk to the female. During the later stages of pregnancy hysterectomy is a more formidable undertaking.

The second alternative is to prevent the pregnancy by means of an estrogen injection (the mismate shot). The hormone works by preventing implantation of the fertilized ova into the wall of the uterus. If you choose this method, take your queen to a veterinarian as soon as possible. The injection must be given *within two to three days* of mating.

One side effect of the injection is that heat is prolonged two to three weeks. During this time the cervix remains open, increasing the chance of a uterine infection. Thus a potential danger exists.

BIRTH CONTROL

The two methods currently available to prevent conception in the female are surgery (ovariohysterectomy or tubal ligation), and artificial stimulation of the vagina.

Birth control pills, which have been used abroad, have not been cleared for use in cats in the United States. They may be available in the future. If so, veterinary counsel will be necessary to ensure proper usage. Adherence to a strict protocol is required.

Chlorophyll tablets, which you can purchase from your veterinarian or pet stores, may help to mask the odor of a female in heat but are not an effective birth control measure.

The two operations used to sterilize the male are castration and vasectomy.

Male sterilization is not an effective population control measure. Another male can fertilize a queen in heat.

Spaying *(Ovariohysterectomy)*

The most effective method for preventing pregnancy is to have a queen spayed. In this operation, the uterus, tubes and ovaries are removed.

Spaying prevents the queen from coming into season and does away with the problem of cystic ovaries, false pregnancies, uterine infection, irregular heat cycles, and the need to keep her confined during her season. Females spayed before they are a year old rarely develop breast cancer later in life.

Contrary to a popular belief, a queen does not need to have a litter of kittens to be psychologically fulfilled. The operation will not change her basic personality, except perhaps to make her less irritable at certain times of the year. The operation will not affect her hunting instincts. A spayed female makes an outstanding housepet. She is able to devote herself exclusively to her human family.

It is also not true that ovariohysterectomy makes a cat fat and lazy. This is caused by overfeeding and lack of exercise. A queen is usually spayed as she enters adulthood. At this time she requires less food. If she continues to eat as before and puts on weight, the tendency is to blame the operation.

The best time to spay a female is at five to seven months of age, before she goes into her first heat. The operation at this time is easy to perform and there is less chance of complication.

After having made arrangements to have your female spayed, be sure to withhold food and water from her on the evening prior to surgery. The operation is done under general anesthesia. A full stomach might result in vomiting and aspiration during induction of anesthesia. Check with your veterinarian concerning other special instructions or precautions to be taken before and after the operation.

Tubal Ligation

In this operation the Fallopian tubes are ligated to prevent eggs from getting from the ovaries to the uterus. It has nearly the same risks as ovariohysterectomy and is only slightly less expensive in most veterinary clinics. It won't stop the queen from going into heat and attracting the male. It does not have the health benefits of ovariohysterectomy. Most veterinarians recommend ovariohysterectomy when an operation is to be performed for sterilization purposes.

Artificial Stimulation of the Vagina

A queen can be brought out of heat by artifically stimulating her vagina. The reasons for this are discussed in the section *Hormonal Influences During Estrus.*

With an assistant holding the cat by the scruff of her neck, raise her tail and insert a smooth, blunt-ended plastic rod or cotton-tipped applicator ½ inch into her vagina and rotate it gently. The queen will probably cry out and exhibit all the signs of actual mating including the post-coital rolling-over behavior.

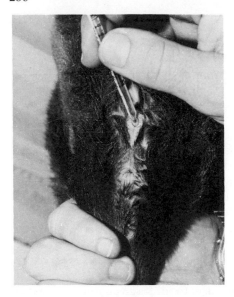

***Artificial stimulation of the vagina* is
a method of taking the queen out of
heat.**   *—J. Clawson.*

She should cease to call in three to four days, but may go back into heat in
about 44 days when the ovaries stop manufacturing progesterone. She should
not be let outdoors while still in heat. If she meets a tom and is accidentally
mated, pregnancy almost certainly will result.

This method can be used when it is desired to postpone breeding for one or
two cycles.

Male Castration

Castration is an operation in which both testicles are removed. The operation is not difficult and the cat can go home the same day.

Castration does not change a male cat's personality except to tone him down
and reduce or eliminate his sexual impulses and the aggressive behavior that accompanies them. His hunting instincts are not affected. He often becomes more
affectionate and more oriented to the company of people.

A neutered male is much less likely to wander and become involved in cat
fights. In most cases spraying, with its accompanying unpleasant smell of male
cat urine, is eliminated. Most veterinarians believe that the best time to castrate a
male is when he is six to seven months old, at which time he is sufficiently mature
so that his growth and bone structure are not adversely affected, but sexual
behavior, if present at all, has not become ingrained.

If a male is castrated before six months, or specifically before his secondary
sexual traits appear, his penis could remain small. This might predispose to
urethral obstruction (see *Feline Urologic Syndrome* in the chapter URINARY
SYSTEM).

When an older male is castrated, and especially if he has mated queens, his
sex drive may remain unchanged, but this is not common.

The same precautions are taken the night before surgery as for ovario-hysterectomy (see *Spaying*).

Vasectomy

Bilateral vasectomy is the treatment of choice when sterilization *alone* is the reason for surgery. In this operation a segment of the right and left vas deferens is removed. These tubes transport the sperm from the testicles to the urethra. A vasectomized tom is able and willing to mate with a queen, but is unable to get her pregnant.

Vasectomy does not disturb the hormone functions of the testes, nor does it influence the mating urge or territorial aggressiveness of toms. It does not reduce spraying.

Breeders who house a number of queens may keep a vasectomized tom. By mating with a queen, he brings her out of heat without the risk of pregnancy. The applications are similar to those discussed in the section *Artificial Stimulation of the Vagina*.

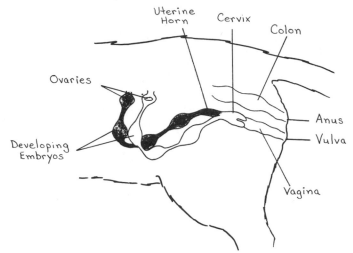

Female Reproductive System.—*Rose Floyd.*

Kittens can be palpated after 28 days.

16

Pregnancy and Kittening

Gestation

Gestation is the period from conception to birth. As reckoned from the first day of successful mating, it averages 65 days. Kittens born on the 63rd or 69th day fall within the normal range. Siamese cats may carry their kittens 71 days. However, if the queen kittens before the 58th day, the kittens probably will be too young to survive.

Determining Pregnancy

During the first three to four weeks of gestation, there are few detectable signs except a slight gain in weight.

By 35 days the nipples begin to enlarge and pinken. Next the breasts enlarge and as the time of birth approaches a milky fluid may be expressed from the nipples. (*Note:* Many queens have breast enlargement after a normal heat period; this alone should not lead to a diagnosis of pregnancy.)

The uterus in cats is a Y-shaped affair with a horn on each side. The kittens are carried in the uterine horns. By 28 days of gestation, an experienced breeder or a veterinarian can tell by palpation whether a queen is pregnant.

How to Palpate for Kittens. Have your queen stand up comfortably. Place your hand under her tummy with your fingers on one side and your thumb on the other to allow the contents of the abdomen to slip between. The structures you should identify first are the two kidneys. They are found at the level of the last rib. Below the kidneys you can feel the colon. It contains soft, putty-like stool. Furthest to the rear, just in front of the pelvis, you can feel the uterine horns and the bladder. The bladder could be mistaken for a pregnant uterus if it contains much urine. By gently pressing with your fingers in this area you may be able to detect firm lumps, which are the kittens growing in the uterine horns.

Palpation must be done with great care. Heavy pressure or too much squeezing could damage a kitten or even cause a queen to abort.

At 28 days kittens are no larger than a small walnut (about one inch in size). At 35 days they are floating in capsules of fluid and are more difficult to detect.

Queens who have been spayed, showing various stages of pregnancy.

Non-pregnant uterus.

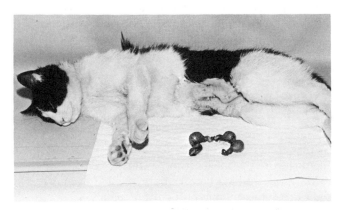

Twenty-eight day pregnancy.

Fifty day pregnancy.

At this time an owner may first notice the queen's abdomen is getting larger. By 49 days kittens are sausage-shaped and their heads are usually large enough to be felt as separate structures.

Unless you are experienced at palpating the pregnant uterus, a negative palpation does not rule out a pregnancy. In this case veterinary examination is desirable to confirm a true pregnancy or establish the diagnosis of FALSE PREGNANCY, a condition more common than most people realize. Signs of false pregnancy usually disappear at about five weeks, but in some cases may continue up to 45 days. Other causes of an enlarged uterus are *Pyometra*; and collections of mucus or fluid in the uterus. The above disorders are discussed in the chapter SEX AND REPRODUCTION.

Other signs of pregnancy are weight gain, abdominal movement which is easily detected during the last two weeks, increased appetite, and sometimes morning sickness.

There is no blood or urine test for pregnancy in cats as there is in people. X-ray of the abdomen can be done later in pregnancy if there is still doubt and it is necessary to know for certain.

Morning Sickness

Cats, like people, can suffer from morning sickness. Usually this happens during the third to fourth week of pregnancy. It is due to hormonal changes, plus stretching and distention of the uterus. You may notice that your queen appears apathetic. She may be off her feed and vomit from time to time. Morning sickness lasts only a few days. Unless you are particularly attentive, you may not even notice it.

Treatment: If your queen seems to be suffering from morning sickness, feed her several meals spaced throughout the day. Your veterinarian may want to prescribe a drug to relax the uterus. Vitamins B and C also may be given.

Prenatal Check Ups

Before you breed your queen it is a good idea to take her to your veterinarian to see if she has any physical abnormalities which might prevent normal mating or delivery.

Be sure to have her checked for periodontitis and dental infections. Bacteria from the queen's mouth can be transmitted to newborn kittens during biting of the umbilical cord. This is one cause of serious navel infections.

Intestinal parasites, if present, should be treated. Tapeworm medications, in particular, can be quite toxic, and should be given only under veterinary guidance.

One week prior to her expected date of confinement make an appointment to have her thoroughly checked again. Your veterinarian will want to discuss with you the normal delivery procedures, alert you to the signs of impending problems, and give you instructions for the care of the newborn.

Be sure to ask where you can get help (emergency service) if needed after hours.

Care and Feeding During Pregnancy

A pregnant queen needs very little special care beyond a boosted diet. It usually is not necessary to restrict her activity. Moderate exercise, in fact, is beneficial. It helps to prevent undue weight gain and the development of poor muscle tone. However, if she is given to climbing, jumping from high places, rough-housing with children and pets, she will need to be watched (especially during the latter part of her pregnancy) and steps taken to prevent excessive physical activity.

During the first four weeks of pregnancy, feed your queen her usual ration of high quality cat food.

Protein requirements begin to increase during the second half of pregnancy. Increase her ration by one-half with an eye to keeping her trim.

Some commercial dry foods may need to be supplemented with canned meat, milk products, eggs, liver or cottage cheese. But if you are feeding a *complete* ration, one formulated to meet all the daily requirements of a cat when fed alone, supplements will not be needed and may be harmful. The queen may then get less of the other things she needs, including fats and carbohydrates (see FEEDING AND NUTRITION). At this time many breeders switch to a ration formulated to meet the nutritional requirements of growing kittens. Ounce for ounce, it is higher in good quality protein.

Excessive weight gain should be avoided at all costs. An overnourished queen is apt to carry fat kittens which can make her labor difficult.

Mineral and vitamin supplements are not required unless a queen is below par from an earlier litter or recovering from an illness. Follow the advice of your veterinarian.

A queen may lose her appetite a week or two before she delivers. At this time her abdomen is crowded with kittens and it may be difficult for her to take in all she needs in one or two meals. It is better to feed several smaller meals spaced throughout the day.

Many drugs cannot be given during pregnancy. They include some of the flea and insecticide preparations, dewormers, and certain hormones and antibiotics. Live virus vaccines (e.g. feline panleukopenia, rabies, feline respiratory virus) should not be given to pregnant females. Check with your veterinarian before starting a pregnant female on a medication.

X-rays of the abdomen should be avoided in the early stages of pregnancy.

Kittening Preparations

Queens should deliver at home where they feel secure. They can easily be upset by strange people and unfamiliar surroundings. This can delay or complicate delivery.

The best place to deliver and care for newborn kittens is in a kittening box. It should be located in a warm, dry, out-of-the-way spot, preferably rather dark— and free from distracting noises.

A suitable box can be fashioned from a strong cardboard container large enough for her to move about in. A rectangular box 24 inches long, 20 inches

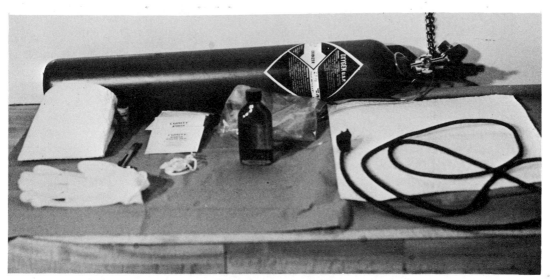

Kittening equipment.

wide, and 20 inches tall is of ample size. You should be able to lift the lid so you can see the kittens and clean the box. At one end cut out a doorway about chest high to the queen, so that she can step in and out without jumping.

Alternately, a reusable box can be made of wood. This has the advantage that inside ledges (two inches high and two inches wide) can be nailed to all four sides. Kittens will crawl under these ledges instinctively and are protected from being accidentally smothered or rolled on by their mother.

Several layers of newspaper are laid on the bottom of the box to absorb moisture and odor. They also give the queen something to dig and scratch up. This she will do instinctively in the way of making her nest. Kittens should never be placed in deep loose bedding such as straw or wood chips which might obstruct their breathing, or be inhaled.

The kittening quarters should be clean, dry, draft-free and warm. Cold damp quarters are the leading cause of early kitten mortality. When kittens are born, the floor temperature should be kept at 86 to 90 degrees F for the first seven days of life. Thereafter it should be lowered five degrees each week until it is 70 degrees F. Keep a constant check on the temperature with a thermometer on the floor of the box.

If the temperature in the kittening room cannot be maintained with the existing heating system, additional heat can be supplied by placing a heating pad, wrapped in a blanket, beneath the box; or by using 250 watt infra-red heat bulbs either suspended above the floor of the open-topped box or mounted in photographer's flood light reflectors (or plant lights). Be sure to leave an area of the box out of the direct source of heat so the mother can rest in a cooler area.

Other kittening accessories include a small box with a towel-covered hot water bottle or heating pad at the bottom to keep kittens in while others are being born; an eyedropper or small syringe to aspirate secretions from the mouths of newborns; artery forceps to clamp a bleeding cord; dental floss or cotton thread for ties; and an antiseptic, such as iodine, to apply to the umbilical stumps. Scissors, clean laundered towels, and plenty of fresh newspapers complete the kittening equipment.

KITTENING

Signs of Confinement

One week before a queen is due to give birth, she begins to spend a lot more time in self-grooming, paying special attention to her mammary and perineal areas. Her breasts become swollen. She may exhibit increased restlessness (or irritability) and begin to search for a place to have her kittens. She often rummages in closets, rearranges clothes in an open drawer, scratches up her owner's bed, and goes about in a flurry of activity which is the ritual of making her nest. Now is a good time to introduce her to the kittening box and encourage her to sleep in it. A queen who has already had litters usually will take to her box without difficulty. If she chooses to have her kittens someplace else, they should be moved to the kittening box as soon as she finishes delivering.

A queen usually eats quite well right up to the day of confinement. After the 61st day of gestation, it is a good idea to take her rectal temperature each morning. Twelve to 24 hours before she is due to deliver, her rectal temperature may drop from a normal of 101.5 degrees F to 99.5 degrees or below. This two-degree drop in temperature can easily be missed. A normal temperature does not mean she will not kitten in a few hours.

As the day of confinement approaches, she should be restricted to the house. If allowed outside, she might decide to run off and have her kittens in a haystack or tool shed.

Labor and Delivery

The uterus of a cat has two horns which communicate with a central uterine cavity. The outlet or cervix communicates with the vaginal birth canal. The kittens, encircled by their placentas, lie within the uterine horns.

There are three stages of labor. In the first stage the cervix dilates which opens the birth canal. In the second stage the kittens are delivered. In the third stage the placenta (afterbirth) is delivered. Queens usually lie on their sides when preparing to give birth.

The first stage, which may last for 12 hours or more, begins with rhythmic breathing and purring which increases as the moment of birth approaches. The queen becomes noticeably more active, digs at the floor, goes to her litter box and strains as if to pass stool, and often cries loudly. As her uterus contracts her abdominal muscles contract at the same time. She may turn her head as if to snap at her groin.

Occasionally a novice queen becomes extremely distressed, runs from room to room, seeks out her owner and cries pitifully. She requires comforting. Take

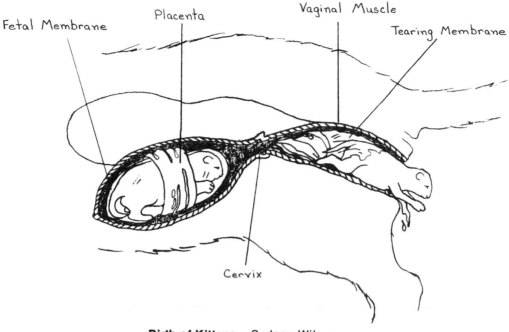

Fetal Membrane   Placenta   Vaginal Muscle
                                              Tearing Membrane

Cervix

Birth of Kittens.—*Sydney Wiley.*

her back to her kittening box and sit beside her. Speak soothingly and continue
to pet her. If this doesn't settle her down, she may need to be tranquilized with
Acepromazine (0.125 mg./lb.).

In the opposite situation a queen becomes upset by having her owner present. She should be left alone in a room with her kittening box and checked on
frequently.

With the onset of delivery, one uterine horn contracts and pushes the presenting part of the kitten down into the central cavity. Pressure against the cervix
causes it to dilate. At complete dilitation, the kitten slides into the vagina. The
water bag around the kitten usually ruptures before the kitten is born, lubricating the passageway. Straw-colored fluid is passed. Then a kitten should be delivered in a few minutes.

After the head is delivered, the rest of the kitten slides out easily. Instinctively the mother removes the fetal membranes, severs the umbilical cord and
begins to lick and clean her kitten. No attempt should be made to interfere with
maternal care. This is an important part of the mother-kitten bond. She is learning that this is her kitten and she must take care of it. If she appears rough it is
only because she is trying to stimulate breathing and blood circulation.

If the queen is occupied with another kitten and forgets to remove the amniotic sac, you should be prepared to step in and strip away the fetal membranes so
that the kitten can breathe (see *Helping a Kitten to Breathe*).

A placenta follows a few minutes after the birth of each kitten. The queen may try to eat some or all of the placentas. It is not essential that the queen consume the afterbirths. The ingestion of several placentas can produce diarrhea. You may wish to remove the placentas from the nest. However, it is important to count them since a retained placenta can cause a serious post-natal infection (see *Acute Metritis*).

If the cord is severed too cleanly or too close to the kitten's navel it may continue to bleed. You should be prepared to clamp or pinch off the cord and tie a thread around the stump. The stump should be cauterized with iodine or some other suitable disinfectant.

When the next kitten is about to appear, remove the first kitten and place it in a box warmed to 85 degrees F by an electric heating pad or hot water bottle. This prevents chilling, or temperature shock, which is a leading cause of newborn deaths.

Between births put the kittens on the nipples. Their sucking action stimulates uterine contractions and helps bring on the colostrum, or first milk of the queen, which contains the all-important maternal antibodies.

Most kittens are born 15 to 30 minutes apart but this is quite variable. Although most deliveries are complete in two to six hours, it occasionally happens that a queen goes out of labor, appears at ease and cares for her kittens, and then 12 to 24 hours later goes back into labor and delivers the rest of her litter. There may be no apparent reason for this seeming interruption. Perhaps the first kittens were delivered from one uterine horn and the remainder from the second. It is important to be aware that this can happen, so that undue anxiety or unnecessary surgery can be avoided. But when a kitten is not born within two hours and the queen appears to be continuously *straining* and in *distress,* then something may be wrong (see *When to Call the Veterinarian*).

After your queen has delivered her last kitten, ask your veterinarian to examine her to be sure there are no retained kittens or placentas. He may administer an injection to clear the uterus.

Assisting the Normal Delivery

When labor is going well it is best not to attempt to aid the queen as she knows by instinct how to deliver her kittens and take care of them by herself. But on occasion a large kitten gets stuck at the vaginal opening. The head or presenting part appears during a forceful contraction, then slips back inside when the queen relaxes. At this point it is wise to step in quickly and complete the delivery. Once a kitten moves out of the uterus down into the vaginal canal, oxygen from the mother gets cut off. Delivery must proceed rapidly.

It is not difficult to complete a partial delivery if the following steps are taken:

As the presenting part appears at the vaginal opening place your thumb and index finger on each side of the perineum just below the anus and push down gently to keep the kitten from slipping back into the mother. Next, grip the

The queen in her kittening box,
beginning to strain.

Getting ready to deliver.

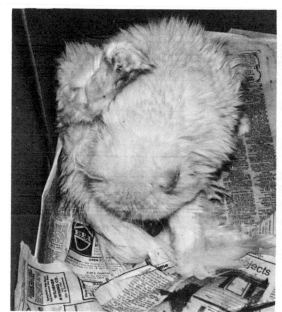

The water bag around the kitten can be
seen bulging through the vulva.

The mother removes the fetal membranes
and severs the cord.

kitten in the birth canal and slide the lips of the vulva over his head. Once this is accomplished the lips hold the kitten in place, giving you a chance to get another grip. Now grip the skin of the kitten with a sterile piece of cloth behind his neck or along his back and draw him out. Apply forceful traction only to the skin, not to the legs or head, as this can cause damage to a joint. Often it is helpful to rotate the kitten first one way and then another, especially when something seems stuck. The birth canal is usually wider one way than the other. If these measures are not immediately successful, proceed as described under *Feline Obstetrics*.

PROLONGED LABOR (Dystocia, Difficult Labor)

The prolongation of any phase of labor is called *dystocia*. It is due to either a birth canal which is too narrow in relation to the size of the presenting part of the fetus (*mechanical blockage*); or to the failure of the uterus to develop enough strength to expel the fetus (*uterine inertia*). Often these two are related, a difficult birth being followed by arrested labor due to uterine muscle fatigue.

Dystocia is much more common in older brood queens and those allowed to become too fat. This is why it is important to keep your female trim and in top condition.

It is also more likely to happen when there are only one or two kittens in the litter since such kittens are apt to be quite large.

Mechanical Blockage

Abnormal presentations can occur at any time but are more likely to arrest labor in the overweight poorly conditioned female. Normally kittens come down the birth canal *nose-first,* with their backs along the top of the vagina. When a kitten comes down backwards, his hind-feet, or tail and rump, are the presenting parts. The hind-foot (*posterior*) presentation occurs about 40 percent of the time. It may be inaccurate to classify it as a malpresentation; it seldom causes difficulties. However, the tail or rump-first position, called the *breech* presentation, can cause a problem—particularly when it occurs in the first kitten. Another position which can complicate labor is a head which is bent forward, or to the side, thereby becoming caught in the birth canal.

A queen who has previously fractured her pelvis is quite likely to have problems delivering because her pelvis is too narrow. It is a good idea to have her spayed.

Uterine Inertia

Uterine inertia is an important cause of ineffectual labor. Mechanical factors which can cause the uterus to become over-distended with stretched-out fibers and loss of power of contraction, are a single large kitten in a small uterus, a very large litter, and *hydrops amnion,* a condition in which there is too much amniotic fluid.

Uterine inertia can be caused by emotional upsets. Sudden anxiety induces a form of hysteria which stops normal labor. This is why it is important for a queen to deliver where she is at ease and familiar with her surroundings, away from casual spectators and other nerve-racking influences.

Some causes of inertia, called *primary,* seem to be due to a deficiency of oxytocin (a hormone produced by the pituitary gland), or calcium, or both. The uterus may respond to an injection of oxytocin (Pitocin) which stimulates stronger contractions. Intravenous calcium may also be given. *Oxytocin is contraindicated if there is a mechanical blockage.* It can lead to rupture of the uterus.

When to Call the Veterinarian

It is certainly better to call your veterinarian on a "false alarm," even if only to gain reassurance, than to delay in the hope that in time the situation will correct itself without help. Often the problem can be dealt with rather simply if attended to at once. However, the same problem, when neglected, becomes complicated—often leading to an emergency operation.

Something may be wrong when:

A queen goes into labor (serious straining) and does not deliver a kitten within two hours. Purposeful straining indicates a kitten is partly in the birth canal. It is a mistake to wait four to six hours as the mother is now exhausted and normal delivery may not be possible even when the cause is removed.

The queen passes dark green fluid *before* the delivery of her first kitten. This indicates separation of the placenta from the wall of the uterus which means the kitten is not getting oxygen from the mother and may die. After the first kitten, green or bloody fluid is normal.

The membranes rupture and a kitten is not delivered in 30 minutes. The passage of yellow fluid means rupture of the water bag (amniotic sac) surrounding the kitten.

Labor stops and there are signs of restlessness, anxiety, weakness or fatigue. Kittens come 15 minutes to two hours apart. Over three hours between kittens is a sign of trouble. This provision need not apply if the queen is resting happily and nursing her kittens without signs of distress.

Feline Obstetrics

If it is impossible to get prompt veterinary help or if the water bag breaks and the kitten is stuck in the birth canal, the following steps should be taken to deliver the kitten:

Clean the outside of the vulva with soap and water. Put on a pair of sterile gloves and lubricate your finger with pHisoHex, K-Y Jelly or Vaseline.

Before inserting your finger into the vagina, be careful not to contaminate your gloves with stool from the anus.

Place one hand under the abdomen in front of the pelvis of the queen and feel for the kitten. Raise him up into position to align him with the birth canal. With your other hand slip a finger into the vagina and feel for a head, tail or leg. When the *head is deviated* and will not pass through the outlet of the pelvis, insert a finger into the kitten's mouth and gently turn his head, guiding it into the birth canal. Now apply pressure on the perineum just below the anus (a maneuver called *feathering*). This induces the queen to strain and holds the kitten in the correct position so he won't slip back into the improper one.

When the kitten is coming as a *breech* (rump-first), hold the kitten at the pelvic outlet as described. With the vaginal finger, hook first one leg and then the other, slipping them down over the narrow place until the pelvis and legs appear at the vulva.

If the mother is unable to deliver a *large kitten coming normally,* the problem is due to a shoulder locking in the birth canal. The head is seen protruding through the vulva. Rotate the kitten first one way and then another so the legs can be brought forward. Insert a gloved finger into the vagina alongside the kitten until you can feel his front legs at the elbow. Hook them and pull them through individually.

Once the kitten is in the lower part of the birth canal, he should be delivered without further delay. To stimulate a forceful push by the mother, gently stretch the vaginal opening. If you can see the kitten at the mouth of the vagina but he disappears with relaxation, grip the skin at the nape of his neck with a sterile piece of cloth and pull him out as described under *Assisting the Normal Delivery.* Time is of the essence, particularly when the kitten is a breech. It is better to take hold and pull out the kitten even at the risk of injury or death since the kitten, and perhaps the others, will die if something is not done.

Sometimes the blockage is due to a retained placenta. Hook it with your fingers and grasp it with a sterile cloth. Maintain slow and steady traction until it passes out of the vagina.

When the uterus becomes exhausted and stops contracting, it is difficult to correct a malposition. Many veterinarians feel that if after two injections of oxytocin 30 to 45 minutes apart, effective labor and delivery do not occur, then Caesarean Section is indicated.

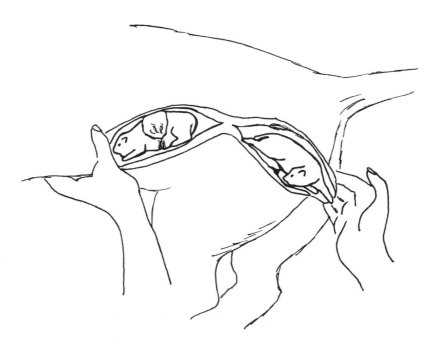

A *deviated head* is a common cause of difficult labor.—*Sydney Wiley.*

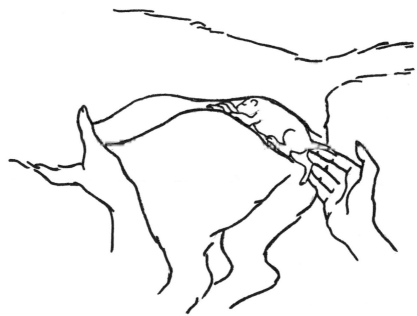

The *hind-foot* or *posterior* presentation occurs about 40 percent of the time.
—*Sydney Wiley.*

Helping a Kitten Breathe

When a kitten is born surrounded by the amniotic sac, it should be removed within 30 seconds to allow the kitten to breathe. If the queen fails to do this herself, you should tear open the sac and remove it, starting at the mouth and working backwards over the body. Aspirate the secretions from the mouth with a bulb syringe. Rub the kitten briskly with a soft towel while holding him head-down to facilitate drainage.

An alternate method of clearing the secretions is to hold the kitten in your hands while supporting his head. Then swing him in a downward arc, stopping abruptly when his nose is pointing to the floor. This helps to expel water from his nostrils. Present the kitten to the mother to lick, sniff and cuddle.

After a difficult delivery, a kitten may be too weak or too flaccid to breathe on his own. Squeeze the chest gently from side to side and then from front to back. If the kitten will not breathe, place your mouth over his nose and blow gently until you see his chest expand. Do not exhale too forcefully as this can rupture his lungs. Leaving his mouth uncovered helps to prevent this complication. Then remove your mouth to allow the kitten to exhale. Repeat this several times until the kitten is breathing and crying.

CAESAREAN SECTION

Caesarean Section is the procedure of choice for any type of arrested labor which cannot be relieved by drugs or obstetrical manipulation. Most veterinarians feel that after 24 hours of unproductive labor, Caesarean Section is indicated. It is indicated *sooner* for a mechanical blockage which cannot be rapidly corrected. The decision ultimately rests with the veterinarian. Consideration will be given to the condition of the queen; length of labor; how many kittens can be delivered by instruments (usually not more than two because of subsequent swelling of the birth canal induced by the instruments); the size of the kittens in relation to the pelvic outlet; failure to respond to injections of oxytocin; and whether the vaginal canal has become dry.

The operation is done under general anesthesia in the veterinary hospital. The risk to a young healthy queen is not great. However, when labor has been unduly prolonged, when toxicity is present, when the kittens are dead and beginning to decompose, or when uterine rupture occurs, then the risks become significant.

Usually a queen is awake and stable and able to nurse her kittens at home within three hours of the operation.

If a queen has a Caesarean Section, she may or may not require a Caesarean Section with her next litter. This depends upon the reason for the first Caesarean Section. Many queens who have had one Caesarean Section are able to have normal vaginal deliveries the next time they become pregnant.

A happy and contented mother with her newly arrived family. —*Sydney Wiley.*

POST PARTUM CARE OF THE QUEEN

Twelve to twenty-four hours after your female delivers, ask your veterinarian to examine her. He will want to check her milk for color, consistency, and quality. (If the milk is thick, stringy, yellowish or discolored it may be infected). Palpation of the uterus rules out a retained kitten or placenta. Many veterinarians prescribe an injection of oxytocin or ergonovine to aid involution of the uterus. This reduces the likelihood of infection.

During the first week take the mother's temperature at least once a day. A temperature of 103 degrees F or higher indicates a problem (retained placenta; uterine or breast infection).

A greenish discharge may be present for the first 24 hours. It is followed by a variable amount of reddish-tinged to serosanguinous (containing both serum and blood) discharge which lasts five to six days. A green, brownish, or serosanguinous discharge that lasts over seven days may indicate a retained placenta or uterine infection (see *Acute Metritis*).

A queen nursing kittens should be kept indoors or taken out only under supervision. During this period she could go into heat. If mated, she may conceive another litter. Breeding should not be allowed at this time.

Feeding During Lactation

During lactation caloric requirements increase sharply up to 300 percent of normal. At this time it is particularly important to be sure that your queen is getting enough to eat. Otherwise, she will fail to produce enough milk to satisfy her kittens. It is virtually impossible to overfeed a queen who is nursing four or more kittens. Nearly all these queens lose some weight, but then regain it when their kittens are weaned.

Feed a good commercial dry cat food ration. (Some veterinarians suggest using a kitten mixture.) Name-brand cat foods are formulated to meet the National Research Council's recommendations for nutritionally complete diets. They provide protein, fat and carbohydrate, along with vitamins and minerals, in correct balance. They are quite suitable for a lactating queen, *if she will eat the required amount.*

Alternately, you may wish to use a canned preparation. Here again, it is important to study the label to be sure that the product is intended as a *complete* diet and not a supplement.

By the second or third week a nursing queen eats three times her normal daily ration, or three full meals spaced throughout the day. Many veterinarians recommend supplementing the kibble with canned meat or cottage cheese in the following proportions: 80 percent kibble to 20 percent canned meat or cottage cheese. Do not exceed this ratio or a correct balance will not be obtained.

Calcium deficiency is the most frequent nutritional disorder in cats. It is particularly likely to occur during lactation. A contributing factor is a meat diet. Raw meat is deficient in calcium. A queen nursing five kittens can lose a third of her calcium stores. Accordingly, a vitamin-mineral supplement containing calcium, such as Pet-Cal, is highly beneficial during lactation. When using canned meat as a supplement, be sure to add extra calcium in the ratio of 0.5 gms. of calcium carbonate to 100 gms. of meat.

Tense, overactive queens, or those with a big litter, may require extra energy. Add three tablespoons of vegetable oil to each pound of dry cat food.

Give Vitamin B supplements to queens with a marginal milk supply.

POST PARTUM PROBLEMS

Problems which can affect the queen following delivery are post partum hemorrhage, acute metritis, mastitis, caked breasts, inadequate milk supply, and milk fever. A few queens have problems accepting their kittens owing to emotional upsets and psychological blocks.

Post Partum Hemorrhage

Vaginal bleeding following birth is not common. When present, it is usually due to a vaginal tear associated with mechanical blockage and a difficult delivery. Excessive loss of blood may produce shock and death. If you see bright red bleeding which persists, notify your veterinarian at once. Surgery may be required.

This should not be confused with the passage of dark red or greenish-tinged blood from the uterus which normally accompanies placental separation.

Acute Metritis

Acute metritis is an infection of the lining of the uterus, having spread upward through the birth canal. It is due to bacterial contamination. Unsanitary kittening quarters predispose to it. Placentas provide an ideal media for bacterial growth. They should be removed from the kittening box after each kitten is delivered.

Acute metritis is likely to occur when part of a placenta has been retained in the uterus. Some cases are due to a retained fetus which has become mummified. Other cases are caused by contamination of the birth canal by unsterile fingers during delivery. A difficult or prolonged labor and a pre-existing vaginitis are other predisposing causes. Vaginitis should be treated as soon as it is diagnosed, preferably before heat and certainly before labor and delivery.

Chronic endometritis and *Pyometra* are other uterine infections which may be confused with acute post partum metritis. They are discussed under *Diseases of the Female Genital Tract* in the chapter SEX AND REPRODUCTION.

Most cases of acute metritis can be anticipated and prevented by a post partum check-up. A veterinarian often will want to clear the uterus with an injection of Pitocin or Ergonovine. Preventive antibiotics are indicated if the birth canal was contaminated during delivery by fingers or instruments.

A queen with acute metritis is lethargic, hangs her head, refuses to eat, and has a temperature of 103 to 105 degrees F. She may cease to keep the nest clean and care for her kittens. They appear unkempt, cry excessively, and may die suddenly. This could be the first sign the queen is ill.

There is a heavy, dark, bloody, greenish or tomato soup-like discharge which appears two to seven days after delivery. It should not be confused with the normal greenish discharge which appears during the first 12 to 24 hours, or the light reddish, serosanguinous discharge which lasts one week. A normal discharge is not accompanied by high fever, excessive thirst or other signs of toxicity such as vomiting and diarrhea.

Treatment: Acute metritis is a life-threatening illness. A veterinarian should be consulted immediately to save the life of the queen. Usually kittens will have to be taken off the mother and reared by hand (see *Raising Kittens by Hand* in the PEDIATRICS chapter). If the infection spreads through her bloodstream, her milk may be toxic.

Mastitis

Two breast conditions affecting the nursing queen are caked breasts and acute mastitis. One often leads to the other.

Caked Breasts (Galactostasis). This is a form of mastitis caused by too much milk in a mammary gland, either because of over-production or because the breast is not being adequately suckled by the kittens. Caking of the breasts can occur during false pregnancy where there are no kittens to remove the milk.

Affected glands, usually the hind ones, are swollen, painful, warm and hard. pH paper may be used to test the acidity of the milk. Normal feline breast milk should test to a pH of 6.0 to 6.5 (colostrum often tests to a pH of 7.0). Milk (not colostrum) which tests to a pH of 7.0 is infected and will make kittens sick (see *Acute Septic Mastitis*). Milk from simple caking of the breasts tests to a normal pH and is okay for kittens to suckle.

Treatment: Apply warm moist packs twice daily and express the gland to draw out some of the coagulated and caked milk. Your veterinarian may wish to prescribe testosterone or a diruetic to relieve the swelling; and may have you

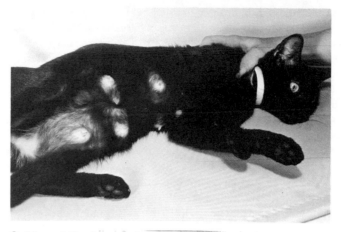

Caking of the breasts is caused by too much milk in the mammary glands.

reduce the queen's intake of food. If the queen has no kittens, the breasts are dried up as described under *Weaning* in the PEDIATRICS chapter.

Severely caked breasts may become infected, thus leading to an acute mastitis. Often this can be prevented by administering a long-acting penicillin, such as Bicillin.

Acute Septic Mastitis (Breast Infection or Abscess). Acute mastitis is an infection of one or more of the mammary glands due to bacteria which get into the breast during nursing from a scratch or puncture wound. Some cases are blood-borne and associated with acute metritis. The milk from an infected breast is toxic and often contains bacteria which can cause kitten septicemia and sudden death. In all cases of sudden death of a kitten, be sure to check the vagina for a

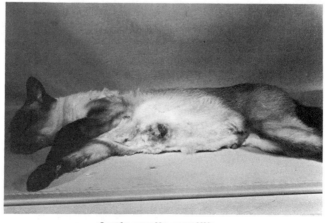

Acute septic mastitis.

purulent discharge and each breast for signs of acute mastitis. The presence of fever supports the diagnosis of maternal infection.

A mammary gland with acute mastitis is swollen, extremely painful, and usually reddish-blue in appearance. Milk may be blood-tinged, thick, yellow or string-like. In some cases the milk will look normal, yet test to a pH of 7.0 or greater. Mothers with acute mastitis refuse to eat, appear listless, and run a high fever (which suggests abscess formation).

Many cases of acute mastitis can be prevented by trimming the nails of kittens when they are two to three weeks old. The hair around the queen's nipples is protective and should not be clipped unless it is matted.

Treatment: Remove all kittens immediately and contact your veterinarian. This disease should be treated by a professional. Routine measures include the use of appropriate antibiotics and gentle massage of the glands three or four times a day, followed by application of warm packs.

In some cases the nipple of an infected gland can be wrapped so the kittens can nurse at the others. If more than one gland is involved, or if the queen is quite toxic, the kittens should be raised by hand as described in the PEDIATRICS chapter. If they are three weeks old, they can be weaned. The procedure for drying up the breasts is explained under *Weaning.*

When milk from an infected breast returns to a normal appearance and tests to a pH of less than 7.0, the kittens can nurse.

Inadequate Milk Supply *(Agalactia)*

The suckling action of the newborn kittens is an important stimulus to the let down of milk. When kittens do not suckle for 24 hours, the milk supply begins to dry up.

The majority of queens will encourage their kittens to suckle as soon as they are born. A novice queen may be too upset by the strain of giving birth to allow her kittens to suckle. Calm and soothe the mother. Lay her on her side and put the kittens to the nipples. Continue this process until she learns to accept them.

Milk can be helped in flow by Pitocin and other hormones. Discuss this possibility with your veterinarian.

A deformed nipple may cause difficulty in suckling. Examine all the nipples to be sure that they are open, fully formed and erect. Discrepancies can be overcome by massaging the nipples to stimulate the flow of milk and then putting a vigorous suckler directly on the nipple.

Occasionally it becomes apparent that a queen is not making enough milk to satisfy her kittens. This is most likely to occur with novice queens and those with large litters. It is most important that a nursing mother receive adequate nutritional support. A deficiency in caloric intake, particularly after the second week when nursing demands are greatest, is a correctable cause of a marginal milk supply (see *Feeding During Lactation*).

Supplemental feedings using artificial queen's milk may be required when the litter is large or the mother is constitutionally unable to produce enough milk by herself (see *Raising Kittens by Hand* in the PEDIATRICS chapter).

Milk Fever *(Eclampsia, Puerperal Tetany)*

Eclampsia is due to an upset in the calcium regulatory mechanism which leads to a low calcium level in the blood. It is called milk fever because it usually occurs during the first three weeks of lactation when there is a drain on the calcium stores in the body. Less commonly it is seen in the latter stages of pregnancy or just before kittening. It is more likely to occur in a queen with a large litter.

Low serum calcium levels cause tetany. The first signs are restlessness, anxiety, rapid breathing, and pale mucus membranes. A queen frequently leaves her kittens and begins to pace up and down. Her gait is stiff-legged, uncoordinated and jerky. Tightening of the face muscles exposes the teeth and gives the face a pinched look. As the condition worsens, she falls down on her side, exhibits spasms in which she kicks all four legs, and salivates profusely.

The temperature is often elevated up to 106 degrees F. This causes more panting, washes out carbon dioxide, raises the pH of the blood, and lowers the serum calcium even further. If there is no treatment within 12 hours the queen will die.

Certain queens seem predisposed to milk fever. If your queen has had milk fever in the past, discuss with your veterinarian the possibility of supplementing her diet with calcium during the last half of pregnancy.

Treatment: Puerperal tetany is a real emergency. Notify your veterinarian at once. Intravenous calcium solutions should be given at the first signs to re-establish normal blood calcium levels. Cardiac arrythmias can occur when calcium is given too rapidly, so this should be done by a professional.

If the rectal temperature is over 104 degrees, treat as you would for *Heat Stroke* while awaiting the veterinarian's arrival.

Kittens must be taken off the queen and fed by hand. If they are three weeks of age, they can be weaned. Younger kittens may be permitted to return to the queen provided she has recovered and you limit nursing to no more than 30 minutes two or three times a day. If there are no adverse effects, these restrictions can be gradually relaxed over the next 48 hours until a normal routine is established. Mothers who must continue nursing should be supplemented with calcium, phosphorus and Vitamin D.

Mothers Who Neglect or Injure Their Kittens

Mothers learn to recognize and care for their kittens as they are born, cleaned and begin to nurse. This bond sometimes is not as strong when the kittens are born by Caesarean Section. Such mothers can have difficulty in accepting their kittens for the first 48 hours. This is less likely to happen when some of the kittens are born before the surgery, or when they are put to the nipples before the sedation wears off.

A novice mother often has difficulty coping with a litter of squirming kittens for the first few hours. This is understandable. With a little help, she can be shown how to nurse her kittens and keep from stepping on them.

A nervous queen could neglect her kittens out of emotional upset caused by excessive noise or too much handling of her kittens by children or strange people. It is important not to allow visitors for the first few weeks, especially when the queen is high-strung and not well socialized to people. Spoiled dependent house-pets who are excessively people-oriented may neglect or abandon their kittens in order to be with their owners.

Due to a hormonal imbalance a queen's milk may not come down for the first 24 hours. During this time the queen may reject her kittens. Milk can be helped in flow by Pitocin. Once the milk comes in, the kittens are usually accepted.

Physical illnesses that may cause kitten rejection are milk fever, breast infection, and post partum uterine infection. A fading kitten whose body temperature has dropped below normal due to sickness or constitutional weakness may be pushed out of the nest. This is nature's way of culling.

A queen may attempt to relocate her nest shortly after delivery. You should return the kittens to the kittening box and stay with the queen, talking softly and stroking her often, until she settles in comfortably. Do not allow her to carry kittens around in her mouth. If she becomes excited or upset, she could bite down too hard.

Cannibalism is a form of abnormal maternal behavior in which the queen consumes her young. It occurs commonly, particularly in catteries. In most cases it is caused by severe emotional stress (for example, a difficult labor and delivery, unsatisfactory kittening quarters, constant interruptions, excessive handling of kittens, and other threats as perceived by the queen).

Queens routinely consume still-born kittens and the products of delivery. While consuming a placenta, a queen might accidentally consume a kitten. A queen might damage her kitten while attempting to sever the umbilical cord, especially if a large umbilical hernia is present. In some cases cannibalism may actually involve the intentional destruction of a constitutionally inferior or malformed kitten.

Rarely, a poorly nourished or half-starved queen might consume her young as a matter of survival.

In summary, most cases of kitten injury or neglect are caused by psychological factors—in particular, those producing emotional insecurity.

Treatment: First identify and remove underlying stress factors. Your veterinarian may then wish to tranquilize the queen with Acepromazine (0.125 mg/lb.). Progesterone has a calming effect and is also useful, particularly to prevent cannibalism. It is given as Depo-provera (50 mg. subcutaneously); or as Ovaban (5 mg. per day until symptoms are controlled; then 2.5 mg. per day for five days).

Nest-seeking can be prevented by introducing the queen to her kittening box two weeks before she is expected to deliver and requiring her to sleep in it.

When the problem is due to maternal infection, the kittens may have to be removed and reared by hand.

Newborn kittens nurse vigorously and compete for nipples, especially those at the chest.

The eyes begin to open at eight to 14 days.

Kittens begin to crawl at 18 days.

17

Pediatrics

NEWBORN KITTENS

During the neonatal period (birth to three weeks of age) a healthy kitten is the picture of contentment. He sleeps about 90 percent of the time and eats about 10 percent. He nurses vigorously and competes for nipples, the preferred ones being those at the chest and the least desirable being the hind ones. For the first 48 hours, a kitten sleeps with his head curled under his chest. While sleeping, kittens jerk, kick and sometimes whimper. This is called "activated sleep". It is normal. It is the newborn kitten's only means of exercise and helps to develop muscles which will be used later.

It is a rare mother who needs help in caring for her kittens. She instinctively keeps her nest clean and her kittens well groomed. By licking the belly and rectum of each kitten, she stimulates the elimination reflex.

It is best to disturb newborn kittens as little as possible—at least until they are a few weeks old and moving about freely. Most queens display anxiety when their kittens are constantly handled. There is a theory that excessive handling interferes with the mechanism by which a kitten learns to identify with, and relate to, his mother and littermates. These interactions are important in establishing the individual's self-awareness as "cat". When these early species associations do not take place, a kitten might exhibit hostility, inappropriate shyness, or fear-biting later in life. However, after six weeks of age, social interaction with human beings and exposure to new and non-threatening situations is essential to the proper development of a happy and well-adjusted pet.

Kittens should be examined when one day old to make sure they are healthy and free of developmental defects. This is a good time to determine their sex (see *Determining the Sex*). Thereafter, change the bedding once or twice a day. This is best done by the same person, preferably while the mother is away from her nest.

Physiology

At one day of age kittens have temperatures that vary between 92 and 97 degrees F. From two to 21 days the heart rate is 200 to 300 beats per minute and the temperature is 96 to 100 degrees F.

A healthy kitten weighs three to four ounces at birth (110 to 125 grams). Rapid weight gain begins a few days after birth, at which time the kitten should gain about 10 grams a day. Most kittens double their birth weight at one week. At five weeks they should weigh about one pound; and at 10 weeks about two.

Kittens are born with their eyes closed. They begin to open at eight days and are completely open by 14 days. The eyes of short-haired varieties open sooner than those of Persians. All kittens are born with blue eyes. Adult colors do not appear before three weeks of age and may take nine to 12 weeks to reach the coloring required by the breed standard. The ear canals, which are closed at birth, begin to open at five to eight days. The tiny folded-down ears become erect by three weeks.

Kittens are sight and sound oriented at 25 days. Usually they begin to crawl by 18 days and can stand at 21 days. Soon after, they begin to walk and can feed from a bowl. They can control the urge to eliminate at four weeks. At this time they prefer the use of papers to soiling the nest.

Most neonatal kittens have little subcutaneous fat. Nor do they have the capacity to constrict their skin blood vessels to retain body heat. Energy for metabolism is supplied primarily through feedings. As there is little margin for reserve, a potentially low blood sugar must be offset by *frequent feedings*. A

Four week old kittens, practicing skills they will need later in life. Mock fighting includes tumbling, paw swatting, clasping with the front legs and kicking out furiously with the hind ones.

kitten who does not eat frequently, for whatever reason, is likely to become chilled. Chilling is the greatest single danger to the newborn kitten.

Kidney function in the newborn is 25 percent of what it will be later in life. As these immature kidneys are unable to concentrate the urine, it is necessary for kittens to excrete large amounts of dilute urine. This obligatory water loss of the kidneys must be offset by sufficient intake of milk, or in the case of kittens raised by hand, by a formula containing adequate amounts of water.

Why Kittens Die

The first two weeks of life present the greatest risk to the newborn. Undoubtedly most deaths are due to lack of advanced preparation—especially failure to provide adequate heat in the kittening quarters, failure to vaccinate the prospective queen, and failure to get her onto a sound feeding program during pregnancy and lactation.

Some deaths can be attributed to birth trauma, maternal neglect, something wrong with the milk supply, and infectious diseases.

Congenital defects are not a major cause of newborn deaths. But when they do occur they may be lethal. Cleft-palate, often associated with hare-lip, prevents effective nursing. Large navel hernias allow prolapse of abdominal organs. Heart defects can be severe enough to produce circulatory failure. Other developmental disorders which may be responsible for the occasional mysterious or unexplained death include esophageal atresia, pyloric stenosis, anal atresia, and malformations affecting the eyes and skeletal system (see *Congenital or Inherited Defects*).

The Kitten Mortality Complex. Although the exact cause of this syndrome is unknown, the virus of feline infectious peritonitis (FIP) has been implicated in a number of cases. In addition to causing newborn kittens to sicken and die shortly after birth, this syndrome is believed to include cases of infertility and habitual abortion. It is discussed in more detail elsewhere in this chapter (see *Kitten Diseases*).

Fading Kitten. This is a kitten, usually under a week of age, who appears vigorous and healthy at birth—but who then fails to gain weight, loses strength and vitality, and with it the ability to nurse. With chilling, failure to nurse and dehydration, the kitten develops a shock-like state due to failure of his circulation. This causes a drop in temperature, heart rate and breathing. As the body temperature drops below 94 degrees F, there is further depression of vital functions. Gradually the crawling and righting ability is lost and the kitten lies on his side. Later, poor circulation affects his brain, causing tetanic rigors and coma, accompanied by breathless periods lasting up to a minute. At this point the condition is irreversible.

There is no general agreement as to the cause of fading kittens. Some cases may be due to immaturity; others to birth defects, environmental stresses, the kitten mortality complex, or an infectious disease.

Early treatment is imperative if death is to be avoided (see *Caring for the Newborn*). Veterinary assistance is advisable.

The Runt. The physiologically immature kitten is at a distinct disadvantage because of his low birth weight and lack of muscle mass and subcutaneous fat. He may be unable to breathe deeply, nurse effectively and maintain warmth in his body. His birth weight may be 25 percent below that of his littermates. Such a kitten is likely to be crowded out by his brothers and sisters and forced to nurse at the least productive nipples.

The most common cause of subnormal birth weight is inadequate nourishment while in the uterus. When all the kittens are undersized, a poorly nourished queen is the prime consideration. When one or two kittens are below par, most likely the fault is one of placental insufficiency, perhaps due to overcrowding or a disadvantageous placement of a placenta in the wall of the uterus. These kittens are immature on the basis of their development rather than their age. If they are to survive, they must be separated from the queen and raised by hand in an incubator as described elsewhere in this chapter.

CARING FOR THE NEWBORN

Newborn kittens are born with limited capacity to adapt to environmental stress. With proper care and attention to the special needs of these infants, many neonatal deaths can be avoided.

Since neonatal kittens do not respond in the same way to environmental stress and illness as do adult cats, a special approach is needed to monitor the well-being of newborns—beginning right from birth. The two crucial factors to watch closely are the kitten's body temperature and his weight. In addition, his appearance, heart rate, breathing rate, sound of his cry, and general behavior can provide useful information as to his overall health and vitality. These perimeters are discussed below.

General Appearance and Vitality

A healthy kitten feels round and firm. He nurses vigorously. His mouth and tongue are wet. When disturbed, he burrows down next to his mother or a littermate for warmth. This is a rooting reflex and is present for the first 11 days.

The sucking reflex is present at birth. Touching the lips and mouth will produce a response. After a few days this reflex is limited to lip contact. An object pushed into the mouth will be rejected. Most neonatal kittens quickly develop a preference for nursing at a particular breast—which they locate by smell. Those that are not used stop producing milk in three days. Newborns spend long hours nursing—often eight hours a day—with sessions lasting up to 45 minutes.

A newborn's skin is warm and pink. When pinched, it springs back in a resilient fashion. Pick him up and he stretches and wiggles energetically in your hand. When removed from his mother, he crawls back to her.

A sick kitten presents a dramatically different picture. This kitten when picked up is limp and cold. He hangs like a dishcloth. He shows lack of interest in nursing and tires easily. Signs of dehydration are lack of moisture in the mouth, a bright pink color to the tongue and mucous membranes of the mouth, a loss of muscle tone, and weakness. When the skin is pinched it stays up in a fold instead of springing back.

Newborn kittens seldom cry. Crying indicates that a kitten is cold, hungry, sick, or in pain. Distressed kittens crawl about looking for help and fall asleep away from the life-sustaining warmth of their mother and littermates. Later, sickly kittens move slowly and with great effort. They sleep with their legs splayed apart and their necks bent to the side. Their mew is plaintive. It sometimes goes on for twenty minutes or longer. Such a kitten is often rejected by the queen who senses that he is not going to survive and pushes him out of the nest rather than waste her energies on him. This can be reversed if the kitten is treated and his body temperature is brought back to normal. The queen will accept him back.

Body Temperature

When a kitten is born his temperature is the same as that of his mother. Immediately afterwards it drops several degrees (how much depends upon the temperature of the room). Within thirty minutes, if the kitten is dry and snuggled close to his mother, his temperature begins to climb back up. A healthy kitten can maintain a temperature 10 to 12 degrees F above his surroundings. But when his mother is away for 30 minutes in a room 70 degrees F (well below the recommended level) his temperature can fall. He quickly becomes chilled, a condition which gravely reduces metabolism.

While chilling is the single greatest danger to the infant kitten, the opposite is also true. Overheating and dehydration can produce many problems. The temperature of the kittening box and the area in which it is kept must be 85 to 90 degrees F during the first week. Thereafter it should be lowered five degrees each week until it is 70 degrees F. The construction of a suitable kittening box is described in the chapter PREGNANCY AND KITTENING.

Warming a Chilled Kitten. A chilled kitten must be warmed GRADU-ALLY. Rapid warming (for example, by immersing him in water), causes dilitation of skin vessels, increased loss of heat, added expenditure of calories, and greater need for oxygen. This is detrimental.

The best way to warm a kitten is to tuck him down beneath a sweater or jacket next to your skin, letting your own warmth seep into his system. If his temperature is below 94 degrees F and he is weak, warming will take two to three hours. Afterwards, he may have to be placed in a homemade incubator (see *Raising Kittens by Hand).*

Never feed *formula* to a cold kitten or allow him to nurse. When so-chilled, the stomach and intestines stop working. If a formula is given it will not be digested. The kitten will bloat and perhaps vomit. A chilled kitten can utilize a 5-10 percent glucose in water solution (which can be purchased at the drug store). Give one half cc per ounce body weight every hour and warm slowly—until he is warm and wiggling about. If a glucose solution is not available, use honey and water; or as a last resort, use household sugar and water: one teaspoonful to an ounce of water.

Importance of Weight Gain

A kitten should gain 10 to 15 grams of weight per day and should double his birth weight in seven to nine days. A steady gain in weight is the best indication that a kitten is doing well. Similarly, when a kitten doesn't gain weight, he should be singled out for special attention. For this reason, kittens should be weighed on a gram scale at birth, daily for the first two weeks of life, and then every three days until a month old.

When all kittens are not gaining weight, you should think of a maternal factor (such as toxic milk, metritis, or inadequate milk supply). A mother who is not getting enough calories in her diet will not be able to produce enough milk to support a large litter. A nursing queen needs two to three times more food than a normal adult cat. In addition, the diet must be balanced to meet the needs of lactation. This subject is discussed in the chapter PREGNANCY AND KITTENING.

A sudden drop in weight with diarrhea is due to water losses. A balanced electrolyte solution is needed. This is the same solution used in correcting dehydration in hand-fed kittens. It is discussed in the paragraph *Common Feeding Problems*.

Kittens dehydrate quickly when they stop nursing. Therefore, dehydration is a factor to be considered whenever a kitten fails to thrive, loses weight, becomes chilled, or is too weak to nurse.

When to Supplement: Kittens who gain weight steadily during the first seven days are in no danger. Kittens who experience a weight loss not exceeding 10 percent birth weight for the first 48 hours of life and then begin to gain should be watched closely. Kittens who lose 10 percent or more of their birth weight in the first 48 hours and do not begin to gain by 72 hours are poor survival prospects. Start supplemental feedings immediately (see *Raising Kittens by Hand*).

If at birth a kitten is 25 percent under the weight of his littermates, you can expect a high mortality. Place this kitten in an incubator and raise him by hand. Many immature kittens can be saved if their condition is not complicated by diseases or congenital defects.

RAISING KITTENS BY HAND

A queen may be unable to raise her litter because of post partum uterine or breast infection, toxic milk, eclampsia, or inadequate milk supply. On occasion a mother might refuse to care for her litter. In such cases the kittens have to be supplemented or hand-fed.

The decision to supplement a kitten is based upon his general appearance and vitality, weight at birth, and his progress in comparison to his brothers and sisters. As a rule, it is better to step in early and start hand-feeding in borderline cases, and not wait until a kitten is in obvious distress. Depending upon the overall condition of the kitten and his response to supplemental feeding, it may be possible to feed him two or three times a day and let him remain with his mother. Others must be taken away and raised as orphans.

If your kitten needs supplemental feeding, calculate his total daily requirement (the method is given in *Calculating the Right Formula*) and assume that a nursing kitten eats four times a day. Give him one-fourth of his total daily requirements at each feeding.

Accurate record keeping is important at all times, but is absolutely essential when kittens are raised by hand. Weigh them on a gram scale at birth, daily for the first two weeks, and then every three days until they reach one month of age.

Three areas of critical importance are: furnishing the right environment; preparing and feeding the right formula; and providing the right management. Feeding equipment should be thoroughly cleaned and boiled. Visitors should not be allowed in the nursery. All personnel should wash their hands before handling the kittens, especially if they have been with other cats. Many diseases can be transmitted to kittens by a person who has recently handled an infective cat.

If the kittens were unable to receive the colostrum, or first milk of the dam, they lack passive immunity and are susceptible to a variety of feline diseases. Vaccinations are then given after three weeks of age.

Since chilling is the single greatest danger to the newborn kitten's survival, you will need an incubator.

The Incubator

You can make a satisfactory incubator in a few minutes by dividing a cardboard box into separate compartments so that each kitten can have his own pen. These pens are important when kittens are fed by stomach tube because, having no nipples to suckle, they tend to suckle each other's ears, tails and genitalia. If you nurse them from a bottle, you may not need to have separate compartments.

Place a small electric heating pad in the bottom of the incubator. One-fourth of it should lie against the side of the box, and three-fourths on the bottom. This permits kittens to get close to the heat when they are cold and get away from it when hot. Cover the pad with a waterproof material such as plastic or rubber. On top, place a baby diaper which can be changed whenever it becomes soiled. This also gives a means for checking the appearance of each kitten's stool, which is an excellent indicator of overfeeding, and an early warning sign of infection.

Another method of providing sufficient warmth is to use overhead infrared heat lights with thermostatic controls. This may not be as satisfactory as a heating pad.

A thermometer should be placed in the incubator to monitor the surface temperature.

Keep the incubator at 85 to 90 degrees F for the first week. During the second week, reduce it to 80 or 85 degrees F. Thereafter, gradually decrease the temperature so that it is 75 degrees F by the end of the fourth week. Maintain constant warmth and avoid chilling drafts.

Keep the humidity of the room at about 55 percent. This helps to prevent skin drying and dehydration.

General Care

Keep the kittens clean with a damp cloth. Be sure to cleanse the anal area and skin of the abdomen. A light application of baby oil should be applied to these areas, and to the coat, to prevent drying of the skin. Change the bedding often to prevent urine scalds. When present, they can be helped by the application of baby powder. When infected, apply a topical antibiotic ointment (Panolog).

For the first ten days, gently swab the anal and genital areas of the kittens after each feeding to stimulate elimination. (This is something the mother would do.) A wad of cotton or tissue soaked in warm water works well.

Hand Feeding

Artificial queen's milk (*Kitten Milk Replacer* or KMR from Borden's) is a suitable formula for feeding orphan kittens as it most nearly approximates the composition of queen's milk. It is available through veterinarians and some pet stores. It has largely replaced the need for homemade formulas and foster mothers.

The composition of cow's milk is such that it is not suitable for rearing kittens.

KMR approximates the composition of queen's milk. It can be fed by tube and syringe, or kitten nurser.

Comparison of Cat, Dog and Cow's Milk

	Solids	Water	Calories /100ml	Protein (gms)	Fat (gms)	Lactose (gms)
Cow	13%	87%	68	3.5	3.9	4.9
Queen	28%	72%	142	11.4	7.9	7.8
Bitch	23%	77%	120	7.5	8.3	3.7
Evaporated (Reconstituted to 20% solids)	20%	80%	115	5.8	6.6	8.2

If artificial queen's milk is not available, one of the following formulas can be used in an *emergency* or as a temporary substitute:

Formula #1:
2/3 cup homogenized milk
3 egg yolks
1 tablespoon corn oil
1 dropper liquid pediatric vitamins

Formula #2:
Evaporated milk reconstituted to 20% solids
1 teaspoonful bone meal per pint
1 egg yolk

These formulas provide one to one and one-fourth calories per cc of formula.

Artificial milks such as KMR come as liquids. They should be prevented from freezing. Follow the directions of the manufacturer in regard to storage.

Calculating the Amount to Feed:

The best way to determine how much formula each kitten needs is to weigh the kitten and use a table of caloric requirements. Daily requirements according to weight and age are given in the following table:

Age in Weeks	Average Weight	Calories Needed Per Pound Weight Per Day	CC of KMR Per Day	CC of Emergency Formula/Day	No. of Feedings Per Day
1	4 oz.	190	32 cc	48	6
2	7 oz.	175	56 cc	77	4
3	10 oz.	150	80 cc	90	3
4	13 oz.	125	104 cc	104	3
5	1 lb.	100	128 cc	128	3
10	2 lb.				

(Note: When using KMR, a kitten needs 8 cc per ounce body weight per day. However, emergency formulas have fewer calories than KMR or queen's milk. Thus, more formula is required.)

To calculate the amount of formula to give at each feeding, weigh the kitten to determine how much formula to give per day and divide by the number of feedings. EXAMPLE: A four ounce kitten during the first week requires 32 cc of KMR per day (i.e., 4 ounces x 8 cc/ounce). Divide by the number of feedings (6), which gives 5 to 6 cc per feeding.

Small, young kittens do best if fed every four hours for the first three to four days. Weak kittens should be fed every four hours. Older, larger kittens can manage on three meals a day. However, if a kitten cannot take the required amount at each feeding, then the number of feedings should be increased.

When a kitten has received an adequate supply of milk, his abdomen will feel full—but not tense or distended. Milk may bubble out around his lips, particularly if you are using a nursing bottle. It is important to avoid overfeeding, which produces diarrhea.

At three weeks most kittens can learn to lap milk from a dish. At four weeks you can mix the formula with small amounts of cat food. Weaning to solids can begin at this time (see *Weaning*).

How to Give the Formula:

Kittens may be fed by medicine dropper, syringe, baby nursing bottle or stomach tube. With any one of these methods it is important to keep the kitten in an upright position so that formula won't be aspirated into his lungs.

A plastic medicine dropper or a syringe is readily available and may be used as an emergency measure in the absence of a baby nurser or stomach tube. Feed slowly, as kittens can choke when formula is dropped or injected too rapidly into their mouths.

The nursing bottle has the advantage of satisfying the urge to suckle but requires that the kitten be strong enough to suck the formula. When using a small doll's bottle or a commercial kitten nurser with a soft nipple, usually you will need to enlarge the hole in the nipple so that the milk drops out slowly when the bottle is turned over. Otherwise, the kitten will tire after a few minutes of nursing and will not get enough to eat. Use a hot needle to enlarge the hole. Warm the formula to about 100 degrees F (slightly warm to the wrist) as you would a baby's. To bottle-feed a kitten, place him on his stomach. (Do not roll him on his back as the formula is apt to run into his windpipe.) Open his mouth with the tip of your finger, insert the nipple and hold the bottle at 45 degrees. The angle of the bottle is such that air does not get into the kitten's stomach. Keep a slight pull on the bottle to encourage vigorous sucking. A bottle-fed kitten will need to be "burped". When a kitten has had enough, bubbles come out around his mouth.

Tube feeding has several advantages. It takes about two minutes to complete each feeding. No air is swallowed (no burping required). It insures that a proper amount of formula is administered to each kitten. *It is the only satisfactory method of feeding immature or sick kittens too weak to nurse.*

If too much formula is injected, or if given too rapidly, it can be regurgitated. This can lead to aspiration of formula and pneumonia. The complication can be avoided if care is taken to monitor the weight of the kitten and compute the correct amount. Kittens fed by tube do not get a chance to suckle and must be kept in separate incubator compartments.

Tube feeding is not difficult and can be mastered in a few minutes. It requires a soft rubber catheter (size 5 French for smaller kittens—size 8 for larger kittens—which can be bought at a drugstore), a 10 or 20 cc plastic or glass syringe, and a gram scale to calculate the weight of each kitten and monitor his progress.

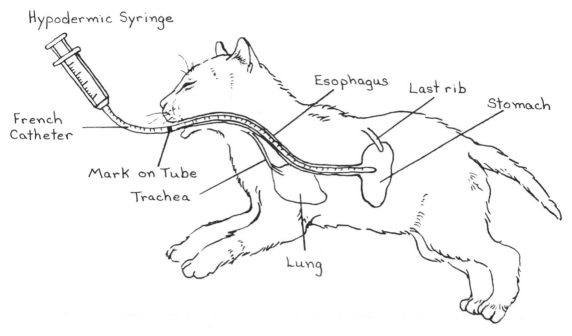

Hypodermic Syringe

Esophagus   Last rib

French
Catheter

Stomach

Mark on Tube

Trachea

Lung

Tube feeding is the best way to feed a weak kitten.—*Rose Floyd.*

A kitten's stomach is located at the level of his last rib. Measure the tube
from the mouth to the last rib and then mark the tube with a piece of tape. Draw
the formula into the syringe and warm it to body temperature by placing it in hot
water. Moisten the tube with formula, and then open the kitten's mouth and pass
the tube slowly over his tongue and into his throat. The tube will be too large to
enter the smaller passage of the windpipe, so there is little danger of passing it the
wrong way. With steady pressure the kitten will begin to swallow the tube. Pass it
to the level of the mark. Connect the syringe to the tube and *slowly* inject the formula down the tube and into the kitten's stomach.

At about 14 days of age the windpipe of many kittens will become large
enough to accommodate the smaller tube. If the tube goes down the wrong way
the kitten will begin to cough and choke. Change to a larger tube (size 8 or 10
French); or by now the kitten may be strong enough to suckle from a bottle.

Common Feeding Problems.

Common feeding problems are *overfeeding* (which causes diarrhea) and
underfeeding (causing failure to gain weight). A steady weight gain at the rate of
10 grams or 1/3 ounce a day, and a normal stool (firm, yellowish), are good indications that you are feeding the right amount.

Experience indicates that owners are much more likely to overfeed than underfeed orphan kittens. The best way to tell if this is happening is to look at the stools. If a kitten is fed four times a day you can expect four to five stools, or about one stool after each feeding.

A loose yellow stool indicates a *mild degree of overfeeding.* Usually it responds to reducing the amount of formula by diluting it one-third with water. As the stool returns to normal you can gradually restore the formula to full strength.

With *moderate overfeeding,* there is more rapid movement of food through the intestinal tract, indicated by a greenish stool. The color green is due to unabsorbed bile. Two or three drops of Kaopectate every four hours, along with a cutback in the strength of the formula, usually corrects this problem.

Unchecked overfeeding leads to a depletion of digestive enzymes and causes a grayish diarrheal stool. Eventually, when there is little or no digestion of formula, the stool looks like curdled milk. At this point the kitten is getting no nutrition and is becoming rapidly dehydrated. Treat this diarrhea by diluting the formula one-third using water; and give Kaopectate three drops per ounce body weight every three hours until the diarrhea is checked.

Dehydration is corrected by giving Ringer's lactate solution mixed half and half with 5% dextrose in water, or a balanced pediatric electrolyte solution such as Pedialyte. These solutions are available at drugstores or through your veterinarian. Give one-half cc per ounce body weight per hour by bottle or stomach tube. Other supportive measures, such as warming a chilled kitten, are indicated. Veterinary administration of electrolyte solutions subcutaneously is highly desirable.

All kittens with gray or white stools should be examined by a veterinarian. They may have a neonatal infection.

Kittens who are being *underfed* cry excessively, appear listless and apathetic, frequently attempt to suckle their litter mates, gain little or no weight from one feeding to the next, and begin to chill. Kittens dehydrate quickly when not getting enough formula. Review your feeding procedure. Check the temperature of the incubator.

Constipation. Some kittens normally have fewer bowel movements than others. This is not a cause for concern unless the stools are firm and the kitten appears to be having difficulty passing them. His abdomen may feel swollen and doughy. If constipation is severe he will appear bloated.

Hand-fed kittens need to have their abdominal and perineal areas massaged with a wad of cotton soaked in warm water after each feeding to stimulate the elimination reflex.

If the kitten is constipated, a warm soap-water enema can be given by eye dropper (two or three dropper-fulls after feeding). Alternately, you can give mineral oil or Milk of Magnesia (three drops per ounce body weight) by mouth. This should be done with extreme care to avoid aspiration into the lungs. If you are feeding a formula containing syrup, give dark syrup which has a laxative effect, instead of white syrup or honey.

KITTEN DISEASES

Toxic Milk Syndrome

Queen's milk can be toxic to kittens for a number of reasons. The chief cause is mastitis, an infection of the milk glands, but post partum uterine infection also can lead to toxic milk. These conditions are discussed in the chapter PREGNANCY AND KITTENING. Kitten formulas which are not properly prepared or stored may become contaminated with bacteria and cause this problem. In some cases the cause is unknown. Presumably there are toxins in the milk which cause digestive upsets in nursing kittens.

Kittens appear distressed and cry continually. Diarrhea and bloating are especially common. The anus often is red and swollen from the continuous diarrhea. One complication of this syndrome is kitten septicemia.

Treatment: The kittens should be removed from the queen and treated for diarrhea and dehydration. Start them off on a Lactate Ringers Solution in 5% Dextrose in water, or Pedialyte solution (see *Common Feeding Problems* in this chapter). Administer Kaopectate (one cc per pound body weight) every six hours. In 24 to 48 hours, switch to Kitten Milk Replacer and hand-feed as described above. Obtain veterinary attention for the queen and her kittens. Do not allow the kittens to return to the mother until this has been approved by your veterinarian.

Newborn Anemia

Iron deficiency anemia affects the offspring of queens who are themselves anemic. It is caused by a low iron content in the milk. This is the most common cause of kitten anemia.

Intestinal parasites also can cause iron deficiency anemia due to chronic blood loss through the gastrointestinal tract, although this is more common in older kittens and adults.

A rare cause of anemia in kittens is a disease called *feline porphyria*. It is due to a defect in the formation of red blood cells. It can be recognized by seeing a peculiar brownish discoloration of the teeth, and a reddish-brown urine.

Kittens with anemia are undersized, grow slowly, tire easily, and have pale mucous membranes.

They should be examined by a veterinarian so that tests can be made to determine the cause. Early detection of iron deficiency anemia is important because this anemia is easily treated by giving the queen and her kittens iron injections and vitamins.

Anemia is discussed in the CIRCULATORY SYSTEM chapter.

Navel Infection

An umbilical stump can be the site of an infection. Predisposing causes are dental disease of the queen (she transfers bacteria to the umbilical cord when she cuts it), contamination in the kittening box by stool and spilled food, and factors which reduce kittens' resistance to disease.

An infected navel looks red, swollen, and may drain pus. There is a direct communication to the liver, which makes even a low-grade infection of the umbilical stump potentially dangerous. Untreated, the signs of kitten septicemia may appear. Prophylactic iodine should be applied to the navel stump at birth to reduce the likelihood of this complication.

Treatment: Cleanse the navel with a dilute solution of hydrogen peroxide followed by a pHisoHex wash. Apply a topical antibiotic ointment (Panolog). Oral or intramuscular antibiotics may be indicated. If the infection does not clear up quickly, consult your veterinarian. This disease can be present in other kittens in the litter.

Kitten Septicemia

Sepsis in infant kittens is caused by infections which spread rapidly and cause signs mainly in the abdomen. They occur in kittens four to 10 days old.

The usual portal of entry is the digestive tract. In newborn kittens, bacteria can penetrate the lining of the bowel just as maternal antibodies can. Infected milk is a major cause of infant sepsis. Navel infection is another.

The initial signs are crying, straining to defecate, and bloating. They are like those of the toxic milk syndrome. At first they may be mistaken for simple constipation. But as the disease progresses the abdomen becomes distended and its skin takes on a dark red or bluish tint. These are signs of peritonitis. Other signs include refusal to nurse, chilling, weakness, dehydration and loss of weight. Death occurs rapidly.

Treatment: The cause must be discovered at once, otherwise the whole litter can be affected. Sick kittens should be treated for dehydration, diarrhea and chilling as described elsewhere in this chapter. They should be given a broad-spectrum antibiotic (Chloromycetin), removed from the kitten box and raised by hand. Septicemia is best managed under veterinary supervision.

Herpes Virus of Kittens

The herpes virus, which produces rhinotracheitis in cats (FVR), and the calici virus, which also produces an upper respiratory infection in adults, both can cause a serious illness in kittens. The two diseases are discussed here together. Regardless of which viral group is responsible for the infection, the signs are similar.

The incubation period is one to six days. Early signs in newborn kittens are abrupt cessation of nursing, weakness, painful crying. At times, kittens may be found dead without apparent cause. Affected kittens may experience sneezing, nasal congestion, eye discharge, coughing and fever. Ulcers of the tongue and palate, and a conjunctivitis which may become complicated by ulcerations of the cornea, also can occur. Illness lasts 10 to 14 days. Mortality rates approach 20 to 30 percent.

Treatment: Veterinary assistance is required. Weak or dehydrated kittens may need to be given intravenous fluids.

Kittens with nasal congestion or mouth ulcers may be unable to nurse and should be tube-fed. Steam vaporization helps to keep mucous membranes from drying out. The eyes should be swabbed gently with a cotton ball moistened in warm water at regular intervals and then medicated as described in the section EYES: *Conjunctivitis in Newborn Kittens.* Idox uridine eye drops are of assistance in this condition, which is caused by a virus.

Prevention of FVR and FVC is discussed in the INFECTIOUS DISEASES chapter.

Kitten Mortality Complex

The virus of Feline Infectious Peritonitis (FIP) recently has been implicated as a cause of sudden neonatal death and fading kittens. Other related problems believed to be produced by this virus are reduced litter size (one or two kittens); repeated abortions; fetal reabsorptions; stillborns; deformed kittens; and infections of the uterus. The entire syndrome has been given the name Kitten Mortality Complex (KMC).

In newborn kittens the signs of KMC include a low birth weight associated with weakness and emaciation and the inability to nurse effectively. In some cases kittens at first appear healthy but then grow weak, lose weight, stop nursing, and die a few days later (fading kittens). Others experience a sudden attack of difficulty breathing, turn blue, and die within a few hours from circulatory collapse and congestive heart failure.

This condition is especially serious in catteries where it can produce a drastic drop in kitten survivals. Preventive measures are discussed in the chapter INFECTIOUS DISEASES (see *Feline Infectious Peritonitis).* Treatment of kittens involves supportive measures as discussed in the section *Caring for the Newborn.*

Neonatal Feline Penleukopenia *(Feline Infectious Enteritis)*

The virus of Panleukopenia can be transmitted to kittens in utero. Like FIP, it may be responsible for fading kittens and some cases of reproductive failure.

Kittens who recover from this infection may develop *cerebellar hypoplasia,* a condition in which the cerebellum fails to achieve normal growth and development. Signs appear at three weeks of age. The kitten develops a jerky, uncoordinated gait. As he jumps or reaches for food, he tends to over or undershoot.

Feline Panleukopenia is discussed in the chapter INFECTIOUS DISEASES.

Skin Infection of the Newborn
(Impetigo; Folliculitis and Pyoderma)

Scabs, blisters, and purulent crusts can develop on the skin of newborn kittens, most often on the bare abdomen. These sores sometimes contain pus. They are caused by poor sanitation and secondary bacterial infection.

Treatment: Keep the nest clean of food, stool and dried debris. Cleanse scabs with a dilute solution of hydrogen peroxide and wash with a surgical soap. Then apply an antibiotic ointment such as Panolog. In severe infections oral or injectable antibiotics may be required.

The eyelids have to be opened in *neonatal conjunctivitis* to remove the pus and treat the infection.

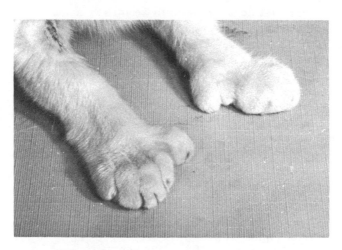

Polydactyly. Extra toes are most common on the front feet.

Navel hernia.

A kitten with *cerebellar hypoplasia*, showing lack of coordination and difficulty moving.

Conjunctivitis of the Newborn

This condition is due to a bacterial infection beneath the eyelids. Some cases are associated with *Herpes Virus of Kittens*. It occurs in kittens before their eyes are open. It is discussed in the chapter EYES.

Congenital or Inherited Defects

Structural defects are not common in kittens. The ones you might be able to recognize are hernias; cleft palate and hairlip; imperforate (absent) anus; polydactyly (extra toes); absent tail; kinked tail; undescended testicle(s); hydrocephalus (enlarged head); strabismus (cross-eyed look); entropion (eyelid rolled-in); and infantile cataracts.

Other defects, which require special studies to diagnose, are malformations in the urogenital tract (kidneys, uterus); pyloric stenosis; sterility in tortoiseshells; deafness in white cats with blue eyes; and cerebellar hypoplasia (incomplete development of this part of the brain).

Birth defects can be inherited, in which case they are produced by genes (i.e., deafness in white blue-eyed cats; sterility in tortoiseshells). Or they can be caused by something which affects the growth and development of the fetus in utero. In either case they are *congenital*—that is they exist at, or date from, birth.

Agents known to produce malformations in the growing fetus include x-rays, cat viruses (FIP; feline leukemia), live virus vaccines, some flea and insecticide preparations; and certain antibiotics.

An antibiotic called Griseofulvin, which is used in the prolonged treatment of ringworm infection, has been found to be associated with severe congenital defects. They include hydrocephalus, spinal cord defects; cats born with missing eyes, cleft palate, imperforate anus, and fused toes. This drug should not be given to pregnant females. It is important to remember this, especially in a cattery where ringworm has been chronic, and where several individuals might be under treatment.

Potentially treatable congenital defects are:

Hernia. A hernia is a protrusion of a portion of the contents of the abdomen through an abdominal wall opening which would normally close in the course of growth. When a bulge can be pushed back into the abdomen, the hernia is said to be *reducible.* When it cannot, the hernia is *incarcerated.* An incarcerated hernia becomes *strangulated* if the blood supply to the tissues in the sac is pinched off. Accordingly, a painful hard swelling in a typical location could be an incarcerated hernia—which is an emergency. Seek professional help.

Hernias have a hereditary basis. There is a genetic predisposition for delayed closure of the abdominal ring in most cases. An occasional navel hernia may be caused by severing the umbilical cord too close to the abdominal wall.

Navel hernia. This is the most common hernia. It is often seen in kittens at about two weeks of age. It usually gets smaller and disappears before six months. If the opening is larger than a pencil eraser, have it repaired. The operation is not serious; the kitten usually goes home the same day. If your kitten is a female and you are planning to have her spayed, repair can be postponed until that time.

Inguinal Hernias. They are not common. The bulge appears in the groin, usually in a female. It may not be seen until she is mature or bred. A pregnant or diseased uterus may be incarcerated in the sac. Inguinal hernias should be repaired.

Cleft Palate. This is a birth defect of the nasal and oral cavities. It is commonly associated with hairlip. It is caused by failure of the bones of the palate to develop completely. This results in an opening from the oral to the nasal cavity, allowing food and liquid to pass between. Usually it is impossible for a kitten to create enough suction to nurse. Survival then can be accomplished only by tube feeding.

A similar condition can occur in adult cats from a blow to the face associated with a fracture of the palate.

Hairlip can occur by itself. It is due to abnormal development of the upper lip. This problem is primarily a cosmetic one.

Cleft palate and hairlip can be corrected by plastic surgery.

Pyloric Stenosis. In this condition the muscular ring at the outlet of the stomach enlarges, narrowing the pyloric canal and preventing food from passing out of the stomach. The deformity tends to occur among related individuals (often of the Siamese breed), suggesting a hereditary basis.

The most characteristic sign is projectile vomiting of partially digested food without bile. It occurs several hours after eating. Vomiting may not occur until weaning-time, when solid food accumulates in the stomach. The diagnosis is confirmed by upper gastrointestinal X-rays which show the typical deformity.

Pyloric stenosis can be treated by an operation which divides the enlarged muscular ring, allowing food to pass through the channel; or by dietary management. This can be determined by your veterinarian.

Another condition, in which the lower esophageal ring enlarges and blocks the passage of food into the stomach, is discussed in the chapter DIGESTIVE SYSTEM: *Swallowing Problems in Kittens.*

Imperforate Anus. This uncommon birth defect is caused by failure of the anal opening to develop along with the rectum. Examination of the perineum will show that the anus is either absent or sealed over by skin. The passage of stool is prevented. Surgical correction may be applicable in some cases.

WEANING

Weaning time depends upon several factors which include the size of the litter, the condition of the queen, and the availability of mother's milk. When necessary, kittens can be weaned at three weeks when they can stand.

A queen may wean her kittens when they are six to 10 weeks old. But if she is left to her own devices and her litter is small, she might continue to nurse them until the birth of her next litter.

If you plan to wean the kittens yourself, start supplementing them at four weeks of age with solid foods as described below. Weaning should be complete by seven weeks. All changes should be made gradually, so as not to cause digestive upsets.

Begin by offering one or two feedings a day of evaporated milk mixed two parts to one part of water. Warm it to body temperature before serving. After a day or two, add baby cereal (oatmeal), and one raw egg yolk (for iron and protein). This should be made up to a sloppy gruel. Feed in a low-rimmed saucer.

Dip your fingers into the gruel and let the kittens lick it off—or smear it on their lips. Once they learn to like it, they will eat from a dish.

To stimulate appetite, remove the queen two hours before feeding. After the meal, let her return to nurse.

Kittens who eat too much gruel are apt to get diarrhea. This is due to overfeeding, or perhaps some degree of intolerance to the milk. Therefore, at least two feedings a day should still be by nursing.

As the kittens start to eat from a pan, there is less demand on the queen's milk supply. You should now begin to decrease her intake of food. This starts the drying-up process.

When the kittens are eating the gruel well (eating more than they are spilling), switch to a name-brand canned meat product specifically formulated to support the growth of kittens. If the label does not give instructions for feeding kittens, assume it is not nutritionally complete and use another. (For information on choosing a nutritionally complete ration see the chapter FEEDING AND NUTRITION.) Some breeders prefer to use a dry ration. This, too, should be a balanced product designed for kittens. Dry rations may be supplemented with small amounts of hamburger, cottage cheese, or strained baby food. These supplements should never exceed 10 percent of the total ration.

Weaning can now proceed rapidly. Discontinue nursing and feed three times a day, as much as the kittens will eat. Once they begin to eat solid foods, be sure to keep water available at all times.

If it becomes necessary to dry the queen up, a drop in her milk production can be accomplished by reducing her food intake. Withhold all food and water the first day. The next day feed her one-fourth the normal amount. The third day feed her one-half the normal amount; and the fourth day feed her three-fourths the normal amount. Thereafter, restore her to her normal ration.

At 10 to 14 weeks of age kittens become susceptible to respiratory and digestive tract infections because they have lost the protective immunity of their mother's milk. Should illness occur, there is a marked reduction in food intake at a time when they should be gaining six or more ounces a week. As a result, they stop growing and become weak and debilitated. This further impairs their resistance to the illness. Such kittens should receive special attention. Every effort should be made to insure adequate nutrition. Appropriate vaccinations during kittenhood will prevent some of these ailments.

THE NEW KITTEN

Determining the Sex

You can determine a kitten's sex during the first 24 hours while you are examining the litter to be sure they are healthy and free of developmental defects; or you can do it before they are sold.

Determining a kitten's sex is more difficult than an adult cat's because their genitalia are smaller and more difficult to see. However there should be no problem if the following steps are taken:

With the kitten facing away from you lift up the tail to expose the anal area. In both sexes you will see two openings. The first opening just below the base of the tail is the anus.

In the female kitten the vulva is a *vertical slit* seen immediately below the anus. In the adult female the space between the anus and vulva measures about one-half inch—but it is closer than that in the kitten.

In the male, the opening for the penis is directed backward. The tip of the penis is hidden in a small *round* opening located one-half inch below the anus. These two openings are separated by the scrotal sacs, which appear as raised darkish areas. The testicles usually are not palpable until the kitten is six weeks old. In the adult tom or neutered male the anus and opening for the penis are more than one inch apart.

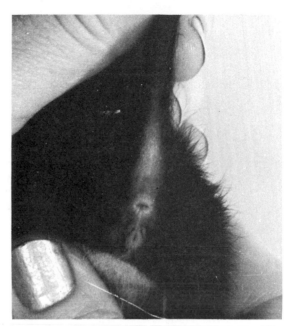

Determining the sex. In the female the vulva is a vertical slit just below the anus.

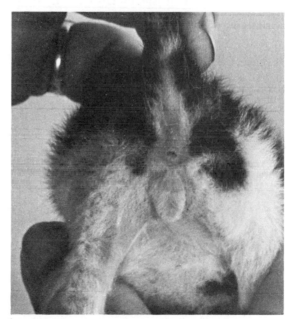

In the male the two openings are separated by the scrotal sacs.

Declawing

This operation may be considered for certain individuals who live indoors and who have developed the vice of scratching and tearing up curtains, upholstery, and expensive furnishings—particularly after attempts to train them to use a scratching post have not been successful (see FELINE BEHAVIOR AND TRAINING).

There is controversy about whether a cat should or should not be declawed. One view is that declawing is unnatural and psychologically harmful. Another is that it does not involve a hardship and that a cat can learn to get along well without them. However, cats who live outdoors should not be declawed. This affects their ability to climb and defend themselves.

Declawing is best done when a kitten is three months of age or older. Many veterinarians suggest that the operation be deferred until a kitten is four to five months old, when it can be carried out at the same time as neutering. Young cats seem to learn to cope without their claws more quickly than do adults.

In most cases only the front claws should be removed. The hind feet are not used for scratching furniture. Leaving the back claws still affords the cat some measure of protection.

The operation, which is done under general anesthesia, involves the removal of the claw to include the nail matrix and part or all of the last bone of the toe. Less complete removal can result in regrowth of the claw or development of a misshapen nail. The feet are firmly bandaged. Dressings are removed in a day or two and the cat can go home. His feet will be tender for several days. The litter box should be emptied and the filler replaced by paper so that the cat won't get sand into his incisions.

18

Feeding and Nutrition

The nutrition of cats has received considerable interest during the past few years and certain large manufacturers of cat foods have conducted extensive research and feeding trials in order to establish nutritious diets that need no supplementation. Federal law requires that all cat food manufacturers provide a listing of ingredients in their rations. Ingredients are listed according to amount: the greatest amount first, the least amount last. However, the required labels do not contain enough information for you to compare one cat food with another. A good indication of quality is a statement on the label that the diet has been found adequate by the Association of American Feed Control Officials (AAFCO).

Another indication of quality is the reputation of the manufacturer. Well-known manufacturers noted for their research generally produce high quality food you can trust.

You can also gauge the effectiveness of a product by observing its effect upon your cat's stool. Poor quality protein passes through a cat's intestinal tract unused, resulting in loose, mushy, or diarrheal stools. Very large stools, on the other hand, indicate excessive amounts of fiber and other indigestibles. Protein quality depends upon the ingredients the manufacturer uses to supply the protein—not upon the type of ration.

When choosing a cat food it is important to determine whether it has been formulated to meet all the daily protein, fat, vitamin and mineral requirements of your cat. The best way to determine this is to look at the label and see if it says "complete, balanced, perfect, or scientific." If it does not, then you can assume it is not a complete diet. Use it only for an occasional treat, or choose another product. When it is designed for the growth of kittens or for nursing queens, the label should tell you this.

Types of Cat Food

There are three types of cat food from which to choose: *dry, semi-moist,* and *canned.*

333

Dry Rations. Dry rations are the least expensive and, because they are abrasive, are the best for the teeth and gums.

Dry cat food is a cereal-based food mixed with meat and/or dairy products. It contains about 10 percent water in contrast to canned foods which contain 70 percent. Complete rations contain added vitamins and minerals.

Some cat owners believe that dry food is less palatable than canned food. However, most cats accept it well. Weight loss due to feeding dry food is unusual.

One advantage of dry food is that it can be left out at all times and the cat can eat when he chooses.

A theoretical disadvantage of dry rations is that they may predispose to the feline urologic syndrome (FUS). This could be due to their low water content which leads to a concentrated urine and an increase in urinary sediment, which might result in the formation of a urethral plug. The amount of ash (magnesium and phosphorus) which a cat takes in each day also could be a factor.

Dry rations tend to lose their nutritional value during storage and should not be used after they are six months old.

Semi-moist Rations. These foods have more eye and taste appeal, but are more expensive than dry foods. They are made up from many protein sources from which a certain meat product (such as fish, beef, liver, chicken) is selected to give the flavoring. The water content is higher than dry ration.

Canned Rations. Canned foods are the most popular and most expensive. There are two types of canned preparation: those sold in the large 12-15 ounce cans; and the specialty or gourmet flavors sold in small flat six ounce tins.

The large cans contain protein derived from meat, fish and vegetable sources along with vitamins and minerals. Many of them are nutritionally complete.

The small speciality gourmet cans offer a high taste appeal. Vitamins and mineral supplements may be added to some of them. They are the most expensive of the cat foods. This doesn't mean they are necessarily the most nutritious. In fact, many are intended to be used as a supplement to a more complete diet, for flavor and taste appeal.

Like the semi-moist varieties, canned rations do not reduce dental tartar. Their primary advantage, aside from taste appeal, is that cats fed canned rations as the major diet may have a lower incidence of urinary sediment formation. This could be due to their high water content. However, like the dry and semi-moist varieties, canned products might not be suitable for cats who already suffer from FUS. This depends on their magnesium content.

To prevent recurrence of FUS, the magnesium content of any cat food should be less than 0.1%, dry weight basis (DWB). Most—but not all—commercial cat foods provide levels of 0.16% DWB or higher. You can consult the product label and in some cases it will give you the percent magnesium—or use a product recommended by your veterinarian. Keep in mind that this provision applies to cats who have had at least one bout of FUS. Special diets low in magnesium are not necessarily recommended for *all* cats. This subject is discussed at greater length in the chapter URINARY SYSTEM (see *Feline Urologic Syndrome*).

A common misconception about cat foods is that in dry rations the protein is of cereal origin, while in canned food it is of meat origin. In fact, both varieties contain protein from meats and cereals. As vegetable protein is the least expensive, the cost of the food is a good index of its protein quality. More expensive cat foods tend to have a greater percentage of their proteins in the form of meat products.

FEEDING YOUR CAT

Food Preferences

Many owners assume that cats eventually will eat a nutritionally balanced diet if given a variety of foods from which to choose. This is incorrect. Many cats will starve rather than eat a product, no matter how nutritious, if they find it unappetizing.

In general, cats prefer meat—older cats, especially kidneys—whether cooked or raw makes very little difference. They prefer food at body temperature, rather than hot or cold. In the wild, mice are the primary food of cats.

Many cats develop a liking for liver. Large amounts should not be given because of its high concentration of Vitamin A. This could produce Vitamin A toxicity. Similarly, raw fish and raw eggs should not be given in excess. Both contain anti-vitamin factors which could produce a lethal deficiency.

Meat alone is not a complete diet. If you feed it primarily, your cat will probably develop a preference to it and stop eating anything else.

Many cats enjoy milk. How much they can consume without experiencing diarrhea varies greatly with the individual. Milk should not sit out for more than two hours (nor should canned food) because of the danger of spoiling.

Food preferences generally are established before a cat is six months old. Accordingly, if you want your cat to be interested in a variety of foods, you should introduce him to them early in life.

Although many cat experts advocate feeding a variety of foods to kittens and older cats (in order to avoid food preference) it may be better to select two or three nutritionally complete rations and then stick with them (see *How to Feed*). There is no reason why a cat should not develop a preference for a particular product *so long as it is nutritionally complete.* The problem arises when a cat develops a preference for a food which is not a complete diet. This could happen when an owner oversupplelments an already complete diet with a highly palatable item such as liver, kidneys, milk, eggs, chicken. The cat then develops a preference for the item and refuses to eat the complete diet. More tidbits are then required and a vicious cycle ensues.

In many feline ailments, the first indications you will have that your cat is not well is when he stops eating. If he has been spoiled and won't eat his base diet, then you can't tell if his refusal to eat is an indication of ill-health or just an expression of food preference.

Other common feeding errors are discussed on the pages that follow.

Choose a balanced diet — don't leave it up to your cat. —*Sue Giffin Litwin.*

How to Feed

Select several nutritionally complete cat foods and offer them one at a time to your cat for several days in succession. Note which ones he seems to like best. Having found two or three products he seems to enjoy, you can use them interchangeably to provide variety and appetite appeal.

If you keep a number of cats, or are unable to feed your cats at regular intervals, a dry or semi-moist ration may be more convenient and certainly will be less expensive. The ration can be left out and fed free-choice.

Canned products should be fed twice daily, at the same time each day.

To learn about various cat foods, see the preceding paragraphs.

Before making a final product selection, you may want to compare the list of ingredients on the label of the package with the "ideal" ration given in the accompanying table. This table also tells you the approximate amount to feed each day.

TABLES OF NUTRITIONAL REQUIREMENTS FOR CATS

Table I—Composition of Various Cat Foods and Amounts to Feed

Variety	*Water*	*Protein*	*Fat*	*Cal/Ounce*	*Amount (Ounces) to Feed a 6 to 8 pound cat per day*
Dry	9-10%	30%	8%	105	2-3
Canned	75%	10%	2%	42	5½-7½
Semi-moist	30-34%	27%	7%	89	2¾-3½
Speciality	75%	10-23%	2-6%	42	5½-7½

(NOTE: 3 ounces of dry food, one level cup, equals 4 ounces of semi-moist or 7½ ounces of canned food.)

Table II—Caloric Requirements

Age	Expected Weight	Calories/Pound	Ounces of Canned Food to Feed per day (685 Cal/lb).
Newborn	4 ounces	190	—
5 weeks	1 pound	125	3 ounces
10 weeks	2 pounds	100	4¾ ounces
20 weeks	4½ pounds	65	7 ounces
6 months	6 pounds	50	7 ounces
Adult	6-10 pounds	40	5½ to 9½ ounces
Nursing Queen	5 pounds	125	14 ounces

Table III—"Ideal Ration"

Age	Water	Protein	Fat	Carbohydrate	Ash	Calcium	Cal/100 gm of Ration
Newborn (0-5 weeks)	72%	9.5%	6.8%	10%	0.75%	0.035%	142
Kittens and Cats	70%	14%	10%	5%	1%	0.6%	150

Adapted from *Gaines Basic Guide to Canine Nutrition* (Chapter on Nutritional Requirements for Cats).

(NOTE: "Ideal" refers to queen's milk for newborns; and food obtained in nature in the case of cats and older kittens.)

Table IV—Recommended Nutrient Allowances*

(Percent or Amount per Kilogram of Food—on a Dry Weight Basis)

Protein	28%
Fat	9%
Linoleic Acid	1%

Minerals

Calcium	1	%
Phosphorus	0.8	%
Potassium	0.3	%
Sodium Chloride	0.5	%
Magnesium	0.05	%
Iron	100	mg
Copper	5	mg
Magnesium	10	mg
Zinc	30	mg
Iodine	1	mg
Selenium	0.1	mg

Vitamins

Vit A	10,000	I.U.
Vit D	1,000	I.U.
Vit E	80	I.U.
Thiamin	5	mg
Riboflavin	5	mg
Pantothenic Acid	10	mg
Niacin	45	mg
Pyridoxine	4	mg
Folic Acid	1.0	mg
Biotin	0.05	mg
Vit B12	0.02	mg
Choline	2,000	mg

*Adapted from National Research Council's *Nutrient Requirements for Cats,* 1978.

Some caveats concerning the feeding of cats:

* Speciality foods and even table scraps can be given as "treats" on occasion—but not until after the base diet is eaten. Cooked meats (liver, kidney), cottage cheese, cooked vegetables, cooked fish, milk, and yogurt are foods with strong taste appeal that cats seem to enjoy.

* Treats should not exceed 20 percent of a cat's total daily ration.

* Uncooked meat and raw fish should not be given because of the danger of transmitting disease (see INFECTIOUS DISEASES).

* Cats prefer to have their food served at room temperature.

* Give your cat something to chew on at least once or twice a week. This promotes good oral hygiene. Usually a cat can be encouraged to chew on a large knuckle bone, especially if a little meat is left on. Avoid long bones such as ribs or chicken bones that can splinter.

Cats have highly selective eating habits. The location of the food dish, noise, the presence of other animals and other threats or distractions can adversely affect how much they are willing to eat. A boarded cat may go an entire week without eating.

Switching Diets: At times it might become necessary to adjust a cat's diet because of a health problem (e.g., diabetes, kidney or liver disease); or in the case of a queen because of lactation. Perhaps a cat may have acquired a singular liking for table scraps or gourmet food items which don't fulfill all his nutritional needs. In such cases, the cat will have to be switched to a more suitable ration.

If he refuses the new diet, the procedure for switching over is as follows: To 80 percent of the original food add 20 percent of the new food, mix together thoroughly, and feed the mixture until the cat accepts it. Once this is accomplished, increase the amount of new food to 40 percent while reducing the original ration. Continue in this fashion until the switch-over is complete.

Common Errors in Feeding

Overfeeding leads to *obesity*. This can be a big problem in cats. If you think your cat may be overweight, determine his ideal weight in proportion to his height and bone. There should be a layer of subcutaneous fat over the ribs, thick enough to provide some padding and insulation, but not too thick. You should be able to feel his ribs as individual structures.

The average cat weighs about eight pounds, but this varies considerably with the breed, age and sex.

Don't box your cat in by letting him get too fat.
—*Sue Giffin Litwin.*

If your cat is overweight, don't leave food out all day long. Decrease his ration by one-third. As he loses weight, weigh him from time to time until he achieves his ideal weight and then maintain it.

A frequently seen error is feeding cats dog food. Cats require twice as much protein and B-Vitamins as do dogs. Cats also cannot convert certain dietary precursors into necessary amino-acids and water soluable vitamins, as can dogs. When a cat is given dog food over a long period of time he can develop Vitamin A deficiency (night-blindness); niacin deficiency (pellegra); retinal degeneration; and other serious or fatal illnesses.

Another common error is to overdose a cat with Vitamins A and D, or calcium and phosphorus, either by giving the vitamins directly, or by oversupplementing his diet with products high in them (such as raw liver or fish oils). Excess Vitamin A causes sterility and loss of hair coat. Excess calcium, phosphorus and Vitamins D can cause extensive metabolic bone and kidney disease. In addition, raw fish contains an enzyme which destroys Vitamin B-1. A deficiency of this vitamin (thiamine) results in brain damage. Fish is also deficient in Vitamin E.

Calcium deficiency is the most frequent nutritional disorder among cats. It may be brought on by feeding meats exclusively, without calcium supplements. Lactation puts an extreme drain on a queen's calcium reserves. Calcium supplements are most beneficial when given during lactation (see *Feeding During Lactation* in the chapter PREGNANCY AND KITTENING).

Feeding Kittens

Most breeders supply a diet sheet with a new kitten. It should be followed, at least for the first few days, since an abrupt change in diet can cause digestive upsets.

Kittens require about twice as much protein and 50 percent more calories per pound than adult cats. Accordingly, it is important to choose a nutritionally complete diet as discussed above, one formulated to support the growth of kittens.

Kittens up to six months of age should be fed three times a day. Labels on cat food packages provide recommended daily feeding amounts. They are useful guidelines but are not applicable to every kitten. As a rule, feed a kitten up to his appetite. The only thing to avoid, which doesn't happen often, is feeding too much. This may produce a loose stool. Also, an overweight kitten is in danger of developing structural defects.

Food preferences generally are established before a kitten is six months old. Therefore it is important to accustom your kitten to a nutritionally complete diet at an early age. You should select two or three products which fulfill these requirements and then use them interchangeably as discussed in the section *Feeding Your Cat.* By offering only products which are nutritionally balanced, you avoid the problem of the "picky" eater who wants to eat just certain highly palatable—but not necessarily nutritious—items.

Vitamin and mineral supplements are not necessary if you are feeding a nutritionally balanced diet. In fact, they may even be harmful. If your kitten is a poor eater and you think he may need these supplements, discuss this with your veterinarian.

Kittens love to play. Provide suitable toys—not balls of string!   —*Sydney Wiley.*

19

Feline Behavior and Training

GENERAL REMARKS

Cats are not social animals by nature. In the wild they avoid direct contact with their own kind except when mating or nursing kittens. More than any other domestic animal, cats are able to fend for themselves.

It has been postulated that the cat's alliance with humans is a dramatic biological decision to swap solitary life in the wild for "the company of men". Perhaps there is that willingness to trade a life of independence for the comforts of food and shelter. But should the cost of these luxuries become too great, a cat will divorce himself from people and retire to his natural surroundings. There is a lot of truth in the age-old expression that a cat adopts you, not you him!

This is not to say that a cat is not able to form strong ties with people and other cats. Such attachments, or dependencies, do develop. The basically asocial nature of cats has been modified by domestication and training. This is especially true of kittens whose initial socialization involves close contact with people. Kittens raised by humans associate man with suckling, warmth, mother's milk, and kittenhood learning play. But even these attachments often are much less than those for the home, yard, and neighborhood—places the young cat has come to know and believe are his own. People are often seen as just an extension of his territory. If forced to make a choice between location and owner, a cat often chooses the location. This can be a problem, particularly when the family moves into a new house. The cat will often try to get back to his former residence.

This singular possessiveness of territory is a major factor behind many behavioral problems which develop when a cat perceives a threat to his established order. Cats are creatures of habit and resent forced changes. Adding a new cat or person to the household can trigger jealousy and a minor psychosis. Just how well the cat is able to adjust depends upon his flexibility and training, his inherited disposition, his sex and state of mind, and his physical well-being. How to deal with these and other behavioral problems that arise in cats is discussed below.

Of all the traits we admire in cats, the one of independence and self-sufficiency stands out the most. Submission, as we see it in dogs, simply does not

341

exist. A cat may retreat or attack, but he will never submit. Administer a stern rebuke, and most cats will hiss in defiance.

The young of all species pass through a period of adjusting to their environment. This is called the period of *socialization,* or the formative period. In kittens it occurs at three to nine weeks of age. A kitten is strongly influenced by the behavior of his mother. It is she who teaches him so much of what he knows. If her knowledge and training are limited, his own education will be lacking.

At five weeks of age a kitten begins to imprint. He begins to see himself as a feline; and to identify with his littermates and mother. If during this period he is removed from the nest, he will identify with people and other animals, if he has contact with them, but may not fully realize his self-identity as a cat. This accounts for many unusual stories, such as cats playing with rabbits.

During the formative period a kitten should have a varied exposure to many new and different experiences. He is then more likely to be flexible and able to make adjustments later in life. This is the hall-mark of a well-socialized individual. The poorly socialized cat has to rely instead on instinctual responses such as the "fight-flight" mechanism. Keep in mind, however, that timidity and aggression are also influenced by heredity.

It is extremely important for pet owners to select kittens who are well-socialized as they make better companions and pets. Qualities to look for in selecting a kitten are discussed in the APPENDIX (see *Choosing a Healthy Kitten).*

TRAINING

General Remarks

Cats, as we have said, are by nature rather independent creatures and, unlike dogs, are not "pack" oriented. Therefore training strategies which rely upon the traditional dominant and submissive roles of master and pet are not likely to be successful in gaining the cooperation of cats.

Striking a cat in anger is definitely inadvisable. This teaches the cat nothing, except to distrust and avoid his owner. Cats have wonderful memories. They do not forgive and forget easily.

Contrary to popular belief, cats are quick to learn if certain basic aspects of cat psychology are taken into account. Cats generally respond to a command only when it is convenient, fun or profitable to do so. Accordingly, the most successful training strategies involve a system of rewards, such as praise and tasty enticements.

Corrective punishment should be administered indirectly. Cats are quite likely to associate punishment with the person doing the punishing, rather than the unacceptable act for which the lesson was intended.

To discourage undesirable behavior, it is best to associate the act with some unpleasant yet seemingly impersonal happening, such as a startling "NO!", or a stream of water from a plastic spray bottle (being careful that the cat doesn't blame the "squirt" on the owner).

Bad habits are easier to prevent than treat. Training a kitten before his bad habits become ingrained is much easier than trying to change the behavior of an adult. To break a bad habit, it is almost always necessary to gradually rechannel his activity into some other acceptable substitute.

Unacceptable behavior often stems from boredom. Cats are fun-loving and playful. They should be given suitable toys with which to distract and amuse themselves. Choose toys that are sturdy and cannot be torn or chewed up. They should be large enough so they can't be swallowed.

In summary, the best results are achieved with patience, steady praise, love, and consistent reward for accomplishments well done.

Housebreaking

Ordinarily this is not a difficult task. A kitten is born with an instinct to bury his wastes. However, he may need to be shown where to eliminate. If his mother was trained to use the litter pan, she will have taught him to use one also. In such a case your job will be made most easy. Train the kitten to use the pan as soon as he arrives.

Satisfactory litter pans can be purchased commercially, or you can use a plastic or enamel-coated tray with disposable plastic liners. A number of different kinds of filler are sold at pet stores. In general they are much more absorbent than shredded newspapers or sand and dirt, and contain deodorizers. Certain cats may find the chlorophyll and/or deodorizing chemicals objectionable and avoid the litter pan. If odor then becomes a problem, you may wish to add a drop of liquid deodorant, sold especially for this purpose, to a tray containing plain filler. In any case, do not use household disinfectants. They can be toxic to the cat, or irritative to his skin and paws.

If the kitten was trained to the litter pan by his mother, select the kind of box and litter he was accustomed to using. After finding a filler he accepts, do not change brands. This could upset his routine and cause a break in training.

To train a kitten to use a litter pan, set him in it whenever he wakes up from a nap, after each meal and anytime he seems to want to eliminate. When he makes a mistake, reprimand him with a loud "NO!" or a squirt of water—but only if you catch him in the act. Never rub his nose in his mistakes.

In the problem case where a kitten was adopted at an early age, or perhaps his mother was not well trained or lived outside, fill the litter pan with what the kitten was accustomed to using (dirt, sand, gravel). Then gradually switch over to a commercial litter. At first, leave some stool and urine in the pan. This will attract the kitten and encourage him to use it. Scratch up the litter with his paws. If these measures are not successful, see *Soiling in the House.*

Once the kitten becomes accustomed to the litter pan it is important to keep it clean. Dirty pans are objectionable to cats. Scoop out solid material once or twice a day and flush it down the toilet. Stir the filler to keep the surface dry. Change the filler every three or four days, or more often if necessary. Wash the pan thoroughly and let it dry out completely before adding new filler. Locate the pan away from heavy traffic so the cat can have privacy. Should it become necessary to move the pan to a new location, make the change in successive steps.

When a well-trained cat suddenly begins to urinate in the house, suspect an illness such as the *Feline Urinary Syndrome.* Other causes of inappropriate elimination can have a psychological basis (see *Soiling in the House).*

Scratching the Furniture

Destructive scratching is one of the most common problems you are likely to encounter. Cats sharpen their claws as a part of their normal grooming activity. In this process the worn-down outer sheath of the claw is caught and removed. This exposes a new inner claw beneath. To avoid damage to upholstery and furnishings, you will need to provide your cat with a suitable substitute, such as a scratching post, on which he can sharpen his nails.

Scratching posts can be bought commercially; or you can make one yourself. Some commercial posts are apt to be too short or are inclined to tip over. The post, either of horizontal or vertical type, should be sturdy and tall enough to let the cat stretch out comfortably. A cat likes to rest on his hind feet while sharpening his front claws.

A satisfactory post can be made by mounting a 30 inch long pine board on a two foot square wooden base. Cover it with tightly woven carpet. A 45 degree slant can be constructed by using a second piece of board to form a triangle. Some people use a wooden box and cover it with carpet. Others tack a piece of carpet to the wall, or simply use a log with the bark still on.

The scratching post should be ready when the kitten arrives. He should be taken to it several times a day, after naps, the first thing in the morning, and whenever he gives signs of wanting to scratch. Insist that he use the post and reward him for good behavior.

If you catch him in the act of scratching where he shouldn't, administer a squirt of water and take him back to the post. He should associate the spray with the object he's scratching—not his owner.

One good way to keep a kitten from scratching at a favorite spot is to place several spring-loaded mouse traps around it upside down. When the kitten steps on the back of the trap, the resulting "pop" provides a scare. Having taken fright two or three times, most kittens will not return. Cat repellants as suggested for spraying also can be used.

An older cat can be trained to use a scratching post, but this takes more time and patience. In some cases the only alternative to giving him up is to have him declawed (see *Declawing).*

Collars and Leashes

Kittens and cats who go outdoors should be furnished with a collar containing an identity tag. Since a cat could get his mouth or a foot caught in the collar, or the collar could get caught on a fence, you should purchase a well-designed collar having an elastic insert that can stretch over the cat's head in an emergency. A bell can be added to alert birds of the cat's whereabouts.

A harness is more secure than a collar for walking a cat.

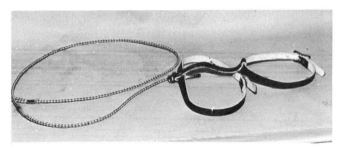

Cat harness and leash.

Walking on a Leash: A harness is recommended for walking a cat on a leash. It is much more secure than a collar. For the first few days, put the collar or harness on only for short periods while the kitten is getting used to it. Then attach a leash which can be dragged behind. Next, pick up the leash and follow the kitten, but don't attempt to control his direction. When he has learned to accept this arrangement, you can start to lead him with occasional firm tugs, interspersed with lots of praise and petting.

Coming When Called

It is important to teach your kitten to come when you call him. As cats normally respond to commands only when it is to their advantage to do so, to get their cooperation you must reward them with tasty treats and affection.

At mealtimes call your kitten by name and follow it with the word "COME". You can repeat this exercise when he comes to you for stroking. With repetition, the kitten will learn to associate the word "COME" with a pleasurable experience. If he refuses to obey, you might try to entice him by throwing a toy nearby.

Don't expect your cat to come to you for something he doesn't enjoy—and never call him to you for punishment.

BEHAVIOR DISORDERS

When an emotionally upset cat begins to act in an unacceptable fashion, in most cases he is suffering from insecurity and/or frustration.

Cats are solitary and independent. They resent intrusions upon, and changes in, their normal routines. Frustration often stems from a change in the living pattern; or the inability to express normal biological drives such as sex, hunting, and aggressive play.

While behavior is strongly influenced by early socialization, it is also modified by genetic determinants which give to each cat his own individual disposition and temperament. It also has its roots in the state of health, age, and sex of the individual.

Some cases of apparently inappropriate behavior are not caused by psychological stress. They are due to improper training or management on the part of the owner. They are a problem to the owner—but not to the cat.

The common behavior problems you are likely to encounter are discussed below.

Soiling in the House

This takes the form of failure to use the litter pan, relapse in a previously housebroken cat, or spraying.

Failure to Use the Litter Pan. The procedure for training a kitten to use the litter pan is described above (see *Training*). If this is not successful, place the litter box in a small area such as shower stall or linen closet and then take your kitten to it after eating, at night, and whenever he seems to want to eliminate. Cats are fastidious by nature and dislike soiling their surroundings. (Keep in mind that cats do not like to eliminate where they eat—so separate the litter box and food bowl.) Usually in five or six days the kitten learns to eliminate in the tray.

One other problem is that of a cat who continually misses the pan. Try using a bigger pan or one with higher sides.

Relapses in a Well-Trained Cat. Here there are several possible causes. Some are health problems (bladder or bowel infection, the confusion of old age, stiffness). Others are caused by spite, revenge, jealousy, emotional insecurity or frustration. One very evident sign of a "piqued" cat is a mess deposited in the middle of his owner's bed.

The odor of urine or feces in the carpet may attract a previously well-trained cat and cause him to select that spot for his future eliminations.

Cats dislike dirty pans. Many refuse to use them unless they are cleaned.

The treatment of a relapse depends upon finding the cause and then taking steps to correct it. A medical check-up may be in order.

Spraying. This is defined as periodic squirting of urine about the house while a cat continues to use his litter pan for routine eliminations. It is most common in the tom cat but also occurs in breeding females and neutered cats of both sexes.

Spraying is an expression of territorial marking. It is associated with the rubbing of body oils (from the chin, tail) on favored objects. It often occurs when a cat feels his territory is threatened by an intruder. Frequently it is an advertisement that sex is available. It increases during the mating season and especially during courtship. It may be brought on by jealousy, insecurity, or a break-down in the relationship between the cat and his owner.

Spraying should not be mistaken for a lapse in toilet training. Spraying usually takes place at ankle height. This distinguishes it from a litter pan problem. The stains and odor are most difficult to remove. This makes the problem all the more distressing.

Treatment: Tom cats and queens who are not going to be used for breeding should be neutered. The operation is effective in 80 to 90 percent of cases, but when performed after the cat starts to spray, it may take several weeks for spraying to disappear. Estrogens in males produce a chemical castration and may be indicated in selected individuals.

The problem in both sexes can be helped by giving a progesterone hormone such as Ovaban or Depo-provera which has a calming effect. When stress is a factor, it is important to identify the predisposing cause and take steps to remove it.

An effort should be made to remove stains from rugs, baseboards and furniture. Otherwise the cat will be attracted back to the same spot. Wash the stains with vinegar or a mild bleach. Products which leave an objectionable odor (to cats) are available through pet stores or your veterinarian. Other substances which may be effective in repelling the cat are moth balls in cloth bags, orange peels, and rubbing alcohol. You can try setting his food dish near the spot. Cats do not like to spray near their feeding areas. Placing upside-down mouse traps around a favorite spraying area, as described in *Scratching the Furniture,* may be of aid.

Energy Release Activities

Cats have natural drives which include hunting, bringing home prey, eating grass, and engaging in play-fighting. When outlets for excess energy are not available, the cat may seek relief in activities which are not acceptable to his owner. Close confinement is a major cause of tension and frustration.

Compulsory Self-grooming. This is an energy displacement phenomenon that occurs rather commonly, especially among Siamese. It affects cats who are hospitalized, boarded at a cattery, or otherwise deprived of their freedom and subjected to long periods of boredom. The signs are excessive licking, especially at the groin. Hair is lost producing bald spots. Skin irritation is mild.

Eating Houseplants. Some cats acquire the urge to eat grass. When not available, they turn to houseplants—some of which may be poisonous (see *Poisoning* for a list of indoor plants with toxic effects). Eating grass might produce a gastric upset but is not a dangerous activity. You can try to satisfy his needs by growing grass in a flower pot to substitute for the plants. As a last resort, give up the plants.

Bringing Home Prey. Cats do not always relate killing with the need to eat, and are apt to deposit a variety of dead or near dead things at your backdoor. Perhaps they hunt to fulfill a primitive instinctual urge, or to exhibit their prowess. If you attach a bell to the cat's collar, it will be more difficult for him to surprise mice and birds. This doesn't always work. Some cats learn to stalk without ringing the bell.

Play-fighting. This energy release mechanism may take the form of biting at the ankles or attacking imaginary objects. It is not the same as aggression. You can provide your cat with toy substitutes, give him more exercise, or allow him to play with another cat.

Eating Disorders

Food preferences. They usually develop in the first six months. This subject is discussed in the chapter FEEDING AND NUTRITION.

Anorexia Nervosa. This is a condition in which the cat refuses to eat, loses weight and begins to starve himself. A deep-seated insecurity or nervous stress usually is at the root of the problem. Keep in mind that loss of appetite is a major sign of many serious feline illnesses. Veterinary examination is indicated.

Entice your cat by offering him treats. Tranquilizers reduce tension and are indicated in the treatment of this disorder (see *Treatment of Behavior Disorders with Drugs*).

Obesity. This can be a big problem. Owners contribute to it by offering cats gourmet foods and tasty treats after meals. Some cases are due to lack of exercise. Others to boredom, or feeding cats together, which encourages competition.

The treatment of obesity is discussed in the chapter FEEDING AND NUTRITION (see *Common Errors in Feeding*). Avoid a sudden drastic reduction in calories. This can produce hunger stress and lead to aggressive behavior. Obesity can be prevented by good feeding practices and by adequate exercise.

Abnormal Sucking Behavior

Animal behavorists suggest that a kitten's habit of sucking on fabrics, people, clothes, and even himself, can be traced to an unsatisfied nursing drive produced by insufficient nursing while in the nest.

Wool sucking is a special case in which the preference is for wool clothing. It may not develop until puberty. It occurs most often in the Siamese.

Treatment: This habit often can be stopped early by catching the kitten in the act and rapping him on his nose with your finger (this is how a queen reprimands). You can try applying some foul-tasting material to the fabric (hot sauce, tobacco juice). Allow the kitten to smell it, then put it in his mouth. Or aim a spray can at the cat so that he smells it and retreats at the hiss. Wool sucking, in particular, is difficult to cure. Progesterone has helped some cases.

Aggressive Behavior

In cats, aggression takes the form of attack behavior. During the process of socialization, a kitten learns to relate to people. His instinctual "fight-flight" behavior comes under the influence of his cortical brain center. He learns to inhibit his self-protective responses. He begins to accept and enjoy stroking and handling.

Many cases of apparently uncalled for aggression are due to a relapse of cortical inhibition, brought on by a heightened state of fear or environmental stress. The cat allows his instincts to rule his better judgment. An upset cat may suddenly attack someone nearby, even though that person played no part in the cause of his upset. A cat who has been in a fight may accept handling by one person, yet attack another who approaches too closely. When cornered, a cat will nearly always take aggressive action.

Some cats, when they are rubbed vigorously under the belly or along the back near the tail, will turn suddenly and scratch or bite. Perhaps this is interpreted as a sex-related act. It usually doesn't happen with gentle stroking.

Cats that develop a hypothyroid problem often become aggressive. Hunger and physical stresses may induce irritable behavior.

Cannabalism is a special kind of aggressive behavior. It occurs in the post partum queen. It is discussed in the chapter PREGNANCY AND KITTENING (see *Mothers Who Neglect or Injure Their Kittens*).

To determine the cause of aggressive behavior, consider how and when it started, the circumstances under which it usually occurs, and what the various attacks may have in common. True aggression should be distinguished from *Play-fighting,* which is discussed above.

Treatment: A poorly socialized cat who resists handling will need to be "tamed". Administer a tranquilizer such as Valium or Librium (see *Treatment of Behavior Disorders with Drugs*). Soothe and pet him. With patience, he may eventually get used to being handled and stroked.

Sexual Behavior

Cats have unusually strong sex drives. One expression of this is mounting. It is a tension release phenomenon in which the individual seeks to gain relief by using queen substitutes—such as furry pillows or perhaps another cat. Spraying, too, is another way of expressing frustration—and advertising that sex is available. It is discussed in the section *Soiling in the House*.

Neutering curbs undesirable sex activity in the majority of cases. However, approximately 10 percent of neutered males retain some overt sexual behavior.

If you plan to use your cat for breeding, you might consider trying hormones (progesterone) which suppresses the libido. They are not without certain side effects. Discuss them with your veterinarian.

Treatment of Behavior Disorders with Drugs

The best approach in treating a cat with a behavior disorder is to identify the underlying cause and seek to remove it. Drugs may be necessary, however, either as primary therapy or to assist during a transition period. In general, it is best to use drugs only when other methods have failed. They should be used under veterinary supervision.

Tranquilizers: Acepromazine has a general depressive effect. It acts on the pain center and also relieves anxiety. *Valium* and *Librium* are less depressive but more selective for reducing anxiety and nervous tension.

Tranquilizers are useful in calming the injured or frightened cat; and in relieving attacks of anxiety brought on by moving, grooming, bathing, mating. A side effect of tranquilizers is that they can block normal cortical inhibitory impulses, so that a cat may stop using his litter pan, or may bite and scratch at the least provocation.

Progesterones: Provera, megace, and other progesterone derivatives have a calming effect and depress the pain center. They are useful in modifying aggressive behavior, particularly when it is sex hormone related. The effects are similar to those of castration.

Progesterones also are effective in treating certain behavior disorders such as spraying, destructive scratching, compulsive self-grooming, anorexia nervosa, wool sucking, and cannibalism. Side effects include weight gain, pyometra, excessive drinking and urination, and the potential for bringing on diabetes.

20

Tumors and Cancers

GENERAL INFORMATION

Most people associate the word *"tumor"* with a growth occurring on the skin or somewhere in the body. However, any sort of lump, bump, growth or swelling (such as an abscess) is a TUMOR. Those which are true growths are called NEOPLASMS.

Benign neoplasms are growths which do not invade and destroy, nor do they spread. They are cured by surgical removal, providing that all the tumor has been removed.

Malignant neoplasms are the same as CANCERS (also called CARCINOMAS, LYMPHOMAS, and SARCOMAS depending upon the cell type). Cancers invade and destroy. They tend to spread via the blood stream and lymphatic systems to distant parts of the body. This is called *metastasizing.*

Cancer is graded according to its degree of malignancy. Low-grade cancers continue to grow locally and attain a large size. They metastasize late in the course of the illness. High-grade cancers metastasize early when the primary focus is still quite small or barely detectable.

Cancers are approached in the following manner: Suppose a female cat has a lump in her breast. Since it is solid, it is probably a neoplasm. It could be benign or malignant. A decision is made to *biopsy* the lump. This is a surgical operation during which the lump, or part of the lump, is removed and sent to the pathologist. A pathologist is a medical doctor who has been trained to make a diagnosis by visual inspection of tissue under a microscope. An experienced pathologist can tell whether the tumor is a cancer. He can often provide additional information as to the degree of malignancy. This serves the purpose of making the diagnosis and, in many cases, gives the rationale for the most appropriate treatment.

351

What is Cancer?

Although much has been learned, the exact cause of cancer is unknown. All cells in the body die and have to be replaced. This process of reduplication is called *mitosis*. A single cell splits into two cells, each identical to the parent. The process is controlled by genes and chromosomes in the cell. Anything which interferes with mitosis at the genetic level can lead to the production of a mutant cell. Many agents are known to do this. They include toxins, chemicals, ionizing rays, viruses and other irritants.

Under appropriate circumstances the mutant cell, which seems to grow much faster than the present cell, reduplicates itself. This, then, could become a cancer. A cancer acts like a parasite. It depletes the host and replaces normally functioning tissue.

It has been suggested that cancers arise more often than we suspect. The theory is that most of them don't get established because the host's immune system recognizes them as "non-self" and so makes antibodies which destroy them.

Long-standing irritants to tissues are a definite cause of some cancers. The irritant agent appears to speed up tissue repair (and therefore the rate of local mitotic activity), and/or interferes with immune mechanisms which destroy new-born cancer cells.

Examples of agents known to increase the risk of cancer in people are: ultraviolet rays (skin cancer); x-rays (thyroid cancer); nuclear radiation (leukemia); chemicals (analine dyes causing bladder cancer); cigarettes and coal tars (causing lung and skin cancer); viruses (causing experimental cancer in laboratory animals); and parasites (a cause of bladder cancer).

Some cancers have a known familial incidence.

A prior injury or blow is sometimes thought to be the cause of cancer. Trauma can be a cause of certain benign swellings. However it is seldom, if ever, the cause of a cancer. The injury calls attention to the area and the cancer is discovered incidentally.

Some benign tumors, such as warts and papillomas, are clearly due to a virus infection. Other benign tumors, such as lipomas, adenomas of the breast and other organs, simply just grow there for reasons unknown at the present time.

There is no evidence that cancer in pets can be spread to people.

Treatment of Tumors and Cancers

The effectiveness of any form of treatment often depends upon early recognition on the part of the cat owner that his pet may have a cancer.

Complete surgical removal of a cancer which has not yet spread is the most satisfactory treatment available. Cancers that have spread to regional lymph nodes still may be cured if the lymph nodes can also be removed. Even when the disease is wide-spread, local excision of a bleeding or infected cancer can provide relief of pain and improve the quality of life.

Electrocautery and cryosurgery are two techniques by which tumors on the surface of the body can be controlled or cured by burning and freezing. This provides an alternative to surgical removal, but special equipment is required.

Radiation therapy is useful in the management of some surface tumors and in deeply situated tumors where control cannot be achieved by surgery. Cures are possible. Radiotherapy must be carried out in a medical center. It requires expensive equipment and the services of a trained radiotherapist.

Chemotherapy employs anti-cancer drugs given at regular intervals. These drugs, even when carefully controlled, have major side affects. They are useful in the management of some widely spread cancers. Hormone therapy and immunotherapy also have been successful in the management of some tumors.

Cancer in the Cat

Cancer is mainly a problem in the middle-aged and older cat, the majority occuring in cats 10-15 years of age. On the other hand, very old cats (19 or 20 years old) seem to have a lower incidence. Perhaps these cats have survived to a ripe old age because of a superior immune system.

The majority of cancers occurring in the cat are not visible by outward inspection. Skin and breast tumors are exceptions. These neoplasms can be detected by inspection and palpation.

The most prevalent cancer in cats is that associated with the feline leukemia virus. Although this virus affects one to two percent of cats in the general population, only a small number actually develop a malignant form of the disease. Common sites of involvement are lymph nodes (*Lymphosarcoma*), and circulating blood cells (*Leukemia*), but any organ or tissue in the cat's body can be affected. Taken together, the feline leukemia virus accounts for perhaps half the internal cancers in cats. It is also associated with other serious diseases which include anemia, feline infectious peritonitis, glomerulonephritis, and toxoplasmosis. The depressed level of immunity associated with feline leukemia virus infection undoubtedly contributes to the high incidence of such secondary diseases.

The skin, which accounts for seven percent of cancers, is the second most prevalent site. Next in frequency is breast cancer (five percent). Tumors of the skin and breast are discussed below.

Other sites for cancer include the digestive and female reproductive tracts. Such cancers may grow to a large size before they are detected—usually by the presence of a palpable mass; or by signs of intestinal blockage. Early detection of these cancers rest upon a suspicion that a symptom caused by some internal disorder could be due to a cancer. You should consider the possibility of cancer when your cat has difficulty eating or digesting his food; or when he has an unexplained bowel disturbance such as constipation or the passage of blood. Cancers of the reproductive tract in females cause few signs, but you should look for vaginal discharge and bleeding.

Tumors of the mouth account for three to four percent of all cancers in the cat. Nearly all of them are malignant (squamous cell cancers). Signs are drooling, difficulty eating, and the appearance of a lump or ulcerated growth involving the tongue or gums, usually. Cancers should be distinguished from infected masses produced by imbedded foreign bodies such as needles, wood splinters, or string cutting into the underside of the tongue.

Cancer of the respiratory tract is rare among cats. The lung is often involved by cancer, but when lung cancer is found it nearly always means that cancer has spread to the lung from some other site. The same thing applies to the liver.

Bone cancer also is rare (3 percent of cancers). The first sign may be swelling of the leg or a limp in a mature cat having no history of injury. Pressure over the swelling causes varying degrees of pain. Bone cancer spreads early and to the lungs.

The bone marrow may be involved by a group of diseases called *myeloproliferative disorders*. In these diseases the marrow stops making red or white blood cells. These disorders are rare and difficult to detect. Symptoms are nonspecific. Diagnosis is made by bone marrow biopsy.

Signs and symptoms of common tumors affecting the internal organs are discussed in the chapters dealing with these organs.

COMMON SURFACE TUMORS

Cysts (Wens, Sebaceous Cysts)

Sebaceous cysts are benign tumors that arise from glands found beneath the skin. They can occur anywhere on the body. Although they are not as common in cats as in dogs, they are still the most common surface tumor in the cat.

A sebaceous cyst is made up of a thick capsule which surrounds a lump of cheesy material called keratin. It may grow to an inch or more in size. Eventually it is likely to become infected and will have to be drained, unless it has already drained spontaneously. This sometimes leads to a cure. Most cysts should be removed.

Warts and Papillomas

These skin growths are not nearly so common in cats as they are in people. They tend to occur on the older cat. Some are on a stalk, but others look very much like a piece of chewing gum stuck to the skin. If they become irritated or start to bleed, they should be removed.

Lipomas

A lipoma is a growth made up of mature fat cells surrounded by a fibrous capsule which sets it apart from the surrounding body fat. It can be recognized by its round, smooth appearance and soft, fat-like consistency. It is not painful. Lipomas are not common in the cat.

Surgical removal is indicated only for cosmetic reasons and to rule out some other tumor, such as a cancer.

A *cyst* in front of the ear.

Hematomas

The hematoma is a collection of blood beneath the skin. It is caused by a blow or contusion. Small hematomas may resolve spontaneously. Large ones may need to be opened and drained. Ear flap hematomas require special care (see EARS: *Swollen Ear Flap*).

Tender Knots

A small knot may be present at the site of an injection and is often present for a few days in kittens who have been given their vaccinations. It seldom requires treatment.

A painful swelling beneath the skin may be an abscess. Abscesses are discussed in the SKIN chapter.

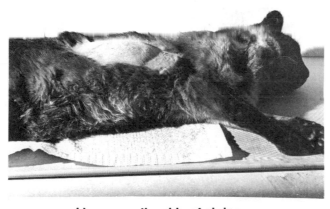

***Lipoma* on the side of abdomen.**

Only a biopsy can establish whether this skin tumor is benign or malignant.

Skin Cancers

Several types of skin cancer can affect the cat. It is important to distinguish cancers from benign tumors. Signs that a growth might be a cancer are: visible enlargement, ulceration of the skin with bleeding, and a sore which does not heal. But physical appearance alone is not always a reliable indicator. Surgical removal or biopsy is often necessary to establish the diagnosis.

The most common malignant skin tumors in the cat are:

Squamous Cell Cancer: This tumor, also called an *epidermoid* carcinoma, appears as a cauliflower-like neoplasm, or hard flat grayish-looking ulcer that does not heal. Size is variable. These cancers tend to occur around body openings and in areas of chronic skin irritation. Hair may be lost due to constant licking.

A peculiar form of squamous cell cancer involves the upper lips of cats who suffer from a condition called *rodent ulcer* (see SKIN). Another type involves the ear tips of white cats exposed to ultra-violet sunlight (see EARS).

Early detection and treatment of squamous cell cancer is important. This tumor is capable of metastasizing widely.

Basal-cell Cancer: Basal-cell carcinomas occur as small nodular growths beneath the skin, often next to each other, producing solid sheets of bumps. They tend to occur on the back and upper chest. Basal cell tumors enlarge locally and spread by direct extension. They do not metastasize. Wide local removal prevents recurrence.

Mast Cell Tumors: Mast cell tumors are single or multi-nodular growths, usually less than an inch in length. The overlying skin may be ulcerated. Look for these tumors on the hind legs, scrotum and lower abdomen. About one out of three is malignant. Cancer is more likely when growth is rapid and the tumor is larger than one inch. Malignant mast cell tumors metastasize to distant organs. Cortisone may be given to temporarily decrease the size of mast cell tumors. The treatment of choice is wide surgical removal.

Melanomas: A melanoma is a malignant neoplasm which takes its name from the brown or black pigment usually associated with it. Often it develops in a pre-existing mole. You should suspect melanoma when a mole starts to enlarge or spread out, becomes elevated about the surface of the skin, or starts to bleed. Melanomas may be found anywhere on the skin, and in the mouth. A suspicious mole should be removed. Melanoma spreads widely, often at an early stage.

This multi-nodular rapidly growing neoplasm is highly suspicious of breast cancer.

Breast Tumors and Swelling

Following heat or false pregnancy, the breasts may remain enlarged or feel lumpy. As you press on the breasts, you may be able to express a yellowish, or at times a milky, fluid. This condition is called *mammary hyperplasia*. It is due to a hormone imbalance. It is seen most commonly in older females who have never had a litter; or in females who have not been bred for some time. It does not occur in females who have been spayed.

Mammary hyperplasia may disappear spontaneously in one to two months, or it may persist; in which case a breast tumor or a problem of the ovaries may be

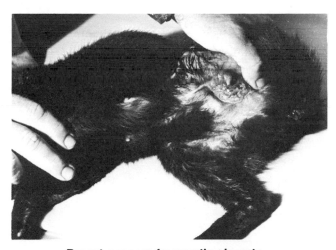

Breast cancers frequently ulcerate.

present (see *Fertility Problems in the Female*). It is then advisable to have your cat checked by a veterinarian.

Nine out of ten true mammary tumors are malignant. The others are adenomas. In cats, breast cancer is a rapidly progressing neoplasm that has a high rate of local recurrence following treatment. It tends to spread widely, with the lungs being the favored sites for metastases. A chest x-ray is advisable to rule out metastases before embarking on radical surgery.

Breast cancer is rare among spayed females, especially those neutered before their first heat cycle.

The leading sign is a painless enlargement or a knot in the breast. Most females so affected are over six years of age. A biopsy is the only way to tell for sure between benign and malignant tumors.

Surgical removal is the treatment of choice for all breast neoplasms. The success of the operation depends upon the stage of the tumor at the time of surgery. The earlier the lump is discovered and treated, the better the outlook. Close follow-up, to detect local recurrence after surgery, is advisable.

You should examine the breasts of your female at least once a month, especially when she is older. If you detect a suspicious swelling or a solitary lump, ask your veterinarian to examine it.

21

Geriatrics

GENERAL REMARKS

A progressive and irreversible deterioration of cellular and organ function occurs in the tissues of all animals with the passage of time. Although its effects are familiar to everyone, the exact mechanism by which organic systems eventually run out of protoplasmic vitality is an unsolved mystery.

Whereas the life expectancy of a cat was once 10 years, cats now are living longer than ever before. The average house cat lives 15 years. It is not uncommon in veterinary practice to see cats 18 to 20 years of age. It is even possible for a cat to reach 25 to 30 years—but this is extremely unusual!

All cats do not age at the same rate. A cat's biological age depends upon many things: his genetic background, his nutritional status, the presence of coexistent diseases, and environmental stresses. Being a purebred or freebred does not by itself influence the aging process.

Of great importance is the care the cat has received throughout his life. Well-cared for pets suffer fewer infirmities as they grow older. But when sickness, illness or injury are neglected, the aging process is accelerated.

The completely outdoor cat in the wild has a markedly diminished life expectancy—only about six years. Accidents, diseases, the trials of securing food, and the stresses of frequent pregnancy all contribute to this shortened life.

The indoor cat on the other hand, who is well-nourished, vaccinated against infectious diseases and protected from accidents, fares the best.

Older cats adjust poorly to physical and emotional stresses. A sudden stress, shock, or even a surgical procedure could lead to organ decompensation. Reduced liver function decreases the capacity to detoxify drugs, a factor which must be taken into consideration when administering medications or anesthetics. An older cat also is less tolerant to extremes of heat and cold. Changes in his diet or drinking water, too, can stress him. His digestive tract and bacterial flora are geared to his present diet.

The senior cat often is a neglected individual. His basic nature is such that when feeling out of sorts and below par, he tends to seek solitude and avoid human contact. Then, too, his infirmities progress so slowly that they may fail to attract attention or, conversely, be passed off as due to old age and therefore unavoidable.

Although aging is inevitable and irreversible, some of the infirmities attributed to old age may, in fact, be due to disease, therefore correctable or at least treatable.

Accordingly, as your cat approaches those golden years of senior citizenship, it is a good idea to set aside a time each month in which to reflect on his general attitude and behavior, and to examine him carefully from head to toe. In this way you will be better able to recognize early signs of disease or infirmity, and take steps to provide for his general health and well-being, as described below.

CARING FOR THE ELDERLY CAT

Behavioral Changes

Older cats are more sedentary, less energetic, less curious, and more restricted in their scope of activity. They seek out warm spots and sleep for longer periods. They become fixed in their habits and are less tolerant of changes in their daily routines. Crankiness and irritability are common.

These behavioral changes are not necessarily due to loss of mental fitness. In most cases they are the result of physical infirmities—such as failing eyesight, diminished hearing and sense of smell, arthritic stiffness and muscular weakness—all of which restrict the scope of a cat's activity, and with it his ability to participate in the life of his family. In frustration, such a cat might withdraw or even seek seclusion; engage in compulsive self-grooming; or begin to eliminate in places other than his litter box.

Providing a warm nesting spot near the center of family activity may stimulate the cat's interest and encourage him to participate more actively, as will a trip outside twice a day when accompanied by his owner.

Boarding and hospitalization in particular are poorly tolerated, in old age especially. Such cats eat poorly or not at all, become overanxious or withdrawn, and sleep poorly. If possible, it is advisable to care for them at home under the guidance of your veterinarian in order to avoid stress and anxiety. Have a neighbor drop by once or twice a day to care for the cat. This may be better than having him boarded.

Behavioral changes which are occasioned by physical infirmities often improve with treatment of the physical infirmities. When such treatment is not possible, abnormal behavior often can be modified or improved through the use of progesterones or tranquilizers as described in the chapter FELINE BEHAVIOR AND TRAINING.

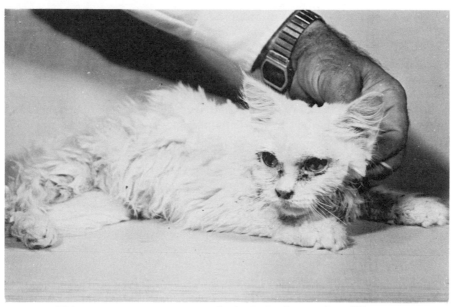

Thin, unkempt appearance, typical of advanced senility.

Physical Changes

The life cycle of the cat can be divided into three parts—kittenhood, adulthood, and old age. The periods marked by youth and old age are relatively short when compared to the length of adulthood. After puberty a cat's physique changes very little until close to the end of his life.

Unless a complete step-by-step physical examination is carried out by the cat's owner, the slowly progressive changes of old-age may not be noticed until they are quite advanced and therefore more difficult to treat successfully.

The Musculoskeletal System. To examine the musculoskeletal system, flex the front and rear legs while noting any stiffness, gritting sensation, or limitation of movement. Compare one side to the other. Look for swollen, painful joints.

The first sign of aging may be loss of muscular tone, especially in the legs. Degenerative changes in the joints and muscles lead to stiffness and intermittent lameness, most apparent when the cat gets up from a nap. His muscles might begin to shake when he exerts himself. He becomes less agile, and perhaps incapable of jumping up to a favorite spot. A stiff older cat may be unable to groom himself thoroughly. Stiffness in the joints is made worse by drafts and by sleeping on cold damp ground or on cement pads. His bed should be indoors in a warm dry spot. He may need to be covered at night.

Moderate exercise helps to keep the joints supple and should be encouraged. However, the older cat should not be forced to exert himself beyond his normal level of activity, which he can best judge for himself. A specific condition (such as heart disease) actually may require that exercise be restricted.

The Coat and Skin. Skin disorders occur with greater frequency in elderly cats. The texture and appearance of the coat are important clues to a cat's general health and mental attitude. A debilitated or depressed cat quickly loses interest in keeping up his appearance—a fact readily appreciated by his unkempt look. Any chronic illness may be reflected in poor coat quality or even loss of hair.

One skin problem that tends to occur more frequently in the aging cat is that of maggots. A cat who has allowed his fur to become soiled and matted becomes a target for flies. Then, too, the infirm individual is less capable of keeping flies away.

Another common skin condition in older cats is feline endocrine alopecia. It is caused by a hormone deficiency rather than a skin irritation. It is typified by hair loss in the groin area and back of the legs. Licking is not associated with this condition.

Careful examination of the hair and skin, as described in the SKIN chapter, may reveal tumors, parasites, and other skin disorders requiring prompt veterinary attention.

The elderly cat should be combed or brushed every day. Frequent grooming and cleaning of his coat with a damp cloth will keep his coat free of parasites and his skin in healthy condition. He will enjoy the stroking and attention which accompanies these daily sessions. A cat who has lost pride in his appearance may once again begin to groom himself as his self-esteem is restored.

It may be necessary to bathe a cat whose coat has become matted or especially dirty. The procedure for giving a bath is discussed in the SKIN chapter. Old cats chill easily. They should be towel-dried and kept in a warm room.

Toenails may need to be trimmed more often unless they are worn down by activity.

The Special Senses. Gradual loss of hearing occurs commonly as cats grow older. Usually it is not apparent before 14 years of age. A cat who has lost his hearing compensates for this by relying more upon his other senses. Accordingly, it is sometimes quite difficult to tell if a cat is going deaf. Techniques you can use to test your cat's hearing are described in the EARS chapter (see *Deafness*).

While there is no treatment for senile deafness, there might be a blockage in the ear canal or some other contributing cause such as ear mites or a tumor which could be improved by treatment. Veterinary examination is desirable.

Loss of eyesight also is difficult to assess in the cat—again, because the other senses become more acute. How to test your cat's eyesight is discussed in the EYES chapter under *The Blind Cat.*

Excessive tearing and eye discharge should be treated if present. They are not usually related to aging.

In many older cats a grayish-white or bluish haze appears in that part of the eye which can be seen through the pupil. It is due to aging of the lens and is called *nuclear sclerosis.* It should not be mistaken for a cataract. While senile cataracts do occur in cats, they are not nearly as common as in man. Loss of vision may be due to retinal disease or another eye disorder.

Surgical removal of cataracts usually is reserved for cats having great difficulty getting around because of loss of vision. Most cats adjust well to a gradual loss of eyesight if they retain their ability to hear. Even when both of these senses are impaired, they are still quite able to adjust to familiar surroundings by touch—using the organ receptors in their whiskers, carpal hairs, and pads of their feet.

Loss of smell can be a serious handicap. A cat uses his odor sensing mechanism as a powerful stimulant to his appetite. The cat who is unable to smell his food often refuses to eat, even though he is hungry. You may be able to gain a clue to your cat's sense of smell by passing an alcohol swab beneath his nose.

Stimulate your cat's appetite by feeding him highly aromatic and palatable foods (see *Diet and Nutrition* in this chapter).

Functional Changes

Changes in eating and drinking patterns, voiding habits, and bowel function occur frequently in older cats. Unless you are especially alert to such changes, you might easily overlook some important clue to your cat's general health. Keep in mind that many cats dislike using their litter boxes in front of their owners. In the case of the cat who goes outdoors to eliminate, some extra effort will be required to see if he is having any problem with his gastrointestinal or urinary systems.

Functional problems are not necessarily due to senility. Many are associated with diseases which, although they afflict aging cats especially, are still correctable or amenable to treatment.

Increased Thirst and Frequency of Urination. Most elderly cats, if they live long enough, develop signs of kidney failure. The kidneys appear to wear out more rapidly than do other organs. The early signs of kidney insufficiency are increased frequency of urination, which is compensated for by more frequent drinking. These are also signs of diabetes, a condition which is more common in older cats.

An older cat who stops using his litter tray or begins to wet in the house may be suffering from cystitis or some other treatable condition, as discussed in the URINARY SYSTEM chapter under *Urinary Incontinence.* Prostatic enlargement ordinarily is not a major cause of urinary symptoms in the cat.

Constipation. This is one of the most common complaints encountered in the care of older cats. Contributing factors are lack of exercise, voluntary fecal retention, improper diet, reduced bowel activity, and weakness of the muscles of the abdominal wall. Along with a tendency to drink less water, this can lead to the formation of hard dry stools which are difficult to pass. Hairballs, which can produce difficulties in cats of all ages, are particularly troublesome in the older individual.

It is important not to mistake straining to void with constipation. Urethral obstruction is an emergency which requires immediate veterinary attention to relieve the cause of the blockage (see *Feline Urologic Syndrome*).

Treatment of constipation and the prevention of hairballs is discussed in the chapter DIGESTIVE SYSTEM.

Diarrhea. Diarrhea often goes unnoticed, especially in outdoor cats. Most cats with chronic diarrhea exhibit irritation of the skin around the anus, dehydration, and loss of condition. Chronic diarrhea in the elderly cat might be a sign of cancer, pancreatic disease, or a malabsorption syndrome. When it is due to old-age, it can often be controlled by diet and medication.

Abnormal Discharges. Abnormal discharges are those containing blood or pus; and those with an offensive odor. Discharges from the eyes, ears, nose, mouth, penis and vagina, suggest infection. In the elderly cat, cancer becomes a consideration.

Pyometra (Abscess of the Uterus) typically occurs in barren older queens, usually two to eight weeks after they go out of heat. Signs are lethargy and depression, loss of appetite, increased thirst, and excessive drinking. They may at first suggest kidney failure, but the abdomen of the queen becomes quite markedly distended and firm. Purulent vaginal discharge makes the diagnosis obvious, but in some cases it may be absent. This is a true surgical emergency. It requires immediate veterinary treatment (see *Uterine Infection* in SEX AND REPRODUCTION).

In summary, the following abnormal findings are danger signals in the elderly cat. The presence of any one is an indication for further investigation by your veterinarian:
1. A sustained increase in temperature, pulse, or breathing rate.
2. Loss of appetite or weight.
3. Unexplained change in behavior.
4. Loss of eyesight, hearing, or sense of smell.
5. Weakness or difficulty getting about.
6. Bloody or purulent discharge from a body opening.
7. Recurrent diarrhea or constipation.
8. Increased thirst and/or frequency of urination.
9. Persistent cough, labored breathing, or shortness of breath.
10. An unexplained growth or lump anywhere on the body.

The Mouth, Teeth and Gums. Examine the mouth as described in the chapter MOUTH AND THROAT. Painful mouth disorders, such as *Periodontal Disease* and *Gingivitis,* are much more common in the older cat. Often they are accompanied by halitosis and drooling. Eating is painful and difficult. A cat with mouth disease eats poorly and loses weight rapidly.

With proper treatment suffering is relieved. The cat is more comfortable, and his nutritional status improves. Loose teeth should be removed. If your cat is unable to chew dry cat food, switch to a semi-moist or moist ration, or feed canned food formulated for older cats. Cats of all ages should be put on a program of good dental hygiene as outlined in the chapter MOUTH AND THROAT.

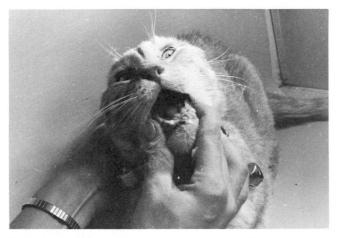

Tooth and gum disease can become a serious handicap in the aging cat.

Anemia is an important consideration in the elderly cat. It is most easily recognized by paleness of the mucous membranes, especially the tongue. Possible causes include liver disease, kidney insufficiency, and cancer.

Changes in Weight. Progressive weight loss is one of the most serious problems encountered in the aging cat. Many cases are due to kidney disease. Others may be caused by cancers or periodontal disease. In some cases the cause is not evident. It is a good idea to weigh your cat each month. A drop in weight is an indication for a veterinary checkup.

Obesity is a serious but largely preventable problem which should be corrected in the elderly cat. Being overweight is a complicating factor in kidney disease, arthritis, and heart disease. An overweight cat is much less likely to exercise and maintain his overall condition and vitality. To prevent and treat this problem, see *Diet and Nutrition* below.

Temperature, Pulse and Respiration. The rectal temperature is an important indicator of the health of the cat. How to take the temperature is discussed in the APPENDIX. Subnormal temperature may be found in debilitated individuals. A rise in temperature indicates an active infection—or a disease not related to old age.

A sustained increase in the heart rate could be an early sign of anemia or heart disease. Treatment of these conditions is discussed in the chapter CIRCULATORY SYSTEM.

An increase in the breathing rate suggests lung disease. In cats, coughing usually indicates bronchitis or airway disease—not necessarily related to old age. Rarely it can be due to heart disease.

Diet and Nutrition

Since an older cat is less active he requires fewer calories than when he was younger. Without a reduction in number of calories, the older cat is likely to gain weight, which puts an added strain on his limited organ reserve. This contributes to a shortened life span.

Caloric requirements for the older cat should be determined on an individual basis. You must take into consideration his *ideal* weight (i.e., that at which he is neither too fat or too thin), how active he is, and what his emotional make-up may be. Active and playful cats require more food than their more sedate counterparts.

In general, an elderly cat of average weight needs only about 35 to 40 calories per pound body weight. Dry ration provides about 105 calories per ounce; semi-moist 89 calories per ounce; and canned ration 42 calories per ounce. Weigh your cat and compute his daily caloric requirements; then determine the amount of ration to feed him each day. (*Note:* Adjust the ration upward or downward depending upon whether your cat is below or above his ideal weight.)

Since the older cat must eat less food, it is extremely important that what he eats be of the highest quality to provide an adequate daily supply of nutrients. The protein quality is especially important. The cost of the food is a good index of its protein quality. This is especially true of a product advertised as a complete or balanced diet.

While high quality protein is important for the older cat, he should not be fed a diet too rich in meat as this creates an increased nitrogen load which must be handled by his liver and kidneys. As weak kidneys are a common problem in elderly cats, they can be thrown into failure by feeding them more protein than they can handle. This might happen when an owner adds meat products to a balanced diet in excess of ten percent of the total daily ration.

High quality protein supplements suitable for the digestive tract of an older cat can be supplied by adding small amounts of white meat chicken, white fish meat, boiled egg, cottage cheese, or skimmed milk. If your cat seems to be losing weight or appears to need more calories, try adding small amounts of carbohydrate (cooked cereals, cooked rice, or farina).

Since the senses of taste and smell usually diminish with age, the tastiness of the ration is also an important factor. Fats increase the palatability of food but they are difficult for the older cat to digest and are high in calories. Some fat is required to aid the intestinal absorption of fat soluable vitamins, and to provide for the manufacture of essential fatty acids, but adequate amounts are supplied by commercial cat foods. Fat supplements should not be added to the ration.

Old cats need more minerals and vitamins. B-Vitamins are lost in the urine of cats having reduced kidney function. In addition, the absorption of vitamins through the intestinal tract diminished as the individual ages. Calcium and phosphorus in correct balance (1.2/1) helps to prevent softening of the bones. Therefore, many old cats probably need a vitamin/mineral supplement. But it should be *balanced* to meet his metabolic needs. Your veterinarian can recommend an appropriate supplement to meet the specific requirements of your cat.

Older cats are more sedentary. Being less active, they require fewer calories. —*Sydney Wiley.*

A ration low in magnesium content (less than 0.1% dry weight basis) is an important consideration for cats suffering from FUS (see Page 256).

It is desirable when feeding an older cat to divide his daily ration into two equal parts and feed the first half in the morning and the second half in the evening. Underweight cats may respond better to three or four feedings a day. Alternately, dry or semi-moist ration can be left out all day long so the cat can "snack" whenever he's hungry.

Special Diets. Prescription diets may be required for cats with heart disease, kidney disease, intestinal disease, or obesity. They should be prescribed by your veterinarian.

PUTTING YOUR CAT TO SLEEP (EUTHANASIA)

The time may come when you are faced with the prospect of having to put your pet to sleep. This is a difficult decision to make—both for you and for your veterinarian. Many an old and even infirm cat can be made quite comfortable with just a little more thoughtfulness and tender loving care than the average healthy cat needs, and can still enjoy months or years of happiness in the company of his loved ones. But when life ceases to be a joy and a pleasure, when the cat suffers from a painful and progressive condition for which there is no hope of betterment, then perhaps at this time we owe him the final kindness to die easily and painlessly. This is accomplished by an intravenous injection of an anesthetic agent in sufficient amount to cause immediate loss of consciousness and cardiac arrest.

22

Drugs and Medications

GENERAL REMARKS

Cats, unlike many other domestic animals, appear to be unusually sensitive to drugs and medications. This applies to drugs used by the veterinarian and those obtained by the cat owner from other sources. It has been suggested that the liver's ability to metabolize drugs is slower in cats than in most other animals, and that this may account, in part, for the cat's tendency to develop toxic reactions. Many drugs and medications which are safe in people, when used according to the manufacturer's recommendations, are not safe for the cat.

Since the margin of safety is often quite small, the size (body weight) of the cat becomes an important consideration.

Your veterinarian will be quite specific in regard to how much medication you should give him, and how often to give it. To avoid the problems of drug intoxication, these recommendations should be carefully observed.

Tranquilizers are discussed in the chapter FELINE BEHAVIOR AND TRAINING.

Antibiotics and Steroids are discussed in the following chapter.

ANESTHETICS AND ANESTHESIA

Anesthetics are drugs used to block the sensation of pain. They are divided into two general categories—locals and generals.

Local anesthetics are used for operations on the surface of the body where they are infiltrated locally into the tissue or into a regional nerve. They may be applied topically to mucous membranes. While local anesthetics (such as *Xylocaine*) have the fewest risks and side effects, they are not suitable for most major operations.

General anesthetics render the cat unconscious. They can be given by injection or inhalation. Light doses sedate or relax the cat and may be suitable for short procedures (such as removing porcupine quills from the mouth). Inhaled gases (such as *Halothane*) are administered through a tube placed in the trachea. Combinations of anesthetics often are used to lessen potential side effects.

The dose of an anesthetic is computed by weighing the cat. Because cats are unusually sensitive to ordinary doses of a drug such as *Pentathol,* veterinarians often administer an anesthetic in sequential small doses—until a desired affect is obtained—rather than giving it all as a single injection.

The removal of an anesthetic agent is by the lungs, liver, or kidneys. Impaired function of these organs can cause anesthetic complications. If your cat has a history of lung, liver, kidney or heart disease, be sure to discuss this with your veterinarian.

A major risk of general anesthesia is having a cat vomit when going to sleep or waking up. The vomitus refluxes into the windpipe and produces asphyxiation. This can be avoided by keeping the stomach empty for 12 hours before scheduled surgery. Accordingly, if you know your cat is going to have an operation, don't give him anything to *eat or drink* after 6:00 P.M. the night before. This means picking up his water dish and keeping him away from the toilet bowl and other sources of water as well.

PAIN RELIEVERS

Analgesics are drugs used to relieve pain. While there are many classes of pain-killers, all of them should be used with caution in the cat.

Demerol, morphine, codeine and other *narcotics* are subject to Federal regulation and cannot be purchased without a prescription. The effect of these drugs on cats is highly unpredictable. Morphine, in a dose appropriate for a small dog, produces apprehension, excitability, and drooling in the cat. When even this minimum dose is exceeded, the cat can convulse and die.

Aspirin, the safest and best analgesic for home veterinary care in the *dog,* is especially toxic to the cat. Small doses produce loss of appetite, depression, vomiting. One aspirin tablet a day for three or four days is sufficient to cause salivation, dehydration, vomiting, and a staggering gait. Severe disturbances in acid-base balance may ensue. The bone marrow and liver may show signs of toxicity. Gastrointestinal bleeding is a frequent complication. All cat owners should be aware of the potential dangers associated with the use of aspirin. It should be given only under veterinary direction. The recommended daily dose for cats is three to 10 mg per pound body weight. (A five grain aspirin tablet contains 324 mg. When given to a five pound cat, this is the same as a person taking seven to 22 aspirins.)

Tylenol (Acetaminophen) is another analgesic which might be inappropriately administered to an ailing cat. A cat who is given two tylenol tablets a day, a child's dose, could develop hemolytic anemia and signs of liver failure.

Butazolidin (Phenylbutazone) is another analgesic often prescribed for horses, dogs, and other animals. When used in these animals, in doses recommended by the manufacturer, it is safe and effective. But when so used in cats, it might produce toxicity much like that of aspirin and tylenol. In addition, Butazolidin causes kidney failure.

In summary, even though analgesics are common household items, they should not be given freely to cats without appropriate indications and then only under specific veterinary direction. At the first signs of toxicity, these drugs should be withdrawn. Discuss this with your veterinarian.

COMMON HOUSEHOLD DRUGS FOR HOME VETERINARY USE

Dose for the Average-sized Adult Cat:

Antacids (Maalox, Mylanta): One teaspoon every four hours for two or three doses.

Charcoal (Activated): Mix one teaspoon in an ounce of water. Give once.

Cheracol-D (Cough Syrup): One-fourth teaspoon every four hours.

Dramamine: 12.5 mg one hour before traveling.

Glauber's Salt (Sodium Sulfate): One teaspoonful.

Hydrogen Peroxide (3%): *By mouth* - one teaspoon every ten minutes for three doses, or until the cat vomits. For *topical application* to wounds: dilute one part to two parts of water.

Kaopectate (For diarrhea)*: One teaspoon per five pounds body weight every four hours.

Metamucil: One capsule—or one-half teaspoon of powder mixed into the cat's food—once a day.

Milk of Magnesia (Unflavored): One teaspoon per five pounds body weight. Give once, or as directed.

Mineral Oil: One teaspoon mixed into the cat's food, once or twice a week.

Panalog (Ear drops and ointment): As directed.

Pepto-Bismol: One-half teaspoon every four hours.

Petroleum jelly (Not carbolated): One-half to one teaspoon, once or twice a week.

---

*Note: Don't use *Paragoric,* which is not safe for cats.

HOW TO GIVE MEDICATIONS

Pills (Capsules and Tablets)

The cat should be wrapped in a towel and held by an assistant, unless he is especially cooperative. Open his mouth as described in the chapter MOUTH AND THROAT. Place the pill over the back of his tongue in the midline or drop the pill deep into his open mouth. Close his mouth quickly. Hold it shut while stroking his throat, or tap him briskly under the chin. This stimulates the swallowing reflex. If he licks his nose, probably he has swallowed the pill.

(*Note:* Avoid breaking up pills, if at all possible. If pills are broken up into powders they make an unpleasant taste which is poorly tolerated. In addition, some pills have a protective coating which is important for delayed release in the intestine).

Medications specifically intended to be given as *powders* can be added to a cat's ration. If the medication has an unpleasant taste, disguise it by adding brewer's yeast, cheese, or strong fish oil.

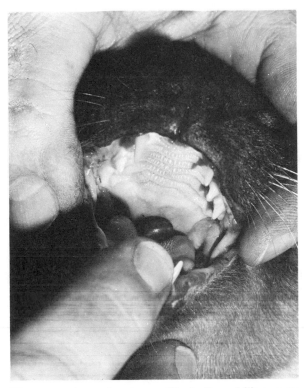

The correct way to give a pill—in the midline, over the back of the cat's tongue. —*J. Clawson.*

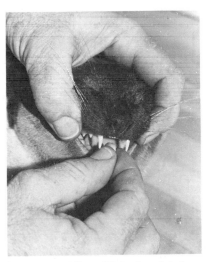

Incorrect. The pill is too far forward. —*J. Clawson.*

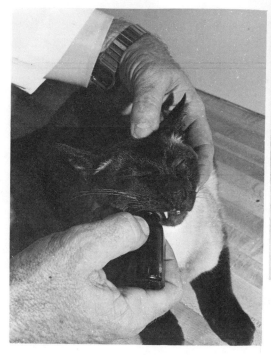

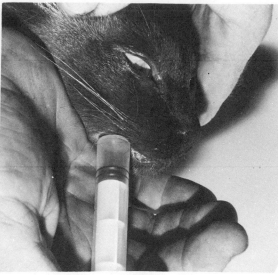

Liquids are administered into a cheek pouch between the molar teeth and the cheek. —*J. Clawson.*

Liquids

Liquid preparations are administered into a pouch between the molar teeth and the cheek. Cats can be given up to three teaspoons of liquid as a single dose. Measure the required amount into a small prescription bottle. It may be easier to use a medicine dropper. Secure the cat.

Tilt his chin up 45 degrees and place the neck of the bottle or tip of the eye dropper into his cheek pouch. Seal his lips around it with your fingers and administer the liquid. When the liquid reaches the back of his mouth, the cat will automatically swallow.

Injections

If it becomes necessary to give your cat injections, it is highly desirable to have the procedure discussed and demonstrated to you by your veterinarian.

Some injections are given under the skin (*subcutaneous*) and others into the muscle. Insulin is an example of the former, and rabies vaccine the latter. Read the directions on the product to determine the route of administration.

Most injections are not painful to the cat, although some intramuscular injections may hurt as the medication is injected. Cats should be secured (see *Handling and Restraint*). A good assistant is a help.

Draw the medicine up into the syringe and point the needle toward the ceiling while pressing the plunger to expel any air.

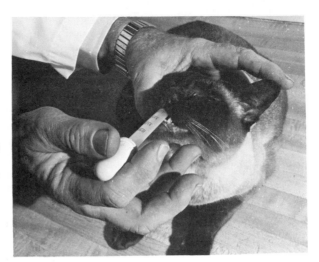

A medicine dropper can be used in this manner.
—*J. Clawson.*

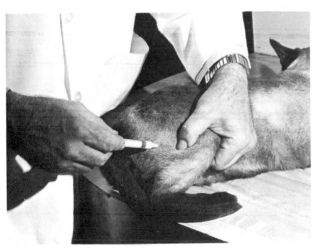

Give *intramuscular* injections into the back of the thigh muscle as described. Avoid hitting the bone (beneath the thumb).
—*J. Clawson.*

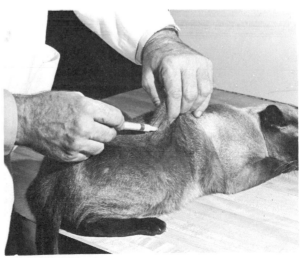

Subcutaneous injections are given beneath the loose skin in back of the shoulder.
—*J. Clawson.*

The technique for giving an injection is to select a site and swab the skin with a piece of cotton soaked in alcohol.

The back of the neck or shoulder is a good place for a subcutaneous injection because here the skin is loose and readily forms a fold when pinched. Grasp a fold of skin to form a ridge. Firmly push the point of the needle through the skin into the subcutaneous fat in a course somewhat parallel to the surface of the skin. Before any injection is given, always pull back on the plunger and look for blood. If blood appears, withdraw the syringe and repeat the procedure. Some medicines could cause death if given into a vessel. In the absence of blood, push in the plunger. Withdraw the needle and rub the skin for a few seconds to disperse the medicine.

Intramuscular injections are given in the muscle of the outside of the thigh behind the femur, half-way between the knee joint and the hip. Injections into vessels, nerves, and joints can be avoided by giving the shot in the described location. Remember to withdraw the plunger and check for blood in the syringe before giving the injection.

Enemas

Enemas are used to treat fecal impactions. The subject is discussed in the DIGESTIVE SYSTEM chapter. Enemas should not be given until a veterinarian has made the diagnosis and prescribed the treatment. Enemas ordinarily are not used to treat chronic constipation as there are better ways to manage this problem.

Suppositories

Medications can be given by suppository when the oral route is not satisfactory (for example, when a cat is vomiting). Or your veterinarian may prescribe a suppository to treat a severe constipation.

The suppository is lubricated with vaseline and slipped all the way into the rectum where it dissolves. Suppositories for constipation contain a mild irritant which draws water into the rectum and stimulates a bowel movement. Dulcolax is a good one for this purpose. You can buy it at any drugstore. The dose for an adult cat is one-half a suppository. Suppositories should not be given to a cat who might have a *Painful Abdomen:* see EMERGENCIES.

Eye Medication

How to medicate the eye is discussed in the chapter EYES.

Ear Medication

How to medicate the ears is discussed in the chapter EARS.

23

Antibiotics and Infections

GENERAL REMARKS

Antibiotics are extracts of basic plants such as molds and fungi. They are capable of destroying some microorganisms that cause disease.

The age of modern antibiotics began with the discovery of penicillin by Sir Alexander Fleming. In 1928, Fleming made a fortuitous and accidental discovery. He observed that a strain of penicillin mold which had fallen on a culture plate could prevent the growth of a colony of bacteria. Although he tried to isolate extracts of the fungus to treat infections, the broths proved too weak.

It remained for a group in Oxford, England, in 1939, under the direction of Sir Howard W. Florey, to isolate potent antibiotic extracts from the mold *penicillium notatum*. The impact of this success on the control of infection sent scientists back to the soil in search of other natural substances having antibiotic activity. This led to the discovery of tetracycline and chloromycetin, as well as many other antibiotics in use today. Taking the basic nucleus of an antibiotic grown in deep broth cultures, researchers added side chains by chemical synthesis. This created a whole new spectrum as synthetic drugs.

Antibiotics fall into two general categories. Those that are *bacteriostatic* (or *fungistatic*) inhibit the growth of microorganisms, but don't kill them outright. *Bacteriocidal* and *fungicidal* drugs destroy the microorganisms.

Bacteria are classified according to their ability to cause disease. *Pathogenic* bacteria are capable of producing a particular illness or infection. *Non-pathogenic* bacteria live on (or within) the host, but don't cause illness under normal circumstances. They are referred to as *normal flora*. Some of them produce substances necessary to the well-being of the host. For example, bacteria in the bowel synthesize Vitamin K which is absorbed into the animal's blood stream and is necessary for normal blood clotting.

Antibiotics are specific for certain pathogenic bacteria. The number now available brings with it new possibilities for animal sensitivity and allergy, and multiplies the potential hazards of mismanagement.

ANTIBIOTICS YOUR VETERINARIAN MAY PRESCRIBE

NOTE: Unless otherwise stated, antibiotics should be continued 48 hours after the cat becomes free of signs and symptoms. If the condition does not improve in 48 hours, check with your veterinarian before continuing the antibiotic.

ANTIBIOTIC	DOSE (By Weight of Cat)	USED IN INFECTIONS OF:	ADVERSE REACTIONS
Penicillin	40,000 u/lb. every 24 hr. I.M.	Skin, Mouth, Tonsils, Uterus, Wounds	Allergy
Ampicillin	10 mg/lb. every 8 hr., orally	Same as penicillin Genitourinary tract Respiratory tract	Allergy
Cephalosporins	Depends on the drug	Urinary tract Respiratory tract	Kidney Damage Expensive
Aminoglycosides: Neomycin	10 mg/lb. every 6 hr., orally Topically 3 to 4 times daily	Diarrhea (orally) Eye*, Ear, Skin (Topically)	Kidney Damage Allergy
Kanamycin	3 mg/lb. every 12 hr., I.M.	Kitten Septicemia	Kidney Damage Deafness Brain Injury in Newborns
Gentamycin	2 mg/lb. every 12 hr., I.M. first day, then once a day Topically 3 to 4 times daily	Skin, Respiratory tract Urinary tract Eye*, Ear	Kidney Damage Deafness
Tetracyclines	8 mg/lb. every 8 hr., orally 3 mg/lb. every 12 hr., I.M.	Respiratory tract Skin	Stained teeth (Unborn kittens) Retarded bone growth (Kittens)
Chloramphenicol	10-25 mg/lbs. every 12 hr., orally Eye preparations, three times daily	Skin, Mouth Respiratory tract Urinary tract Eye* (topically)	Bone marrow depression (Do not use high doses more than 5 days)
Panolog	Topically 2 or 3 times daily. Drops and ointment.	Ear Skin	
Erythromycin	5 mg/lb. every 8 hr., orally	Penicillin substitute when cat is allergic to penicillin	Rare
Lincomycin	7 mg/lb. every 8 hr., orally 5 mg/lb. every 12 hr., I.M.	Skin, Wounds Penicillin substitute	Diarrhea

—continued

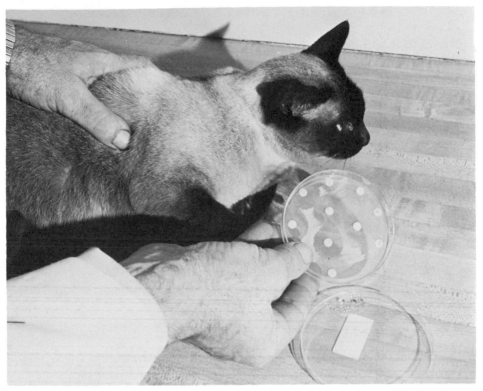

Discs containing various antibiotics on a culture plate, showing which antibiotics inhibit growth. —*J. Clawson.*

ANTIBIOTICS YOUR VETERINARIAN MAY PRESCRIBE—(continued)

ANTIBIOTIC	DOSE (By Weight of Cat)	USED IN INFECTIONS OF:	ADVERSE REACTIONS
Tylosin	5 mg/lb. every 8 hr., orally	Same as Erythromycin	Same as for Erythromycin
Sulfa Drugs	Depends on the drug	Urinary tract Gastrointestinal tract Eye*	Forms crystals in urine. Anemia. Allergy
Furacin	Apply 2 to 3 times daily (topically)	Burns Kitten vaginitis	
Griseofulvin	10 mg/lb. daily for 4 to 6 weeks	Ringworm	Don't use in pregnancy (Teratogenic)
Nystatin	100,000 u/lb. every 6 hr., orally for 7 to 14 days	Thrush	

*Preparations used in the EYE must be labeled specifically for ophthalmologic use.

WHY ANTIBIOTICS MAY NOT BE EFFECTIVE

Misdiagnosis of Infection

At times, signs of inflammation (such as heat, redness and swelling) can exist without infection. Sunburn is one example. Infection can be *presumed* to exist when one sees inflammation *and* purulent discharge (pus). Usually there will be an offensive odor. Other signs are fever and elevated white cell count. Specific infections are discussed in other chapters.

Inappropriate Selection

An antibiotic must be effective against the microorganism. Sometimes a choice can be made on the basis of the character of the illness. The best way to determine susceptibility is to recover the organism, culture it, and identify it by colony appearance and microscopic characteristics. Antibiotic discs are applied to the culture plate to see if the growth of colonies is inhibited. Antibiotics are graded according to whether the microorganism is *sensitive, indifferent* or *insensitive.* Unfortunately, laboratory findings do not always coincide with results in the host. Nevertheless, antibiotic culture and sensitivity testing is the surest way of selecting the best agent.

Inadequate Wound Care

Antibiotics enter the blood stream and are carried to the source of the infection. Abscesses, wounds containing devitalized tissue, and wounds with foreign bodies (dirt, splinters), are resistant areas. Under such circumstances, antibodies can't get into the wound. Accordingly, it is important to drain abscesses, debride or clean dirty wounds, and remove foreign bodies.

Route of Administration

An important medical decision rests in selecting the best route for administration. Some antibiotics have to be given on an empty stomach, and others with a meal. Insufficient absorption from the gastrointestinal tract is one cause of inadequate blood levels. Some antibiotics are not absorbed when taken with antacids or milk. In severe infections antibiotics are given intravenously, or by intramuscular injection, to circumvent this problem.

In the treatment of urinary tract infections, other substances may have to be given by mouth to change the acidity of the urine and assure that the antibiotics won't be inactivated.

Dose and Frequency of Administration

The total daily dose is computed by weighing the cat, then dividing the dose into equal parts and giving each at spaced-out intervals. When the total dose is too low, or not given often enough, the result is less favorable.

Other factors which have to be taken into account when computing the daily dose are the severity of the infection, the age of the cat, his overall health and stamina, whether he is taking another antibiotic, and whether he is taking drugs which could depress his ability to fight infection (such as cortisone).

COMPLICATIONS OF ANTIBIOTICS

All drugs should be viewed as poisons. The side effects of a drug could be more dangerous than the disease.

Antibiotics should never be given without justifiable indications. Common complications of antibiotics are discussed below and listed in the accompanying table. (This list is by no means complete.)

Allergy

Antibiotics, more so than any other class of drugs, can cause allergic reactions. Allergies are discussed in the SKIN chapter. Signs of allergy are hives, rash, itching and scratching, and watering of the eyes. Wheezing, collapse and death can occur.

Toxicity

There is a certain margin of safety, sometimes rather small, which lies between the therapeutic dose and a dose toxic to the cat. Toxicity is due to overdose, or impaired elimination. With age, and advanced liver and kidney disease, these organs fail to break down and excrete the antibiotic.

Young kittens require a lower dose by weight than adult cats because their kidneys are immature.

One cause of overdosage is giving an antibiotic for too long a time.

Toxicity can affect one or more systems:

The ears — Damage to the otic nerves leads to ringing in the ears, hearing loss, and deafness. Loss can be permanent.

The liver — Toxicity can lead to jaundice and liver failure.

The kidneys — Toxicity causes nitrogen retention, uremia, and kidney failure.

The bone marrow — Toxicity depresses the formation of red cells, white cells, and platelets. Fatalities do occur. Chloromycetin is especially at risk.

Signs of toxicity are difficult to recognize in the cat. They can be far advanced before they come to the owner's attention.

Secondary Infection

Antibiotics can alter the normal flora which serves as a protection against pathogens. Harmful bacteria can then multiply and cause disease.

Severe diarrhea follows the use of certain antibiotics which change the normal flora of the bowel.

Emergence of Resistant Strains

Strains of bacteria which are resistant to the antibiotics evolve when antibiotics are used: (a) for a long time, (b) in too low a dose, and (c) when the antibiotic is bacteriostatic. Microorganisms resistant to one antibiotic often are resistant to others of the same class.

Use in Pregnancy

Certain antibiotics can affect the growth and development of unborn or newborn kittens. Tetracyclines, griseofulvin, and kanamycin are three of them. They should not be used in pregnancy if substitutes are available.

ANTIBIOTICS AND CORTISONE

Cortisone and other steroids have an anti-inflammatory effect—that is, they reduce the size of the swelling, redness and tenderness, but do not treat the infection. They help to relieve the pain and irritation associated with an inflammation. Cortisone is used frequently to relieve itching, particularly that associated with allergies and skin diseases. It is often combined with antibiotics, particularly in topical preparations for use in the eye, ear, and on the skin.

Because they have anti-inflammatory properties, steroids mask the signs of infection while giving the impression the cat is getting better. At times, this can lead to continuation of tissue damage. Preparations containing steroids should not be used in the eye except under medical supervision.

Steroids have another side effect which is particularly undesirable. They depress the normal host immune response. This may allow infections to go unchecked.

Other untoward effects of steroids are discussed in the SKIN chapter under the heading *Cortisone Excess.*

Appendix

NORMAL PHYSIOLOGIC DATA

Normal Temperature:

Adult Cat: 100-103 degrees F (rectal). (Average: 101.5 degrees F.)
Newborn Kittens: see PEDIATRICS: *Physiology.*

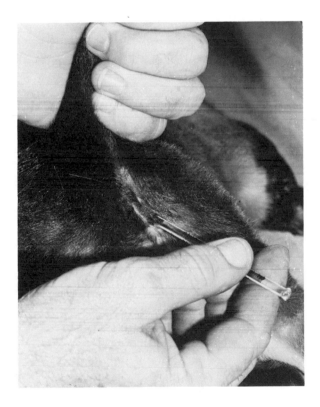

How to Take Your Cat's Temperature:

The only effective way to take your cat's temperature is by rectal thermometer. Shake down the thermometer until the bulb registers 96 degrees F. Lubricate the bulb with vaseline. With your cat standing, raise his tail and hold it firmly to keep him from sitting down; then gently insert the bulb into his anal canal with a twisting motion. Insert the thermometer one to one and one-half inches, depending upon the size of the cat. Hold the thermometer in place for three minutes. Then remove it, wipe clean, and read his temperature by the height of the silver column of mercury on the thermometer scale.

Clean the thermometer with alcohol before using it again. This prevents the transfer of diseases.

(Note: Should the thermometer break off, usually because the cat sits down, do not attempt to find and extract the broken end. Notify your veterinarian.)

Pulse

Normal: 110-140 beats per minute at rest. (Average 120.)
(Note: To learn how to take your cat's pulse, see CIRCULATORY SYSTEM: *Pulse).*

Respiration

Normal: 20-30 breaths per minute at rest. See RESPIRATORY SYSTEM.

Weight

Intact males (toms) — Eight to 15 pounds.
Neutered males and females — Five and one-half to 10 pounds.

Gestation

63 to 65 days. (Normal range 59 to 69 days.)

CAT FANCY AND REGISTRATION ORGANIZATIONS

American Cat Association, 10065 Foothill Boulevard, Lake View Terrace, California 91342

American Cat Fanciers Association, P.O. Box 203, Point Lookout, Missouri 65726

Canadian Cat Association, 14 Nelson Street West, Suite 5, Brampton, Ontario L6X1B7, Canada

Cat Fanciers Association, 1309 Allaire Avenue, Ocean, New Jersey 07712

Cat Fanciers Federation, 2013 Elizabeth Street, Schenectady, New York 12303

Crown Cat Fanciers Federation, 1379 Tyler Park Drive, Louisville, Kentucky 40204

Governing Council of the Cat Fancy, Dovefields, Petworth Road, Witley, Surrey GU85QU, Great Britain

The Independent Cat Association, 211 East Olive (Suite 201), Burbank, California 91502

United Cat Federation, 6621 Thornwood Street, San Diego, California 92111

This kitten is showing the instincts of a born stalker and hunter.
                                                    —*Sydney Wiley.*

GUIDE FOR
BUYING A HEALTHY KITTEN

The best age at which to buy a kitten is when he is about eight weeks old. At this age kittens start to become self-reliant. You can usually tell whether an individual is going to be a good show or breeding prospect or, in the case of a pet, a representative example of the breed you have chosen.

Kittens two months old are formative. Most new owners prefer to take charge of the care and training of their kittens while they are still young and impressionable.

Good sources for free-bred kittens are newspaper ads, some of the better pet shops, veterinarians, and animal welfare organizations. But for a pedigreed animal it is much better to go to a specialist breeder. Many of the leading cat publications (for example, *Cats Magazine,* P.O. Box 37, Port Orange, Fl. 32019; or *Cat Fancy Magazine,* 5509 Santa Monica Blvd., Los Angeles, Ca. 90038) carry classified advertisements for the various breeds, or, you can write to one of the cat registration organizations listed in the appendix of this book and request the name of the secretary of the breed club of your choice. They, in turn, may be able to mail you a listing of breeders.

After you locate several breeders who have the kind of kitten you are looking for, write to each and explain whether you are interested in a male or female, plan to breed or show, or are just looking for a family companion and pet. A sincere inquiry providing the breeder with some information about the prospective buyer is much more likely to elicit the type of information you are looking for than a hastily scribbled note.

It is wise to insist upon buying the cat on the approval of a veterinarian. Emotional attachments develop rapidly. This can make the return of a kitten to a breeder a difficult task. Conscientious breeders, who are proud of their stock, are willing to stand behind them. They will not object to this request. No breeder should be expected to offer you a guarantee that the cat will win in the show ring. Picking a future champion at eight weeks of age is extremely difficult, even for breeders with considerable personal experience. Although many qualities show up clearly, others cannot be determined in the very young kitten. The care, training, feeding, medical care and socialization of the kitten after the purchase are every bit as important as the genetic background of the parents.

Many buyers prefer to visit a cattery and make their own selection. There is no need to panic when, on the appointed day, you find yourself standing before a litter of bouncing kittens and find that all appear to be equally lovable. Most kittens appear healthy at first glance but a closer examination may disclose a potential problem that could make the individual undesirable.

Here are the things you should look for in a healthy kitten:

Examine the kitten first head-on. The nose should be cool and damp. Sneezing or a nasal discharge may indicate a respiratory virus infection.

Look inside the mouth. The gums and mucous membranes should be a light pink. A pale color is a sign of anemia.

The baby teeth should be clean and bright. The incisors should meet edge to edge. If a match head can be inserted between the upper and lower incisors, the bite is either undershot or overshot and probably won't correct itself.

The eyes should be clear, bright, and free of watery discharge and matter. There should be no white spots on the surface of the eye which could be scars from injuries or infections. Redness or protrusions of the third eyelid also may indicate a chronic eye ailment or poor health.

Permanent adult eye color is apparent at this age. Avoid a kitten with a blue iris, especially if his coat is white, as there is a strong possibility that he will be deaf. The eyes should look straight ahead. A cross-eyed look is undesirable. This is especially common in Siamese.

The ear canals should be clean and sweet-smelling. A build-up of wax with a rancid odor could be caused by ear mites. Head shaking and tenderness about the ears indicate an infection of the ear canal (again, usually mites).

Feel the stomach. If it is swollen, this would indicate poor feeding or possibly worms. A bulge at the navel is most likely an umbilical hernia.

The skin and hair around the anus and vulva should be clean and healthy-looking. Signs of irritation are discharge, redness, and hair loss. They indicate the possibility of infection, chronic diarrhea or worms.

In male kittens both testicles should be present in the scrotum.

The coat should be fluffy, glossy, and free of mats. Excessive scale, sores, itching and deposits in the fur indicate fleas, mites and other external parasites. Moth-eaten bare areas are characteristic of ringworm and mange.

Next examine the kitten for soundness and correct structure. The legs should be straight and well formed; the feet cupped and the toes well-arched. The gait should be free and smooth. Avoid the kitten who is stiff-legged or lame.

Kittens at eight to twelve weeks should weigh about two to three pounds. The thin, bony, underweight kitten is not desirable, nor is the one who is overly large or too plump. The most desirable kitten is the one who appears in correct proportion for his age and size.

The most important consideration when selecting a kitten for a family pet is his personality and disposition. Kittens who remain with their littermates and mothers until eight to ten weeks of age learn to relate to people and to other cats by watching how their mother reacts to them. Once a pattern of primary socialization has been established, it tends to become fixed and doesn't change later in life. Heredity also can influence a kitten's disposition. For these reasons, you can tell a lot about a kitten's sociability by observing the queen and how well she handles interactions with strangers.

The well-socialized kitten, when talked to, appears eager for attention. When picked up he settles down and relaxes. When stroked, he may begin to purr. These are good indications.

See if he follows you about when you set him down. Dangle a piece of string in front of him, or throw a wad of crumpled paper, and see if he wants to play. Clap your hands or stamp your feet. After being briefly startled, see if he recovers quickly.

A kitten who is inactive, withdrawn, who does not interact well with his littermates, who shrinks when spoken to or resents being picked up and remains tense, may be timid or in poor health. Taking a chance that he will overcome his shyness later usually is not worthwhile. He is unlikely to make a good family pet. (However, he may be suitable for a couple without children.)

As good health and good disposition so often go hand in hand, it is perhaps wise, in making the final selection, to pick the sturdy individual with bright eyes who is full of life and bursting with self-confidence.

Check to see that your kitten has received his all-important first vaccinations. Be sure to ask for and receive his registration papers and pedigree (if purebred), a diet sheet, and a vaccination schedule.

After you have made your purchase, you should receive advice and counsel in future weeks. Any guarantees concerning the kitten should be discussed and agreed upon *before* the check is signed.

Grooming, Feeding and Training

Begin grooming your kitten as soon as he settles into his new home. At this age it is easier to accustom him to a daily routine. The process of grooming and handling is a good socializing experience, particularly if you plan to show him later. It may be difficult to groom an older cat who has not had this training early in life.

Daily handling also gives you the chance to check your kitten's eyes, ears, teeth, and the condition of his skin. Fleas and other parasites should be treated. Check his teeth to be sure the adult ones are coming in normally. This is the best time to start a program of good oral hygiene as described in the section *Teeth*.

Trimming the front nails may be considered for kittens who are going to live as house pets. How to groom the coat, and care for the nails, is discussed in the SKIN chapter.

Most breeders supply a diet sheet with a new kitten. It should be followed, at least for the first two weeks, since abrupt changes in diet can cause digestive upsets. To learn about cat nutrition and the feeding of older kittens, consult the chapter FEEDING AND NUTRITION.

You should begin to teach your kitten how to use a litter pan and a scratching post soon after he moves into his new home. You might also want to teach him how to walk on a leash and to come when called. The training of cats is not like that of dogs, owing to differences in character and personality. It is advisable to read the chapter FELINE BEHAVIOR AND TRAINING to learn about these differences.

The front paws are sometimes used as spoons to eat food or "drink" milk.   —*Sydney Wiley.*

General Index

NOTE: Pages shown in boldface contain detailed coverage of the item.

Abortion, 270, **278**
Abscess, 114, 143, 173, 230
Abscessed tooth, 157
Acne, 113
Adrenal glands, 113
  (*See also:* Cortisone)
Aggressive behavior, 77, 225, 227,
  272, 308-9, 342, 348, **349**
Aging, 359-60
  a cat by his teeth, 166
Allergies, 36, **105-9,** 145, 156, 185,
  189, 209
Allergic reactions, 36, 105-9, 178,
  209, 379
Alopecia, feline endocrine, 111, 362
Anal
  glands, 195-7
  sac abscess, 198
Anemia, **219-20**
  causes of, 51, 56, 72, 75, 80, 81,
    98, 152, 160, 210, 323, 365, 369
  (*See also:* Feline infectious
    anemia)
Anesthesia, 368-9
Anorexia nervosa, 348
Antibiotics and Infections, 375-80
Antibodies, 60-1
Antidote, universal, 39
Antiserums and venoms, 46, 61,
  65, 71, 77
Anus and Rectum, 194, 329
Appendix (of book), 381-2
Appetite, 151, 161, 335
  (*See also:* **Index of Signs and
    Symptoms**)
Arterial thromboembolism (clot
  in artery), 218
Arteriosclerosis, 215
Arthritis, 230, **243-4**
Artificial Insemination, 283
Artificial Respiration, 23-5
  in newborn kitten, 302
Ascites (fluid in abdomen), 72, 186,
  198
Asphyxiation, **27-8,** 369
Aspirin, 185, 244, **369**
Asthma, 209

Bacterial diseases, 64-6
Balance, 139
  lack of, 42, 140, **149,** 225-6, **229,**
    369
Bandaging, 48-50
Bathing, 90-3
Bee stings, 36
Behavior
  change in, 77, 225, 269, 277, 283,
    294, 308, 311
  disorders of, **346-50**
  normal feline, **341-2**
  of elderly cat, 360
  strange (unusual), 38, 41, 77,
    152, 200-1, 225-7, 269, 277, 383
Birth Control, 284-7
Birth of kittens, 294-302
Bite (occlusion), 168
Bites, care of, 48, 77-8, 143, 163
Biting, prevention of, 28-31
Bladder
  diseases of, 247-9, **253-8**
  worms, 59
Bleeding
  control of (wounds), **47-8**
  gastrointestinal, causes of, 43,
    56, 80, 185, 188, 194, 198, 353,
    364, 369
  post partum, 304
  spontaneously, 42, 155, 198
Blind cat, 134-7
Bloating (swelling of abdomen),
  185-6
Blood clot, in artery, 218
Blood sugar, low (hypoglycemia),
  200, **226,** 312
Boarding a cat, 338, 347, 360
Bone and joint problems, 233-46
Bones for cats, 170, 176, **338**
Brain, 222-7
Breast
  cancer, 357-8
  infection, 305-7
Breathing
  abnormal, 201-2
  rate, normal, 382
  tubes (trachea, bronchi), 207-9

Breech delivery, 298, 300
Breeding, **261-5,** 271
  (*See also:* Mating; Infertility)
Breeds of cat, 259-61
Bronchitis, 207-9
Brushing and combing, 88-9
Burns, 26
  chemical, 43, 163
  electric, 28
  of mouth, 163
Buying a healthy kitten, 383-5

Caesarean Section, 302
Caked breasts, 305
Calcium deficiency, 304, **308,** 339
Calicivirus, 66
Call (heat, estrus), 268-70
Cancer, 352-8
  (*See also:* Tumors)
Cannibalism, 309
Cardiomyopathy (heart muscle
  disease), 216-8
Cardiopulmonary Resuscitation
  (CPR), 23-5
Carrying (picking up) cat,
  technique for, 30
Castration, 225, **286**
Cat foods, 333-5
Cataracts, 135, 362-3
Catnip, **152,** 276
Cavities (dental caries), 169
Cerebellar hypoplasia, 325
Cerebrovascular disease (stroke),
  225-6
Chiggers, 101
Chilling, 26, 362
  in kittens, 313, **315**
Chlamydia, 66, 130
Chlorophyll, 284, 343
Circulation, 211, 214
Claws
  trimming, 89-90, 307
  removing (declawing), 332
Cleft palate, 328
Cloudy eye, 132
Coat, **85**

appearance, unkempt, 161, 163, 169, 170, 173-4, 362
care of, 86-9
  elderly cat, 362
  poisonous substance on, 39
  (*See also:* Hair)
Coccidiosis, 80
Cold, exposure to, 26
"Colds", 68, 153
Colitis, 188
Collars and Leashes, 28, 99, **344-5**
Colostrum, 61, 296, 305, 317
Coma (loss of consciousness), **228**
  causes of, 35, 38, 40-2, 45, 78, 105, 198, 200, **222-6,** 252
  treatment of, 229
Come, teaching to, 345
Concussion, brain, 222
Conformation, 234, 264
  kitten, 385
Congenital defects, 327-9
  (*See also:* Genetic disorders)
Conjunctivitis, 130-1
  of newborn, 132, 327
Constipation, **191-2,** 374
  in kittens, 322
  in elderly cats, 363
Convulsions, **227-8**
  causes of, (*See:* Fits, *Index of Signs and Symptoms)*
  treatment of, 228
Cornea, disorders of, 132-4
Cortisone, 51, 61, **112,** 133, **380**
Cough, 203
Coughing, (*See: Index of Signs and Symptoms)*
  home treatment for, 204
Cross-eyed, 125
Cutaneous larvae migrans, 57
Cuts and lacerations, **47-9,** 78, 143, 163
Cystitis (bladder infection), 257
Cysts of skin, 97, **354**

Dandruff, 100-1
Deafness, **149-50,** 262, 362
Death, signs of, 225
Declawing, 332
Dehydration, **27,** 64, 315, 322
  in kittens, 313, **315,** 322, 324
Dental hygiene, 170
Dermatitis, 38, **106-9**
Deworming, 52-4
Diabetes (sugar), 135, **199-200**
Diarrhea, **186-9,** 364
  causes of, (*See: Index of Signs and Symptoms)*
  in newborns, 316, 322, 323
Diet, switching from one to another, 338
Diets, for treating:
  constipation, 192

diarrhea, 189
FUS, 256-7
kidney failure, 252
obesity, 339
upset stomach, 184
(*See also:* Feeding; Vitamin and Mineral deficiencies)
Digestive System, 179-200
Dips, insecticide, 104-5
Disc, ruptured, 230
Distemper (feline panleukopenia), 69-72
Drooling, **176**
  (*See also: Index of Signs and Symptoms)*
Drowning, 27-8
Drugs, accidental overdose with, 44
  (*See also:* Medications)

Ear(s), **139-50**
  cleaning and medicating, 141-2
  discharge, 146-8
  foreign bodies in, 148
  mites, 101, **146**
Ear flap, 143-6
Eating grass and plants, 347-8
  (*See also:* Poisoning, by plants and shrubs)
Ectropion, 128
Elizabethan collar, 40
Emergencies, **23-50**
Emergency medical kit, 22
Encephalitis (brain inflammation), 77, 81, 184, **225**
Enemas, 191, 374
  how to give, 192
Enteritis, infectious, 69-72, 187-8
Entropion, 128
Epilepsy, 227-8
Esophagus, 180-2
  foreign body in, 181
Estrogen (female hormone), 270, 277, 347
Estrus (heat) cycle, 268-70
  abnormal, 276-7
Euthanasia, 367
Eyes, **117-137**
  color of, 118-9, 264, 312, 384
  discharge from, 129-30
  foreign body in, **126,** 132-3
  how to apply medicine to, 122
  how to examine, 120-1
Eyelashes, 118, **126-7,** 133
Eyelids, 118, **125-8**
  third, **128-9**
Eyesight, 117-8, 121
  testing for, 134

Fading kitten, **313,** 325
False Pregnancy, 283-4

Fecal impaction, 189, 192
Feeding
  adult cats, 335-6
  growing kittens, 340
  lactating queens, 303-4
  old cats, 366-7
  orphan kittens, 316-22
  pregnant mothers, 292
  weaning kittens, 329
  (*See also:* Diets; Vitamin and Mineral deficiencies)
Feeding and Nutrition, **333-40**
  common errors in, 338-9
Feline Infectious Anemia (FIA), 64
Feline Infectious Peritonitis (FIP), **72-4,** 278
Feline Leukemia Virus Disease Complex (FeLV), **74-6,** 278,
Feline Panleukopenia (FPL), 69-72
  in kittens, 325
Feline Urologic Syndrome (FUS), 253-7
Feline Viral Respiratory Disease Complex (FVRD), **66-9,** 129, 130
Fetal reabsorption, 278
Fever, high, (*See: Index of Signs and Symptoms)*
Fishhooks, extraction of, 175
Fits (*See:* Convulsions)
Flatus (passing gas), 188, **193**
Flea(s), **98-9**
  allergy, 106-7
  collar, 99
Flehman, 152
Flies, 103
Flukes, 58, 199
Food
  allergy (or intolerance), 106, 185-6
  poisoning, 43
  preferences, 335
  (*See also:* Cat foods)
Foreign body in:
  ears, 148
  esophagus, 181
  eyes, 126, 132-3
  intestinal tract, 190
  mouth, 174-5
  nose, 155
  stomach, 185
  throat, 176
  tongue, 171
  voice box (larynx), 206
  windpipe, 207
Formulas, for newborns, 318-22
Fractures of bones, 155, 230, **238-41,** 245
Freebred cats, 259
Frostbite, **27,** 145
Fungus diseases, 79

Fungus infections of:
   brain, 225
   ear, 145, 148
   eye, 122, 130
   mouth, 173
   sinus, 157
   skin, 109-10
FUS (Feline Urologic Syndrome),
   253-7

Gastritis (upset stomach), 184-5
Gastroenteritis, 187-8
Genes and chromosomes, 261-5
Genetic disorders, 125, 128, 135,
   137, 149, 166-8, 236, 238, **262,**
   276, 313, **327-9**
Geriatrics, **359-67**
Gestation (duration of pregnancy),
   289, 382
Glaucoma, 136
Grooming
   coat care, 86-9
   equipment for, 86-7
   kittens, 385-6
   lack of self (unkempt appear-
      ance), (*See:* Coat)
Growths (*See:* Tumors)
Grubs, 103
Gums, 164

Hair (coat), 83-4, 262
   (*See also: Hair* in *Index of Signs*
      and Symptoms)
Hairballs, 86, 159, 183-5, **190-2,** 363
Halitosis (bad breath), 161, 164,
   169, 173-4, 251, 364
Hand feeding, kittens, 318-22
Handling (to prevent biting), **28-31**
   restraining for treatment, 29-30
"Hay fever", (*See:* Pollen allergy)
Head and neck abscesses, 178
Head injuries, **222-5**
Hearing, 139-41
   diminished (*See:* Deafness)
Heart
   arrhythmias, 212, 308
   diseases, **215-9**
   failure, 214-5
   massage, **23-5**
   murmurs, 214
   rate (*See:* Pulse)
Heartworms, 219
Heat (estrus) cycle, 268-70
   abnormal, 276-7
Heat stroke, **34-5**
Heimlich maneuver, 206
Hematoma, 143-4, 355
Hemorrhoids, 194
Hernia, 328
Herpes virus, 66, 78
   of kittens, **324-5,** 327
Hip dysplasia, 236

Hives, 106, 126
Hoarseness, 204
Hookworms, 56
Hormone diseases, **111-2,** 244, 277
Housebreaking, **343**
   (*See also:* Wetting in house)
Hunting and bringing home prey,
   347-8
Hydrocephalus, 227
Hyperparathyroidism, 244-5
Hypoglycemia (low blood sugar),
   200, 226, 312
Hypothermia (loss of body heat),
   26
   (*See also:* Chilling)
Hypothyroidism, **111,** 276-7, 349

Immunity and immune system,
   60-1, 105
Impotence, 276
Inbreeding, 262, 264-5
Incontinence (loss of control of):
   bladder, 230
   bowel, **193,** 230
Incubator, how to make, 317
Infectious Diseases, **60-81**
   of kittens, 323-5
Infertility, 275-82
Injections
   adverse effects of, 232, 355
   how to give, **372-4**
Insecticides, 43, **104**
Insect Parasites, **98-105**
Insect stings, 36
Insulin, 199-200
Intestines, **186-93**
   blockage of, 189-90
Itchy skin disorders, 95-6

Jaundice, 64, 72, 81, **198**
Joint injuries, 238, 243

Kitten(s)
   buying a healthy, 383-5
   determining sex of, 330
   deworming, 53
   feeding, **340,** 385
   grooming, 86, 385-6
   newborn, 311-16
   training, **342-5,** 386
Kittens, rejected by mother, 308-9,
   315
Kitten diseases, 245, **323-9**
Kitten Mortality Complex (KMC),
   74, 313, **325**
Kittening (giving birth), **294-8**
Kittening box, 292-3
Kidney diseases, 249-50
Kidney failure (uremia), 42,
   250-2, 369

Labor, prolonged or difficult,
   298-300
Labyrinthitis (inner ear infections),
   149
Laryngitis (loss of voice), 204-5
Larynx (voice box), 204-6
Laxatives, 190, 192, 374
   for hand-fed kittens, 322
Leukemia virus, **74-6,** 278, 353
Lice, 102-3
Lick sores (granulomas), 115, 162
Limping (lameness), **236,** 243-5,
   354
Lipoma (fatty tumor), 97, 354
Lips, 161-3
Liquid medications, how to give,
   372
Litter pans, 343, 346
Liver failure, 72, 81, **198-9,** 369
Lockjaw (tetanus), 65
Lumps and bumps, 97, **354-6**
Lungs, 209
   fluid on (pleural effusion), **210,**
      214
Lungworms, 58-9
Lymph nodes, 61, 75, 81, 160
Lymphosarcoma, 75, 353

Maggots, 103, 363
Malabsorption of foods, 188, 199
Mange, 100-101
Many-tailed bandage, 49
Mastitis, 305-7
Mating, procedures, 272-4
Medications, drugs and, **368-74**
   antibiotics (table of), 376-7
   common household, for use on
      cat, 370
   dewormers, 52
   ear preparations, 142
   eye preparations, 122
   for behavioral disorders, 350
   how to give, **370-4**
   insecticides and dips, 104
   intoxication by, **44,** 149, **379**
   poisoning by, 44
   vaccinations, 63
Melanoma, 356
Meningitis, 79
Meowing (crying), 203
   kittens, **315,** 323-4
Metabolic diseases, 226, **244-6**
Metritis (infection of uterus), 304-5
Middle ear infections, 149
Milk
   artificial queen's, 307, 318-9
   as food, 186, 335
   of queen
      inadequate, 307
      infected, 305-7
      toxic, 323
Milk fever (eclampsia), 308

Mismate shot, 284
Mites, **99-101**
   ear, 101, **146**
   head, **100, 145**
Morning sickness, 291
Motion (sea) sickness, 184
Mouth, **159-75**
   foreign bodies in, 174-5
   how to examine, 160
   lacerations of, 163
Musculoskeletal System, **223-46**
Muzzling, 46

Nails, 84
   (*See also:* Claws)
Nasal discharge, 153
Nasal infection, 156-7
Navel infection, 323-4
Navel (umbilical) hernia, 328
Nephritis and nephrosis, 250
Nerve injuries, 230, **232**
Nervous System, **221-32**
Newborn kittens, 311-16
Nose, **151-8**
   foreign bodies in, 155
   polyps, 158
Nose-bleeds, 155
Nuclear sclerosis, 135, 362
Nutrition (*See* Feeding; Vitamin
   and Mineral deficiencies)
Nutritional requirements for:
   cats, 336-7
   kittens, 245
   queens
      lactating, 303-4
      pregnant, 292
   old cats, 366-7

Obesity (getting fat), 292, 348, 365
Obstetrics, **294-300**
Oral hygiene, 170
Osteomyelitis, 243
Osteoporosis (thin bones), 245
Ovaries, cystic, 277
Ovulation, 270
   failure of, 277
   inducing, to bring out of heat,
      285

Pain relievers, 369
Painful abdomen, 36-7
   (*See also: Index of Signs and
      Symptoms*)
Pancreas, 199-200
Panleukopenia (*See:* Feline
   Panleukopenia)
Panting, 202
Paper Bone Disease, 245
Paralysis, **229-32**
   (*See also: Index of Signs and
      Symptoms*)

Parasites, control of, on premises,
   105
Parathyroid glands, 244
Pediatrics, **311-32**
Pedigrees, 259-61, **264,** 385
Penis, 279-80, 330
Periodontal disease, **168-70,** 364
Photophobia (light hurts eyes), 77,
   121, 133
Picking up cat, technique for, 30
Pills, how to give, 370
Pinworms, 58
Placenta, 296
Plants, toxic, 38-9
Play-fighting, 348
Pneumonia, 209-10
   causes of, 42, 55, 68, 79, 81, 182
   viral (pneumonitis), 62, 69, 209
Pneumothorax (hole in chest), 23,
   28
Poison Control Center, 39
Poisoning by:
   carbon monoxide, 28
   drugs and medications, 44
   insecticides, 43, **104**
   plants and shrubs, 38-9
   rat baits and chemicals, 40-2
   spoiled food (garbage), 43
Poison ivy, 107
Pollen allergy, 105-6, 156, 208
Polyps, nasal, 158
   rectal, 198
Porcupine quills, extraction of, 175
Porphyria, 323
Post partum care of queen, 303-9
Pregnancy, **289-94**
   accidental, 284
   determining, 289-91
   drugs during, 292, 380
   false, 283-4
Premises, control of parasites on,
   105
Prenatal care of queen, 291-3
Progesterone (pregnancy
   hormone), 282-3, 347-8, **350**
Prostate gland, 363
Protozoan Diseases, 80-1
Pseudorabies, 78
Pulse
   absent, 23, 225
   how to take, 212
   rate, 382
      abnormal, 212, 216
      of newborn, 312
   weak, 46, 214
Pupils, 118
   (*See also: Index of Signs and
      Symptoms*)
Purebred cats, 259-61
Purring, 203
Pyloric stenosis, 328-9

Pyometra (abscess of uterus), **282,**
   364

Queen, 265-6
   deworming before breeding, 53,
      291
   post partum, care of, 303-9
   pregnant, care of, 291-2
   spaying, 285
   vaccinating, before breeding, 61,
      63

Rabies, **76-8,** 161
   vaccine, 62-3
Ranula, 178
Rectum and anus, **194,** 329
Registration for cats, 261, **382**
Regurgitation, 180-1
Respiratory System, **201-10**
Restraint (*See:* Handling)
Retinal Diseases, 137
Rhinotracheitis, (*See:* Feline
   Viral Respiratory Disease
   Complex)
Rickets, 245-6
Ringworm
   of ear flap, 145
   of skin, 109-110
Rodent Ulcer, 115, **161-2**
Roundworms, 55-6
Runt, 314

Salivary glands, 176-7
Salivation (*See:* Drooling)
Salmonella infection, 64-5
Scabies, 100
Scratching post, 344
Seizures, 227-8
   (*See also:* Convulsions)
Sexual behavior, 268-9, 272, 347,
   349
Sex and Reproduction, **259-87**
Sexual intercourse, 272
   diseases transmitted by, 279, 281
Shampoos and powders, 93, 99,
   104, 107
Shedding, 85
Shock, how to treat, **46**
   electric, 28
Shots, how to give, 372-4
   (*See also:* Vaccinations)
Sinusitis, 157
Skin, **83-115**
   abscess, 97, **114**
   allergies, 36, **106-9**
   cancer, 97, **356**
   care of, 86-9
      elderly cat, 362
   diseases, diagnosis of, 95-7
   infection, 97, **113-4**
   lumps or bumps, 97, 354-6
Skin rash, in kittens, 325

Skunk oil, in hair, 93
Sleep, putting a cat to, 367
Smell, sense of, 151-2
  diminished, 156, 363
Snake-bites, 45-6
Sociability, **342**, 346, 349, 360, **385**
Sore throat (pharyngitis), 175
Soundness, 234
Spaying, 285
Sperm, 266, 271, **275**
Spinal cord, 229-30
Sprains, 237
Spraying, 266, 286, 347
Standard (of breed), 259
Still-born kittens, 278, 325
Stomach, **182-5**
  worms, 59
Stomach tube, 320-1
Stones, bladder, 257
  urethra (FUS), 253-7
Stool(s)
  average number, 191
  appearance of, **187**, 333
  (*See also: Index of Signs and Symptoms*)
String
  around tongue, 172
  in mouth, 174
  swallowed, 190
Strokes (Cerebrovascular), 225-6
Stud (tom), 266
  neutering, 286-7
Stud tail, 114
Suffocation, 27-8
Sunburn, 26, **145**
Superfecundity and superfetation, 271
Suppository, how to give, 374
Surgery, preparations for, 369
Swallowing problems in kittens, 181-2
  (*See also: Index of Signs and Symptoms*)

Tail, 233, 241, 262
  (*See also:* Stud tail)
Tapeworms, 57
Tar in hair, 93
Tartar (dental calculus), 168-70
Tearing mechanism, 129-30
Tear stains, **129-30**
Teeth, **164-70**
  incorrect number, 166
  care of (oral hygiene), 170
Teething in kittens, 166
Temperature
  drop before kittening, 294
  how to take, 381
  normal, 381
    kitten, 315

of incubator, 317
of kittening box, 293
Tendon injuries, 237
Testicles, 280-1
Testosterone (male hormone), 276
Throat, **175-6**
  foreign body in, 176
Thrush (candidiasis), 110, 173
Thyroid gland, 111
  (*See also:* Hypothyroidism)
Ticks, 102, 148
Toad poisoning, 43
Tom (male cat), 266
Tongue, 159, **170-2**
  foreign bodies in, 171
  string around (strangulation), 172
Tonsillitis, 175
Tooth decay, **168-70**, 364
Tourniquet, 45, **47-8**
Toxic milk, 323
Toxoplasmosis, 80-1
Training, **342-5,** 386
Tranquilizers, 350
Transporting an injured cat, 34
Trench mouth, 173
Trichinosis, 58
Tubal ligation, 285
Tube feeding, 320-1
Tuberculosis, 65-6
Tumors (growths), **351-8**
  anal area, 198
  brain, 149, **226**
  breast, 357-8
  ear, 146
  esophagus, 181
  eye, 123, 128
  intestine, 190
  kidney, **252**
  leukemia, 75, 353
  lips, 162
  lymphosarcoma, 75, 353
  mouth, 175
  nasal cavity, 158

Ulcer, stomach, 183, **185**
Umbilical cord, 296
Undescended testicle, 280-1
Uremic poisoning, 250-2
Urethra, **253-7**
Urinary System, **247-58**
Urinary tract infections, 247-9
Urinating with difficulty (*See: Index of Signs and Symptoms*)
Urine, **247-8**
  blood in, 42, **249**, 253, 257
Uterine infection, 278, **282**, **304-5,** 364
Uterus, during labor, 294, 298-300
  removal of (spaying), 285

Vaccinations, 61-3
  vaccines, when to give, 63
Vagina, artificial stimulation of to prevent pregnancy, 270, **285-6**
Vaginal cytology (to predict ovulation), 274
Vaginal discharge (*See: Index of Signs and Symptoms*)
Vaginal infection, 281, 305
Vasectomy, 287
Vestibular syndrome, idiopathic, 229
  (*See also:* Balance)
Virus Diseases, **66-78**
Visceral larva migrans, 55
Vitamin and Mineral, deficiencies, 226, 245-6, 304, 335, 339
  indications for supplemental use, 292, 304, 308, 366
  overdosing with, 246, 339
  table of requirements, 337
Voice box (larynx), 204-6
  foreign object in, 206
Voiding, disturbances of, **249**, 258, 346-7, 360
Vomiting, **182**
  common causes of, 183-5
  home treatment for, 184
  (*See also: Index of Signs and Symptoms*)
Vomiting, how to induce, 36

Warts, 97, **354**
Watery eye, 129-30
Wax in ear, 141, **146-8**
Weaning, 329-30
Weight
  adults, 382
  ideal, **338**, 366
  kittens, **312**, 316
  loss of (*See: Index of Signs and Symptoms*)
Wetting in house, 249, 258, **346-7**, 360
Whipworms, 58
Whiskers, 84, 150, **152**
Windpipe, foreign body in, 207
Wool sucking, 348
Worming (deworming), 52-4
Worms (intestinal parasites), **51-9**
  how to control, on premises, 53-5, 105
Wounds, care of, **47-50**, 378

Yellow Fat Disease (pansteatitis), 246